DATE DUE

NOV 1 0 1982			
MAY - 4 1983			

The

Philosophy and Theology

of

Anders Nygren

EDITED BY

Charles W. Kegley

SOUTHERN ILLINOIS UNIVERSITY PRESS

CARBONDALE AND EDWARDSVILLE

FEFFER & SIMONS, INC.

LONDON AND AMSTERDAM

CONTENTS

PREFACE

THERE ARE several features of the thought of Anders Nygren, and of its examination in this volume, which I should like to identify. Some of these may be fairly obvious to scholars, although not necessarily so to students of theology and philosophy and to the general reader. Other characteristics are sufficiently unique to deserve "reading into the record" at this point.

First, Anders Nygren, like other major creative minds in our day —Paul Tillich was also an excellent example—is a paradigm case of a borderline thinker: he moves easily and constantly between the theological and the philosophical fields. This phenomenon itself has several aspects. For one thing, Nygren, like other contemporary giants in these two fields, is a philosophical theologian, or probably more accurately, a theologically-oriented philosopher. Because the adjective sometimes swallows the noun, one should be at pains to emphasize that Nygren's pioneering works, as well as his latest writing, have been clearly *philosophical*. The sometimes suppressed or incidental, often open and central thrusts of his work, however, have a clearly religious orientation. Interpreting "religion" and "theology" broadly, as continental and especially Scandinavian scholars usually do, Nygren has persistently wrestled with the questions of what man *is*, of what and how he can *know*, and of what he can *become*. The last is not the least of his major queries and includes the question of man's place in the universe. Clearly, these are some of the central issues both in philosophy and in theology. Equally clear is the propriety, therefore, of examining his thought in a fashion similar to the way in which the thinking of Tillich, Niebuhr, Brunner, Wieman, and Bultmann have been treated in volumes in The Library of Living Theology.

Another aspect of this borderline character attaches to the word "examination" which was deliberately used above. Although a Festschrift has an honorable place in the academic world, the present study seeks, without any false modesty, to engage in a much sterner and more productive task, namely, to analyze and ruthlessly criticize Nygren's thinking, and to elicit Nygren's response to his interpreters and critics. This unique structure originated in 1939 when Professor Paul A. Schilpp, then of Northwestern University, set out to clarify the issues in contemporary philosophy through a series of books—there are now thirteen massive volumes—entitled The Library of Living Philosophers. It is a pleasure to acknowledge, here again, our debt to Professor Schilpp, not only for the general plan of the volume, but also for his never-failing friendly advice over three decades and with our intro- duction to and association with Southern Illinois University Press.[1] It is a source of deep satisfaction to the present editor that the aim of this volume, as of its predecessors, was achieved thanks to the scholars from all over the world who generously participated. There *is* honest and clearly stated disagreement, there *is* clarification, and there are lines of inquiry opened for more profitable future study. From this, theology, philosophy and related fields may be expected to benefit.

Still another aspect of the borderline stance should be cited. If, as many believe, a break is occurring between these two historic disci- plines—and there is abundant evidence that it is not merely a break but often is open warfare—any major and competent effort to rebuild the lines of communication between philosophy and theology may be valu- able. To cite a single respect in which this is demonstrated, Nygren, on the one hand, recognizes and practices the kind of quest for clarity and analysis of meaning so highly and rightly prized by philosophers. On the other hand, he is equally emphatic in emphasizing the demand for rational and faith-ful religious and ethical judgments. Accordingly, he rejects at once both the old-fashioned, metaphysically speculative phi- losophies, and the presently popular varieties of anti- or irrationalistic theologies. As a result, discussion of his thought opens up a "free-for- all" into which anyone in the contemporary battle can enter.

A second feature of Nygren's thought is suggested by the preced- ing statements. This is the central role which language analysis, the quest for motifs, and the concern with contexts of meaning jointly play in Nygren's thought. Because these elements are discussed in this book so often, and with reference to a variety of issues, it is best here simply to call attention to their continuing importance, and to hint—I hope not unfairly or discourteously—at a possible consequence. Do they re- sult in a tendency to relativism, and if so, is this accidental or is it logically involved in the above-mentioned ways of thinking? Nygren is clear and firm about the objective character of motif research in identifying, for example, motifs in history, in literature, and in Platonic, Stoic, and biblical thought. When one turns, however, to the normative fields—for example, to ethics, political philosophy, and aesthetics—there is a growing suspicion that the purely analytical approach exhibits a neutrality which has serious implications. It is often said today that "clarity is not enough," and that the analytical approach has a built-in elimination of truth claims in any but the empirical sciences and, by extension, in mathmatics and logic where validity and certainty are possible by virtue of their purely formal character. But what about theology, ethics, and god-talk generally? Each reader will find here a major problem for further reflection. Hopefully, he will do so with additional light shed by the interpreter's work and by Nygren's response in the following pages.

A third feature, and, by a kind of irony a problem in Nygren's thought is this: one of its chief claims to world-wide and increasing fame—its analysis of the forms of love in *Agape and Eros*—threatens to lead to a misunderstanding of Anders Nygren, the philosopher-theologian, and of his work. This tends to occur in two ways. First, the sheer brilliance and erudition of that study has misled some into thinking that this is his only major contribution. That this is *not* the case, the present volume should once for all make clear. Second, there is an impression abroad that his notion of love puts the emphasis far too strongly on the marks of the holy, the austere, what some would call the non- or transhuman character of love at the expense of an understanding and exhibition of warm, personal love. This Preface furnishes neither the space nor the appropriate setting in which to argue the case on theological and philosophical grounds. It does, however, permit me to record that, to the degree that Emerson was correct when he wrote, as regards action versus words, "What you are speaks so loud I cannot hear what you say," Anders Nygren, the man, expresses a humaneness and capacity for rapport which is unfailingly warm, and winning. In the decade during which this volume was in preparation, it was an unceasing privilege and pleasure to know him and to work with him.

Finally, it should be pointed out that Nygren, unlike the subjects of previous and similar volumes in The Library of Living Theology, occupies a unique status, i.e., as a Bishop of the Church of Sweden, and so not merely as a distinguished professor of philosophy or of

theology. This occasions a question because to some it is a commenda-
tion, to others a kind of condemnation. It may give to his work an
aura of reverence, a suggestion of authority, even the assumption that
he will, of course, be a defender of the faith. It may induce some
to an initial rejection on the ground that organized religion, if it
doesn't kill genuine freedom of thought, is likely to depress and in-
hibit that freedom. That this has and can happen is undeniable. That
no authoritarianism and special pleading infects Anders Nygren's
works is also clear. He writes with an intellectual honesty, a scientific
caution, and a scholarly modesty, as regards religion in general and
Christianity in particular, such that the pro- or the antireligious must
admire his achievements. His open-mindedness and deep commitment is
a combination too rarely found in the second half of this century.

GRATEFUL acknowledgement is given to the following publishers for
permission to quote from certain of the published works of Anders
Nygren.

To the Society For the Promotion of Christian Knowledge of
London, for permission to quote various passages from *Agape and
Eros*.

To the Student Christian Movement Press of London for permission to quote from *The Gospel of God*.

Full documentation of these books is contained in the bibliography and notes.

Charles W. Kegley

Wagner College
Staten Island, New York City
January 1970

NOTES ON CONTRIBUTORS

EXTENDED comments on a group of distinguished scholars tend, like long introductions, to be embarrassing to all concerned. Hence, the following notes are limited to identification of the contributor by title, position, and citation of only those publications by which he is most likely to be known.

RAGNAR BRING is Professor Emeritus of Theology at the University of Lund, Sweden. German, Danish, Finnish, and American Universities have honored him with degrees and published his lectures. His publications in English include: *Commentary on Galations* (1961), *Preaching the Law* (1960), and *How God Speaks to Us* (1960). His leading position in Swedish theology as well as his prominent role in ecumenical theology bears fruit in the present extended study of Anders Nygren's thought.

JOHN BURNABY is Professor of Divinity, Emeritus, Cambridge University. The scholarly world knows his now classic, *Amor Dei,* as it also knows that when one wishes the discrimination of the specialist on "amor," "caritas," and "agape" in Augustine and others, one turns invariably to Professor Burnaby's works.

ERIK M. CHRISTENSEN is senior Lecturer in general and comparative literature at the University of Odense, Denmark. Formerly at the University of Aarhus, he has increasingly established himself as a perceptive interpreter of the kinds of problems dealt with in his essay in this book.

BERNHARD ERLING is Professor of Religion at Gustavus Adolphus College, St. Peter, Minnesota. His dissertation studies led to the publication of *Nature and History, A Study in Theological Methodology with Special Attention to the Method of Motif Research* (1960). He gave invaluable assistance to the present volume in translation and general editorial advice.

NELS F. S. FERRÉ is Ferris Professor of Philosophy, College of Wooster. His internationally known scholarship is perhaps most quickly recognized by citing *The Universal Word, A Theology For a Universal Faith* (1969), and his special competence for participating in this book is seen in his *Swedish Contributions to Modern Theology*, with William Johnson (1968).

THOR HALL is Associate Professor of Preaching and Theology at the Divinity School, Duke University, Durham, N. C. He will be identified by students of theology with his book, *A Theology of Christian Devotion: Its Role in the Modern Religious Setting* (1969). The scholarly world is at present welcoming his major new work, *A Framework for Faith*. This is a study of the *Lundensian Theological Methodology in the Thought of Ragnar Bring*, to cite its sub-title (1969). As this is written he is concluding a sabbatical leave spent in Sweden and devoted, in part, to a study of contemporary trends in Swedish theology.

J. W. HEIKKINEN is Professor of New Testament Interpretation and Theology at the Lutheran Theological Seminary, Gettysburg, Pa. He combines two main interests, the ecumenical and the biblical. The former is evidenced in his membership on the executive committee of the National Council of Churches (U. S. A.) on Faith and Order; the latter in his book, *Helping the Youth and the Adult Understand the Bible*.

SØREN HOLM is a Professor at the University of Copenhagen, his official area of scholarship being systematic theology. Of his almost forty books in the area of theology and philosophy, he may best be known for his work on *Schopenhauer's Ethik*, his two volume study of religious philosophy in the twentieth century which appeared in Danish in 1952, and his works on Kierkegaard, Christian Ethics, and Religious Philosophy, all of which have also been published in German editions.

PAUL HOLMER is Professor of Theology at the Divinity School, Yale University. He needs no introduction to American readers. Beginning in 1946, when he published *Faith and Reason*, through the sixties (e.g. *Philosophy and the Common Life* 1964), he has produced a steady stream of books, articles, and monographs. All who have read the present book in manuscript form have cited his present essay as of outstanding importance.

RUDOLF HENRIK JOHANNESSON, former Assistant Professor of Systematic Theology at the University of Lund, is now Lektor (Senior Master) in the College, at Stockholm. His most important book is *Person och Gemenskop* (1947). Several of his most important articles appear in *Religion in Geschichte und Gegenwart*, third edition.

CHARLES W. KEGLEY has been Professor of Philosophy at Wagner College, Staten Island, N. Y. for twenty years. In 1970 he became Professor of

Philosophy and Chairman of the Department of Philosophy and Religious Studies, California State College, Bakersfield. Author of *Protestantism in Transition* (1965) and coauthor of *Religion in Modern Life* (1957), he has edited *The Theology of Emil Brunner* (1964) and *The Theology of Rudolf Bultmann* (1966, 1967) and coedited with Robert W. Bretall volumes on Reinhold Niebuhr and Paul Tillich in The Library of Living Theology series.

ERNST KINDER is Professor of Systematic Theology at the University of Münster and is associated with the Institute for Ecumenical Theology of the Westphalian Wilhelms University of Münster. His works include: *Der evangelische Glaube und die Kirche* (1958) and *Was ist evangelische?* (1961) which also appeared in English (1968) under the title, *"Evangelical" —What Does It Really Mean?*

VALTER LINDSTRÖM is Dean of the Cathedral, Karlstad, Sweden, and formerly was Assistant Professor of Systematic Theology of the University of Lund. He is a specialist on Kierkegaard and has published *The Theology of the Stages* (1943). In addition to other works, his study of the theology of the following of Christ in Kierkegaard's writings, *Efterföljelsens teologi hos Sören Kierkegaard,* appeared in Stockholm in 1956.

ULRICH E. MACK is a teacher of Protestant Theology at Kurfürst-Friedrich-Gymnasium, Heidelberg. His competence extends far beyond the exhaustive Bibliography of Nygren's work which appears exclusively in this volume. The latest of his publications is *Anders Nygren* in Tendenzen der Theologie im 20. Jahrhundert (1966).

JOHN M. RIST is Professor of Greek, University College, University of Toronto, Canada. Both linguist and philosopher, he has written on the problems of this book in *Eros and Psyche* (1964), *Plotinus: The Road to Reality* (1967), and most recently in *Stoic Philosophy* (1969).

VILMOS VAJTA is Research Professor at the Institute for Ecumenical Research, Strasbourg. He is author of *Die Theologie des Gottesdienstes bei Luther* (1952) and a shorter version in English, *Luther on Worship*. He is also editor of *Studienbänden-über Lutherforschung, das lutherische Bekenntnis und das Problem der Abendmahls-Gemeinschaft.*

FR. VICTOR WARNACH, O.S.B., is University Professor for Philosophy at the University of Salzburg, Austria. He symbolizes in his positions the title of the present book, for in addition to being Director of the Institute for Philosophy at the Faculty of Theology of the University of Salzburg he is at present also Pro-Dean of the Faculty of Theology. He is probably best known for his extended study, *Agape: Die Liebe als Grundmotiv der neutestamentlichen Theologie* (1951).

PHILIP S. WATSON is Professor of Systematic Theology at Garrett Theological Seminary, Evanston, Illinois. His position is unique as it concerns this book because he is translator and editor of Anders Nygren's *Agape and Eros* (1969) and of Nygren's *Essence of Christianity* (1960). His international reputation was established by works such as *Let God Be God* (1960) and *The State as a Servant of God* (1946). His translation and assistance in the production of this book places the scholarly world deeply in his debt.

Two distinguished British scholars have rendered invaluable translation services:
LANCE GARRARD is Professor of Philosophy and Religion, Emerson College, Boston. His name is internationally known as former editor of *The Hibbert Journal* and Principal of Manchester College, Oxford.

PETER W. RUSSELL, while engaged in the translation of Anders Nygren's "Intellectual Autobiography," was Tutor in New Testament, Trinity College, Umuahia, E. Nigeria. He is now with Epworth Theological College, Salisbury, Rhodesia.

Intellectual Autobiography

INTELLECTUAL AUTOBIOGRAPHY

Anders Nygren

IT IS HARD to write a biography. Great insight and a considerable understanding of the particular cultural situation are required to put the subject in his proper setting, and an ability to enter sympathetically into his life and times, if the essentials are not to be lost in the mass of data. In short both proximity and distance are at the same time demanded.

But if to write a biography is difficult, to produce a trustworthy autobiography is much more difficult, indeed scarcely possible. It has often, and truly, been said that it is almost impossible to write the history of one's own times. The reason is simple and obvious: one is standing too close to see clearly. In the midst of the events, the writer lacks historical perspective. He shares the assumptions which appear self-evident to his contemporaries; their prejudices are his also. Just because they are self-evident they pass unnoticed and yet it is these very assumptions that set the deepest mark on an epoch. A later age for which not our ideas but others were self-evident would more easily be able to discover what were the unspoken assumptions by which we lived, and would therefore have a much better chance of giving an accurate historical picture of our day.

This is all the more true of autobiography. Here, of course,

TRANSLATED BY PETER W. RUSSELL

distance is completely lacking, but so also, paradoxically, it would seem is the close sympathy, for sympathy presupposes an element of objectivity, a distinction between subject and object, which is of course impossible when subject and object are the same. Moreover, it is a matter of experience that the writer of autobiography is threatened by many dangers; he is all too open to the temptation to make retrospective adjustments, to file down the jigsaw pieces of which life is made up, in order the better to fit a desired pattern. In the end autobiography may become simply an *apologia pro vita sua*, not to mention the fact that the autobiographical form gives to the "I" a central position which does not belong to it.

The burden is somewhat lightened when the task is limited to "intellectual autobiography," for the function of such an essay in a publication of this sort can only be to provide some autobiographical remarks to show how the author has approached his problems, something not directly indicated in his writings, but which can possibly be of help in understanding them. Thus the question becomes easier to answer since it is concerned with concrete empirical matters. The works are before us, the problems dealt within them are before us, and when one is faced with the problem of how one came to be interested in these problems and to concentrate upon them, one does not have to delve deep into hidden levels of the past, consciousness, even though one is often carried far back in time.

For one whose work has been concerned with the historical, structural, and systematic analysis of different ideas, and the clarification of their original meaning and internal relationships, and the changes of form resulting from these relationships, a curious situation arises when he is required to turn the searchlight on his own work. The immediate result of such an examination, if it is rightly and conscientiously carried out, can only be that everything generally said to be original dissolves into nothing, in as much as nearly every ingredient has in one way or another been given and received. Of course there can be individual differences, but for myself I have more and more come to see the truth and wide validity of the saying, "What have you that you did not receive?" This is so not only because of the nature of the material as something given in history and tradition, but also because the systematic principles by which the given material is ordered in a new form and a new perspective, are also anchored in something given and would be impossible without it. I shall attempt to illustrate this in what follows.

It is a psychological commonplace, continually confirmed by observation, that the impressions received in childhood and youth are of
decisive importance in determining the later development. Perhaps it
has been too little noticed that this is also true in the highest degree of
intellectual development. Nearly every problem I have dealt with in
the course of the years, can be referred back more or less clearly to
such early impressions. Of this I shall give examples later; first a few
words about my home background.

My father, who was Principal of the Elementary Teachers' College in Gothenburg, had pursued advanced studies at Lund University,
and an academic appointment had seemed to be within his reach. He
was however compelled for economic reasons to enter the world of
teaching, and this he never later regretted. As head of the college of
Gothenburg, and teacher of Christianity and educational method, he
set his mark for many years on the training of teachers in western
Sweden. He had a large and well-stocked library, and if it was particularly strong in theology, philosophy, and history, yet such subjects as
the history of art were not neglected. It was a goldmine to delve in,
and so it was quite natural that the world of books became my world.
Both of my parents were profoundly Christian people, but this did not
mean that the atmosphere of our home was at all narrow. The Christian
faith included the whole of life, all human life in its breadth and
richness. Church life in Gothenburg at the turn of the century was
extremely vigorous. If one wanted a seat in church, it was not enough
to be there when the church doors opened half an hour before service
time; one had to queue outside the church at least fifteen or twenty
minutes earlier, and even then it could happen that one had to be
content to stand. I can never be grateful enough that right from the
beginning at home and in the worship of the congregation I got to
know the Christian life from within. This was a tremendous gain, *even
on the purely intellectual level.* A person who has had this experience
has been freely given much that anyone who approaches the subject
from outside must work hard to attain. To use a convenient illustration, anyone who has visited the Cathedral at Chartres and has seen
from within the glow of color and experienced the wonderful effect of
the sun shining through the stained glass windows, would immediately
realise how difficult, if not indeed impossible, it would be for anyone
who had only had access to the window from outside to form an
adequate picture of the meaning and effect of these great masterpieces,
however carefully he studied the material available to him. There are

things which can be understood only from within, and which cannot be discussed meaningfully without this understanding. It is this that renders so much of the current debate about religion so sterile and unfruitful: the approach is made to religion and to Christianity without any attempt to clarify the meaning of the subject under discussion. That I myself have been able from the beginning to experience Christianity and its significance from within has for me had the consequence that I have never had to "demythologize the New Testament." If from the beginning no mythological world view is falsely read into it, then there is nothing to demythologize. But the risk in first mythologizing and then, demythologizing, in order to correct the error thus made, is that it becomes all too easy to demythologize away the Christian reality itself, and to be left in the end with just your own myth.

And now I must give some concrete examples to show how early impressions directed my attention to problems that I was to deal with many years later.

It might be asked how I first met the problem of "Agape and Eros." Of course it is impossible to give a complete answer to this question, but the moment when the very first seed was planted is quite clear. I can remember perfectly the first time I heard the word "agape" and the impression it made on me. My father was in conversation with an acquaintance, and I was sitting and listening eagerly. A great deal went over my head, but I caught something here and there, and in particular a sentence of my father's "But Christian agape means something quite different." I will not hold my father responsible for anything I have written since then, but his remark provided a nucleus around which my thoughts could be gathered and arranged. Of course it was at first only a general questioning and a feeling that it would be rewarding to discover what sort of thing this "agape" might be, indeed that it was essential to discover this. Not until twenty years later were my ideas in order and the material ready. "Eros" and "nomos" and a great deal more besides had come within the scope of the inquiry, but it was all for the purpose of understanding what the Christian idea of agape means and does not mean. Of course nothing of this was there at the beginning, but if that first seed had not been sown from outside, would there have been any treatment of "agape and eros"?

There is room only for one or two further examples of early impressions that have remained with me and born fruit many years later. Teacher that he was, my father was not content to order our daily family prayers in the traditional way. He used, for example, passages from Luther's sermons, and this seed fell on good ground in my brothers and me. However, it was also the cause of a disaster: when we came to one of those extravagant, not to say grotesque, expressions of Luther's, we three boys could not keep straight faces, but could not help but giggle. Father did not say a word, but the next day Luther had given way to another book; to our great sorrow, as Luther was much more fun and more exciting than the usual devotional books. Fortunately, Luther was not long in coming back. The only comment I would make on this is that long before there was talk of a Luther renaissance in the world at large, there was one in full swing in our home at the turn of the century.

Another book used on such occasions was *Apostelen Paulus's Breve* – The Letters of St. Paul[1] – by the Norwegian theologian F. W. Bugge, orally translated into Swedish. The particular passage chosen dealt with the letter to the Colossians; why this letter in particular I do not know. It was fascinating to hear of Paul's mighty struggle against gnosticism's, or rather the gnostic heresy's, distortion of the Gospel, and above all his affirmation of Christ's universal primacy over all rule and authority, of Christ as at the same time Head both of the Church and of the universe, and of the Church as the Body of Christ. When *This is the Church* (*En Bok om kyrkan*) was published in the early 1940's, it was no accident that my introductory essay was entitled "Corpus Christi" [The Body of Christ]. The connection with my early impressions is obvious.

The subject for the conference for the clergy of Gothenburg Diocese in 1903 was the doctrine of the atonement. The paper to be discussed was the work of an old and respected rural dean, outstanding among those who were reputed pillars of the diocese. There was a mighty debate. In the preceding years the Church of Sweden had been shaken by a great struggle over the doctrine of atonement, which had resulted in the separation of the Swedish Mission Covenant Church. Moreover in the years about the turn of the century the theology of Ritschl had made its entrance, admittedly a tentative and cautious entrance, into our theological faculties. These two factors made the atmosphere somewhat heated, and the discussion became stormy. Some thought they detected the influence of the new "errors" in the chairman's paper, and there was no lack of voices to brand the old patriarch as a heretic. I was among the visitors in the gallery, and it was naturally an experience for a twelve year old to hear the disputation of the learned clergy. The matter was thrashed out thoroughly, and Hebrew and Greek words like *kaphar, kipper, kapporeth, hilasterion* flew about.

In this context what gripped me most of all was the combination *Kapporeth-Hilasterion.* When I began to study the letter to the Romans seriously some years later, I noticed that our old version of the Bible followed Luther in keeping this combination, when in Romans 3:25 Paul is made to describe Christ as "The Mercy Seat," while this interpretation was in general rejected by modern exegetes. Who had interpreted the apostle's meaning correctly? The question was constantly before me, but more than thirty years were to pass before I had the opportunity in my *Commentary on Romans,* to set out my view of it. This may seem to be a matter of mere unimportant detail, but it is closely tied up with Paul's whole view of the Old Testament and of Christ as the central point of all scripture. When I was invited some years later to contribute to the memorial volume for Ernst Lohmeyer, it was natural that my contribution should be on "Christ—The Mercy Seat." I have mentioned this small point since it is a typical example of how an early impression has been able to stay with me and be effective for half a century.

One more thing belongs here: namely how it came about that I was caught up with philosophy. This too had its quite concrete starting point. About this time I happened to come across a collection of essays by the German philosopher J. E. Erdmann among my father's books. It was of course a Swedish translation, and it had the promising title *Filosofiska Miniatyrer—Philosophical Miniatures.* A better or more persuasive introduction to philosophy would be hard to find. This was no dry exposition of the problems of philosophy; instead various interesting questions arising out of concrete examples were subjected to a fresh philosophical analysis as far as possible within the limits of the essay form. In a witty and attractive way the author took up one question after another and illuminated not only the central point, but also a great deal of the surrounding territory. In a chapter called "Conflicts of Duty" for example, he not only introduced the reader to the subject promised by the title, but also to a number of those conceptual traps and logical paradoxes, with which the history of thought is so rich. However, the essay that most deeply impressed me was the one with the provocative title "Stupidity." The starting point of the author's analysis of the nature of stupidity was an experience he had had while sitting one day at the Hamburg railway station. Near him a family was also sitting and waiting, and he understood from the conversation that they were travelling by rail to a family celebration in the little village of Kyritz. When the time for the train to depart approached and a great crowd of travellers streamed in, the smallest boy exclaimed "Whatever are all these people going to do at Grandfather's in Kyritz?" "Don't be stupid," shouted the elder brother. Wherein did the stupidity lie? The boy travelling to Grandfather's at Kyritz, and with his limited experience he could not imagine any other reason for travelling by train, and supposed that all these people were going to Grandfather's at Kyritz. He peeped, so to speak, through his own little keyhole, and that was where his stupidity lay.

To imagine that there is nothing else in the world than what I can discover by looking through my own keyhole, and to suppose that a statement must be meaningless if I cannot at once understand it without feeling my way into the subject in question, that is stupidity. The truth and the wide validity of this argument struck me immediately. I had been given here the key to philosophy. Its task is to give us the wide perspective, to free us from too narrow views and to clarify the perspective we must have in order to understand at all what is under discussion. The seed was now sown that was to determine the nature of the later growth; here was the organizing principle around which all further philosophical ideas could be ordered and could grow.

In this connection it ought perhaps to be added that Erdmann's particular approach to philosophical analysis is to "ask questions of the use of language," just of the ordinary use of language. Even though he warns us against the idea that "the use of language can solve all problems," he nevertheless firmly maintains the principle that "one who pays attention to the use of language will see how man is accustomed to think." That this was my *initium*, my entry into philosophy, may perhaps to some extent explain the affinity there is between my philosophical ideas and the semantic-linguistic philosophy of recent years. In both cases the task of philosophy is seen to be the clarification and analysis of the meaning and use of language.

Such was my first encounter with philosophy. When later I read in the *Confessions* of St. Augustine what effect the study of Cicero's *Hortensius* had had on him, I could see that what he described there was exactly my own condition—I too was gripped by philosophical eros. Naturally there were some important differences; I had never thought that philosophy could be a way to God. Philosophy is not a function of religion, it is a human activity, but as such it is one of the most important, because it is concerned for clarity of thought and breadth of view, as against confusion and narrowness of mind.

When my father died—I was fifteen at the time—our family

moved to Lund, where we three brothers were in due course to study at the University. So it came about that for two and a half years I was pupil at the Cathedral School in Lund, one of the oldest educational institutions in the country with traditions going back to the High Middle Ages.

My years as a student at Lund were overflowing with interest. There was so much to learn and assimilate. Naturally my studies were chiefly concerned with philosophy and theology. It was a turning point from old to new. Guest lecturers from other countries were not as common then as now, but we were the more careful to take the opportunities that were offered, and it was like a breath from the great world when in our little Lund one was able to hear such great scholars as Adolf Harnack, Ulrich von Wilamowitz-Moellendorff and Frantz Cumont. I cannot say that the actual university teaching made any decisive impression on me. The important thing was the private studies and the books where one could come into contact with the great masters of other times. The rebellion common to students was in my case deliberately restrained in the knowledge that there was in the last resort so little one could achieve on one's own. I never forgot that it is a sign of stupidity to make cocksure judgments about things from the way they look through one's own private keyhole. One naturally presupposed that a qualified writer had seen problems in a wider perspective, and one had not one's self understood the matter rightly. The situation was nevertheless rather ambivalent, since in my school-days I had come across an argument in a book that seemed very doubtful, and had later read a review by a well-known scholar in which this very passage had been singled out for criticism. This obviously strengthened the self-reliance which was at the same time being kept in bounds by the thought of "stupidity." Whenever I was disposed to query something I came across in my reading, this gave me an incentive to go further into the matter in order to try to form a well-founded opinion.

My student days partly coincided with the period of the great religious debates. I was a silent observer, but was for this reason better able to study the "keyhole" tactics which were characteristic of the attacks on religion and the Christian faith. I noticed this particularly in one of the leading representatives of this tendency—*nomina sunt odiosa* —who enjoyed a great reputation as a debater. His particular method of approach was to cite passages from theological writings, but to read a different meaning into them and then tilt against these distorted creations of his own imagination. This attack rarely failed in its effect on those who were unacquainted with the works in question, but as I was acquainted with them the speaker stood before me unmasked. Either he had not understood what he had read, or else for propaganda purposes he deliberately distorted them "for the good of the cause." Probably it was a mixture of both. For one who was interested in the philosophy of religion these discussions were extremely rewarding, at least as a study in method, if not because of their content.

As I have said, I was chiefly interested in the philosophy of religion and systematic theology, but I had also a strong inclination towards the New Testament. About this I will mention only two things both of which had a certain significance for the future. In our lectures on New Testament exegesis Adolf Jülicher's great book, *Die Gleichnisreden Jesu* [The Parables of Jesus], which was then newly published, received careful and detailed treatment. His main thesis, that in the parables of Jesus we were dealing not with allegories, but with direct speech, was immediately convincing. On the other hand, I found it hard to accept his subsidiary idea that Jesus' parables were intended as *proofs* to compel the assent of the listeners with incontrovertible argument. In other words, in his parables Jesus was saying "This is the way things are in real life, and you cannot deny it; now carry this over to the spiritual realm and refer it to God's relationship to man." This I just could not agree with. It fitted so badly with the picture the gospels gave of Jesus; in the gospels Jesus did not deduce God's attitude from human models and seek to persuade men by means of logical proofs. Nor did it do justice to the particular material. Is the master who employed workers in his vineyard and gave a full day's wages even to those who had worked for only one hour, really an example of the way things actually should be done in the world, an example that could therefore be used as a premise for determining God's attitude? Much later I had occasion to develop this criticism in an essay "Till förståelsen av Jesu liknelser" [Towards the Understanding of the Parables of Jesus] and afterwards in a systematic context in *Agape and Eros*.

I was especially interested in the Letter to the Romans, and tried to penetrate its meaning by reading several commentaries simultaneously. In this way I gathered a great deal of valuable detailed knowledge, but I was left with a question: is it not sometimes possible for the wealth of detail and the various rival interpretations to obscure an argument and a message that are in themselves quite clear? Can one in fact fail to see the woods for the trees? Quite clearly it is not because the linguistic problems presented by the Scriptures are so much more interesting that we study them so much more carefully than other texts. But the question does now arise of whether this detailed study of purely linguistic questions, a study of extraordinary importance and often quite decisive for interpretation and understanding, has not taken the center of the stage at the expense of the context of thought and subject matter, which are the real aims of our study? It was thoughts and experiences like this which in time matured and gave rise to the series of commentaries, *Tolkning av Nya Testamentet* [Interpretation of the New Testament], with its special form and purpose.[2]

However, the philosophy of religion was already taking a prominent place in my studies. At that time it was not an independent subject in the theological faculty at Lund, but a rather subordinate part of the study of history of religions, and even this subject did not have its own professor but only a docent.[3] This was Docent Torgny Segerstedt later editor of *Göteborgs Handelstidning* and famous as one of the most energetic and consistent opponents of National Socialism. When Nazism was at the height of its power he succeeded in greatly irritating and angering Hitler and his circle with his journalism, which was always frank and penetrating. He also gave the Swedish government many difficult moments. However, we are concerned with him here as a teacher in the university. He most generously went out of his way to meet my wishes, and allowed me to concentrate on those problems which were nearest to my heart. When examinations were past, it was he above all who encouraged me to go on to further studies, and unknown to himself spurred me on to those studies both in a positive, and more particularly in a negative way. He was asking me about my plans for future study, and I told him that as well as philosophy of religion I wished to go further in systematic theology (dogmatics and moral theology) and New Testament exegesis. He then advised me most strongly against systematic theology, saying that what was of value in systematics could be much better derived from philosophy of religion, as this was the scientific form of systematic studies, with dogmatics and ethics as its unscientific counterpart. This did not accord at all with what I had come to understand by either philosophy of religion or systematic theology. A philosophy of religion which tries to take over the task of systematic theology is a travesty. It can have this purpose if and only if it is to be a metaphysical philosophy of religion, and if it is metaphysical it thereby becomes unscientific.[4]

Nevertheless I derived untold benefit from this conversation. Precisely because of this contrary advice, my previously vaguer research program became more clearly formulated and my desire stimulated. I was thus able to finish my time as a student with a fully developed research program. The possibility of a purely scientific, nonmetaphysical, philosophy of religion had to be fundamentally explored, as well as the scientific basis of dogmatics and moral theology. Those who know this "prehistory" will see at once what my program was for the next few years and how it led to the publication of three works. The first was my thesis on *Religiöst a priori, dess filosofiska förutsättningar och teologiska konsekvenser*, 1921 [*The Religious a priori, Its Philosophical Basis, and Theological Implications*], where an attempt is made to establish the philosophy of religion as a purely critical, scientific discipline, while repudiating every form of metaphysics. (*Den metafysiska filosofiens betydelse*, 1918 [*The Significance of Metaphysical Philosophy*] and *Det religionsfilosofilosofiska grundproblemet*, 1919, 1921 [*The Basic Problem of the Philosophy of Religion*] in which there is a confrontation between metaphysical and scientific philosophy of religion, were preparatory studies for this work.) The second major work deals with *Dogmatikens ventenskapliga grundläggning*, 1922 [*The Scientific Basis of Dogmatics*] and the third with the problem of *Filosofisk och kristen etik*, 1923 [*Philosophical and Christian Ethics*]. Here, however, we have crossed the border into the next period, and must retrace our steps.

In 1912, when only twenty-one years old, I was ordained to the ministry in the Diocese of Gothenburg. At that time there was an acute shortage of ministers, and the lower age limit of twenty-three was freely waived. In later years I have often mildly regretted that I did not spend the time before I reached this minimum age in study abroad. My studies hitherto had had a bias towards Germany; what might have been the results if I had been able to complement this with study in England and the consequent mastery of English? It would have obviated many later difficulties, but in those days visits to other countries were not so common for young people, and my route lay directly towards the work of the ministry. Perhaps it was better so, for a journey abroad at that point might have been a distraction.

The years of my ministry from 1912 to the beginning of 1920 were a time of concentration. It might be thought that the work of the ministry with the regular Sunday preaching and the continual contact with people would involve a serious disruption of study. But the opposite was the case. Even from the intellectual point of view the work of the ministry is extraordinarily stimulating. I have never found my tension between the pastoral office and the scientific task of scholarship. It is not a matter of mutual tolerance, but of a fruitful interrelationship. To stand in the Christian congregation with the task of presenting the Gospel to modern man gives a firm anchorage at the central point of Christianity, and to be immersed in a scientific study of the biblical message has the same effect. What else can the Church want than that the truth and nothing but the truth about the meaning of the Gospel shall become manifest? Theological scholarship certainly provides many examples of men falling into error, misled by the prejudices of their day. It is here, however, that scientific criticism can make its best contribution in correcting such aberrations, and just at this point philosophy and the philosophy of religion can play their most valuable roles, in exposing false presuppositions and unconscious confusion of categories—things that often lie in the background when a science falls into error.

The main question that concerned the philosophy of religion when I was a student was that of the "religious a priori," which had been raised by scholars like Ernst Troeltsch and Rudolf Otto. Since in my studies I had begun to conceive of a quite different form of the philosophy of religion, a scientific, critical form, a reckoning with the idealist, philosophical theories of these authors was inevitable. An exhaustive analysis of the concept of a priori would have to be undertaken to get to the heart of the problem and to understand the ideas that lay behind and found expression in these statements about a religious a priori. This was the purpose of my doctoral thesis, which was called *Religiöst a priori*. This was to some extent an unfortunate title, because it was understood in some quarters to be the outline of a program of research, whereas in fact it was only intended to state the problem, and the direction in which its solution, or rather its dissolution should be sought.

When my work was nearing completion, I undertook something that could be called empirical, or rather quite simply, experimental theology and philosophy. It has always struck me as curious to write about the work of living authors without first giving them an opportunity to express their views on the objections to be brought against their ideas. Why not discuss your objections with them and thereby both ensure that you are rightly interpreting their ideas and also discover their reaction to the objections? In 1920, therefore, I travelled to Germany and was able to discuss the problems personally not only with Troeltsch and Otto, but also with a number of other scholars among whom Carl Stange should particularly be mentioned; he had not directly dealt with the question of a priori, but his philosophy of religion did approach the critical, scientific type. I found in full measure what I was looking for on this journey, but it also brought me something much greater and much more important in my life. Like Saul the son of Kish, who went out to find his father's asses and found his kingdom, I went to discuss my theological and philosophical problems with a number of German scholars, and amply found what I was looking for, but I also found something else I was not looking for; I found my kingdom—my wife. Even before we were engaged she helped me (she had herself studied under Troeltsch at Berlin University) to translate my plan of attack on Troeltsch into perfect German, and this gave me an excellent starting point for my conversation with him. And since then she has always helped me through; everything I have written we have thoroughly discussed together, and the greater part of it she has translated into German.

In the year 1921 I became Docent in the Philosophy of Religion at the University of Lund. This gave the subject a rather more independent status than it had previously had, even though for purposes of examination it was still combined with history of religions. When I became professor of systematic theology (especially ethics) three years later in 1924, the philosophy of religion was in due course included in my responsibilities. To look ahead a moment, when I retired from my professorship in 1948, two professors were appointed in my place, one for ethics and the other for philosophy of religion, and thus philosophy of religion had its own independent professorship within the Faculty of Theology.

My university appointment meant in one way a tremendous change for me, but in a deeper way there was, paradoxically enough, no change at all. What had previously been my hobby became my work and what had now become my work nonetheless remained as my hobby. What was new was the obligation to give lectures; but the way "docent lectures" were arranged made them in fact just an extension of my research work and a happy stimulus for it. In general I was exceptionally fortunate with my docent lectures. To have a smallish group of students who took the course not because they were obliged to, but purely out of interest, could not but be stimulating in the highest degree. There was no need to adapt the presentation to the nature of the audience, since they wished for nothing better than that the lectures should be concerned solely with the nature of the problems. Thus the very lectures became a powerful driving force for my research, and a splendid help with my writing. Unfortunately this fruitful period of docent work lasted only three years, but these three years gave rise to two fairly major works already mentioned as *The Scientific Basis of Dogmatics* in 1922 and *Philosophical and Christian Ethics* in 1923, and there was also the preparatory work for further studies. Both these books arose directly from my docent lectures, but they were of course made possible by the previous years' work, and took further the view of philosophy and theology which already appeared in *Religiöst a priori*. In the interests of clarity it should be said that when in this context I speak of the "Kant-Schleiermacher presentation of the problem" there is no question of adopting either Kant's position or Schleiermacher's. I strongly dissociate myself from both of them, and have demonstrated their untenability. It is a question only of taking up a quite definite, carefully delimited line of thought which could be made fruitful in the attempt to lay a scientific and methodologically valid foundation for philosophy and theology. This is the line of thought and method that Kant described as the "transcendental method," but which is better and more clearly described as the "logical analysis of presuppositions." We have no use for an arbitrary and unscientific philosophy or theology. Both secular philosophy and the philosophy of religion, as well as theology, are all threatened by the same sickness, namely metaphysics, and it is to prevent this that we need the "logical analysis of presuppositions." All my work on problems of method has had this one end constantly in view: to lay down a solid basis for theology and philosophy and in both these fields to overcome the threat of the metaphysical and the arbitrary. Apart from this, philosophy and theology work with quite different presuppositions and under different conditions, but at this point both are under the same threat.

I count it among the most stimulating experiences of this period that I was involved in the founding of the Lund Philosophical Society, and was made its first president. This brought about a number of fruitful contacts, both in Sweden and beyond. Strangely enough, it was the contacts within Sweden that were weakest at this time. Even at the time of writing my thesis my knowledge of Uppsala philosophy was very limited. Philosophically, Uppsala and Lund represented two separate and distinct worlds, and without direct access to the oral tradition of Uppsala, it was difficult to follow the philosophical thinking that was being done there. Axel Hägerström's *Das Prinzip der Wissenschaft* seemed to me far too involved with metaphysical ideas, and I had therefore not gone further in this direction. Through the Philosophical Society I now had the chance to hear and to get to know personally both him and more especially his younger colleague Adolf Phalén, a most acute thinker. My view of the task of philosophy as the analysis of concepts was further strengthened by my contact with these men, but the suggestion sometimes made, that my work has deeper affinities with Uppsala philosophy, is an invention that needs demythologizing.

When in 1924 I became one of the two professors of systematic theology in Lund, I became part of a unique working team. These were happy years for the faculty and its members. There was great enthusiasm for the work and a rich output of scholarship, and the personal contacts and friendships were rich and satisfying. When I think back to the faculty in which I was privileged to take my place, I picture it above all as a great family in which every member made his contribution to the happiness of all. In particular I must mention the closest of my professional colleagues, Gustaf Aulén, with whom I shared the teaching of theology. I had first met him about ten years before at one of the first seminars for licentiates in theology held by him after his appointment as professor. My assignment on that occasion was to give an exposition of the famous section four of Schleiermacher's *Der Christliche Glaube*. This was my first opportunity to present my ideas on the Kant-Schleiermacher presentation of the problem, ideas which were later to play a central part in *Religiöst a priori* and to be comprehensively treated in *The Scientific Basis of Dogmatics*. Even at that first meeting I had been struck by the openness and generosity which were characteristic of Gustaf Aulén's thought, and which now as his closest colleague I was able to enjoy. There is no doubt at all that the co-operation that then began was something quite unique. I can never be too grateful that for the first ten years of my professorship I had Gustaf Aulén beside me. Nor am I any less grateful than when he gave up his professorship to become Bishop of Strängnäs, his successor was Ragnar Bring, with whom the same spirit of co-operation continued down the years. He and I had become acquainted quite early on when, after finishing his basic studies in philosophy at Uppsala, he came to study theology at Lund. Through him I gained many insights into the Uppsala philosophy. Both philosophically and theologically we stand very near each other, and so he, as no one else, has been able to give a sympathetic account and exposition of the main outlines of my philosophy of religion in the first essay in this book.

Because of the philosophical and methodological studies of the previous years, even though they were not really adequate for so great a subject, the way was now clear for the treatment of those problems which concern the subject matter of theology. These had, of course, been present throughout, for method is nothing without the subject matter and content, which one is seeking to order. On its own, method has no value. The whole of the later part of *Philosophical and Christian Ethics* was devoted to the problem of the unique character of the Christian ethic, a problem of the content of theology, not of theological method. My purpose was to show that the person of Jesus Christ is central to the Christian faith, and how in Him God meets us as self-revealing, judging, atoning, and fellowship-creating Love, and it is this that gives the Christian ethic its specific character: life in Christ is life in love. But at this point another problem had arisen. It was my old problem: what is meant by agape in a Christian context.

Since the time of Augustine it has been agreed that Christianity is the religion of love, but what exactly do we mean when we thus speak of love? To some this seems a wholly superfluous question; when Christianity speaks of love it surely means just love! Yes, indeed—but the matter is not quite so simple. What exactly we mean by it is a more complicated question. Surely no one can overlook the fact, to take but one example, that when Augustine speaks of amor he means something quite different from what Paul means when he talks of agape. If we use the word *love* to translate both, this must not be allowed to lead us into a confusion of ideas. Yet to talk simply of Christian love is in fact to accept this confusion. The word is used without any particular meaning being given to it. For one person it will mean a demanding love, for another sentimental love, for a third some sort of sublimated eros, for a fourth the agape of the cross, and so on. The only way forward is through a careful analysis of concepts and motifs.

From a wide range of possible and actual confusions I selected one complex, the one that has decidedly played the greatest and most fateful part in the history of the Christian Idea of Love, the complex "Agape and Eros." It was the actual course of the history of Christian thought with its conflicts and syntheses of Biblical and Hellenistic ideas that dictated this approach. Moreover there was a more personal factor involved. For many years I had been fascinated by the personality and writings of Plato, with which I had become acquainted partly in Swedish translations, and partly in Schleiermacher's celebrated translations. Because I had this positive interest in the legacy of Plato's thought, I hoped I might be able to carry through this analysis of the influence of Biblical thought, on the one hand, and of Platonic, Aristotelian and neoplatonic thought, on the other, with due strictness and without falling into the usual evaluative comparisons. Such evaluations were not intended nor needed. The task of scientific scholarship is to describe not to evaluate. Again and again in my work it is emphasized that the terms agape and eros are not used as value judgments, but purely and exclusively as descriptions. It is all too easy for us to use words like "Biblical," "New Testament" (in its adjectival meaning), and "Christian" as evaluations. Once when lecturing in Norway I used a very forcible illustration to repudiate this confusion of description and evaluation. Imagine a plainsman from the flat homely agricultural province of Scania in Southern Sweden, who out of pure local patriotism has got into the habit of using the word "Scanian" to describe all the things he most values. Take him to Norway and show him the grandeur and majesty of the Norwegian mountains; what are we to think when he expresses his feelings in the words "Isn't that just a real Scanian landscape"? This is exactly what innumerable writers are doing when they persist in describing as Christian, ideas which clearly belong to and get their meaning from non-Christian contexts and motifs. Why do they do this? Simply because they themselves value these ideas. Is there nothing of value to be found outside the realm of Christianity?

In the later 1930's exegetics and systematic theology had drawn so near to each other in Swedish theology that it was possible to establish an even closer co-operation. My old idea of a new sort of commentary on the New Testament was now revived in a more concrete form. My colleague in systematic theology, Professor Ragnar Bring and I, with three exegetes, Professor Anton Fridrichsen of Uppsala and Professors Johannes Lindblom and Hugo Odeberg of Lund, co-operated to start the series of commentaries *Tolkning av Nya Testamentet* [The Interpretation of the New Testament]. The principle in this series was that in the preparation the authors should work their material with all the rigor of strictly scientific scholarship, but in the presentation they should, as it were, keep all this scholarly apparatus to themselves, so that no scaffolding should be allowed to obscure the structure and thought of the New Testament text.

In working on *Agape and Eros* and *Commentary on Romans* I

came to a clearer understanding of the fundamental importance of a few great and simple principles of research, which can be summarized under the three following heads:

1] Always begin with the sources. Do not be distracted by the secondary literature from the primary concern with the sources. If the secondary literature is allowed in too soon, it prevents clear perception of what the sources really contain; one can only see and recognize what others have found there.

2] When through personal investigation you have come to know the sources through and through and have a clear idea of what their purpose and meaning is, then and only then can the secondary literature be of tremendous help. You can compare what you yourself have seen with what others have seen, what you yourself have discovered in the texts with the discoveries of others. Such a comparison can greatly enrich the investigation; what other scholars have seen can complement and correct your views, and what you have seen can be the starting point for a critical survey of what has already been done in this field.

3] Look for all possible objections to your own theory. *Search out instances of negative evidence*—the more the better. If your theory is wrong, the best thing that can happen is that you yourself discover this as soon as possible, and reject the false theory, to start over again, one experience the richer. If on the other hand, the theory is basically sound, it will certainly be far too rigid in its first form, and contradictory examples can be a valuable help in refining it. Only a theory that has withstood the refining fire of such negative criticism can claim to be a scientific-based hypothesis. Within the realm of science we cannot go beyond hypotheses.

For all their simplicity these principles are an effective way of freeing oneself from the overwhelming power of a tradition that can, nevertheless, at times be completely wrong. To escape from tradition in this way is urgently necessary. For example, in fairly modern histories of doctrine we can find some quite peripheral utterance used to sum up the teaching of one of the Fathers, as if it were one of his central and most characteristic ideas. The reason for this is quite simply that this view is supported by a long-standing tradition. If we follow this tradition back through the years, it may turn out to be centuries old, perhaps going back to the thirteenth or fourteenth century, when theology used the *sic-et-non* method, and tried to find authorities to support a particular view. Any statement in one of the Fathers that seemed to support the view in question was eagerly grasped, even though in its context it was not a central idea. For the particular occasion the statement was of great importance; for it was not a question of a historical interest in discovering the author's characteristic ideas, but simply of a dogmatic interest in finding authorities to support a particular view. But why should we continue this error since in the context of our historical interest it is pointless, and the only reason for it is that for centuries the Father in question has been connected with this idea? I am not, of course, implying that the modern historian of doctrine has not read the Fathers; of course he has, but when he came across this saying, in the joy of recognition he concluded that the facts of the matter were just what the traditional view maintained. This is one example of the necessity of escaping from it by means of the simple methodological principles enumerated above.

The years of my professorship saw the rise and fall of the "Third Reich." About the time of the Nazi *coup d'état* I frequently visited Berlin for several months to read in the *Staatsbibliothek*. In this way I had the opportunity of following in detail the developments in church and state, and was able to appreciate the horrors that were in store. On my return to Sweden I contributed a number of articles to the Swedish press exposing various aspects of the new regime. In November 1933 I gave an address in the Great Hall of the Students' Union in Lund on the new situation in Germany. The hall was, of course, crowded, but after the lecture I gathered from the questions of the audience that they had difficulty in believing that the situation really was as I had described it—it was just not possible. Yet there was worse to come. This very idea, so widespread throughout the world, that the thing was not possible, was in fact one of the factors that made it possible.

In this context I think particularly of my friend Birger Forell, minister of the Swedish congregation in Berlin, who made his home a refuge and meeting place for many persecuted Germans. Through him I was able to meet many of the leading opponents of Hitler and even occasionally to take part in their meetings. Since the Germans had officially no freedom of speech, I felt it incumbent upon me to speak in their stead, and in this connection visited various German ministries, a remarkable experience. In the Ministry for Interior Affairs I received a concrete experience of the new Nazi concept of truth, that is, "Truth is what is to the advantage of your own people." The official who received me outlined the new situation, but all that he said was what we ordinary mortals call untrue. When in the course of our conversation he realized that I was well acquainted with the situation, his whole approach changed. He accepted my point of view and tried as far as possible to put things in a favorable light. He seemed no whit troubled by his "double-think," and indeed why should he? Measured by the new concept of truth he had spoken the truth both times. If a foreigner who apparently knows nothing, should come, it is "to the advantage of your own people" to pull the wool over his eyes. If it appears that he is well acquainted with the situation, it is "to the advantage of your own people" to try to put things in as favorable a light as you can. From such negotiations one returned with an increased affection for our old honest concept of truth. It was also a great joy to me to see how young students who had been fed for a long time on the new concept of truth and had accepted it, after some hours of discussion came over to my, that is to say our common western, idea of truth. Human intelligence will not let itself be smothered! This gives hope for the future too.

Some of my articles on the German question I collected in a book *Den tyska kyrkostriden,* 1934, and Edition 1935, *The German Church Conflict,* which was also published in English and Dutch, but naturally *not* in German. My articles nevertheless were not unknown in Germany. They circulated among the opposition, and more than that, when I visited the *Reichsinnenministerium* they brought out from the files my articles—translated into German! Not only the Germans were under supervision! The books and the articles, however, cost me four years *Reise-und Redeverbot* (ban on travel and public speech) in Germany. I had been invited to give a series of lectures there, but this had to be withdrawn on orders from Berlin which described me as *"dem Deutschen Staate nicht tragbar"* (*persona non grata* to the German state). The satisfaction of having this in black and white easily overcame my disappointment at being unable to give the lectures.

After the collapse of Germany in 1945 I seized the first possible opportunity to renew my broken contacts. Travel was difficult in Germany at that time; the railways were destroyed and trains had to be redirected over long diversions, and in spite of many months of negotiations I had not managed to get a visa for the East Zone. By order of the Allies and on an allied troop train I was able to pass through the East Zone, and on arrival in Berlin was able in ten minutes to get the long desired visa from the Russian military command. It was moving to see how great was the longing of the Germans for fellowship after the long years of separation. Although the lectures I was to deliver dealt with subjects of no great attraction and under normal circumstances would have drawn only small audiences, it was now necessary to use the *auditorium maximum* or the Great Hall of the universities in which I lectured. It was neither the lecturer nor the subject that formed the attraction, but the simple fact that someone from outside had managed to penetrate the dividing curtain. It was like Noah's dove returning with the olive branch, the first sign that the Flood had begun to ebb from the earth and normal life was beginning again.

There was in England after the war one prison camp that was unique, Norton Camp. Its uniqueness lay in the fact that there were assembled here a hundred or so theological students and a number of theological teachers, all prisoners of war, who formed a theological school or faculty, or what you will. The "principal" was Professor Gerhard Friedrich, the present editor of Kittel's *Theologisches Wörterbuch zum Neuen Testament*. For a prison camp this was a most brilliant and humane arrangement, and it had come about partly through the good offices of Birger Forell, whom I have spoken of already. There was, however, a shortage of teachers. One more professor was needed for the students to have this period officially recognized as part of their studies. With the permission of the competent authorities I was able to concentrate my teaching in Lund so as to leave the necessary time free for Norton Camp. In three weeks I gave fifty lectures there, half in New Testament exegesis and half in dogmatics. This period of concentrated association with the students and their teachers was for me a unique high point in my life. My farewell was also unique; I received a document which conferred on me the honor of *Doctor Captivitatis*. The seal was made of a piece of barbed wire. And there was something else unique too: the camp had its own printing press. Shortly before my journey to England I had been commissioned by the Lutheran World Federation to prepare an official paper on "The Word, The Sacraments and the Church" to be presented to the Lutheran World Conference in Lund in July 1947. This paper in its original form was first printed at the Norton Camp printing office.

One more thing must be mentioned from the time of my professorship. At the Lutheran World Conference in 1947 I was made President of the Lutheran World Federation for the next five-year period. I must emphasize that this was done while I was still a professor, since it seems to me to be significant that the choice of the first President of the Lutheran World Federation was not from the ranks of the church leaders but from among the professors. It is a reminder that in Lutheran theology scholarship has always held a central place.

The Lutheran World Federation made possible a great number of valuable personal contacts and brought a tremendous widening of outlook, as well as travel to various parts of the world. In my last year as professor I spent five months in the United States and Canada, the first months to become acclimatized and the remainder to deliver lectures in about twenty theological faculties and seminaries. This was an unparalleled way of getting to know the theological and church life of America, restricted as I was to the theological world.

In November 1948, I was appointed Bishop of Lund. A new era in my life had begun, yet from another point of view it was not so new, and did not wholly lack continuity with the past. When I took my seat as Bishop of Lund's Cathedral Chapter, it was just twenty-five years since I took my seat as a member of the same Cathedral chapter—the chapter in those days consisted of the members of the theological faculty. For a quarter of a century I had taken part in the administration of the diocese with great interest, and knew the diocese well. And that which had to do with pastoral responsibilities was my first love. Nevertheless I had never thought of a bishopric. When I had been offered one in other dioceses I had declined out of regard to my work as a scholar, which I understood to be the duty I had to fulfill. Now that Lund was in question the situation was rather different. The demands of my journey to Germany, England, and the United States had meant that after completing my *Commentary on Romans* I had not seriously resumed the work of scholarship that lay waiting for me, and my involvement in the Lutheran World Federation and my ecumenical duties cast a long shadow over the future. I was therefore unable with complete conviction to present the same reasons for a refusal. Moreover, the fact that it was Lund made a difference, for there I could maintain the old contact with the theological faculty.

The diocese is an excellent organization inherited from the past, which we could never have invented. Certainly the Bishop's visitations do not give a direct impression of the daily life of the parish; this comes to him through the minister's report at the time of the visitation. But the significance of the visitation is not so much that it is a check on the life of the church as an inspiration to it. The congregation is always well represented at the visitation service and the church crowded with people. Since the visitation is a great church festival it gives the congregation an opportunity to show itself as it ought and wishes to be, but often is not. The discussion with the parish's representatives and the presentation of the result to the parish as a whole makes it possible for the bishop—just because he comes from outside—to say a word of exhortation and encouragement to the parish in a way that the parish's own minister cannot. The visitation breaks into the everyday and the parochial and arouses the parish's awareness of being a part of a greater whole, in the last resort part of the whole church on the earth, of the Body of Christ. Not the least important task of the bishop is that of *consolator pastorum*. This was for me a particularly congenial task, as most of the ministers I met in the parishes were old pupils of mine from Lund.

My participation in ecumenical work covered practically the whole of my time as professor and bishop and some years beyond. More active participation began with the World Conference on Faith and Order at Lausanne in 1927. That first meeting was marked, on the one hand, by clear desire for brotherly encounter, and on the other hand, by a great ignorance and lack of positive understanding of each other. In these circumstances it was not easy to make any contribution. My only contribution was limited to something wholly negative: to the scotching of a proposal to work out a new confession of faith (with a Ritschlian flavor). A confession of faith should never be drawn up on the basis of a passing theological outlook, least of all when it is nearing its dissolution. I am convinced that if this proposal had been taken to the assembly, it would have been rejected there. But already concern with such unreal proposals had become a handicap to the newborn ecumenism.

Ten years later in 1937 the churches met again, this time in two world conferences, first "Life and Work" at Oxford, and shortly afterwards "Faith and Order" at Edinburgh. It was naturally the latter with its concentration on the central question of belief that interested me most. By now the climate had changed to some extent. The churches had still rather hazy ideas about each other; one very often came across the idea that Lutheranism would be a nuisance ecumenically and uninterested in the unity of the church, an idea that was apparent even in the preparatory material for the conference. This was a complete surprise to me. From my earliest years I had learnt from St. Paul that the church is the Body of Christ, and that all divisions are therefore an injury to Christ Himself: "Is Christ divided?" From Luther himself I had learnt always to direct my gaze on "die ganze Christenheit auf Erden" (The Church of the Third Article, *tota ecclesia in terra*). To bring some light into the situation Professor Jens Nørregaard, the Danish church historian, and I were commissioned to give some guiding lectures on Lutheranism, he on the historical aspect and I on the systematic. This cleared the air; people realized that Lutheranism does not consist of abstruse doctrines, but of simple Christian faith. Moreover this directed the work of the first section to the central point of the Gospel and to Christ, the center of the Gospel, and the result was that we came at last to complete unity. It was a historic moment, and the members of the section broke spontaneously into a *Te Deum*. One of the chief contributors to this happy result was the Orthodox theologian N. V. Arseniev. Later this report, alone among the sectional reports, was unanimously accepted by the Assembly. How had this surprising unity been achieved? I answered this question with the phrase "The way to the center is the way to unity," a phrase which later became an ecumenical slogan.

In comparison with Edinburgh, the next World Conference was almost a step backwards. On the level of organization, Amsterdam had great significance in the setting up of the World Council of Churches, in which Life and Work and Faith and Order came together in a greater whole. But the theological thinking also was too much in terms of organization; how do *we* agree or disagree with one another? Particularly disturbing was the attempt to present the churches as two blocks, the Catholic, which holds to continuity, and the Protestant, which asserts discontinuity. I protested against this and demonstrated the untenability of the idea by explaining that I (the president of the Lutheran World Federation!) must attach myself to the "catholic" side since I believe in continuity in the Church: Christ is present in His Church not as an occasional event now and then, but "always, to the end of time." This subject of "catholic and protestant" gave rise to strong disagreement in the Assembly, and I was asked if I were willing to be in on the setting up of a new commission on "different sorts of continuity." This came to grief because several proposed members were unable to free themselves for this work. The question was, however, to arise once more in an improved form at the next Faith and Order Conference at Lund in 1952.

Meanwhile the idea had gradually crystallized that the ecumenical task should begin not in our attempts to bring about the unity of the church, but rather in the unity of the Church *already given in Christ*. Ecclesiology, that is to say, must be brought back to Christology (and to Pneumatology). This idea was strongly supported by such theologians as T. Torrance of Edinburgh and E. Schlink of Heidelberg. The Lund Conference therefore resolved to set up a new "Theological Commission on Christ and His Church" in two sections, one in America and one in Europe. I was chairman of the latter and thus was able over a period of ten years to work together with Schlink, Torrance, G. Florovsky, the Orthodox theologian, and a number of other theologians of different confessions. The subject was, of course, too big and comprehensive to be completely worked out in the available time, but fortunately the commission also received a special mandate, namely the question of baptism. The terms of the mandate were to begin from the fact that the majority of churches acknowledge each other's baptism, and to show the ecumenical implications of baptism for the unity of the Church. But this did not work at all. The first report of this commission was shot to pieces at the Faith and Order Commission meeting at New Haven in 1957, and it was as well that it was, for the unity of the Church is not based on our recognition of each other or of each other's baptism. The question was referred back to the theological commission, this time with no restrictions. We are now able to take up the question from its own central Christological starting point; the baptism of Jesus as consecration to his Messianic vocation, our baptism as incorporation in the Messianic community, in the Body of Christ, with all the light that is shed from this central point on the *meaning of baptism*—something about which every church has an endless amount to learn with respect to its own understanding of baptism. And indeed when this central point was reached, the Edinburgh experience was repeated. There was a great unanimity in spite of the fact that the commission included such varied members of Anglicans and Lutherans, Greek Orthodox, Presbyterians, Congregationalists, Methodists, Baptists and Quakers. At the Faith and Order Commission meeting at St. Andrews in 1960 the reception was as positive as it had been negative at New Haven in 1957. When there was the right starting point, then, unity too was achieved. If the New Haven meeting gave a negative proof, that of St. Andrew gave a positive proof for the statement, "The way to the center is the way to unity." The ecumenical situation can be illustrated thus: if every church will only dig sufficiently far down towards the center of the Christian faith, they will meet at one point, in Christ. The Church is the Body of Christ.

In speaking of the ecumenical, I also include the Lutheran World Federation. It is not a gathering of like-minded people of a sect. It is churches of the Reformation gathered around the Gospel that belongs to the whole Church on earth. And the particular ecumenical task of Lutheranism is constantly to point to the center, Christ alone.

There is much more that could be told from the ecumenical field, for example, from the Lutheran-Roman Conference at Berlin-Herms-dorf in 1934, with twelve theologians from either side (this was a forerunner of the present conversations between Roman and Lutheran theologians). For over a week we met to talk together on "Justification and Grace" and had a truly profound discussion. I could mention too the Lutheran-Reformed conversations of later years. In every case there is the same experience: the nearer you get to the center, the more easily do you achieve understanding and unity.

Finally, a brief word about my present occupation; in my last years as professor I was planning to take up again the problem of the philosophy of religion, because there was still a great deal there that was left undone. Both theology and philosophy have suffered great harm through not being on speaking terms with each other for so long. After my retirement, my plans, which had to be set aside while I was a diocesan bishop, once more demanded my full attention. An incredible amount has happened in the realm of philosophy, and as it has turned out the compulsory postponement has actually favoured my plans. With respect to my problems, time has worked only to advantage. In recent years, everything that we call philosophy has begun, though with quite a different intention and orientation, to concern itself in one way and another with the analysis of meaning. Thus, there is a wealth of new material to illuminate my old problems of the analysis of concepts and meaning, of contexts of meaning and motif. In an essay entitled "From Atomism to Contexts of Meaning in Philosophy" (published in *Philosophical Essays dedicated to Gunnar Aspelin*, Lund, 1963) I have outlined the development that has taken place, using Ludwig Wittgenstein, perhaps the foremost thinker of our age, as an example. The flood of new philosophical literature that has poured forth in recent decades, and demands attention, is practically impossible to take in. In the near future I shall present the results of my work in a study entitled "Meaning and Method: Prolegomena to a Scientific Philosophy of Religion."

Just when I had begun the preparatory work for this study, I received an invitation to give a term's lectures on the philosophy of religion in the University of Minnesota, and then to work a year thereafter as "resident scholar" at the Ecumenical Institute in Evanston (one term of which was to be spent as visiting professor at Chicago Divinity School), all this with the generous support of the Danforth Foundation. Nothing could have fitted in better with my plans. My visit to the United States in these favorable conditions afforded me extremely valuable personal contacts, as well as insights into Anglo-American philosophy that were of exceptional value for my work. For this I can never be too grateful.

THEOLOGIAN AND MINISTER—in the service of scholarship and of the Church!

In the midst of human life with all its richness and all its tragedy, the Gospel of Jesus Christ is heard, God's "yes" to his mankind, giving them a new beginning and a new hope. The theologian interprets and the minister proclaims this gospel. Here is a twofold vocation for which one cannot help but be grateful.

Anders Nygren

Lund, Sweden
1969

Philosophy of Religion

I

ANDERS NYGREN'S PHILOSOPHY

OF RELIGION

Ragnar Bring

EVER since the Enlightenment, the problem of the relationship between the truth of the Christian faith and what philosophy affirms
has been constantly in the foreground. This problem, expressed in
other terms, was of course present much earlier. During the Middle
Ages one sought to determine the right relationship between reason
and revelation. Thomas Aquinas, who thought in Aristotelian terms,
conceived of revelation as the fulfillment of reason; revelation completed and raised all human knowledge to a new and higher plane.
Within Occamistic philosophy of religion, revelation was not merely
a higher grade of knowledge than reason, but reason and revelation
were conceived as two different kinds of knowledge, which accordingly did not stand on the same level. Luther rejected Aristotle and
could appear to have been an Occamist. Although he never developed
his own philosophy of religion, it is nonetheless possible to note indirectly how he thought. Reason for him was in part something good
and necessary, especially when human and temporal relationships were
concerned. But reason could also become an enemy to faith, if man
sought thereby to determine his relationship to God. A tendency in
this direction, always to be found in man, made it evident that man
was a part of the fallen world.

TRANSLATED BY BERNHARD ERLING

After Luther, through an Aristotelian and Greek dominated scholastic philosophy, an earlier scholastic view of the relation between philosophy and Christianity returned. Certain articles of faith were based on both reason and revelation, making for a kind of "natural" theology, while other articles were based on revelation alone. In the theology of the Enlightenment, "natural theology" was expanded until all of Christianity was so understood, and since no effort was made to distinguish Christianity from other religions, it could be called "natural religion." This changed the meaning of natural theology, and revelation became equivalent to that which was rationally given. This understanding of reason and revelation came to have great influence upon philosophy of religion. Even in our days it has showed its strength, as among those who insist that religious propositions must be established as true before the bar of reason if they are to be valid.

It was Schleiermacher who first of all directed a critique against the Enlightenment's view of natural religion. We can begin our presentation of Nygren's philosophy of religion by examining this critique. The basic concept of the theology of the Enlightenment was that Christianity was a natural religion in that in its essence it gave expression to something wholly rational and universally moral. It was, therefore, as Tindal put it, as old as the world. It expressed the rational and moral content of the human spirit. When Schleiermacher, however, addressed his *Speeches on Religion* to the cultured despisers of Christianity of his time, he made no attempt to develop an apology for Christianity on the basis of such an understanding of the essence of religion. He maintained, on the contrary, that there was no natural religion; each religion was *historical* and *concrete*. There were many religions, each having its own structure, its own message, that which for it was central. Thus each religion could be studied with respect to its ideational content. Since each individual religion actually had its own aims and purposes, all its ideas cohered together and had one center. Each religion formed what Schleiermacher called an "individuality," i.e., it represented an organic whole, a structure with a definite center. This annulled one aspect of the idea of natural religion, the notion that there was basically only one religion. But another aspect of natural religion, that religion should coincide with knowing (ratio) and be identical with morality, was also thereby annulled. For if there were many religions, which were all independent, each having its own core, its own essence, they could not all coincide with knowledge, nor all represent the same moral outlook.

The chief result of Schleiermacher's critique was that the general concept of religion was seen to include completely different religious outlooks, and the problem arose as to how these were related to each other. Beyond this there was not one unified concept of morality, but different moral outlooks. Finally, the content of religion, morality, and knowledge could not be said to be a priori identical. Nygren, who proceeds from such an interpretation of Schleiermacher, has in his book, *Dogmatikens vetenskapliga grundläggning*,[1] sought to develop Schleiermacher's critique of natural religion even further. The mixing together of morality, religion, and knowledge leads, according to Nygren, to metaphysics. While a connection with metaphysics may have been acceptable in the case of some religions, Nygren holds that there is a decided difference between what Christianity and metaphysics signify. Nygren regards metaphysics as a mixing of religion and knowledge, the validity of which the philosophy and the theology of the Enlightenment may at times have supported, but which is untenable.

As far as Schleiermacher is concerned, Nygren holds that despite Schleiermacher's rejection in principle of the concept of a natural religion, he actually finally made use of certain of its ideas in a new form. "The feeling of absolute dependence" became for him that which characterized all religion, and when this feeling of absolute dependence was conceived in psychological terms, it itself became a kind of natural religion, which united the different religions with one another. It then would still be necessary to define the theoretical content of this feeling, the thoughts and ideas bound up with it, and to compare these with science, or to point out the extent to which they gave expression to theoretical truths. In *Dogmatikens vetenskapliga grundläggning* Nygren has demonstrated how Schleiermacher, despite his intention to present the feeling of absolute dependence as a purely formal concept (as a category), instead inconsistently let it be conceived as determined in its content (as an emotional experience common to all religions), and thus he himself ended up with a new form of "natural religion."

As has already been pointed out, Nygren can be said to make use of the conclusions attained in Schleiermacher's *Speeches*. Nygren regards it established that the concept of natural religion in the form it took in the period of the Enlightenment is impossible. But he regards Schleiermacher's solution as on the whole untenable, although it is wholly correct that each religion represents an organic unity, an "individuality." [2] The question then becomes: How are the different religions related to each other? Do they have anything in common? And how shall one understand the relation between religion (especially Christianity) and science?

Here Nygren has been able to make use of certain Kantian ideas. Kant's basic problem was epistemological. He inquired as to the possibility of the *validity* of knowledge. How can the knowledge which we gain empirically receive a certainty, a validity, comparable to the certainty of mathematical knowledge? Kant examined the presuppositions of knowledge, and arrived at what he called the transcendental presuppositions of knowledge: space, time, and the categories. These provided not only the presuppositions, but also the boundaries of theoretical knowledge. With these presuppositions it followed that metaphysics, which was regarded as closely connected with religion, could not have scientific validity.

But does not religion then fall; is not all religion impossible? Many thought so. Kant did not in the final analysis have this opinion, but his understanding of Christianity tended to remain within the framework of the theology of the Enlightenment. Nygren has a wholly different understanding of Christianity from Kant, but builds upon his philosophical ideas and seeks to explain how religion and science are related to each other. Metaphysics seeks to let the concept of God represent the highest reality, and this in such a way that one can gain a scientifically modeled knowledge of God. But this becomes philosophically impossible after Kant. Nygren follows Kant and rejects all metaphysics; there is no science of that which is beyond space and time. To this radical, apparently positivistic thesis he adds the affirmation that not only is theology not metaphysical knowledge, but that Christianity also, as *religion*, has nothing to do with metaphysics. He insists that metaphysics is actually an impossible confusion of religion and science. Its religious side can, however, be dominant and constitute the nerve of a strong and intensive religion, as is the case in Neoplatonism.

But how then can the relation between Christianity and philosophy, or more generally between faith and knowledge, be understood? In answering this question, Nygren begins with certain positive results which he believes Kant achieved, quite apart from his critique of metaphysics. It is now common to regard Kant as wholly antiquated and his ideas unusable in modern philosophy. To be sure, much in his system, as well as in Neo-Kantianism, may be considered obsolete, representing thinking which modern philosophy must entirely abandon. At the same time one need not, therefore, conclude that there are no proposals in Kant which are usable and which could be developed further. When Nygren makes use of Kant, this is what he does: he takes certain ideas from Kant and gives them further development. Kant had analyzed the presuppositions of knowledge. He assumed that there were judgments, the validity of which could not be doubted. Such judgments were to be found in mathematics and the natural sciences. It was necessary only to find their presuppositions, and Kant found them in the forms of sensibility, space and time, and in the categories. Nygren makes use of this train of thought, but he develops it further. He notes that the presuppositions, which Kant proposed for knowledge, applied to knowledge in space and time, of which mathematics and natural science provide examples. The general question, which all the judgments here imply, has to do with that which is valid or true in the reality to be found within space and time. Judgments which have to do with this reality have the categories as presuppositions.

Here one could be tempted to propose, as is often done, that religion has to do with another reality. This seems to be a simple solution, but it leads, according to Nygren, to metaphysics, for in this manner we get two realities mutually limiting each other, both of which must be defined theoretically and scientifically. But any definition of reality beyond space and time would be metaphysical. There is, however, a tendency in Kant to let philosophical analysis apply primarily to knowledge and judgments, rather than to reality. Nygren develops this idea further and makes the point that the concept of reality can never be made central for philosophy. If one does this, one lands in metaphysics, either in idealism's assumption of another reality in addition to spatiotemporal reality, or in positivistic metaphysics, which in rejecting idealistic metaphysics makes spatiotemporal reality a reality in itself. If one assumes that a *certain* reality represents *all* reality, or reality as such, one is thinking metaphysically. This applies equally when one rejects a transcendent reality, conceiving spatiotemporal reality as reality in itself, as when one assumes another reality in addition to spatiotemporal reality. Materialism thus has just as much of a metaphysical character as idealism, even though the materialistic program calls for the rejection of metaphysics.

Instead of the concept of reality, Nygren makes the concept of validity central. This means that the decisive question has to do with the meaningfulness of judgments. In what manner and under what conditions are they valid? The actual correctness of a judgment is therefore not bound to its relation to spatiotemporal reality, but can refer to conditions under which something is valid and can claim to be correct or factual without being spatiotemporal. There can, accordingly, be kinds of judgments wholly different from theoretical judgments.

There has long been a distinction between the true, the good, and the beautiful, as between different kinds of values, different domains of human awareness. This suggests to Nygren that there are different domains of experience, in which different kinds of judgments can be found, each having validity in its domain. If Kant identified the transcendental presuppositions for the judgments in mathematics and the natural sciences, and found what must be the case if theoretical judgments (judgments affirming what is true with respect to that which can be defined in terms of space and time) are to be valid, then judgments which have to do with the good and the beautiful are equally valid, but in a different way. The fundamental questions which lie behind these judgments and which can be said to be connected with their transcendental presuppositions are: "What is beautiful?" and "What is good?" just as in the theoretical domain one asks: "What is true within space and time?" What is valid when, for example, we must presuppose that there is a relationship which we call cause and effect? In a similar manner one asks in the ethical domain: "What is good?" and in the aesthetic domain: "What is beautiful?" The answer to these questions remains undetermined; it is not hidden in the question itself, nor can it be derived from the question. All that must be presupposed is that the question is meaningful. It is not meaningless to ask about something good or something beautiful; there actually is something which we call good and beautiful, however our opinions as to what is good or beautiful may differ.

Nygren now sets up the question about religion as parallel to the above named basic questions. Religion in its various forms always touches upon the eternal, and thus Nygren holds that one can reckon with a domain where the judgments have to do with the eternal, and provide different answers to the question as to what is eternal. One could perhaps also say that the question has to do with the God relationship, to the extent that one finds this concept in every religion. For Buddhism, however, it is perhaps better to remain with the question of the eternal; nirvana refers to something eternal, even if one does not speak of any God. And one can also quite possibly conceive an atheistic religious orientation.

Nygren sees all judgments within the life of the human spirit as falling under certain transcendental presuppositions, which can be rewritten as universal questions concerning what is true in a theoretical sense, good in a moral sense, beautiful in an aesthetic sense, and eternally valid in a religious sense. Human experience can therefore be divided, according to Nygren, into different domains, and each domain has its special presuppositions. In the theoretical domain, the transcendental question concerning what is true in space and time applies, and *the different special sciences* provide answers to this question. It is, of course, possible that a science may give certain answers which later must be corrected. The answers can be changed, but they all receive their *meaning* in that they are designed to set forth what is true, what is valid when one asks about the domain with which the sciences are concerned. In the same manner quite different answers can be given to the question as to what is good. Out of the question itself—at the universal level, where one deals with that thinking or acting, which concretely affirms something *good*—no answer can be derived. Different ethical "basic motifs" and ideals can be affirmed. Here in the emotional domain, where feeling and will and also the unconscious have their place, different conceptions of what is good must be able to contend with each other; no theoretical demonstration can here be decisive. Here, at the level of what Kant called "the practical"—that which has to do with willing, feeling, and acting—a personal decision is necessary.

Something comparable is also the case, according to Nygren, where religion is concerned. The different religions cannot be reduced to certain common ideas; there is no natural religion in *this* sense. Each religion gives its own answer to the basic religious question. As Schleiermacher pointed out, each religion represents an organic unity. That which was called "the essence of religion" is not something with a defined content, but only an abstract viewpoint, a fundamental question, a transcendental presupposition for the religious ideas and the behavioral expressions to which it gives expression. One can, however, speak of the essence of an individual religion, e.g., the essence of Christianity. For an individual religion is an answer to the universal religious question, and these answers are always concrete and definite in their content. A religion has a definite center, something which colors all individual ideas in this religion. Together with "ideas" one could also say *decisions or patterns of behavior*. Ideas and patterns of behavior constitute a unity; when a person's ideas are not in accord with the behavioral pattern of a given religion, they become inappropriate expressions of this religion. A concrete religion, e.g., Christianity, has a definite center, and the task of theology is to find and clarify its content. Nygren calls this center the *basic motif* of the religion in question, i.e., the idea or the certainty, the emotional attitude, the spiritual conviction affecting one's whole orientation, which puts its stamp on everything. As far as Christianity is concerned, Nygren has defined this basic motif by fixing upon the New Testament message about God's agape, i.e., the love of God which in Christ has overcome that which opposes it, and triumphs through self-sacrifice. According to Nygren all Christian ideas cohere with this idea.[3]

There are, then, according to Nygren, different domains of experience, behind which are to be found different transcendental presuppositions, or, in other words, the contents of these domains can be understood as different answers to the basic questions which are the constituting presuppositions of these domains of experience. If it is a question of moral judgments, i.e., of ideas about good and evil, one cannot meaningfully ask about their truth or falsity in the same sense that one seeks the truth in the area of the natural sciences. Nevertheless, it is not meaningless to talk about good and evil, but the point of departure, the interest in putting the question, is wholly different from what is the case in the natural or other sciences. This is also the case with respect to religion. That which a religion has to say is not to give information about the natural sciences, but something else. It speaks of salvation, of a new life, of that which can never be wholly understood without making reference to something beyond that which is given in space and time.

Quite another matter is the fact that co-operation can exist between answers to different basic questions. In our time this is perhaps most apparent in the area of psychology. The Christian message about salvation has relevance for man's total behavior. Psychiatry's understanding of the unconscious, its techniques for carrying on a helpful conversation with a suffering individual, whereby release can be gained from that which binds the psyche, can provide answers to theoretical questions, but also at the same time be of the greatest importance for the religious question of salvation, and religious answers can also be of the greatest psychological importance.

We might further develop and describe this principle through discussing our relation to the Bible. We must, on the one hand, scientifically investigate the Bible, but it must then be clear to us, that the context in which we have put it is that of historical science, in which we receive answers only to historical questions. No historian through his research can reach God and his acts, any more than a natural scientist can find God in nature, if he remains on the scientific level. On the other hand, no science can render meaningless the message of the Bible—its religious meaning. For we can also read the Bible, putting it in the context of religion, and letting it answer, not the questions of history or science, but the questions of eternity. As God's Word the Bible speaks to us in a manner in which no science can speak or refute.

But at the same time it must be emphasized that the scientific and the religious approaches to the Bible (the Bible as a historical source and the Bible as God's Word) are two understandings of the Bible which do not contradict each other, but on the contrary can complement each other.[4] It was precisely through historical and philological investigations of the meaning of the concept of the righteousness of God that Luther broke through to the understanding that God in Christ is a giving love and his righteousness is not only demanding and condemning. And certainly Luther's understanding of the Word of God and the salvation it offers has something to contribute to psychology and psychiatry.

Thus, insights within the different domains of experience can be made to work together. But a presupposition for this possibility is that the separate aspects are basically distinguished and not confused. If they are confused no good results are possible. If Luther had not let philology be what it is, he would not have reached his reforming insight. And, on the other hand, if one does not let God's Word, e.g., the message about Christ's divine work, be what it is, but changes Christ into a Rabbi or an ideal man, then one destroys the very nerve of Christianity itself. Thus, the fact that judgments from different domains of experience can work together does not alter the fact that one must in principle separate them from each other. Science, religion, morality, and aesthetics represent different forms of the life of the human spirit, and each must first of all be understood for what it is in itself, from the viewpoints constitutive for its domain. Thus, one cannot do justice to a religious statement by pretending that it is scientific (theoretical) in nature, nor can one prove a moral thesis, e.g., that it is good to give oneself for others, since self-affirmation can appear equally reasonable. If one is to understand religious or moral judgments, one must view them in their own contexts, taking into account what they are trying to say, what they really mean.

This basic meaning must be grasped if one is to understand certain judgments. If, for example, one examines the ancient church's doctrine of the two natures of Christ, this doctrine would become meaningless if one were to conceive it in purely philosophical and scientific terms. It becomes, on the other hand, highly meaningful if one sees it in the context of the Bible's witness about the salvation of mankind through God's act in Christ, in the context of that act through which he lets man be incorporated in a new fellowship, a fellowship which is also eschatological in character, having its goal in eternity. That God lets man participate in his life through Christ is entirely meaningful in the context in which this idea appears in the Bible.

It is a truth which has become more and more clear for modern philosophy, that one can only understand a word in and through the context in which it is placed. In and by itself a word can ordinarily have many meanings. One must understand its place in a sentence and even in a broader context in order to grasp its function. Only through insight into its concrete function can it be rightly understood. This simple semantic insight is very similar to Nygren's attempt to distinguish between the different domains of experience, which in his later writings he prefers to call *contexts of meaning*. The result is that religious (as well as moral and aesthetic) judgments must be understood in the contexts in which they are given. Much critique that is directed against Christianity is based on the presupposition that Christianity claims to be a kind of science, as if, e.g., the creation account were a quasi-scientific description, or God a philosophically definable concept. But when interpreted in this manner Christian affirmations cannot be understood at all. It is their point of orientation which must be understood. What Nygren has sought to do is to define how all religions are so oriented that their judgments neither should nor can be understood as rational judgments.

Simple observation should teach us that religious judgments cannot be negated just because they do not provide answers to scientific questions or appear to be paradoxical. If there is validity for religious judgments, it is not of a theoretical kind. Just as Kant could affirm that valid knowledge (synthetic a priori judgments) were to be found in the natural sciences, whereupon it was necessary to discover their presuppositions, in order to determine their scope, so one can at once affirm that religious judgments cannot be neglected, but clearly have something specific to say. Their role cannot be taken over by other functions of the human spirit. It is therefore necessary to determine the presuppositions of these judgments.

Nygren's thought opens large perspectives and suggests a great many tasks. How shall one more specifically define such a transcendental deduction of religious judgments, which has only been sketchily proposed? What results can be gained through cooperation with philosophy, e.g., of the analytic kind? How shall the basic religious question, its category, be more specifically formulated—that which defines the context of meaning within which the different religions can be included, so that their affirmations become meaningful as different answers to the basic religious question? This category must itself be wholly without content, presenting only a universal viewpoint. It must never itself become the "essence" of religion, only a viewpoint such that all religious judgments can be subsumed under it.

IN the foregoing we have given a general survey of Nygren's philosophy of religion. We shall seek now to look at it more closely and in this connection raise some critical questions. We begin with Nygren's position with respect to metaphysics, perplexing to many, which position has already been touched upon in the foregoing.

If one raises the question as to the relationship between theology and metaphysics, the answer that one will certainly most often receive is that theology is a kind of metaphysics, yes, a typical metaphysical pattern of thought. Some will probably simply identify theology and metaphysics. By metaphysics one, in such a case, presumably means the assumption of a supersensual existence, and it appears self-evident that theology must reckon with such an existence. Is not the task of theology that of developing what the Christian is to believe about a higher, supersensual existence?

The positivistic philosophy, which denies all metaphysics, rejects Christianity for just this reason, that Christianity affirms a supersensual reality. In reply to such a formulation Nygren could say that it is precisely the positivistic denial of a supersensual reality which involves metaphysics. For this is to make this reality into reality in itself, absolutizing spatiotemporal existence. Christian thinkers have very likely also often presented metaphysical ideas, when they have spoken of a reality other than the spatiotemporal as a scientifically definable reality. But according to Nygren neither theology nor Christianity in and of themselves involve metaphysics. First of all, theology is not at all knowledge or science of God and the supersensual, and second, Christian faith in God is not of such a nature that it can be changed into a science of that in which one believes. Faith, according to

Nygren, does not operate in the sciences. But it is certainly not for this reason something arbitrary or meaningless. On the other hand, Nygren would probably add that metaphysics is actually something meaningless; it is quite simply a false science, neither faith nor knowledge.

Such a statement would certainly astonish many and shock some. What then does Nygren mean by theology? What does he understand by faith? And how can he exclude metaphysics so totally from the sphere of both Christian faith and Christian knowledge? Some who have looked into Nygren's first major work, *Religiöst a priori*,[5] without really grasping its meaning would be even more surprised by the assertion that he rejects all metaphysics, for this book deals with the religious a priori, and most of the books with this theme have sought to demonstrate the metaphysical nature and necessity of religion. The train of thought has been that religion is rational and that it has the same nature as science; it involves a demonstrable necessity. It has its roots in a philosophically or psychologically provable facticity. If one looks more closely at Nygren's work, however, one finds that his train of thought is wholly different from the ordinary. One could say that Nygren actually denies a religious a priori in the usual sense of the word. Instead he wants to affirm an a priority in religion of a different kind from that commonly supposed.

A metaphysical philosophy of religion can regard itself as religion raised to the form of thought. For Nygren, philosophy of religion is not religious in its function, but is a scientific analysis of the nature, role, and place of religious experience in man's spiritual life. It is therefore its validity which must, first of all, be investigated, and then the relation between this validity and the validity which we ascribe to other experience, theoretical knowledge and ethical judgments about good and evil. This is to say, one must explain what truth and meaning religious propositions have, compared with scientific judgments.

The first question then becomes: How is religious validity conceived? Here one must carefully distinguish between two different things. The validity which belongs to religious propositions has its basis in a possible validity which can only be shown in a transcendental manner (i.e., religious propositions are not meaningless or arbitrary). This validity does not have any religious character of its own, any more than the presuppositions which make it possible for us meaningfully to make aesthetic or ethical judgments are aesthetic or ethical in character. All that is established through these presuppositions is that one can meaningfully make religious judgments. Therefore, it may possibly have been misleading to use as a book title the expression "The Religious a priori." The religious is not a priori, and the a priori is not religious. The title intends only to affirm that religious affirmations are meaningful, which is to say that they can be put into an intelligible context.

One factor which can make for certain difficulties in the understanding of Nygren's book, *Religiöst a priori*, is that he defines the religious category as the *category of eternity*, and that in general he identifies the eternal with validity. One therefore easily gets the impression that one is to think in a manner which could suggest a Platonic schema. Highest in such a schema would be an eternal validity which in its essence was religious, and this would provide the basis for all the domains of experience, though religious validity would, so to speak, be closer to the ultimate transcendental presupposition for everything than would the validity of the other domains of experience.

It can appear as if a certain shift were observable in Nygren's way of thinking about the category of eternity itself. The line of thought which he developed in *Religiöst a priori* was worked out in an intensive encounter with a number of German writers. These writers had generally been influenced by idealistic patterns of thought and eagerly sought in one way or another to demonstrate the truth of Christianity. Nygren's main task in his first major writing was to show the untenability of these lines of thought. The a priori one could rightly talk about was of a transcendental nature, and this meant that judgments in the religious domain could be meaningfully affirmed and that therefore a possible validity was to be found in this domain. But any possibility of scientifically demonstrating that some concrete religion, e.g., Christianity, had more validity than other religions was specifically repudiated. Scientifically one could only state that religious judgments have their own meaning. One can investigate what each religion means, but thereafter it must be a question of struggle between the different religions, which takes place at a level where science is unable to provide a decisive word. For, if science were able to do this, religion would not be an independent life form, but the content of religious judgments would be dependent on what could scientifically be defined as factual.

This correction of common German trains of thought is carried out in *Religiöst a priori*. But the book's ambiguity seems to lie in the fact that one can receive the impression (by virtue of the starting point that was chosen) that the religious a priori, as representing the category of eternity itself, is thought to be set above the other a prioris. It can appear as though Nygren meant that the religious a priori was identical with an a priori placed over all the other domains of experience, or, in other words, that the validity which the judgments of each domain of experience have was something which in a sublimated form was represented in the presupposition of religious judgments, which was the idea of eternity. Other judgments (theoretical, ethical, aesthetic) would then, not in the same sense, represent pure validity, but in their case validity would be limited in some way.

The shift in Nygren's way of thinking, or the clarification of his intentions, which appears in his later writings, makes it quite evident, however, that he does not place the religious a priori above the other presuppositions of experience, but thinks of the a prioris of the different domains as mutually interdependent, so that if one should be destroyed, the others would also be destroyed.

The impression perhaps sometimes gotten from the presentation in *Religiöst a priori* could be illustrated in this way:

The a priori—the category of eternity

RELIGIOUS	ETHICAL	AESTHETIC	THEORETICAL
a priori, the presupposition of religious judgments (the eternal).	a priori, the presupposition of ethical judgments (the eternally existing category of good-evil).	a priori, the presupposition of aesthetic judgments (the eternally existing category of beautiful-not beautiful).	a priori, the presupposition of theoretical judgments (the eternally existing category of true-false).

In this schema the difference between the religious a priori and the other a priori concepts could be thought to be such that the religious a priori is identical with the category of eternity itself, while the other a prioris are not so directly related to it. But in his later writings it becomes clear that Nygren thinks of the different concepts of the a priori as wholly parallel. Thus the religious a priori is not conceived as placed above all the domains of experience. Instead one domain presupposes the other, so that rejection of the validity of one makes impossible the validity of the others, wherever one might happen to begin.

This also means that the way has been opened for defining the religious a priori in other ways than by specifying it as the eternal. One can understand that Nygren has been strongly opposed to all attempts to accept a *psychological* a priori, e.g., in the manner of Rudolf Otto.

This has made him extremely cautious in specifying the religious a priori in any particular way. Critics have called attention, however, to the difficulty that thereby has arisen, that the uniqueness by which religious judgments are distinguished from other judgments cannot simply be the fact that these judgments make the claim of always being valid. That this validity has to do with something eternal is correct, but this idea of eternity would seem to have a quality, which perhaps should have been more exactly specified.

One can, however, easily understand that Nygren would approach such questions with the greatest caution, since they very easily lead to the old attempt to define the "essence of religion." According to Nygren, that which binds different religions together is the fact that they are different answers to one and the same fundamental question. The fundamental ethical question is, "What is good?"—the religious question, "What is eternal?"—the aesthetic question, "What is beautiful?"—and the theoretical question, "What is true?" But since in all the forms of the a priori the thought of validity and thereby of eternity enter, the demand for a particular form of the specifically religious idea of eternity or validity arises. And thereby the problem arises as to how to avoid conceiving the essence of religion as this was done during the eighteenth and nineteenth centuries; how one is to formulate a correct understanding of it, an understanding which does justice to each religion's own empirical validity.

It could be pointed out that the idealistic philosophy itself, which Nygren already criticizes in *Religiöst a priori*, but the terms and frames of reference of which he nonetheless uses in his argument, can easily lead to the mistaken view that he has given the concept of eternity three meanings, or let it have three functions in his system, even if he has wanted to identify the first two. Thus, it can appear as if the different domains of experience were subordinate to an ultimate concept of validity, which can be called "eternity." This would be one meaning of eternity, eternity (*1*). In addition to this, each of the different domains of experience would have its own validity, its eternity, which would certainly be a formal validity, but nonetheless specified in its function, an eternity (*2*). Back of all theoretical judgments there would be one concept of eternity, i.e., that they are valid with space and time as their presuppositions; back of all ethical judgments would stand as a necessary, transcendentally given question, the question of good-evil (or, from a Christian point of view, the category of fellowship), which would be still another specified form of eternity

(2). In the same way the question beautiful-not beautiful would be a transcendental question for the aesthetic domain, which expressed yet another form of eternity (2). Now since the concepts of validity or eternity which lie beyond the different domains of experience as their transcendental presuppositions would all be forms of eternity (2), but at the same time were to be distinguished from each other, they could be designated as eternity (2a) (the validity of religion, a transcendental concept of eternity), eternity (2b) (the theoretical domain's eternity or transcendental validity, the question true-false in its scientific meaning, eternity (2c) (the ethical domain's eternity or transcendental validity, from the Christian viewpoint regarded as the category of fellowship, or else as a general question about good-evil or right-wrong), and eternity (2d) (the aesthetic domain's eternity or transcendental validity, the question of beautiful-not beautiful).

The term eternity becomes even more ambiguous in that it can be used to designate the eternity which exists in the Christian religion, a concept which is content filled and thus not formal, a concept of eternity which in its Christian form is to be distinguished from the concept of eternity in all other religions, each of which has its own special form of this concept. We would then have a content-filled concept of eternity, an eternity (3), and this concept could again be divided into the concepts of eternity of the different religions, eternity (3a,b,c,d,e, etc.).

At the same time these many meanings of the concept of eternity do not indicate that Nygren has confused the different meanings. His train of thought is understandable, and the different meanings of the word "eternity" become clear from the context, especially if one studies his later works. Nygren's understanding of the relationship between what has here been designated as eternity (2) and eternity (3) is that these are related as question to answer, as form to content, as transcendental presuppositions to the concrete judgments which fall under them. Nygren's understanding of the relation between what has here been called eternity (1) and eternity (2) would seem to be the following. Since in each domain of experience it is presupposed that something is valid, the result of a dissolution in principle of that which is valid with respect to one domain must be the dissolution also of the validity of other domains. It is in this sense that the various domains presuppose each other's validity. The dissolution in principle of theoretical validity would also destroy the validity of the religious domain.

It is impossible, for example, to argue that because our knowledge is incomplete, one can just as well affirm one thing as another, for thereby the validity of the theoretical domain would be abolished, and thereby, it would also follow that religious judgments would become invalid or arbitrary. That which is the opposite of validity for Nygren is always arbitrariness. If arbitrariness should be made dominant in one domain, the judgments of another domain would also become invalid. Thus the *appearance* that eternity (*1*) were a special, independent form of eternity, separated from eternity (*2*), would seem to be connected with the difficulty of clarifying the mutual dependence, in which the different domains or groups of judgments stand in relation to one another. Here, however, further clarification by Nygren himself would be desirable. Thereby the value of his contrast between validity and arbitrariness could also be further elucidated.

At times Nygren has been regarded as a crypto-apologete, as if his interest were only to show that religious judgments could be valid. Actually his ideas have a wholly different meaning. First of all, he destroys all apologetic maneuvers by which one does not take scientific criticism, e.g., of the Bible, seriously since one argues that because there are always differing opinions, scientific judgments do not have any assured validity. If this idea were developed to the point that it was affirmed that one could say what one pleased and that scientific results were a matter of indifference as far as religion was concerned, this according to Nygren would mean that all validity would be destroyed, and that then the validity of religious judgments would also be destroyed, with everything becoming purely arbitrary. It is pecisely against this and all tendencies in this direction that Nygren's effort is directed. In the realm of justice it is, of course, evident that positivistic tendencies have appeared annulling the validity of the question regarding good-evil, or right-wrong, so that the state's coercive decrees or custom and convention are thought to be constitutive for what one calls right-wrong. This would mean that here different kinds of arbitrariness were given free play. It is just in opposition to this that the "transcendental" validity in principle of the different domains provides a defense, the value of which should not be underestimated. On the other hand, it also follows that one cannot in a positivistic manner regard religious judgments as in principle arbitrary, for then the validity of theoretical ideas would also be destroyed.

It is especially to be noted that one would be led to a radical misunderstanding of Nygren if one placed too much emphasis on the

terminology of German idealistic theology which he uses. The idea
referred to above, that one could be led to interpret him in such a way
that there was an ultimate validity and that the religious a priori (but
not the a prioris of the other domains) could be directly identified with
it, is connected with idealistic (Neo-Kantian) terminology. But Nygren has specifically rejected this idea in *Filosofi och motivforskning*.[6]
If one, for example, should seek to conceive Nygren's pattern of
thought in such a way that above everything there was a general a
priori, from which could be derived the a prioris of the different
domains of experience, and that the a priori of the religious domain
stood closer to this highest a priori than the a prioris of the other
domains, one would be led to a view completely opposite to Nygren's.
Then, in an idealistic manner a highest idea would be assumed, actually
conceived as an active power, and from this the ideas subordinated to it
would be thought to be produced. The highest a priori would then, as
it were, produce out of itself the a prioris with lower grades of
validity. Such a view of an idea actively producing other ideas and of
lower ideas emanating from a higher idea is diametrically opposite to
Nygren's way of thinking. What is difficult for some to understand is
that Nygren uses idealistic terminology, but his own thought is a
radical critique of idealism. It is wholly foreign for him to think of
deriving subordinated ideas from superordinated ideas, or that higher
ideas should be able to bring forth lower ideas. It is just such a
procedure that he rejects, and one reason he speaks of validity rather
than reality as that which is to be subjected to philosophical analysis is
that one easily tends to think metaphysically of different grades of
reality, when the concept of reality is made the central problem of
philosophy. One can, however, speak of a primary and a secondary
validity without falling into metaphysics. Therefore, in order rightly
to understand Nygren's basic idea, it is important to understand that
according to him, that which distinguishes the theoretical a priori from
the religious a priori, the ethical from the aesthetic, must be a formally
different way of putting the question, but not a qualitatively different
content. Therefore, for example, Rudolf Otto's idea of a psychologically determined concept of religion must definitely be rejected. Similarly all tendencies, such as occur in existential philosophy, to let the
feeling of guilt take the place of the formal question, have led, according to Nygren, inescapably to metaphysics and to untenable theories.

Nygren's position is illuminated by his opinion that the validity of
the different contexts of meaning or domains of experience can be

mutually placed above one another. In *Filosofi och motivforskning*, Nygren has explained the meaning of philosophy as he conceives it. He distinguishes between philosophy as a world view, which is not scientific, and scientific philosophy. Such a philosophy must carry on concept analysis and undertake an analysis of the transcendental presuppositions of experience. This analysis leads to the necessity of assuming different domains of experience or contexts of meaning. This transcendental analysis does not, however, have anything to do with the idea of principles valid in themselves. "Only in relation to experience is it meaningful to speak of principles," he says. "The validity of the principles has no other meaning than that they are implicit in experience as its logical presuppositions. There can thus be no possibility of principles valid 'in themselves.' " [7] He is also aware that one now must root out every remnant of metaphysics more thoroughly than Kant himself was able to do. With respect to Kant's philosophy, he is of the opinion that one cannot deny that there the transcendental presuppositions really became principles in a metaphysical sense, that is, magnitudes out of which validity, so to speak, emanates. [8] This idea Nygren radically rejects.

One should observe the change in terminology which can be noted if one compares Nygren's earlier and later writings. In the later writings he prefers the expression "contexts of meaning" to "domains of experience." Thereby it becomes clearer as to what is meant by the different groups of judgments. With this terminological change is connected also the fact that the concept "eternity" in the later writings is less markedly used as a characteristic of the religious context of meaning. The religious context of meaning refers simply to the God relationship or the relation to the eternal. When there is reference to eternity in connection with the transcendental presupposition of religion, it is, however, important to note that the concept of eternity then does not refer to the Christian, content-determined concept of eternity, but to a question which is shared by the several religions (a general question having to do with the God relationship). The Christian understanding of eternity is one of the possible answers to this question, and one must then set forth this content-filled, Christian concept of eternity in such a way that it expresses Christianity's basic motif, and thus has to do with God's agape. The general question about eternity, or religion's transcendental presupposition cannot be used to distinguish one religion from another; this occurs through the answers which set forth the central meaning of each religion. The transcendental category of eternity thus marks out the difference between religious, theoretical, ethical, and aesthetic judgments, but does not indicate the difference between the concepts of eternity in Christianity as compared with other religions.

With respect to the concept of validity it should be observed that it can consistently be interpreted in different ways, depending on that to which the concept more specifically refers, whether it is the presupposition for the validity of judgments itself, or the validity of a particular judgment. Nygren has expressed this more precisely in *Filosofisk och kristen etik;* where what he has there written is so illuminating for his train of thought that we cite the following:

> When we designate a judgment as valid, we intend thereby to attribute to it a special validity: the relationship affirmed in the judgment is not only an assertion, but a justified assertion. But it is apparent that not all such valid judgments are situated at the same level. Rather one should be able to construct a scale of validity, where the lower judgments for their validity must presuppose the validity of the proposition, "The sun warms the stone," presupposes the validity of the causal law. That which stands highest on the scale of validity and which thus does not point beyond itself to an even higher validity we can designate as having primary validity. Again, that which occupies a lower position on the scale of validity and can only maintain its validity on the presupposition that certain other judgments are valid has secondary validity. We must in other words distinguish between . . . a validity of primary and another of secondary dignity. Thus the causal law, if it is valid at all, has primary validity, while the individual causal judgment, "The sun warms the stone," has secondary validity.[9]

Here again it must only be remembered that Nygren has never thought of validity as a metaphysical principle, from which valid judgments could be thought to emanate.

If we now turn to the "secondary validity" of judgments within the *Christian* religion, it must be understood that these by belonging to the religious category certainly have meaning, but their correctness depends on the fact that they rightly express that answer to the fundamental religious question which Christianity gives. Their Christian "correctness" can therefore, according to Nygren, not be derived from the religious category. Nygren means to say that those judgments which express that interpretation of Christianity which he calls a synthesis between "eros" and "agape" and thus involve a distortion of the gospel, contain just as meaningful an answer and belong just as much to the religious category (or the religious context of meaning) as those which in his opinion express a correct interpretation of Christianity, i.e., those which express the concept of agape. Whether the latter is a "correct" interpretation of Christianity and the former "incorrect" is a matter to be determined systematically and historically. Systematic theology works together with the history of ideas and seeks to find what the New Testament and the biblical message it contains has to say. This, according to Nygren, seen from one viewpoint, is God's love revealed in Christ's deed, God's agape.

One can say that Nygren's philosophy of religion has the metaphysician as its chief opponent. Metaphysics represents an attempt to work together the different domains of experience into one system, so that each religious judgment at the same time receives scientific character and validity. It destroys that which is specific in religion and makes its understanding of reality receive the same character as scientifically demonstrable reality (reality in space and time). More generally, metaphysics turns from the concretely real to the universal and adds to it the character of reality. From this a tendency towards conceptual realism follows, and a tendency to see reality as such realized in universal concepts, as in the "ideas" of Platonism. And in so far as these concepts are thought to be realized in something concrete, metaphysics tends to identify the concept of reality with some particular reality.

Platonic idealism represents a typical metaphysical system. The highest idea is the highest reality, and it includes the highest value. The ideas of the true, the good, and the beautiful ultimately culminate in the highest idea. Nygren's philosophy of religion radically opposes this tendency to let everything issue in a highest idea, which at the same time signifies a reality. One could say that there is a twofold metaphysical tendency in Platonism, the tendency to identify reality and value, and the tendency to identify the idea of something real with some concrete reality. Both of these identifications are most radically rejected when the basic philosophical question is made to deal with validity rather than reality. Thereupon it becomes natural to distinguish between different forms of validity (primary and secondary validity). In this way it is also possible to avoid the modern tendency to make the question of the relation of reality to space and time central and paramount. One can speak of spatiotemporal reality without for this reason having expressed oneself about any metaphysically conceived reality. Nygren recognizes that affirming as well as denying another reality than that given in space and time must lead to metaphysics.

At the same time taking a position with respect to such a system of thought as Platonism clearly becomes very complicated from Nygren's point of view. In terms of modern logic it becomes necessary to reject Platonic idealism as logically meaningless or as contradictory. Reality as such cannot be something concrete, nor can it be a definite idea, no matter how generally its content is conceived. Reality and thought cannot coincide, nor can reality and value. In many ways it can be shown that Platonic metaphysics, in purely intellectual terms, leads to absurdities. When Nygren, however, in his greatest work, *Agape and Eros*,[10] discusses Platonism, he discusses it from an entirely different point of view. Platonism is also a religious system of thought, the backbone of a basically religious orientation and a pattern of life corresponding to it. And Nygren well knows that one cannot from a purely logical point of view reject a religion. From such a perspective the meaning of its affirmations will not be clarified. It is rather the case that that Platonism, which from a logical point of view can appear as self-contradictory and therefore meaningless, can receive a clear meaning if it is recognized that Platonism represents a religious system, an answer to the question of the way to salvation. This answer does not in and of itself become incorrect because it has become connected with a logically unreasonable metaphysics, nor is its meaning, which becomes apparent when viewed from a religious perspective, lost because of this connection with a logically untenable metaphysics. If a Platonist wanted to unite his understanding with modern demands of logical consistency, he would have to change the logical structure of the Platonic system of thought, but the answer to the question of salvation itself does not become impossible by virtue of its connection with metaphysics. Modern logic can put philosophical problems and tasks before Platonism insofar as it is a living phenomenon, but it cannot on logical grounds declare the Platonic idea of salvation impossible.

It is important to emphasize this lest one draw the incorrect conclusion from Nygren's attack on metaphysics that he thereby had produced an indirect proof for the truth of Christianity, in that only Christianity is free from metaphysics, in the sense that metaphysics has been described. It must be noted that when Nygren contrasts eros and agape in *Agape and Eros*, there is never any attempt to show that the idea of eros is unreasonable. On the contrary, its meaning is most effectively set forth. Indeed it is made evident that it is actually easier to develop a system of eros religion than one of Christian love, in that the "unmotivated" nature of the latter makes it more difficult to illustrate its meaning.

We return however to a consideration of the basic outline of Nygren's philosophy of religion. With respect to Nygren's first writings, the wish could be expressed that the plan for a transcendental deduction of religion, which was there presented, had been concretely carried out. The pattern for such a deduction comes most nearly from Kant. We begin, therefore, with a consideration of Kant's thinking at this point. Kant's question was, *How* are synthetic judgments possible a priori? What is necessary (according to the interpretation of Kant which Nygren follows) is not to show *that* synthetic judgments are possible a priori. That this is the case is the point at which Kant begins. Such judgments are acknowledged to be valid. They do not need to derive their validity from a superordinated validity. But one can investigate the presuppositions which must exist, that which must always be presupposed when such judgments are affirmed. The answer becomes space and time, which are the a priori forms of sensibility, and the categories. If, for example, the category of causality were invalid, no concrete causal relationship could validly be affirmed. This does not mean (at least according to one train of thought in Kant) that a concrete causal relationship *derives* its validity from the category of causality, but only that in the affirmation of a causal relationship the category of causality is in fact presupposed. What Kant sought to define were thus the universal presuppositions which must always in fact exist when valid judgments are affirmed.

The transcendental deduction means an elucidation of the presuppositions which consciously or unconsciously are assumed in every causal relationship. If one can establish that space, time, and the categories have not been presupposed, one can also conclude that valid theoretical knowledge does not exist. Since space, time, and the categories are not presupposed in metaphysical judgments, these judgments are invalid.

But what then does the transcendental deduction of *religious* judgments mean for Nygren? Nygren has not spelled this out in detail, and therefore one must draw one's own conclusions as to his thinking at this point. In correspondence with the Kantian line of thought, according to which it is not a question of deriving validity from a higher validity, but only of examining the presuppositions of the generally accepted validity of the judgments in mathematics and the pure natural sciences, Nygren must have assumed the actual validity of religious judgments (i.e, that there are religious judgments which are meaningful and not arbitrary). One can then presume that Nygren as-

sumes that religious judgments express conceptions which represent
something inescapable, something the importance of which cannot in
principle be doubted. They must be accepted as having an empirically
evident importance in the cultural life, so that they cannot simply be
pushed aside as meaningless, no matter how much one may attack individual judgments or how much one religion, from its vantage point,
may reject other religions. Thus, Nygren's point of departure would
seem to be that religion actually cannot be rejected as mere nonsense.
Nygren makes no attempt to prove that religion is not nonsense.

The transcendental deduction of religious judgments, then, must
be regarded as meaning that the presupposition for religious judgments
is the concept of eternity. This concept must have been thought to
express something comparable to space, time, and the categories. The
observation, in *Religiöst a priori*, that the concept of eternity seemed to
be conceived as placed above other forms of validity, would then mean
that the concept of eternity, more directly than other transcendental
presuppositions, can be regarded as expressing the concept of validity
itself in its abstract purity. As has been indicated, this seems difficult,
however, to maintain, since, as the transcendental presupposition for
religious judgments, it must nonetheless have its own specific nature.
Just as space, time, and the categories certainly do not have any
psychologically fixed or any concrete content, but just the same are
definite presuppositions for concrete theoretical judgments, the possible validity of which is assumed, so also the religious a priori must
have some characteristic which distinguishes it from the presuppositions which stand back of the theoretical, ethical, and aesthetic judgments.

If the category of eternity is the transcendental presupposition of
religious judgments in the sense that, if this category were abolished
these judgments would also lose their meaning and validity, it itself
becomes a way in which these judgments are bound to each other.
Instead of assuming an essence of religion which could be defined in
and through certain ideas or through certain feelings which were
common to all religion, here the cohesive bond becomes a transcendental viewpoint, a universal question, which has meaning with respect to certain judgments, while it does not have meaning with respect to others. While space, time, and the categories present a question concerning judgments about a reality existing in these forms and
relationships within this reality, the religious category poses a question
concerning eternity. The answers may differ greatly, since eternity in

the different religions has wholly different meanings and is differently conceived. But the question concerning eternity has meaning for all religions, while with respect to relationships within space and time it lacks meaning. In a comparable way, a categorical question concerning that which is beautiful has meaning for judgments which deal with some form of beauty, while it lacks relevance for other domains in the sense that judgments in these domains do not derive their meaning from being answers indicating what is beautiful.

In Nygren's later writings, where he has more and more engaged in concrete investigations in the history of ideas, his religio-philosophical theories have received an application in the way in which he has concretely developed the context of meaning within the Christian thought complex. These thoughts would often be meaningless from viewpoints such as are natural from a theoretical point of view. Christian love, agape, is unmotivated, a fact which from a theoretical viewpoint can make this love appear meaningless and wasted. If, in a logical system, one reckons with goals, thoughts of Christ, his relationship to God, and his atonement, these seem difficult to understand rationally or to explain in a theoretical system. In the context in which they stand and from the vantage point of the New Testament understanding of God they become, however, wholly intelligible. If one comes to these thoughts with the correct approach, the one that corresponds to the purpose which these thoughts intend to express, they become not only intelligible, but clear. (The same applies also to such ideas as the resurrection of Christ and to other ideas which in our times have been regarded as impossible to understand in any other way than as myths.)

The original contribution of Nygren's philosophy of religion is thus, chiefly the fact that it makes it evident that the fundamental questions to which religious ideas can be said to constitute answers are "transcendental" in nature, which is to say that they are presuppositions for meanings and ideas, not only within the Christian faith, but in all religions, no matter how separated and in strife with each other these may be. If these presuppositions themselves were to have a concrete content, this would mean that they received a metaphysical significance, much like the idea of the "essence of religion" of the period of the Enlightenment. In our day, metaphysics easily creeps in under the guise of psychology. If, for example, one were to assert that a feeling of guilt was common to all religions, this would be a typical metaphysical affirmation. It is not true empirically that the feeling of guilt is common to all religions, and those feelings of guilt which can appear in certain religions are wholly different in kind from the Christian feeling of guilt, which presupposes the idea of God's law, his love (agape), the work of Christ. The Christian feeling of guilt belongs to the answer which Christianity gives to the fundamental religious question. To confuse the answer with the question is a confusion of the same kind as the confusion in the theology of the Enlightenment of the universal essence of religion with that which was typically Christian. A general feeling of guilt is an obscure concept which can only develop as one, in an unclear manner, mixes together a vague Christian feeling of guilt with certain general ideas to be found within existential philosophy. According to Nygren, religion forms a special domain of experience, and its ideas are connected in a context, the meaning of which appears as an answer to a categorical question; and by such a question Nygren means the general viewpoint by which several religions can be held together in a unity.

How then does Nygren conceive the relation which exists between the different contexts of meaning? One difficulty that could arise, especially when the theoretical context of meaning is separated from the atheoretical contexts of meaning (religious, ethical, and aesthetic), is that one could easily conclude that these, e.g., religious judgments, were wholly illogical, or that logical patterns of thought had no place in these contexts. Yet one could say that Nygren's thought tends in just the opposite direction. It is, therefore, especially important to understand how he has conceived the so-called theoretical context of meaning. That which characterizes it is, first and foremost, that here judgments may not have value traits, while this is the case in the atheoretical contexts. But more must be said, for judgments within the atheoretical contexts of meaning can assuredly be said to be value characterized, but they are certainly not for that reason without an inner logic. In one sense, like all judgments which have any meaning at all, they could be said to be theoretical. But the context of meaning which Nygren calls "theoretical" is not only characterized by the fact that there logic orders the judgments. Nygren has built upon certain of Kant's ideas, and thus for him, theoretical judgments refer to spatiotemporal reality and function within Kantian categories, which means that they are all placed under a definite presupposition. They specifically refer to spatiotemporal reality and beyond this they have no validity.

Here we must again consider how, according to Nygren's view, metaphysics develops and functions. Kant rejects metaphysics as a science, since metaphysical judgments do not have space, time, and the categories as presuppositions. Beyond this there have been many different opinions about Kant's position regarding metaphysics. For Nygren, metaphysics as a science is also impossible. But this does not mean that judgments which refer to the beautiful, the good, or the eternal (or to the God-relationship) should be held, a priori, to be meaningless. Nygren refuses to use the concept of reality as a universal point of orientation, for this easily leads to the view that only theoretical judgments receive meaning and validity, since they alone refer to spatiotemporal reality. If one assumes that the characteristic of valid judgments is that they must have to do with spatiotemporal reality, this, according to Nygren, leads inescapably to metaphysics, for this would mean that one reality would be designated as that which was in and of itself real. But that a certain reality is identified with reality in and of itself, that which as such is real, is typical of ontological metaphysics. Thinking of reality as the basis for the validity of judgments must lead to an ontology which involves metaphysics, which also applies when one assumes that spatiotemporal reality is reality as such. If on the basis of this idea that logical judgments are defined as those which refer to this reality, all value judgments must be understood as merely subjective and arbitrary. In this way their meaning and objectivity, in every sense of the word, would become impossible. Tendencies in this direction are to be found in the Swedish philosopher, Axel Hägerström.

It must, however, be noted that spatiotemporal reality conceived as reality in itself, reality as such, actually thereby becomes a limited reality at the same time that it is intended to be the total reality. For it is defined as limited to space and time, by which a boundary is drawn as over against every idea of any reality other than the spatiotemporally defined reality. It is wholly natural that if one begins with this idea, one must regard as unreasonable any reality other than the spatiotemporally given reality. This would be a "reality" which was not a reality, for it was assumed at the outset that reality as such was spatiotemporal reality. What one thereby does not note is that this spatiotemporal reality also becomes metaphysically defined; one gets a spatiotemporal metaphysics, which excludes all conceptions of reality other than the spatiotemporal, as well as all judgments whose logical meaning has not been defined in terms of the spatiotemporal context.

When Nygren rejects the concept of reality as the ultimate point of orientation for thought, he escapes the dilemma in which one finds oneself, whether one accepts or denies a reality in addition to spatio-temporal reality. To begin with the concept of validity not only saves one from metaphysical tendencies, it also opens the possibility of affirming the meaningfulness of judgments within the atheoretical contexts of meaning, as well as opening the possibility of establishing a relationship with recent tendencies in analytic philosophy.

But we return to the observation that logical judgments, according to Nygren, are certainly not limited to the theoretical domain. These judgments could be said to have a special kind of logic. To the extent that all meaningful judgments must be logical, religious, ethical, and aesthetic judgments are also logical. If, as did Kierkegaard, one speaks of paradoxical judgments as far as the Christian faith is concerned, by this is not meant meaningless judgments. The term "paradoxical" has been much misused. It has been forgotten that Kierkegaard sought by the use of such judgments to provide a place for the uniqueness of Christianity as over against the rationalism of the Hegelian philosophy. Thus, he intended precisely to develop a form of meaningful Christian judgments; these, from the viewpoint of the philosophy then dominant, appeared to be unreasonable.

Nygren's theory of the different domains of experience or contexts of meaning, thus, is by no means an attempt to say that religious (or ethical, or aesthetic) judgments can escape the demand that they be logically meaningful. Instead it represents an attempt to find the vantage point which makes it possible for the meaning they have to reach expression and become intelligible. But, if this is to happen without a perversion of their content, this vantage point must differ from that of theoretical judgments, since these judgments have quite another purpose, at the same time that they in their own way are also logical.

In our day philosophy of religion has taken many different courses. German theology has tended to follow existential philosophy, which seems to have helped theology to achieve a new understanding of many problems, but which can also lead in directions which make impossible a correct understanding of the message of Christianity and God's agape, since man is placed in the center. The Neo-Thomists go another way, but they remain bound to Aristotle's patterns of thought and to Greek metaphysics. Modern analytic philosophy has to a large extent taken a positivistic attitude toward religion. It has commonly revealed a great lack of actual theological insight as to what the Christian religion means, and has easily slipped into a this-worldly metaphysics, for when spatiotemporal reality becomes reality as such, justice is not done to the claims to validity of ethical, religious, and aesthetic judgments; these appear as subjective and arbitrary. The difficulties of this position become apparent in the realm of the philosophy of law. Thus, the risk of landing in the form of positivism, represented by thinkers who maintain that the state determines what is right, a theory which suits all dictators all too well, has led many philosophers of law in the direction of natural law theories, and so also to a metaphysics which stands close to the conception of natural religion.

Quite a different approach is to be found in Nygren's thought. If his intentions were to be followed out, a philosophy of religion and a philosophy of law could be developed in which metaphysics would be overcome, but at the same time the value and the validity of juridical as well as religious affirmations could be maintained. Beginning with that which is concretely given (those situations where the difference between right and wrong factually exists and where religion is found to be inescapable), one can work back to the most general presuppositions for these phenomena and indicate the contexts in which these propositions are meaningful. The idea that every concept has its meaning in and through the concrete context to which it belongs, is close to certain observations that have been made in modern analytic philosophy. If Nygren's idea of different contexts of meaning were further developed, it should be possible to relate it to ideas within modern analytic philosophy, insofar as these are based on actual observations of different meanings of words and are not expressions of a positivistic metaphysics.

Nygren has opened a door to wider research. It is not important to insist that his system is wholly adequate in every detail, but to go through the open door and press on with the research that he has begun. Nygren himself has sought to relate his ideas to certain viewpoints in modern analytic philosophy, according to which it is pointed out that a word does not have a fixed meaning as designating a certain concrete reality, but must be understood in the context to which it belongs. In his recent essay, "From Atomism to Context of Meaning in Philosophy," [11] he has sought to show how Wittgenstein's thinking developed in this direction.

It has been emphasized that for Nygren it is utterly essential that the basic philosophical question concern itself not with that which is *real*, but with that which is *valid*. One might wonder why he does not ask about what is *true*. This is due to the fact that the question of truth, and the discussion of the so-called truth criterion has tended to lead to metaphysics, because truth has commonly been identified with spatio-temporal reality, and thus with that which has to do with relation-ships within this world. To think in terms of two realities, one within this world and a higher reality transcending this world, would mean that, on the one hand, one let this "second" reality be thought of in this-worldly terms and concepts, but at the same time also thought of it as being something else. This is an old metaphysical idea; metaphysics always confuses faith and knowledge, or, speaking theologically, this age and its conditions with the age to come.

Nygren, therefore, relates himself to philosophical tendencies which do not investigate reality as such, for this leads to metaphysics, nor a particular reality, for this is the task of the special sciences, but the context in which judgments appear, the sense in which they are meaningful. He investigates the presuppositions which must exist in order that a judgment is to have meaning. This presuppositional anal-ysis leads to a new attempt to understand the nonarbitrary nature of even atheoretical judgments, i.e., their validity. It is the task of philoso-phy of religion to analyze the presuppositions of the validity of reli-gious judgments, just as philosophy must also examine the presupposi-tions for the theoretical judgments given in the special sciences, and philosophical ethics, the validity of ethical judgments. Philosophy, according to Nygren, in addition to its general task of concept analysis, has the task of analyzing the transcendental presuppositions of judg-ments, i.e., what has been presupposed as valid when one has assumed the possible validity of certain judgments. Philosophy is therefore a science of first principles, but not in the sense that it seeks to define principles eternally valid in themselves; this would be a metaphysical train of thought.

According to Nygren, philosophy must begin with experience, with the judgments given in the special sciences, and it must seek to find the presuppositions of these judgments. In this way the transcen-dental validity of the theoretical domain of experience is established. The concrete judgments which affirm various causal relationships pre-suppose, for example, the category of causality, the basic fact that we can understand spatiotemporal reality under the schema of cause and effect. That this relationship has often been and is conceived in a faulty manner does not prevent us from meaningfully speaking of cause and effect. Hume criticized the concept of causality and sought to point out the contradictions involved in the common understanding of the causal relationship. But he did not achieve an explanation of the necessity of the concept of causality. Hume instead dismissed the causal relationship as contradictory.

For Nygren, it is the task of all philosophy to get behind the judgments which we make to their transcendental presuppositions. This applies also in the atheoretical domains, not least in the case of religious judgments. It is empirically evident that they cannot in a positivistic manner quite simply and generally be regarded as arbitrary; they play too large a role in all cultures for this. But it is the task of philosophy of religion to investigate what one has assumed in making such judgments, i.e., to examine their transcendental validity. In this way no individual judgment is declared to be correct; only a possible validity is indicated. Correctness of individual judgments must be determined on the basis of their coherence with the central ideas or the message of the religion in question, and this becomes the task of theology. Philosophy of religion, like all philosophy, works, as it were, backwards and examines the presuppositions of religious judgments. Theology, on the other hand, investigates concrete subject matter, such as oral and literary expressions of the Christian faith.

It has been common practice to unite theology, philosophy and religion. Philosophy of religion has sometimes been seen as a more scientific, philosophical form of theology, which replaces theology's naïve expressions with ideas and terms drawn from philosophy. And theology itself has been conceived as an attempt to make a science out of the Christian faith. This mixing together of faith, theology, and philosophy of religion has often been supported by the thought that reality cannot be understood in a noncontradictory manner, but that ordinary science ultimately leads to contradictions. Philosophy, then, should show that one ultimately is confronted by antinomies. This should make it possible for theology, conceived as a relatively scientific form of faith, to develop into a speculative philosophy of religion, beginning with the contradictory nature of reality, and adding to this certain ideas regarded as valuable and appealing to the feelings gotten from some form of Christian faith.

Nygren does not begin with any such assumed antinomies. He takes it for granted that the special sciences are to explain the problems of spatiotemporal reality, and that this reality is therefore logically intelligible, even if one is able to understand only a very small part of it and the task of understanding remains infinite. One cannot, however, without landing in metaphysics, declare the world as such unintelligible. One is, therefore, not to assume that judgments about the world must be contradictory. Metaphysics and the feeling of the inadequacy of science most commonly arise because no formula has been found for exhibiting the validity of atheoretical experience, for the fact that religious, ethical, and aesthetic judgments do not have to be arbitrary, even though they do not give expression to anything that can be scientifically proved or conceived.

If philosophy of religion, like all the branches of philosophy, according to Nygren, is to investigate the presuppositions of experience, or the conditions under which any meaningful judgment may be valid, theology, on the other hand, turns to a historically and empirically given material and investigates its structure. Christian theology turns to Christianity and investigates it. Here the material is concrete and historical. The basic source of the Christian religion is the New Testament, and behind it, the Old Testament interpreted through the New Testament, which is the way in which the Christian church has understood the Old Testament. Theology seeks to analyze and set forth the Christian understanding of the Bible as God's revelation. That the contributions of purely secular historical research to an understanding of the biblical writings are also helpful is evident. In his essays in *En bok om bibeln*, Nygren has applied his understanding of the difference between faith and knowledge to the interpretation of the Bible. One must distinguish between the purely historical investigation of the Bible, which in and by itself is wholly necessary, and the Christian understanding of the Bible. Both of these approaches to the Bible fructify each other, but they must not be confused. A purely historical investigation cannot express itself about God and his will. Yet the Christian faith sees behind the words of the Bible God's revelation, his activity, his way to men to save them from the power of sin and death, his struggling and triumphing agape.

Theology is a systematic-empirical *science*. It must set forth what is meant by the Christian understanding of God's revelation. Theology is, thus, not proclamation; it investigates and interprets religious ideas, but it is not itself religion. Nor does theology involve a spiritual interpretation of the Bible. This would be a confusion of faith and knowledge and would therefore result in metaphysics. Science, in its approach to the Bible, must first of all carry out a purely historical investigation, using the same methods which are common to other historical research. When this is done, the Old Testament writings can never be interpreted with the help of the New Testament. A historical document can be understood with the help of contemporary or earlier documents, but not through later documents. But theology must also set forth how the Christian church, on the basis of a definite faith, has interpreted God's revelation in the Bible. This revelation is the revelation of his agape. Agape is not a static quality, but is to be understood dynamically, as God's love which struggles onward and breaks down opposition. It breaks down the legalism into which God's revelation here on earth has constantly been perverted; it breaks down that law which has been distorted in that it has been made a means whereby egocentric man seeks to make himself meritorious before God. On the other hand, God's true, undistorted law is always included in God's agape. God *wills* something, and this is expressed in his law. But this can rightly be understood only in and through God's acting in love. Christ was God's agape, but for this reason he had to struggle and give himself in suffering and death. He was at the same time an incarnation of God's fulfilled law, the law rightly and perfectly understood, which Christ brought to its fulfillment, the law of the Messianic kingdom. We find this law in the work of Christ, which for us has reconciling and redemptive significance.

It is important to understand that theology, when it sets forth the meaning of the Christian idea of love, is an *empirical historical* science. It is certainly systematic in kind, but this by no means diminishes its scientific character. It belongs to the theoretical rather than the religious "context of meaning" or "domain of experience." Faith belongs to the religious context of meaning, but theology's presentation of the meaning of faith belongs to the theoretical domain or context of meaning. The fact that theology involves a systematic historical analysis does not change this, nor take away at all its theoretical character. On the contrary, the highest level of historical investigation, when the material in question can at all be handled in terms of the history of ideas, is precisely a systematic investigation. Here are sought the leading ideas which were capable of bringing together many different ideas into a total outlook. A task of this sort is precisely empirical and historical as well as systematic. The leading ideas form a context which is organized into what Nygren calls a "basic motif." When such a motif is presented, it is not essential to recount or present all the ideas which have played or are playing large roles in the Christian faith. What must be done is to present that which makes for a coherent whole, that which makes the Christian faith-outlook a historically given continuity, an organic whole. That this can be set forth in a historical-systematic manner by no means removes faith's living character and its contemporary significance—quite the contrary!

It is important, however, to put the questions in such a way that one actually reaches such a basic motif and correctly sets it forth. Here philosophy of religion plays a decisive role. For it contains the presuppositions for religion in general. These can be rewritten as a universal question, fundamental in its nature. What is the relation to eternity in the Christian religion? How is the God relationship there structured? What is meant by that which, in the Bible, is called revelation? Philosophy of religion has to do with all that is connected with defining the question. The question must be put in such a way that Christianity as an organic unity can provide an answer to it. If one does not ask correctly, one cannot get a correct answer. The question must be put in such a way that in the answer to it, all that is constitutive for Christianity, the message of salvation at its core, can be presented. The content of the answer can never be derived from the historically given material, first of all from the Bible, but also from the whole history of Christian thought.

It must always be remembered, if Nygren is to be understood, that wholly different, even contradictory answers can be given to a categorical or basic question, with full recognition that these answers, nonetheless, belong under the same universal question. The answers which a concrete religion gives provide the way in which it is characterized. To the extent that a religion is conceptually unified, its answers to the categorical question are clear and univocal. The categorical question, on the one hand, distinguishes all religious judgments from judgments related to other fundamental questions, and, on the other hand, makes possible the definition of the particular answer each concrete religion gives. It is the task of theology to indicate the answer which Christianity gives to the fundamental religious question.

A basic motif can be defined as an answer to a categorical question. This answer must, as concretely as possible, indicate a given religion's deepest intention, its "essence," that which characterizes it. Ever since the theology of the Enlightenment the term "essence," as applied either to religion or Christianity, has been suspect, and this is quite natural, for one sought thereby to indicate something common to all religions, certain ideas which were always the same, e.g., ideas about God, virtue, and immortality. The concrete religions had adapted themselves to patterns of thought current during the periods of their development; in this way, it was believed, differences among them could be explained. Nygren's theory of basic motifs, however, as has been indicated, represents a radical critique of such ideas. The concept "essence" therefore comes to have a new meaning. It can only indicate a concrete, historically given religion's intent and content, that which binds together all ideas within it and gives them unity and meaning.

It was pointed out earlier that Nygren, more consistently than Schleiermacher, has argued that there is no "natural religion." In the conception of natural religion, theoretical, ethical, and religious propositions were bound together as if they represented truths of the same kind. Nygren distinguishes in principle between different contexts of meaning or domains of experience, which makes impossible the traditional conception of natural religion, in which an attempt was made to unite theoretical thought, religious faith, and moral conviction. It also makes impossible the conception of an essential core, common to all religions. One could therefore say that for Nygren the religious category or the transcendental question takes the place that the idea of the essence of religion had in the system of natural religion. But the transcendental question is purely formal, without any content, a frame within which wholly different contents can be inserted, and it is the content which can be designated as the "essence." One can therefore, according to Nygren, never speak of the essence of religion, but one can very well speak of the essence of an individual religion, e.g., of the essence or the basic motif of Christianity. When this is said, it should be evident that the word "essence" as so used, has for Nygren a meaning quite different from its meaning in the thought of Adolf von Harnack. According to Harnack the essence of Christianity had a meaning closely related to the essence of religion, as the latter was conceived in the period of the Enlightenment.

Motif research represents a method which can in principle be applied to every religion, insofar as such a religion has expressed itself in a manner which can be characterized or be found to have a definable meaning. Nygren has carried out the method only with respect to Christianity, but here it has been done all the more thoroughly. The chief example of the application of this method is in Nygren's great, now classic work, *Agape and Eros.*

For the sake of clarity, it should probably be pointed out that this understanding of theology, according to which its task is to analyze systematically and historically "basic motifs," means that the term "theology" is given a different meaning from that which it has often received. Historically, theology has often been understood as one aspect of the Christian proclamation, the proclamation presented in scientific terms. For Nygren this means that one has incorrectly confused faith and knowledge. The earlier dogmatics often did this; it was assumed that one should develop the doctrines of the Christian faith in an edifying manner. This was especially common in the period of Pietism. In this manner the Christian message was not presented in its purity; instead theology became a one-sided proclamation presented with false claims. The Lutheran orthodoxy which preceded Pietism had understood that a correct presentation of the Christian faith required thinking through the problems which belong to the philosophy of religion, such as the relation between reason and revelation. But its manner of carrying out this task remained within the context of the scholastic philosophy of that time. Indeed, it represented, in part, a revival of the Aristotelian or scholastic philosophy, which Luther had decisively rejected. Luther himself had not worked out any philosophy of religion, but in practice he distinguished between reason and revelation in a brilliant manner. One could almost say that in his writings a philosophy of religion is presupposed, though never coherently thought through or developed by him. It would be a fruitful project to examine more closely the suggestions of such a philosophy of religion in Luther, for example, in his understanding of the relation between reason and revelation, between creation and redemption, or between temporal and spiritual authority.

Nygren has made use of Kant's insight about the necessity of abandoning metaphysics, and he has drawn implications from this through his theory of the different contexts of meaning, which go further than those drawn by Kant. Nygren has built upon the results of modern research in the history of religions, regarding the meaning of different religions. It would now be an important task to test the method of motif research by applying it to different religions, determining in this way the extent to which a unified outlook can be found within them. In addition to this Nygren has, through his standard work, *Filosofisk och kristen etik*, which unfortunately thus far remains untranslated, given a clear application of his understanding of the relation between the work and tasks of philosophy and theology insofar as Christian ethics is concerned. In his *Commentary on Romans* [12] he has tried to show what Paul's basic ideas are. Even earlier than this, in *Agape and Eros*, he applied the method of motif research to the very center of Christianity, and thereby also gave, through a survey of the history of Christian thought, an insight into the meaning of Christianity, as this is to be found in the Bible and has developed in the dramatic struggle of its basic motif (agape) and the basic motif which issues from the Greek-Hellenistic religiosity (eros), but which has sometimes been synthesized with Christianity. In many shorter writings Nygren has further developed his basic ideas. As a bishop and ecumenical churchman he has also been able to put into practice his conception of Christianity, and work for a correct understanding and application of the gospel in practical church life. Sometimes these practical contributions have come so into the foreground, that there has been a tendency to forget his fundamental work in philosophy of religion. It is the latter, however, which constitutes the foundation for all of his later contributions. It provides the basis for continued work for anyone who is willing to make the effort to understand it, and independently seek to develop it further through critique growing out of such understanding, developing relationships with new patterns of thought and the new presuppositions to be found in the results of recent philosophical research.

It should be mentioned that Nygren himself in the last decade has been occupied with investigations about just these problems. In a new book, which is to be published at the end of this year, with the title "Meaning and Method: Prolegomena to a Scientific Philosophy of Religion," he gives an extensive investigation of the central problems of Philosophy and of Philosophy of Religion. Here he also discusses—positively and negatively—the contributions of modern American and English philosophy.

2

NYGREN

AND LINGUISTIC ANALYSIS

LANGUAGE AND MEANING

Paul Holmer

A MANIFEST feature of Nygren's work in theology is that he has mostly enjoyed it. He was never the professor or the bishop (or the retired bishop-professor) long-bored with his subject. Even though his writings were polemical and novel in his early years, even though he has been subjected to severe criticism early and late, Nygren is not one of those theologians whose concern with theology, early or late, is tense or defensive. Without much trumpeting and long before widespread enthusiasm for ecumenical theology, Anders Nygren helped make Lundensian theology, which was Swedish, Lutheran and parochial in origin, international, ecumenical and catholic. His extreme and constant interest in theology, which has been invariably professional, has also been combined with a light and deft touch; and he has been, consequently, enlivening both to himself and to others. Oddly enough, his extremely professional interest has also made him a force in the lives of Christians.

Some of us must use a volume such as this to discharge our obligation to Nygren for a lifetime of thoughtful preoccupation with Christian things and for his venturesome books. My library includes most of his books, many of them used when preoccupied with fighting my way out of terrifying indecision, awesome doubts and confusions, compounded of metaphysics, positivism and vague religious beliefs. Even in youthful days, when my Swedish was painfully inadequate, his pages were a call to intellectual integrity as well as Christian faith. Now, with long exposure to the temptations of the professionals who write about religion and philosophy, I can only thank him for his achievements in both respects. For he has put the abstract and concrete together in an extraordinary way.

When others have been attaching themselves to one or other of the warring theological schools, Nygren has pursued an individual way. He has not enrolled under any of the patent banners, neither has he regarded any theological emphasis of the present as beyond the pale, nor has he made for himself a mere theological patchwork of bits and pieces. All through his authorship, now of almost fifty years, he has given new ideas, as well as old, a run for their money, assessing and developing them by his own creative and critical intelligence. In all of this, Nygren's alert tolerance, coupled with his trenchant argument, has been of great benefit to theology and to his readers.

Of course, there has also been the wide range of his theological work. For he has moved from certain kinds of detailed category study, almost in the tenor of modern philosophical analysis, to criticisms of metaphysics, from lengthy historical studies of the Christian idea of love to a bishop's pastoral letters, from the foundations of dogmatics to the foundations of ethics, from questions of demythologizing scripture to a lengthy commentary on the Epistle to the Romans, and from essays in an antimetaphysical temper, akin to Hägerström, to a late essay highly appreciative of the later Wittgenstein. So, in one man, we have adeptness in scriptural studies and responsible historical learning, albeit put to characteristic and strong uses. His philosophical work has been absolutely critical for him, giving him his tools as well as delimiting and defining his numerous tasks. To have done the latter marks him off as an exception.

Also, one must note that Nygren has preached and practiced the principle that theologians and preachers must avoid obfuscation. Among other things, this has meant getting rid of most murky German metaphysics. This must not have been easy, for he is veritably steeped in nineteenth-century German thought. On the other hand, Nygren has not been loathe to use technical terms, nor technical concepts, but only in strictly scholarly contexts and for such guarded purposes that their meanings are clear and their use justified. He is refreshing because he shows that pretentious jargon is not an essential element in any work, theological or philosophical, that aims to be profound.

These things have been said to put the remarks which follow into the right perspective. Without ever once proclaiming the virtues of "synthesis," of "dialogue," of "relevance," or even "ecumenicity," Nygren has traversed very abstract philosophical topics, learned from critical historians, and simply made sense with the hardest kind of work and the most disciplined of learning. This is what makes him worth reading; this is what makes him worth arguing with too. But his work is not perfect; but like most efforts of integrity, it is perfectible. Therefore the criticisms.

My critical remarks will be addressed to him and his pages in the spirit which he enjoined in an essay of 1958. There he urged that more attention be paid to questions in the philosophy of religion.[1] He alluded to the new problems raised by logical empiricists, semanticists, and the existentialists. In a way that is still rare for a theologian, Bishop Nygren has addressed a large range of tough-minded questions, almost continually since he began writing in the second decade of this century. Instead of meekly fitting theology into the regnant philosophical metaphysics or world views, Nygren has worked his own way into very difficult logical and epistemological matters, by and large, the kind of issues otherwise left to the most professional of philosophers and discussed only in professional journals. Furthermore, he has not only read others, he has concluded for himself and in print. Thus, he has said all kinds of things about difficult concepts like "validity," "reality," "category," "value judgments," "facts," and "metaphysics." It is not my theme that he has always concluded correctly, but it is my contention that he has treated these matters in a style befitting a professional modern philosopher. Small issues have been important to him. Besides, he has put this acumen to theological uses.

Furthermore, because he has argued over the years that theology ought to be free of philosophical components, especially metaphysical views, he has also looked for such a method as would "succeed in reducing the philosophical presuppositions to a minimum."[2] The matter of expunging these pieces of early philosophies, of getting rid of metaphysics, of using only chaste and pure categories, allies Nygren rather firmly in temper with those philosophers we call analytic and critical, rather than with those who are speculative and metaphysical.

In what follows, I want to ally in part with this temper too. And I do not wish to quarrel with Bishop Nygren's program. Least of all do I want to argue, in the manner of Professor Wingren, about false anthropological presuppositions, in Nygren's pages, which somehow entail false hermeneutical presuppositions.[3] Instead, I want to push Nygren's philosophical analysis a little further. It seems that Nygren, probably following Hägerström and other critical thinkers, saw clearly the absurdities of the older metaphysics getting entangled with theology, ethics, science, and esthetics. Just as the sciences are now prosecuted without getting one's metaphysics straight, either before or after, so Nygren helps us not only to do theology as professional work within the universities, but also to believe in God and become responsible Christians, without first declaring our metaphysics or even resolving our metaphysics surreptitiously.

So much is to the good. But there is more work ahead. If part of the effort in recent years in philosophical arenas has been to get rid of illusions and the spell of subtle intellectualist convictions, then I am certain that Bishop Nygren would welcome more stringency. Without mitigating in the least the importance of what he has done, I wish to push further several of his analyses. For he has really substituted one kind of philosophy, a critical logical kind, for the metaphysical varieties. But it seems to me that a closer analysis of the language of several of his philosophical claims will show that he does not need even his sparse philosophical scheme in order to do theology. Therefore, we will examine in turn: first, those big concepts, "True," "Good," "Beautiful," and "Eternal"; second, the notion of validity; and, third, a few specific theological issues.

FIRST, we shall say something about major philosophical "problems" that Nygren treats with such deference. One gathers that the words "truth," "good," "beauty," and "eternal" are in some way or another fundamental to him. They are said to be fundamental because they are the minimal terms for irreducible forms of spiritual life. Nygren makes philosophy a "geometrical locus," a kind of placing of these forms, within the life of the spirit.[4] And right here we have an interesting facet of his thought, one which is perhaps slightly misleading. He uses "forms" and other spatial (and logical) expressions when talking about "categories," "problems," and "questions." Almost like Kant, he likens philosophy, not to one more subject-matter field among others, nor quite to an activity without doctrines or any kind of resolution (e.g., in the manner of Wittgenstein), but to a kind of deduction, almost geometrical, transcendental to be sure, of the concepts, principles, problems, perhaps questions (these seem to him to nest together) which are necessary, universal and, hence, valid.[5] In a later section, we shall note in particular some issues respecting Nygren's conception of validity, but right here one topic is this farrago, "truth," "good," "beauty," and the "eternal."

The issue I wish to raise has little to do with Professor Gustav Wingren's criticisms. He is sarcastic about Nygren's wishing a supposedly neutral philosophical scheme and says, "It is presupposed that the categorical and fundamental questions have already been defined in another discipline." [6] He contends, therefore, that other kinds of presuppositions of an anthropological sort are introduced in this neutral and descriptive philosophical guise, and, besides, that theology and theologians do not depend upon another and alien discipline. Wingren makes an ardent plea for theology altogether independent of Nygren's neutral philosophizing, insinuating that "the underlying reason for this procedure has been the feeling that theology lacks scientific prestige, and that we must secure this prestige for it." [7]

As Nygren's writings unfold, the case against metaphysics of the systematic idealistic and materialistic (also scientific) sorts seems to become decisive. He finds metaphysical concepts to be esthetic, expressive, unverifiable, subjective, and simply irrelevant, if not distorting, when introduced into science, into ethics, and into theology.[8] Here Nygren's hand is very sure and his aim very accurate. He is at pains to show that concepts in ethics, esthetics, science, and in theology, too, are not also and simultaneously concepts in metaphysics. Usually, however, Nygren is prone to talk less about the concepts and to stress that one need not believe in a world view in order to believe and do other things, or that theology or ethics, as a whole, does not depend upon a metaphysics. In other words, Nygren frequently uses rather large and sweeping terms, e.g., "ethics" and "theology," despite his supposedly analytic bent. Nonetheless, the result is a major clarification, for which one can be grateful.

But now we come to something like this:

> If we take a broad survey of the history of human thought, we get a lively impression of the truth of the old saying that there is nothing new under the sun. . . . Quite early in the history of thought we find the great fundamental questions asked, concerning the True, the Beautiful, the Good, and above all, the Eternal: the problems, that is to say, of Knowledge, of Esthetics, of Ethics, and of Religion. For our Western civilization the classical statement of these questions is that of Plato. . . . And in spite of all the changes which history has made in the forms in which the questions are asked, we may yet say that mankind is still occupied with these same great questions.[9]

Through a variety of writings, long and short, over a period of many years, Nygren has tried to show by both a kind of deduction in Kant's special sense, that there are these transcendentals and by a kind of description, not quite so dependent upon Kant and a priori deductions, that there are these inescapable, nonmetaphysical and nonscientific questions.[10]

Nygren takes seriously these large terms, "True," "Good," "Eternal," and "Beautiful." They seem to me to be at the most only rhetorical and obfuscating and needing explanation rather than providing it. He uses these terms to explain something about the concept, "agape," in Christianity and to get at the persistent component, the essence, of Christianity. But these terms are not the names of anything at all. Let us take this notion of truth. Nygren seems to believe that there is one master concept of truth at work in all these different circumstances: [11]

1] If I "refer any phenomenon to its causes" ("smoking causes coughs");

2] if I "make any statement" ("Churchill was a Tory") or "think any thought" (e.g., Aristotle's four causes)

3] "the demand for consistency in thinking" (when I say, "Don't exaggerate—I won't know when to take you seriously").

When one tries to use "true" or "truth" in connection with even these three circumstances, I doubt that there is any core of meaning, any master concept, actually at work. If one only confines himself to what Nygren calls theoretical language, I still do not believe that the many kinds of statements, descriptions, beliefs, that pass as theoretical, could be subsumed under "truth," as if "truth" referred in turn to something they all had in common.

Nygren is inclined to put together the many different things called "theoretical," "descriptive," and "scientific," as if they all had TRUTH in common. In the first place, there are too many different things under "description" or any of these labels to be said to have any one thing in common. Besides "description" is really many concepts, not one. So, too, with "theory" or "theoretical." "Science" is also many things—many concepts. One must not be misled by the common word to assume there is a common concept. Secondly, it may be that Nygren is misled by the fact that we give to descriptions, theoretical interests, and sciences some common linguistic forms. So we can say: "I know that ———" and fill in whatever we please. This makes us think that knowing is one thing, describable by whatever logical canons we can discern for sentences of such a form. But this does not bring the differences any closer together, except in a deceptive way. Perhaps something of the same consideration applies to Nygren's notion that we have also "inescapable questions." [12] For in what sense or senses, we have a meaningful use of "question" covering ethics, science, religion, and esthetics quite escapes me. But once we get "question" working, it "seems," but only seems, to denominate something in common. At this juncture, it is wise to remember the multiplicity, the variety itself, the kinds of activities, words, and sentences, in order not to be misled by what logicians and others oriented to formal matters have said about underlying structures and similarities.

One of the reasons philosophers have had so much trouble defining "truth *qua* truth" is precisely that that word, when assumed to have its life and vitality in every kind of intellectual endeavor, becomes impossible to define. Where it has to do so much work as this, it finally does not do any. Therefore, philosophers have disagreed violently about truth, some saying it is a semantical word, some a transcendental, some that it is a matter of consistency, others that it is a question of correspondence between thought and things. But, is it not the case that "telling the truth" involves often a concept of "truthfulness," not "truth"; so if we hear a fantastic dream and the dream gets too complicated, we doubt the "truthfulness" of the dreamer (he did not dream what he said he dreamed). Is the same concept of truth at work if we also say, "Despite the pleasantness of your dream, I'll wager you are glad it was not true"?

My charge is that a general concept of truth is really an invention of people who like to generalize. I do not believe that it is deduced, even in Kant's plausible way, nor discovered as Plato would have one believe. Furthermore, that general concept of truth is not the one that is working for us when we speak, write, or think in various contexts. In fact, if Nygren is really doing a neutral philosophical kind of description, as he says, I believe he would have discovered something else, namely, that there are many concepts of truth at work in the many ways in which we talk, write, and think. So, Wittgenstein noticed that when

> longing makes me cry "O, if only he would come!" the feeling gives the words "meaning." But does it give the individual words their meanings?

But here one could also say that the feelings gave the words their "truth." And from this you can see how the concepts merge here.[13]

But I am not accusing Nygren of wanton generalizing or simply failing to describe. Most of us are also victims of philosophical habits, and because Nygren is so gifted and so many-sided in interests, these habits come very easily to him. Besides such habits seemed to fit something — the many concerns which he had and the range of phenomena that were so easy to classify. Of course, there are also these subtle matters of overlooking the differences and seeking the formal similarities.

But is not this the point, namely, that the formal structures, the classification, or categories ("the categories," Nygren says, "are basic questions") [14] are not quite relevant either? The concepts "truth" and "good" merge and so do "meaning" and "truth" (as the Wittgenstein reference showed). It has not been my interest to distinguish clearly Nygren's use of "category," "question," "concept," and "problem." But I gather that he thinks a range of activities and "a group of questions" can be summed up as "the ethical question," [15] so we get a category. Also there is, then, in the range of activities and questions, be they esthetic, cognitive, ethical, or religious, the fundamental question. Appearance aside, "the old question still remains, but it is stated in a new form." [16] So, the philosophical point is almost extra-ethical, esthetic, religious, and cognitive. Philosophy "categorizes," forms the questions abstractly, and, of course, delineates the concepts involved. Philosophy is a critical activity, about these other activities, in fact, analytic of them.[17] But this is an instance of a philosopher "subliming" and projecting the ideal proportions of these activities rather than a strict disciplined analysis.

Thus far, Nygren seems to be very clear indeed, in fact, too clear. He wants to get rid of metaphysical world views in which these must somehow fit and of the notion that their concepts are, on the face of it, actually metaphysical concepts. But Nygren does not leave matters there. And the fault is not quite that he all the while has another world view himself. Instead, Nygren is too much the intellectualist. He makes a clarifying concept by which to orient himself. This keeps him from describing either human behavior as it is in all its miscellaneous diffusiveness or the working concepts as they are with all their specificity and differences being kept clearly apart. He lumps activities and questions, pursuits and human happenings; and he, following other critical philosophers, thinks that they can be meaningfully categorized. Perhaps we should say that they can be, but only for various purposes. Nygren makes the categories fundamental so that they will fit all purposes. And here is where clarity becomes his bane. He is misled by the fact that because a rough word like "ethics" can be used to aggrandize a range of activities and statements, to believe that there is a formal and proper question or concept to go with it. So too, with his other fundamentals.

More than this, he is unable to resist the temptation to look at all the working concepts, within one of his categories or domains, except as expressions of master concepts like "True," "Good," "Eternal," and "Beauty." Let me take an example of this temptation. Suppose one categorizes esthetic statements and discovers that "beautiful" is used about a poem, a sunset, a piece of reasoning, a Scriabin sonata, and a woman's figure. We have then, we are tempted to say, "five uses of beauty." It is easy to assume that taking all of esthetic experience (all these examples plus many more) together calls for the elucidation of a single inclusive concept, "beauty." Nygren is a wise man, indeed, for he refuses to pontificate about what the large concept will be; and by this one can be instructed, for he is surely discriminating here. But he does take seriously the formal likeness even though he cannot further specify. My point is that he is wrong to erect a category here, to posit a single question, to even seek a master concept. For there is none at all except as a result of this idealization that goes on in his pages. And this is a matter of being misled by an ability, not a lack of an ability, to thinking that there is something to think about, corresponding to that formal property.

Only the study of language itself is needed here to explain how we get into the notion that there are these catgories, questions, and concepts. For the person who wants to know what beauty itself is, is perhaps discontented with understanding that there are many concepts, not one, and that the ambiguities and differences of meaning are not a fault at all. It makes great sense to learn how to call each of these things beautiful; it only makes for confusion and bad philosophy to ask for the clear, exact, unambiguous definition of beauty—especially when there isn't any. "Beauty" is a word with meaning only in a context; and the context is not esthetics. There are many contexts—evening and the sunset is one; listening to music is another; looking at a woman is another, etc. Nygren's philosophizing is neither as empirical as he wants it to be—he thinks about the categories not the individuals—nor as analytically descriptive—he quickly gets to those big formal concepts that can only work in his artificial contexts, not the real contexts of everyday life.

Nygren has, therefore, too great a role for philosophy, not least the philosophy of religion, in his systematic reflections. A remark of Wittgenstein's which Nygren notes in a judicious article about him says that most problems and questions of philosophy result from the fact that we do not understand the logic of our language. "And so," Wittgenstein says, "it is not to be wondered at that the deepest problems are really 'no' problems." [18] It seems to me that there are no big questions, categories, and concepts of Nygren's sort either.

BUT there is another kind of big philosophical word in Nygren's vocabulary. I think it a very dubious word indeed in the philosophical contexts he proposes for it. The word is "validity." Again he seems to have given it a general meaning such that it applies to all of esthetics, ethics, religion, and cognition. It is a truly philosophical concept, and by that I mean that it occurs only in philosophical discourse in the specialized meaning he notes. Something like religion or ethics is "valid" in the philosophical context, so too is knowledge and esthetics. Part of the bite which Nygren gives this expression is polemical. He makes the claim in order also to show that ethics, esthetics, knowledge, and religion are not to be judged metaphysically, as if they all approximated reality in varying degrees, or as if they were all true or false relative to the same objective stuff, or as if they were variously correspondent to a transcendent order of being. So, he says philosophy has to do with validity, not reality.[19]

Once more his moves against the metaphysical interpretation of all these kinds of discourse and activities are fully justified, and his articles still read as an impressive series of diatribes against sloppy thinking, and somewhat fanciful concept formation. He is still a model for would-be theologians. Again, though, Nygren is too much the philosopher himself. He still wants a subject matter, and he again supplies something as a substitute for what he has destroyed. He takes away reality and supplies validity. Of course, he has precedence and terribly good company; for Kant and Hägerström do something of the same. And it is not fair at this point to say that Nygren is only practicing metaphysics on his terms, for that is to equivocate badly on the term; he does this because he is not critical enough.

However, one is not here criticizing Nygren for being philosophical if one means analytic, intelligent and even rational. Nor is one asking him to be more theological or purely theological, or ethical only, or only commonsensical instead of sophisticated. Neither is this to say that being naïve is better than being complicated or that a bumpkin is superior to a professor. The issue is elsewhere and is not intended to be an *ad hominem* at all.

It is important to mark Nygren's consistencies here. In an essay on the nature of philosophy, Nygren defended the view that philosophy was knowledge and really a science, while simultaneously repudiating unequivocally the idea that it was ontological.[20] Philosophy is primarily a logical discipline whereby one discerns the underlying components and structure of the major cultural activities we know as knowledge, ethics, esthetics, and religion.[21] The result is that philosophy does not produce any new knowledge or new ethics, religion, or art—no new disclosures of reality; but it does show that each of these big transcendental concepts is independent, universal, and necessary. Apparently this is where "validity," in turn, begins to mean something.

"Validity" is a logical term initially. We use the word "valid" to describe an argument in which the inference is justified. An inference is warranted, logicians have said, when there is an implication already obtaining. So, there have been those who have argued that thinking, which is mostly made up of psychological processes, needs an objective warrant; and this is what is declared in the notion of there being, or not being, an implication (a nonpersonal, nonpsychological, logical relation). Two plus three makes five, we are prone to say, whether you think so or not; that it must be so, is a matter of validity. Thereby we say something about a logical relation.

To the extent that philosophy discerns what makes doing sums, placing bets, manufacturing speedometers, counting steps, measuring the field, and subtracting pence from pounds "possible," Nygren would, I take it, say that all of these depend upon the validity of two plus two equalling four. Without that one could not have the others. The dependence is logical, not always chronological—first the number then the measuring, etc. But, again we have the strange business of making too much out of "validity." For granted that we might say something about the concept of validity even in the instances of using numbers, it seems to me most dubious to suggest that validity is so general a concept that it works equally in the other areas. If I say to someone who does not know how to count or to use numbers in certain simple ways, namely, that he ought not to try to subtract ten pence from ten guineas, my reasons are straightforward and clear. There is a dependence here, and I can make sense of the notion that an elaborate business of subtraction can only be carried on with rules for numbers—we might call these concepts—otherwise the whole "game" breaks down. And one might say, too, that unless these rules are valid, unless they obtain, one cannot do these other things. Then "validity" gets its conceptual worth again in a specific context.

However, it is difficult to see that there is the same kind of dependence of practical endeavors—the whole of ethics—upon any one idea, say of the Good. For one thing, ethics, esthetics and religion are not any one kind of thing. Each of these terms is a loose kind of coverall that is not the least bit clarifying. It is right and proper that these terms should be that way, for we use them for rather crude and approximative purposes. Furthermore, it is hard even to see that they have as much in common as Nygren says they do when he calls them "fundamental values" or when he says they are atheoretical instead of theoretical.[22] We have to say, instead, that each of these is many activities and that it is a mistake to suggest that there is any one game of life called ethics, another called religion. Therefore, there is no "one" concept or no one rule within each either. In what sense are these "values"? What is being told us about all of them by such a use of terms?

Apparently "validity" is something that a logically trained and critical philosopher sees as a characteristic of these interrelated cultural activities. Of course "validity" is a concept; and as a concept it must be a meaning-complex that refers. But to what does it refer? I submit that Nygren is inventing this concept of validity, not discovering it at all. The concept does not refer to any common characteristic or group of characteristics. When we say this or that is valid, I propose that the word "valid" may very likely be exceedingly meaningful in a given context. But Nygren is proposing that philosophy provides concepts for the life of the spirit, and that means for all of human culture ("the system of culture").[23] Human life is no one game and no one context; neither are ethics, esthetics, religion, and knowledge. For this reason, we have no warrant for saying that all of ethics is dependent upon the idea of the good or that even that the concept of the good is, therein, a rule. Now we know that there is no philosophy for everything that has passed as ethics, because there are no common concepts, principles, presuppositions, rules in such a miscellany. This is the way it is with ethics, and the attempts even at a single philosophy of science (lately we have seen that there are many concepts within history, different from physics, biology, philology, and the rest) or a single scientific method are clearly abortive.

"Validity" is supposedly a common characteristic of Good, Beautiful, True, and Eternal. Here the notion of there being something in common is pushed to the most extreme level. Apparently this concept gets its vitality and meaning because it marks "necessity" and "indispensability." Everything which Nygren (and Hägerström) has said about the word "reality" could here be said about "validity." At one time philosophers dignified certain partial and arbitrarily selected aspects of their experience by calling them "reality." Nygren has shown, too, how "reality-talk" is in the philosophers' context (in contrast to that within specific contexts) essentially subjective, unprincipled, and honorific.[24] Is it not the case that he is doing the same thing with "validity"? What has a limited significance in the context of a certain kind of logic, perhaps within a kind of discussion involving numbers, is pushed to the extremes we have noted. It does not seem to me that there emerges, therefore, anything at all specific or precise, certainly not enough to suggest a special philosophical concept.

"In such a difficulty," Wittgenstein says, "always ask yourself: How did we 'learn' the meaning of this word ('good' for instance)? From what sort of examples? in what language games? Then it will be easier for you to see that the word must have a family of meanings."[25] If one does this with "validity," "good," "beauty," "eternal," and "truth," it seems to one that the supposed philosophical concept proves not to be part of any game whatsoever. What Nygren did so well with "reality," "being," and a few other terms dear to metaphysicians, he and his students could well afford to do to these terms. That Nygren did not do it is not surprising, granted the role and status that a kind of logical philosophy had in Hägerström and most of the best philosophy (the most technical, difficult, and acute) of the past generation.

The difficulties here are obscure, not least because they involve such a widespread tendency among the nonmetaphysical and logically-oriented philosophers. It must arise in some such way as this: namely that a thinker like Nygren wants to compare the practices and related uses of words in ethics, esthetics, and religion with those in logic where we do have fixed rules and precise uses. Because we can say in a rather obtuse way that there are principles of validity therein, we are inclined to believe all these more ordinary ways of speaking must be formally proper too—if we could only isolate the formal properties.

Then Nygren's task becomes one of stating their logical structure; and this is what he does in his transcendental deductions. No wonder then that a characteristic, "validity," is proposed for all of these in turn; for it is applicable if there is the logical structure Nygren claims. But this logical structure is an ideal, something posited and not discovered. Again perhaps Wittgenstein's self-criticism applies also to Nygren.

> All this, however, can only appear in the right light when one has attained greater clarity about the concepts of understanding, meaning and thinking. For it will then also become clear what can lead us (and did lead me) to think that if anyone utters a sentence and "means" or "understands" it, he is operating a calculus according to definite rules.[26]

And his general concept of validity only works if there are general logical structures for even ethics and religion.

IN THIS section I would like to discuss a few smaller issues, most of which are again closely related to the issues of language and meaning. On page 23 of *Christ and His Church*,[27] Nygren says:

> Consequently the question of Christ and his relationship to the gospel has also entered into a new stage, for "Christ" and the "Kingdom of God" are interchangeable concepts. What holds true of the Kingdom of God holds true also of Christ.

In his essay "Corpus Christi," [28] Nygren argues that the Church is Christ and that the body of Christ (which is what Christians call the Church) is Christ himself. These things are said also in order to refute what Nygren holds to be mistaken views. Thus he is against saying with Kant that the Kingdom of God is "a society concerned for the preservation of morality" or "a republic under moral law." [29] Accordingly, one can understand and profit greatly from learning that moral language, talk about law, duty, right and wrong, good and evil, does not feed the concept of the Kingdom of God. Nygren is here an analytic kind of logico-descriptive theologian, showing us rather pointedly why moral expressions and behavior are not the places where several distinctively Christian words derive their meanings.

This is all to the good, and his negative case is a splendid one. His positive aim seems clear enough too. He wants to show how the "Kingdom of God" concept feeds on the distinctive Christian sources. So he says that the New Testament concept is altogether different from Kant's.

> There it cannot exist other than in immediate connection to the
> head of the Kingdom, to Christ. It is not built by men, and it does
> not come into effect through human decision; it comes through
> an act of God. It follows upon God's decree. . . . And all the
> New Testament's message comes to just this, that this event has
> taken place through Jesus, who is therefore called the Christ.[30]

Therefore, there is no Church without Christ.[31] Moral laws and high
hopes, imperatives and happiness are not enough. And one gathers that
in large part this is another illustration (as is his *Agape and Eros*) of
how theology works. Theology does not prove doctrines to be true,
but it does legislate by showing that certain doctrines are not proper
because they put together incommensurate components. Theology
puts the concepts which are together, e.g., in Christian scripture, also
together in the doctrines. Theology in this sense has to do with logic,
the compatibility, rather than the truth of doctrines.

But Nygren is not content to put them together and show how,
for example, the concepts of Church and Christ depend upon each
other and a host of other practices and beliefs. Instead he makes the
case stronger by saying that the concepts are interchangeable. Now
this is a kind of meaningless thing to say. Frege's famous example of the
concepts of "Evening Star" and "Morning Star" referring to Venus yet
clearly not being identical as concepts is appropriate. But certainly the
"Kingdom of God" and "Christ" are not different concepts referring
to the same thing. When are they interchangeable? When not? There
may be some cases when they are interchangeable, but that does not
say that they are so without qualification. And the instances where we
can speak truly about the Kingdom of God will not be coextensive
with the instances that one can speak truly about Christ. Furthermore,
there must be all kinds of reasons for two concepts arising even in
Biblical times.

A second issue has to do with Nygren's acceptance of the distinction between value judgments and theoretical descriptive judgments.
There seem to be dogmas lurking in this distinction that mitigate the
effort to be logically discerning. For one thing, are not "value judgments" and "theoretical judgments" too pat? I wonder whether this
distinction is not almost meaningless as it stands. For it supposes that
we know also the logic of all kinds of statements whereby we can say
whether they are one or the other, or neither. But what kind of
knowledge is that? Is that philosophy? Here Nygren again is too clear.
His logical interest is too well defined and he makes artificial the issues.
Furthermore, do we not have to learn to use sentences to ascertain this

kind of thing? Can we look at sentences and know their meaning? That would be true only if we could trust their "form." But that is what we know to be deceptive.

On matters of faith, Nygren is very intent upon showing that beliefs of Christians are not intrinsically metaphysical or just one more world view.[32] One can understand his case quite well. But once he has said that much about theology he wishes to show that ethics, esthetics, and science are not metaphysical either. However, by insisting upon the separation of these, it seems to me he omits the problem. The fact is that often people moved by pangs of conscience describe the world differently than the blasé and Christians describe the cosmos differently than the pagans suckled by other creeds outworn. Because the different kinds of speech of different kinds of people have sometimes overlapped and sometimes not, a certain mystique about language and what it means has developed. No one does metaphysics on purpose except a few professors of the subject, and usually their offerings are not very impressive. The reason we have metaphysics at all is that all kinds of people speak out of different dispositions and in different ways about what we like to think is the same world. There would be no problem if we spoke valuationally at 7:00 A.M. and theoretically at 7:00 P.M. The point is that people do all kinds of things, including "describing" in ethical, esthetic, and religious contexts too. Theoretical-like and des-criptive-like judgments occur just everywhere and anywhere in the mouths of babes, saints, rakes, fops, and sots. Logical types get distrib-uted rather widely.

People imbued with ethical passion describe the whole world in a certain way. It seems to me downright silly to say that ethical language is one thing or the other, for example, imperative-like or evaluative, rather than descriptive. Likewise, religious men do their ethics differ-ently, probably some do their esthetics differently too; but the point is that there is a language of esthetic living which becomes also an esthetic performance. Likewise, there is a language of faith which is itself part of the religious life. But there is only a philosophical dogma which says that these ways of speaking can also be divided according to logical canons, as if some were descriptive, others not, etc. These logical typifications which make up so much of recent philosophy have not grown out of close empirical study. Instead they are part of a long philosophical heritage—really excess baggage. They elude us about the real similarities and differences which crisscross over the material in an enormously complex way.

Of course, Nygren is right in wanting to give a conceptual justifi-

cation for, in his case, Christian theology. He saw that it did not have
to be metaphysical the way systematic philosophers had said. But he
seeks the justification in a scheme of logical types. This is one more
intellectual mishap. His actual performances in his purely religious
writings are, I believe, much better than his abstract reflections. For,
in the former, he has repeatedly reminded us of piety, of guilt, of con-
trition, of the way of a Christian life, and these are also the contexts
in which Christian theological concepts are born; but in the latter, he
makes their theological typification an actual clue to their meaning.
The fact is that he does not really need the latter scheme at all. He is
wrong because he thinks he does.

He has said about theology that "på samma gång måste den vara
positivt kristlig och sträng vetenskäplig," [33] ("at the same time it must
be positively Christian and strictly scientific"). Actually he has succeeded despite his philosophizing. He has kept his theology, by and
large, true to the New Testament, but he has misdefined the task by
supposing that theology must be of one logical type. Actually the New
Testament itself shows us that the language of the faithful is not
valuational only nor theoretical only—it is a mixture of types just as
common everyday language is.

The third briefer issue is the strange category "the eternal." [34] We
are told that Christians find the revelation of the eternal in Jesus
Christ.[35] The eternal, one must remember, is inevitable and fundamental for the life of the spirit and validates the place of religion in human
life.[36] Christ is the place where the eternal "breaks in" for Christians.
But Nygren argues that this concept of the eternal is the means by
which one can now understand compound names like, "Jesus the
Messiah," "Jesus is the Son of God," "The Lord," "The Logos."
Furthermore, one can understand, too, the "dogmatic constructions"
built upon these names.[37] Apparently this is the case because Christians
are "expressing," in those names and in the dogmas, that the eternal is
revealed, judges them, reconciles them, and provides fellowship—all in
Jesus Christ.

There are several things wrong with this. If a man uses "Lord" for
Jesus, who is Nygren or anyone else to say what he means? Was he
thinking: "Aha, the eternal," but saying: "Lord"? If not, how does this
"eternal" business work? As a question? Sometimes Nygren says that,
but apparently as a question which a man does not phrase for himself.
It takes a philosopher to phrase it and quite a while after. In either case,
the "eternal" has a priority—it makes a man seek out historical "an-

swers," even Jesus Christ. I wonder if Nygren is in any position to tell anyone about this. Or does he know how our thoughts work before our language gets going by expressing the thoughts? Is this what knowing the logical validity implies?

He says that "names" and "dogmatic constructions" are expressions. This says something about the way our language works too. But here there is a strange convention among us, namely, the one which likens word to "expressions," as if they were partial, like tears are said to be not the whole of the grief but only "expressions" thereof. Nygren puts the religions of the world, their names and their dogmas, in the category of expressions. This seems to me to be a conventionalism which elides a few plain matters. It suggests that one need not look at the use of "Lord," whether the man submits as he says it or obeys him subsequently, but rather that one peer into his consciousness or the structure of the language to discern that "eternal" component, concept, question or category. And we cannot ask most men, for they do not know about the "eternal" anymore than most men know about the "good" or "beauty" or "truth." (It took Plato to state these.) Therefore, I suggest that "express" is misleading. Words and dogmas do not express meaning. If they are not simply idle, certainly we can ascertain what they do for their user. If they do nothing, have no antecedents or consequences, then they might well be useless and meaningless. Occasionally they may "express" too, but not invariably nor often. Nygren is perhaps misled by the notion that what is behind the word, the logical structure, is more important than the words or the dogmas. If so, this is a devastating assertion and certainly false.

Everything previously noted about Nygren's considerable prowess as a technical thinker is borne out by a new and long book recently from his pen. Its title is "Meaning and Method: Prolegomena to a Scientific Philosophy of Religion," but the title does not begin to tell the story nor provide a clue to Nygren's agility as a thinker and intellectual craftsman—this despite his advanced age. In a way that is, to say the very least, almost frighteningly anticipatory of the kind of criticisms that have been noted, Nygren here is trying to refurbish his philosophical schematism and bring up to date his Kantlike views of "eternal," "validity," "presupposition," and other erstwhile fundamental categories and concepts.

In brief, this last book (not yet published in Swedish or any other language and available to me only in typescript) is a very impressive account of recent technical philosophy. It deals with what the European tradition calls "theoretical" philosophy rather than with "practical" philosophy. Roughly this means that he is concerned with critical philosophy, with developments in logic and epistemology, where technical competencies prevail and where there is genuine professionalism. He is not writing here about most existentialists, neometaphysicians, views of life, or even the moralizers, like Toynbee, who pass for philosophers. And there is scant attention paid to Tillich, Rahner, theological system-makers, and those obviously helpful and earnest writers who want to tell us what is what. No, here as always, Nygren is the highly professional writer, who believes that there are "grundlig" matters, difficult and even obtuse, but upon which significant effort like even doing theology, does depend. As impressive as such a judgment sounds, and I mean to make it so, if for nothing else, to express admiration for such a fine mind as Nygren has and for such discipline that it takes to get such mastery, still, it seems to me that this view is deeply wrong. And the reasons are, even after carefully perusing his newest pages, still those noted in our previous criticisms.

But, more of that later. Here, let it be noted, what this last book is about and just how the same issues as we have noted are now addressed. It is no secret that Nygren found Axel Hägerström's philosophy highly suggestive and a positive aid to his own intellectual formation. But Hägerström wrote almost as a loner, without the support of a rich and thickly textured philosophical culture, save an historical one. Since the second decade of this century, there has been, of course, an enormous development of the very kind of critical and nonmetaphysical philosophy that Hägerström was proposing. In the past few decades, that kind of philosophizing is not done any longer simply against the philosophies of Kant and earlier metaphysicians. Neither is it the case that "idealism" is the sole focus, as it was for both theologians like Barth and Brunner and philosophers like Hägerström and Mach. The debate has become more refined, the focus more specialized. The issues now are "meaning," the nature of "concepts," the concept "fact," whether there are "rules" and "criteria," etc. So, Nygren's book addresses that vast corpus of technical philosophical literature, roughly since 1920 through the sixties, with the more practised eye of the highly sophisticated student exposed in some detail to genuine advances in the discipline. Thus, we read here about Wittgenstein, both of the *Tractatus* and the *Investigations*, about Ryle, about Strawson, about Feigl, Popper, Toulmin, Black, Quine, Frege, Austin, Russell, Collingwood, even Gustav Bergmann.

This litany of the greats in the philosophy that is called "analytical" and/or "linguistic analysis" would do credit to any philosophy professor; and it is a positive shock to find a theologian, and a Bishop at that, who discusses them so candidly and so well. There is nothing cheap nor histrionic about this survey and certainly it is not done merely for effect. Nygren purports to be taking a wider look around. He is still worried about the status of both philosophy and theology, how they are, in Kant's term, "possible." He tells the story of technical philosophy with the very special interest of correcting and bearing out, if such can be done, his earlier account. Hence, he concerns himself with refining the case against metaphysics, using this time considerations brought to light by logical positivism and its critics; and he worries in detail about the newer kinds of epistemologies, the range of issues covered by "induction-deduction," the controversies about "description," but to such effect that here Nygren is using recent literature to correct the overly-formalized views of his earlier years and also those of Hägerström. But as he moves on he comes also to those tantalizing issues of "meaning," of informal versus formal "logic," and to the radical reconsiderations of the very nature of philosophy that we are familiar with in Wittgenstein and Ryle. I think it fair to say that Nygren, careful as he tries to be, is not doing justice to the later Wittgenstein (nor to Ryle, Austin, and others) when he edits their pages to the effect that "a great deal of what they have to say is really a kind of analysis of presuppositions." Nygren makes their concerns with language, with meaning, with ordinary usage, somehow coalesce around the notion that, after all, this is very much like clarification and statement of what was anterior, namely, presuppositions. The effect, again, is a little smothering—too much is put into that comprehensive notion of "presupposition." And, what is novel and distinctive, hard to understand though it be, is now compressed into something familiar and almost bland. Nygren's citations of Collingwood help him put the incongruities together.

It is almost as if the philosophy of the past few decades makes Nygren's systematic case, his kind of deduction, his claim for "validity," for the persistent and abiding features that are "eternal," even more sophisticated and explicit. It is as if modern "linguistic analysis" has given more substance to and more material by which his expression theory of dogmas and theological statements can be construed. Wittgenstein's "forms of life" become for Nygren something like "presuppositions," almost as if they are what is being "expressed." Now,

Wittgenstein never said anything like that. Though there are analogies here that are suggested to one, it seems to me that Wittgenstein's cryptic case against the notion that there is a "spiritual" or mental activity corresponding to the words, by which one can say that words "express" what one had in mind, inveighs heavily against the presupposition view, too. Wittgenstein's notion of "language-games," of "use," of "forms of life," etc., were helps in the direction of freeing one of the apparatus that epistemological philosophy had invented. So, once again, where Ryle and Wittgenstein would help us sweep clean the philosophical stable, getting rid of surely some things called metaphysics and most certainly of that business called "epistemology," Nygren reads them to make his case for epistemology even more refined.

Despite, then, the masterly display of erudition and clever deployment of editorial and critical skills, I do not find Nygren's latest efforts in the direction of foundational philosophical matters at all convincing. It seems to me that Nygren must have been touched by the kinds of criticisms he has read through the years, both the criticisms of the older radical antimetaphysical philosophies and those of his writings; but, instead of moving with those philosophical critics who have come to see that there are no foundational matters to be disclosed, either metaphysical or epistemological, Nygren wants to keep the latter. His analyses and restatements seem to me to suffer in consequence. He makes judgments about recent philosophy that seem to me to be wrong —almost as if he can see the upshot and significance in relation to these matters that are foundational when Wittgenstein and Ryle could not. Maybe he is right; but to say that is to admit that another kind of philosophy is operative, the kind which is speculative and declarative, almost pontifical and dogmatic. With that, one finds that his pages are not quite in the descriptive character so long associated with his name.

IT IS the case that Anders Nygren has been one of the most gifted of philosopher-theologians in the past fifty years. He uses Christian concepts with Christian purposes—to the instruction and edification of men in the new life in Christ Jesus, our Lord. That he can do this so well is a testimony to his Christian understanding. But he has also been a technical theologian, interested not only in using these concepts but also in describing them. Furthermore he has tried to place them in relations with other fundamental concepts, show how all could be deduced, and even to distill there from the essence of Christianity. For Nygren there was a science of the essences of ethics, esthetics, knowledge, and religion. I believe that this science, philosophy, is no science at all. Here Nygren has gone wrong. He has proposed some doctrines about these things. But most of these are as meaningless as the metaphysics against which he rails.

Nygren has been right in thinking there is an essence, but he is wrong in thinking there is a science of essences (e.g., a philosophy of religion by which to deduce that essence). There is certainly an essence but it can only be understood in the rules, the concepts, the beliefs, the practices associated with Christianity, Jesus and the Church. It is not something in all of these—it is these. Therefore, it is quite enough for a theologian to describe these in great detail. Nygren has, of course, done much of that already and very admirably. But he is inclined to think that these descriptions are like clues to a more fundamental and exact logical structure. There he was wrong. He was bewitched by the thought of a logic, a more ideal structure, open to a philosophical discernment. Instead of positing this logical apparatus by which to get at the essence of so many important things, it would have been quite enough to say with Wittgenstein that all that was needed was "a grammar."

Nygren's practice in his theological writings was very close to seeing the concepts only in the practice, rules, and protocol of the New Testament and Christian people. His abstract writing, anxious to refute the philosophical conventions of the day, substituted logical doctrines for metaphysical doctrines. He thought he needed these doctrines to make theology intrinsically Christian and "*vetenskaplig*," but he did not. The grammar of the faith is quite enough.

Motif Research

3

THE METHOD

OF MOTIF RESEARCH

Valter Lindström

P HILOSOPHY should, according to Nygren, consist in a general theory of experience. It should start from the actually existing knowledge as an accepted fact. It should ask the question, how and on which conditions the existing knowledge is possible. By means of analysis philosophy has to try to find its way backwards to the fundamental conditions of our knowledge, with which we operate not only in our daily experience but also in every scientific investigation. Inevitably we use such concepts as true and false, real and unreal, cause and effect, etc. It is by means of presupposed concepts like these that the particular propositions get their logical connection and meaning.

Philosophy should, as a general theory of experience or as a logical analysis of the presuppositions of thought, try to find its way back to these conditions of our knowledge. In this way philosophy ought to have the character of a critical theory of knowledge. But theory of knowledge is only one part of philosophy, because experience is not exhausted by an exclusively theoretical statement of existing circumstances. We encounter sentences and propositions, which externally have the form of theoretical propositions of experience, but which obviously lose their meaning when they are subordinated to the presuppositions or categories of theoretical knowledge. So it is, by way of example, in regard to the ethical or to the religious concepts. When in an ethical proposition a deed is characterized as good, this proposition in its linguistic form does not differ from an ordinary theoretical proposition. But *the meaning* is quite different. This is also true in regard to the religious propositions. These propositions stand under other conditions and are obviously determined by other categories than the theoretical propositions.

Thus we have to do with several dominating contexts of meaning or universes of discourse, every one of which is governed by specific categories. It is, according to Nygren, the task of philosophy to perform its analysis of propositions in each of these spheres and in this way proceed to a comprehensive doctrine of categories.

When, through its analysis of presuppositions, philosophy has managed to reach back to the presuppositions or categories which underlie the propositions of several kinds, the question of the different contexts of meaning seems to have got an exhaustive answer.

The whole of the complex of propositions, which are subordinated to a certain category, thereby forms a unitary context of meaning and every proposition within that universe of discourse gets its unequivocal signification by being placed in this context.

But this is applicable only to the theoretical concepts, where it is possible to go directly from the categories to the particular proposi-tions and to win from them an absolutely unequivocal meaning. This, however, is not possible within the atheoretical contexts of meaning. The religious universe of discourse does not constitute any unequivocal context of meaning. Within the historical religions we meet a few typical answers to the categorical religious fundamental question, answers which neutralize each other, leaving their mark on all con-nected particular conceptions, propositions and valuations.

In the religious and in the ethical sphere the fundamental answers to questions of categorical character give a certain color to all particu-lar propositions. An ethical proposition, for example, receives a quite different meaning, if you start from one or another ethical ideal. And, as Nygren has demonstrated, a word like "love" gets a quite different signification, if the context is dominated on one side by the Hellenistic motif of eros and on the other side by the Christian motif of agape.

Thus an intermediate link is inserted between the general category and the particular ethical or religious proposition and the particular propositions get their unequivocal meaning only through this interme-diate link. Nygren calls this intermediate link a *basic motif*.

Thus, within the atheoretical contexts of meaning we have to do with several secondary universes of discourse, running along with each other, everyone of them determined by its own basic motif. Only within the secondary contexts, where not only the general category is considered but also the basic motif, do the particular propositions receive their unequivocal signification.

Thus, according to Nygren, the basic motif of a way of thinking is the fundamental answer which it gives to a question of categorical character. He calls an investigation, which is meant to get back to the basic motif, dominating a certain way of thinking, *motif research.*

The error of trying to understand a statement in isolation arises when due deference is not paid to the observation that no word, no proposition has a meaning in itself, only in its context. A statement must be seen in its immediate context, in the wider context of which it is part and finally in the comprehensive context of meaning, which expresses the sort of context in which the word stands and through which it ultimately receives its meaning.[1] An investigation of this kind operates on the boundary between philosophy and history. The question is put in the philosophic manner, but the answer must be derived from the historical facts. Thus, the motif research includes at the same time a philosophical and a historical problem. As regards the starting point, it is connected with the philosophic analysis of prerequisite conditions and the doctrine of categories resulting out of it. But the answer to the question about the fundamental conditions of a way of thinking can not be concocted by means of philosophy, but must be derived from history. The basic motif of a certain way of thinking can be established only through immediate observation of historical phenomena. The motif research has no right to exempt itself from the general conditions of historical investigation.

But does this method of proceeding not mean an outrage on historical facts? Who has said that historical matters must inevitably react on a question, asked in this manner? And if one proceeds with the presumption that such must be the case, is not then the risk of unhistorical construction impending?

Nygren denies emphatically that motif research should prevent a right understanding of the historical material or make it impossible. First of all, the categories are not arbitrary assumptions but necessary and inevitable conditions. The very thought that an ethical thought should not react on the ethical category of good and evil and the question involved in it is so absurd that there is no need of confutation. If every relation to the ethical category is lacking, this is only an evidence of the ethical irrelevance of the view in question. It then must be considered from another categorical point of view, which brings out its real sense.

But, in the second place, it is pure fiction that it should be possible to hold to the immediately given facts without any viewpoints at all. On the whole there is no such material immediately given, untouched by all viewpoints. As a matter of fact the historical reflection consists in assigning a place to the material under some leading points of view.

The viewpoint adopted by the motif research must be more objectively inevitable and better anchored to the historical material than any of the viewpoints, which can be assumed by the historical reflection.

As regards the acquiring of a picture of the chaotic multiplicity of meeting impressions, it is possible to strike off into two different directions. You can try to enumerate as completely as possible the elements included in the given multiplicity. This manner of procedure is characteristic of *the chronicle*. But even the chronicle must make a selection, although this is often done arbitrarily and unconsciously. But you can strike off into a contrary way too. Instead of seeking to attain a complete reproduction of the immediately given multiplicity, you can pick out certain particular striking features. This is done in *caricature*, where conspicuous features are arbitrarily brought into strong relief. If the arbitrary viewpoints are replaced by more essential ones, it is possible to rise from the chronicle to a *historical reflection* and from caricature to *characterization*.

A real overcoming of the arbitrariness, however, can be attained on both lines only by fitting the phenomena into a wider connection. Not until the particular historical event is seen in its place in the contemporary setting, not until the particular way of thinking is arranged in the more comprehensive historical connection of ideas, can this event or way of thinking be understood in a way which actually comes in close touch with reality. And not until the particular phenomenon, which you try to characterize, is arranged in a wider systematic connection, does its typical feature and distinctive mark appear clearly. The characterization grows into *systematics*.

In the motif research the two mentioned lines run together to a unity. The basic motif replies to the highest systematic question from the widest point of view within the history of ideas. The categorical question about the context of meaning here gets its answer on a historical basis.

Nygren has used the method of motif research chiefly within the theology of systematics. The method makes it possible to give an objective, strongly scientific character to this branch of theology. In his great work *Agape and Eros*, Nygren has shown that the basic motif of Christianity can be summed up in agape. The distinction between the two kinds of love, agape and eros, has proved to be of eminent importance in the field of the history of Christian thought. But the motif research in this specific formation has been of great value not only within the limits of theology but also in the history of literature in general and in the hands of literary men, too.

Criticism passed on the method of motif research, however, has not failed to appear. Thus the basis of the method, worked out in the field of philosophy of religion, has been criticized. Several investigators have maintained that Christianity is interpreted by Nygren as the positive content of the religious a priori category of universal applicability. The science of motif research corresponds to the idea of positive religion as a realization in history of the religious category. But thereby, the critics say, a certain view of the essence of Christianity, stamped by cultural idealism, is presupposed. This view, according to the critics, must inevitably influence the investigation of the Christian message. In other words, the method of motif research is affected by a hidden metaphysical presupposition and this is the idea of religion as a product of culture, which as a matter of fact is a religious concept, pregnant with meaning, which necessarily must come into conflict with the content of Christianity. Of course Christianity is a piece of culture, too, the critics say, but Christianity as a message is, in the interpretation of Nygren, absorbed by Christianity as an idea.

This criticism is to a certain extent justified in regard to earlier writings of Nygren in the field of philosophy of religion. But later on he has removed those traces of idealistic transcendentalism which could be found there. In the work *Filosofi och motivforskning* [Philosophy and Motif Research], nothing of that kind can be noticed. There he has reached a pure logical analysis of presuppositions, which starts from really existing knowledge, from real ethical positions and from real religious statements.

The criticism, which has been made of Nygren's own application of the method of motif research in *Agape and Eros* is closely connected with the remarks in the sphere of philosophy of religion upon the method as such. Generally the criticism has the purpose of showing that his exposition is dominated by a touch of intellectualism. It is in a higher degree the question of the *idea* of love than of the revelation of

God as interventions and actions in history. Furthermore agape is vindicated in a way which seems to exclude every assertion about the law of God and about longing for God from a genuine Christian teaching.

It is possible to derive statements from Nygren himself, which are directly intended to prevent an interpretation of his intentions in the direction just mentioned. Nevertheless, there are reasons for the question, if, perhaps, Nygren's way of thinking has certain characteristics, which let the indicated objections appear as not quite unexpected.

It is more than probable that Nygren deliberately puts forth those points of view, isolated, which have a direct importance to his analysis of the idea of agape. But it seems as if the kind of criticism at which we have hinted here could have been avoided, if Nygren had constantly inserted the idea of agape in the tension between the demanding law of God and the gospel of self-sacrificing love. This remark, however, is not an objection against the method of motif research. It is quite in accord with Nygren's intentions to state that the basic motif of Christianity must not necessarily be summed up in a single concept. It can just as well be summarized for instance in the tension between law and gospel.[2]

4

MOTIF RESEARCH AS A GENERAL

HISTORICAL METHOD

Bernhard Erling

ALTHOUGH the historical method of motif research, as Nygren has developed it, has thus far been applied primarily to theological subject matter, in this essay the broader historical relevance of this method will be explored. It will be necessary, however, before examining its broader relevance, to understand its theological use. This in turn requires that some consideration be given to Nygren's philosophy of religion, with which the origins of the method of motif research are closely related.

The close relationship between philosophy of religion and historical method is indicated in one of Nygren's earliest essays, "Det religionsfilosofiska grundproblemet" (1921), where he states that two steps are required in developing a theory of religious experience: a definition of the religious a priori, and a description of the historical realization of religion.[1] Since the concept of the a priori was current in the philosophical discussion of the first two decades of this century, Nygren used this terminology and devoted his doctoral dissertation, *Religiöst apriori, dess filosofiska förutsättningar och teologiska konsekvenser,*[2] to an attempt to define the religious a priori. He was critical, however, of the various attempts that had been made to define the a priori. That which he found of value in the various conceptions of the a priori which he examined was the presupposition of the validity of various forms of experience, but he was not satisfied with the way in which this factor of validity was identified. Nygren argued that for this purpose the Kantian transcendental method should be used, which he defined as follows: "That which must be valid if experience is to be possible at all is necessarily and universally valid." [3] Nygren understood this method as involving careful critical analysis designed to identify and define the presuppositions implicit in the various domains of experience. In a recent essay, "The Religious Realm of Meaning," [4] Nygren has again discussed the problems to which he devoted his attention in his earlier writings, but he no longer finds it necessary to use the term "a priori," which indicates that this terminology is not essential for a definition of his method. He observes that the philosophical climate has changed in the past decades, so that one must now relate one's thinking to the terminology of logical empiricism, semantics, and existentialism. Yet he still finds it useful to speak of the logical analysis of presuppositions and of the various realms of meaning which become identified when such logical analysis takes place.

Such analysis, according to Nygren, is the chief task of philosophy. Philosophy is to serve as a kind of universal science, analyzing and defining the distinctive character of the various domains of experience which constitute the life of the human spirit.[5] Nygren suggests that human existence can be understood as involving the asking and the answering of certain fundamental questions. Man inescapably asks: What is true? What is good or right? What is beautiful? As far back as we can go in human history the relevance of these questions is recognized. These questions are, furthermore, distinctively different, so that answers to one of these questions do not at the same time serve as answers to the others. Yet these answers, though distinctively different, do have something in common. To identify this common factor which the different answers to the fundamental questions share Nygren uses the term "validity." [6] In the method of transcendental deduction the fact that such validity exists in each of the domains of human experience is presupposed and, through critical analysis, an attempt is made to define more specifically the nature of this validity.

In *Religiöst apriori* Nygren states, however, that the transcendental deduction of the religious category must necessarily differ fundamentally from the transcendental deduction by which other areas of experience are defined.[7] This is because, in Nygren's opinion, the validity of religious experience cannot be assumed. He explains that this difference between religious experience and the other forms of experience is due to the essentially passive or receptive nature of religious experience, as contrasted with the active and productive nature of experience in the theoretical, ethical, and aesthetic domains. Due to the active and productive nature of experience in the cultural (theoretical, ethical, aesthetic) domains, those who will not accept the presuppositions of these domains cut themselves off from the fellowship constituted by the activity in these domains, which can lead to intolerable situations. Religious experience, however, differs in that it is essentially passive or receptive. The fellowship it represents, accordingly, can presumably be abandoned without the objective consequences being such that the untenability of such a position is immediately apparent. Therefore, in the analysis of the validity of religious experience one cannot, as in the cultural domains, begin by assuming such validity exists, but in order to establish the validity of religious experience one must show that its validity is one of the necessary presuppositions of the validity of the experience of the cultural domains.

Nygren seeks to do this by subjecting the concept of validity itself to further analysis.[8] As has already been indicated, the judgments by which the questions defining the theoretical, ethical, and aesthetic categories are answered all make claims to validity. But Nygren holds that in so doing they appeal to a category which transcends each of these categories singly, as well as all of them collectively. This transcendence may be illustrated, Nygren argues, by pointing to its relation to space and time. Truth, for example, the validity presupposed in the theoretical domain, is according to Nygren independent of space and time. The fact, therefore, that truth has validity presupposes that such transcendence of space and time is conceivable. But this presupposition by which human life is raised from the realm of the temporal to the realm of the eternal is, Nygren points out, fundamentally religious in nature. The concept of the eternal is not essentially cultural but religious in its significance. In philosophical terms the eternal may be identified as validity, whether of truth or of values, raised above the limits of space and time, but in religious terms it may also be identified as that which participates in the life of God. According to Nygren it follows, therefore, that we must reckon not only with this spatiotemporal world, but we must also recognize an eternal world. Yet this eternal world is not antithetical to the spatiotemporal world, so that one must leave the spatiotemporal world in order to participate in the eternal. Rather it is the art of piety to seek in all that is and happens the aspect of eternity, and the stronger piety is, the less of the temporal is lost. In this way the religious dimension of every part of life is recognized, as all existence is placed *sub specie aeternitatis,* under the aspect of eternity.[9]

If the category of eternity is the religious category, the religious question may be phrased as follows: What is the eternal? Stated in theocentric terms this question becomes, What is God? or, What is the God relationship? The purpose of the more general statement of the question is, however, to make it applicable to religions which do not affirm the God relationship, such as Buddhism. In identifying the category of eternity as the religious category and defining the religious question, philosophy has reached the limit of its competence as far as its relation to religion is concerned. In its role as a universal science philosophy can examine the nature of validity in the religious domain. It can define this validity as having to do with an inescapable dimension of human experience, which, if man is not directly aware of it, can be indirectly identified by analyzing the ultimate presuppositions of other areas of human experience. It is thus possible to define the religious question as constituting an inquiry as to the nature of this ultimate dimension of human experience. But beyond this point it is not possible for philosophy to go, for the answer to the religious question is not to be found in or derived from further analysis of the question. The category of religion, like the other categories, is as a category strictly formal. It represents religious experience only in the most general terms and is given content only in the history of religions.[10]

BECAUSE the content of the religious category must be historically defined, Nygren heartily approves of Friedrich Schleiermacher's rejection at the beginning of the nineteenth century of the philosophy of religion of the Enlightenment, according to which there was a natural religion containing the core of the rational religious truth to be found in all religions, while the positive, historically conditioned supplementary material in addition to this inner essence to be found in the several religions was viewed as only negative in its significance. Schleiermacher insisted that there is no natural religion, but that all true religion is instead positive and historical, so that the variety and differentiation which the several religions manifest is necessary and inescapable, proceeding from the essence of religion. Nygren does not believe, however, that Schleiermacher was wholly successful in his efforts to describe the various historical religions. According to Nygren,

Schleiermacher used a speculative rather than a purely critical approach, so that the most significant differences among the historical religions became identified with different levels of cultural development, or the kind of relation existing between the religious realm and the natural and ethical realms. Nygren therefore concludes that as far as specific religious content is concerned there is actually little difference between Schleiermacher's religious category of the feeling of absolute dependence and the natural religion of the Enlightenment against which Schleiermacher so strongly reacted.[11]

How then does Nygren propose to describe the differentiation which the history of religion reveals? He suggests that a critical method be used which, taking its point of departure in the universal category of religion, accepts the empirically given historical religions as they are and does not seek to reconstruct them philosophically. The religious category and the religious empirical reality are to be critically brought together, so that by means of the religious category the chaotic variety of the various religions is in some measure overcome, but the historically given content of these religions is to be fully acknowledged.[12]

An illustration of the use of this method can be found in one of Nygren's early monographs. In *Det bestående i kristendomen* (1922) [13] Nygren states that religion as it appears historically contains these elements: All religion claims to unveil the eternal, which revelation, in turn, constitutes a judgment upon man. There is accordingly the need for reconciliation, and reconciliation then leads to the experience of fellowship with God. In Christianity these elements receive their distinctive form through Jesus Christ.[14] Thus Christianity, while containing the same basic elements as other religions, is at each point distinctively different, and the same can presumably be said also of other historical religions.

How Nygren at this period understood the distinctive character of Christianity is indicated in *Filosofisk och kristen etik* (1923), where he outlines the way in which the revelation of the eternal in Jesus Christ determines the Christian ethical ideal.[15]

The basic religious relationship is the relation between the eternal and the temporal. Where this relation is one of fellowship, the religion is ethical, since the nature of the God relationship influences the content of the ethical ideal. Fellowship between God and man can be understood in different ways, however. The relationship may be one of power, where God is the despot and men are his slaves. The relationship may be legalistic, characterized by privileges and duties. The relationship may also be a love relationship, which is the God relationship revealed in Jesus Christ. The God relationship of love is like the power relationship in that it is theocentric. It differs from the law relationship in that it is spontaneous. Within the law relationship there can also be love, but it is limited to the deserving. That this is not the case in Christianity is considered unreasonable and unjustified from the legalistic point of view. Christianity, therefore, gives us an experience of God in which God in self giving love spontaneously enters into fellowship with man.[16]

The Christian God relationship, however, necessarily involves judgment upon man, because man in his natural estate has a disposition quite opposed to the spontaneous love of God revealed in Jesus Christ. For the natural man the individual self is at the center and no Lord is recognized by which the self may be freed from its egocentricity. When the natural man is charged with sin, it is this egocentricity that is meant, which egocentricity derives its characteristic meaning from its lack of a God relationship.[17]

In every religion there is need for reconciliation, but religions differ in the way in which such reconciliation takes place. If, therefore, the Christian God relationship is characterized by spontaneous, unmotivated love, that love must reveal itself at this decisive point. And so the New Testament witnesses that it has. Reconciliation as described in the New Testament is not the result of human sacrifice or ethical achievement, but is a work of God. God enters into fellowship with sinful man, thus giving him a God relationship and breaking the dominion of evil. This fellowship involves necessary conflict between the divine love and human selfishness, and in the vicarious suffering that results, much of this love is "lost love." Yet the "lost love" revealed on the cross is also triumphant, and has become the unshakable foundation of Christian fellowship with God.[18]

The consequence of this fellowship with God is that man no longer is isolated and egocentric, but finds himself in a fellowship determined by God's spontaneous love. In so far as there are Christians in the world, this spontaneous love is at work, and non-Christians can to this extent experience God. Since the Christian God relationship is not achieved ethically, but is a gift which expresses itself in neighbor love, there is no tension between the God relationship and the neighbor relationship. Instead the Christian God relationship makes neighbor love possible. While the Christian life is at every point characterized by fellowship with God, the Christian God relationship manifests itself in human neighbor love and cannot help but so manifest itself.[19]

In summarizing the foregoing description of the Christian religion in its relation to other religions, it could be said that religions differentiate themselves by being ethical or nonethical, depending on whether the God relationship is conceived in terms of fellowship or not. Where the God relationship is conceived in terms of fellowship, this relationship may be despotic, legalistic, or a love relationship. Nygren speaks of the natural man as egocentric in that he lacks a God relationship. Christian reconciliation involves overcoming this natural human egocentricity. Religion, therefore, so conceived is necessarily theocentric rather than egocentric in its orientation. Indeed there are references in Nygren's writings in this earlier period which would seem to exclude egocentric religion from the religious category altogether.[20]

IN THE method of motif research as illustrated in *Agape and Eros*, we find further development of the critical method by which Nygren seeks to describe the characteristic uniqueness of the several religions. The method of motif research makes it possible to deal more comprehensively with the broad range of differentiation which the various religions represent. Thus, for example, there are no difficulties in terms of this method in recognizing egocentric religion as a formally adequate answer to the categorical religious question. This method also makes it possible to interpret more adequately the distinctive character of the several religions. The content which history provides for the religious category is not characterized simply by the individual uniqueness which all historical phenomena are found to have. The several religions in addition to possessing this kind of uniqueness also, it appears, reveal a limited number of distinctively different ways of answering the religious question.

The three motifs Nygren has described bear the names agape, nomos, and eros. In the agape motif the self-giving love revealed in Jesus Christ is the predominant factor. The nomos motif is characterized primarily by law and a system of rewards and punishments, while in the eros motif man aspires toward what are regarded as the higher values. Nygren is not suggesting that these motifs either do or should exist in a pure form. He does argue, however, that the agape motif, at least, resists synthesis with the other motifs, and must assert its predominance in a given religious orientation in so far as it encounters elements characteristic of these other motifs.[21] It is possible that there may, however, be various forms of synthesis between the nomos and the eros motifs, and there may also be other motifs in addition to these three. Nygren's method is not speculative so that the entire range of historical possibility can be predicted in advance. It is only as this method is used and applied to the available historical data that the question of the number of the basic motifs can be answered.

The motifs represent a way of interpreting human value experience. Nygren has always distinguished between the domains of experience which deal with values and the theoretical domain, which in his opinion does not, sometimes calling the former domains of experience "atheoretical" in nature.[22] The important difference between the theoretical and the atheoretical domains is that in the purely factual judgments of the theoretical domain it is possible to abstract from human relationships, while this is not possible when the value judgments of the atheoretical domains are considered. Values require a valuer.[23] This is not to say that value experience does not require an objective component, but the subjective component is always essential. Nygren does not explain what the objective component in value experience is, but in the religious and ethical domains it could be argued that the possible answers to the religious and the ethical fundamental questions represent this objective component. These answers must be chosen by individuals or groups. A religious or ethical decision must be made before these answers become historical data, but once such a decision has been made, and this fact is remembered and recorded, such answers can be described as possible alternatives even in situations where they have not been elected.

These alternate possibilities represent contexts of meaning which Nygren calls "fundamental motifs." By a fundamental or basic motif Nygren means an answer to a question categorical in nature in which many individual judgments, values, and existential decisions cohere together.[24] This definition appears to be quite general in its reference. In *Agape and Eros,* after defining what he means by a fundamental motif, Nygren adds that in order to develop its full meaning the whole doctrine of the categories would have to be outlined. He does indicate, however, that the categories are defined by the four fundamental questions concerning the true, the beautiful, the good, and the eternal, and adds that when we speak of a fundamental motif we are moving in the realm of these ultimate questions.[25] In the discussion which provides the context for the definition of a basic motif in *Filosofi och motivforskning* it is evident that motifs are, furthermore, primarily related to the atheoretical domains.[26] Strictly speaking there is no such thing as a theoretical motif, for in this domain one finds only factual relationships. The answer to the theoretical question, What is true? is the description of a causal nexus or a purely factual situation, and the problem of values and existential decisions, which occasions the development of motifs, does not arise. This leaves us with the aesthetic, ethical, and religious domains. Obviously there are aesthetic motifs. Nygren states that the primary associations of the term are to be found in the realm of art.[27] Yet it is questionable as to whether one could single out any aesthetic motifs as "basic motifs." In any case, Nygren's suggestion that the *associations* of the term are to be found in the aesthetic domain indicates that its primary significance, as he uses it, is not to be found there.

This leaves us with the ethical and the religious questions. In Nygren's view these two questions are organically related to one another, the religious question referring to man's relationship to the eternal or God, and the ethical question referring to man's relationship to his fellow man. Thus these questions share the common problem of man's relationships with other persons and the more ultimate relationship which may be called the relationship with the eternal or the God relationship. These questions have not been arbitrarily chosen. The philosophical method of transcendental deduction by which they are defined has been described above. Nygren is of the opinion that these questions represent inescapable presuppositions derived from critical analysis of given areas of experience without which these areas of experience cannot be properly understood.[28] Motif research, therefore, in Nygren's view stands between philosophy, understood in this critical sense, and history. It works with questions defined by philosophy and seeks answers for them in the given historical reality. Motif research may thus be described as a critical philosophy of history. As such Nygren believes that it is related to earlier metaphysical philosophy of history in much the same way that the critical epistemology is related to the metaphysical epistemology which preceded it.[29] Thus, it is apparent that Nygren claims relevance for this method, not only with respect to the phenomena of religion, but with respect to history in general.

Nygren claims this general historical relevance for the method of motif research because he is of the opinion that relationships, coherence, or connectedness are constitutive for history. He insists that an event cannot be understood in isolation from its context. Should a historian seek to stick only to facts, abandoning all interest in interpretive patterns and the presuppositions of a given period, he would be forgetting that the relationships of events are also empirically given.[30] Indeed Nygren goes so far as to say that an atomistic conception of history is nonhistorical, since to understand a given historical phenomenon is to place it in its proper context, where it has a meaning it could not have in some imagined timeless sphere.[31] As other designations for research which examines this connectedness of historical events Nygren suggests "typological research" or "structural research."[32] These structures exist consciously as well as unconsciously. They play a very important role when they operate unconsciously as self-evident presuppositions.[33] Nygren therefore finds much more significance in what thinkers of a given time took for granted than in what they argued about.

In an essay entitled "Det självklaras roll i historien,"[34] Nygren states that while historical understanding of a past epoch can be defined in terms of Leopold von Ranke's celebrated phrase, "Wie es eigentlich gewesen ist," this means that the past must be understood in terms of its own context. In order to provide this context the self-evident presuppositions of the period being studied must be defined. In order to grasp these presuppositions, which may have been so self-evident that they were not even subject to discussion, both distance from them and congeniality with them is required. There must be enough distance from the period so that its self-evident presuppositions are not also shared by the historian. On the other hand, the period being studied must not be so foreign to the historian that he is unable appreciatively to recognize and define the presuppositions of the period. Historical understanding therefore requires creative tension between such distance and congeniality.

The goal of historical study is to avoid anachronism, for historical time is not quantified clock time, where every unit is like every other unit. Instead, each period has it own uniqueness and is characterized by its own self-evident presuppositions. There are two kinds of anachronism, one in which a person or a thing simply becomes placed in the wrong milieu, which is quite easily discovered and corrected. More serious is what Nygren calls *fundamental anachronism*, where a given historical period is interpreted not in terms of its own presuppositions, but in terms of the self-evident presuppositions which the interpreter happens to have. If one asks how one can be sure that one has

discovered the self-evident presuppositions in terms of which a historical period is to be understood, Nygren suggests that the adaptability of
the material being studied will indicate whether one is interpreting it in
terms of its own presuppositions or not. If the material is resistant, not
permitting itself to be ordered in the way one seeks to order it, this is
very likely a sign one has approached it with the wrong presuppositions. When the correct presuppositions have been found, Nygren
holds that this will be evident as the clear meaning of the material being
studied becomes manifest. Nygren suggests, therefore, that the great
thinkers of the past be approached with a certain humility. One should
not so readily accuse them of inconsistencies and self-contradictions,
for the difficulties one encounters in interpreting them may simply
indicate that one has not yet identified the presuppositions in terms of
which these thinkers are to be understood.

A second part of this essay consists of examples of such self-evident presuppositions. Nygren identifies three which have extended
over long periods of time and which have together dominated almost
the entire history of Western civilization. These are the Greek-Hellenistic views of existence expressed in Platonic dualism between the
world of the ideas and the sense world. Another is the Christian
concept of the two ages, which are not ontologically opposed as in
Platonic dualism, but are engaged in historical struggle, the decisive
encounter between them taking place in the Christ event. The Alexandrian world scheme, in which all proceeds from God in order to
return to him again, represents a compromise between the Christian
and the Greek-Hellenistic views of existence, though the Neoplatonic
element in the Alexandrian world scheme appears to be more dominant
than the Christian element in it. According to Nygren, it is in terms of
the Alexandrian world scheme that Thomas Aquinas, the medieval
mystics, and Dante's *Divine Comedy* are to be understood.

The third of these existential outlooks appears in the Renaissance
and becomes fully expressed in the Enlightenment. Here man is made
the measure of all things and becomes divine. Examples of this view are
to be found in Marcilio Ficino, in philosophical subjectivism, political
Machiavellism, the theory of the social contract, nationalism, the evolu-
tionary optimism of the Enlightenment, and positivism. Nygren finds
this presupposition expressed in Friedrich Nietzsche's words, "If there
were Gods, how could I endure it to be no God! Therefore there are
no Gods." [35] Nygren holds that we are now, however, living in a time
of transition. The events of the past century have robbed the human

god of his self-evidence, though it is not yet clear what the self-evident presuppositions of the coming age will be.

HOW THEN are the self-evident presuppositions which are fundamental to historical understanding identified? This the method of motif research is designed to do. While it is not certain that the self-evident presuppositions discussed above (Platonic dualism, the Christian concept of the two ages, man divinized and made the measure of all things) can be equated with the motifs of eros, nomos, and agape, the motifs are clearly examples of self-evident presuppositions. Thus, motif research should be understood as a method for identifying such self-evident presuppositions, whether they be religious motifs appearing in different forms in every age, or self-evident presuppositions more specifically identified with a particular age.

In describing the method of motif research, Nygren speaks of two lines which may be followed in historical research, one of which he calls the "historical" line and the other the "uniqueness" line.[36] In each of these lines one begins with the chaos of uninterpreted events and moves through ever-broadening stages of research until finally the two lines come together in the grasping of a fundamental motif. It is important to note the fact that the research in both instances begins with the chaotic variety of impressions of persons, things, and events. This must mean that Nygren is defining a method which can be used not only in the interpretation of documents, but which can also be used in the interpretation of historical data in a much broader sense.

What Nygren calls the historical line of research begins when there is an effort to chronicle that which has taken place. However, already at this level a principle of interpretation enters, for even such historical description involves selectivity. All events are not described. The moment a given amount of material is called historical a certain selectivity has already occurred. What factors, however, govern this selectivity? How is arbitrariness escaped? Apparently certain events are described because they are believed to be more significant than other events. But this significance is not a purely factual datum. The recognition of this significance constitutes a decision for which some account must be given. Even in the most strictly theoretical approach to historical phenomena, such a factor of decision is inescapable.

This selective factor is more clearly evident in the parallel approach to history where significant form is seen in historical events, and an effort is made to describe it. Here one may illustrate the meaning of the material being studied by way of an illuminating caricature. Again there must be an attempt, however, to escape the extent to which the meaning illustrated has been arbitrarily chosen. In both of these lines of historical study one seeks, therefore, to move toward a broader context. Thus, one moves from chronicle to history, and from caricature to that which is characteristic. Nygren insists that this effort to work toward a broader and more systematic context does not take one away from the phenomena being described, but actually closer to a real understanding of them. This process continues from history to the history of ideas, where history is seen in the context of a given historical epoch, and from the isolation of the characteristic to its being seen in a wider systematic context. It is at this point that the two investigations come together in motif research, which unites in itself the grasping of uniqueness and individuality in the broadest possible historical context. It is in this way that "a fundamental motif gives answer to the highest systematic question from the most widespread outlook of the history of ideas." [37] In this way the categorical quest for structures of meaning receives its historically conditioned answer.

It has already been indicated that the two lines of historical research which converge to form the method of motif research both begin as interpretation of events. As such they begin with what may be called history-as-actuality. Historiographers distinguish three meanings which history may have. One may speak of history-as-actuality, history-as-record, and written-history.[38] By history-as-actuality is meant all that has been felt, thought, imagined, said, and done by human beings as such and in relation to one another and to their environment since the beginning of human existence on this planet. Quite obviously only an infinitesimally small part of history-as-actuality is preserved in history-as-record, nor is there any reason why all that occurs should be remembered. Yet when any attempt is made to interpret the meaning of history-as-actuality, all of this history is relevant to such an interpretation, and one may properly ask whether the most significant aspects of this history have been remembered. Certainly in so far as such an interpretation is based on one's own experiences and observations, one must take care lest highly significant data are ignored. Fortunately history-as-record includes not only what historians judge to be significant, nor is it limited to literary records. Thus, to the archeologist, potsherds can speak eloquently about a vanished civilization, though no one ever intended that such a record of the past should be preserved.

Written-history, finally, while purporting to be about history-as-actuality, is or should be based on history-as-record, except in so far as
the personal observations and experiences of the historian may also be
used. The distinction between written-history and history-as-record
can not, however, be sharply drawn, since written-history can itself
become history-as-record for a later historian.

How, then, is motif research related to these three meanings of
history? First of all, motif research, like all other forms of written
history, must interpret history-as-actuality. Nygren is aware that this is
the ultimate reference of the motifs which he describes. Yet there are
indications that he thinks of this method primarily in its use in the
interpretation of the texts studied by the historian of ideas. Thus in his
essay describing the method of motif research, he illustrates its use by
discussing the problem of interpreting two apparently similar statements in Luther and Thomas Aquinas, showing how basically the
meanings of these statements differ when they are seen against the
background of the differing motifs implicit in the thought of Luther
and Thomas.[39] Nygren speaks of the connectedness of events as constitutive for history and as empirically given, but at the same time he
argues that motif research does not have to contend with certain of the
difficulties to which historical-genetic research is subject. The connections in historical-genetic research, he points out, are often difficult to
establish, while the place and importance of a motif in a given outlook
may be unmistakably clear.[40] Where a motif came from and whether
there is actual dependence of one outlook upon another may be difficult to determine, but the content of a motif may be described without
any such difficulties. This suggests that the connectedness which historical-genetic research seeks to describe is not empirically given, while
apparently the connectedness which the motif represents is empirically
given. In discussing how the self-evident presuppositions of a historical
period can be identified, Nygren speaks of "the resistance of the
material," stating that in this way a hypothesis regarding these presuppositions can be empirically tested.[41] Yet here he must be thinking of
written texts rather than the sequence of events which history-as-actuality presents. If one distinguishes between history-as-actuality, on
the one hand, and history-as-record and written-history, on the other,
it would seem that if one is thinking of history-as-actuality both
historical-genetic research and motif research share a common problem. For both, the connectedness between events may be difficult to
grasp, though the difficulty may take different forms in these two
types of historical research. Once there are records and written history

it may be easier to recognize motifs that are implicit in these records than to explain their origins, but until such records exist this connectedness must be intuited and remains a hypothesis as far as the events it is designed to interpret are concerned.

Nygren argues as follows: "Historical reflection consists precisely in ordering the material under certain major viewpoints, and it is first through such ordering that the material is given historical significance. Actually the viewpoint which motif research adopts is more objectively inescapable and anchored in 'the historical material' itself, than any of the other viewpoints which might be adopted in the study of history." [42] He then describes the process outlined above by which it is possible to move from the immediately given chaotic variety of impressions of persons, things, and events to the motif. Interestingly enough he interprets the movement towards the motif as a way of overcoming the arbitrariness necessarily involved in the selection which occurs in the first stages of historical description. Yet if one begins with history-as-actuality, is one necessarily led to *one* motif as the "answer to the highest systematic question from the most widespread outlook of the history of ideas"? [43] Is there, in other words, one motif that provides the clue to the meaning of history-as-actuality, or might more than one motif be considered when this meaning is to be defined?

Nygren does believe, as has already been indicated, that each historical period has its own uniqueness and is characterized by its own self-evident presuppositions, but he has not discussed the relation between what he terms the self-evident presuppositions of a given age and the motifs. [44] Some of these self-evident presuppositions are closely related to motifs. The Christian concept of the two ages is closely related to the agape motif and Platonic dualism is closely related to the eros motif, while the Alexandrian world scheme, which Nygren describes as the result of a compromise between Christian and Neoplatonic tendencies, may be related to both the eros and the agape motifs. But whereas the self-evident presuppositions appear to be related to a process of cultural development and thus succeed each other, the motifs appear to coexist, while at the same time influencing the cultural development in those periods and areas in which they are in the predominance. The motifs, therefore, would seem to represent fundamentally different, yet alternately possible ways of interpreting human existence which do not change, though the manner in which they are expressed in different periods is affected by the self-evident presuppositions characterizing those periods.

Nygren, of course, might avoid the problem of distinguishing between the relations of the self-evident presuppositions of a given age, on the one hand, and the motifs, on the other, to history-as-actuality by saying that he is interested only in describing what others have said the meaning of history-as-actuality is. Thus he may be interested only in defining the motif or motifs implicit in the Bible, or in the Platonic dialogues, or in the writings of Augustine and Luther. There is a kind of historical research which consists of describing the ideas of other historians, and undoubtedly such research is needed, but it would seem that the historical method most adequate to such a task would be a method which was itself able to begin in its interpretation with history-as-actuality. But in such a case it might appear that more than one motif could be defined as an answer to the fundamental religious and ethical categorical questions. The same events might not be capable of such diverse interpretations, but if one is seeking answers for such fundamental questions, the whole range of history-as-actuality is relevant, and while one might believe that the answer was to be found in one "salvation history," one would have to grant the possibility, at least, of other salvation histories, quite differently conceived, providing also different answers. In addition to such answers one would furthermore have to recognize the possibility that the meaning of history-as-actuality could be sought in a nonhistorical manner, that is, one might hold that the meaning of human existence is not to be sought in the interpretation of any sequence of revealing events, but instead through some process of ontological speculation. Only if these different possibilities are recognized does it seem possible to explain why there are at least three motifs, the agape, nomos, and eros motifs, which are not simply the self-evident presuppositions of past ages, but continue to remain as living religious and ethical options. The agape and nomos motifs can be regarded as ultimately appealing to events and thus as historical answers to the question of the meaning of human existence, while the eros motif would seem to be nonhistorical in its orientation. It shares the same categorical questions as do the other two motifs, but it does not find the answers to these questions revealed in the historical process.

How then are the motifs ultimately to be understood? One possible interpretation of the motifs is to regard them as differing understandings of historical causality. By historical causality is meant, on the one hand, the way in which man's behavior as a causal agent is to be understood, and, on the other hand, the way in which the causal efficacy of that which ultimately stands over against man is to be interpreted. The motifs in such a case present possible ways of understanding how man behaves and how God acts, if indeed man is confronted in that which stands over against him by an acting God, and if not, how the causal efficacy of the impersonal value structure which stands over against man is to be conceived. If the motifs are so understood, they are not only of interest to ethicists and theologians. Every historian must be concerned in one way or another with the dynamics of human behavior. R. G. Collingwood speaks of the historian's task as involving the re-enactment of past experience, and uses in this connection the analogy of a detective solving a crime by imaginatively re-enacting on the basis of the evidence available what may have taken place.[45] Such re-enactment must, however, necessarily involve presuppositions about what the motivations of the persons involved may have been. So also the changes that have taken place in historiography in recent years are related to differing theories of human causality, to whether human freedom is affirmed or denied, and if affirmed, how it is understood, as well as to the more ultimate causal efficacy which may be attributed to God, or to whatever is conceived in a given world view to function as the equivalent of God.

The method of motif research can be interpreted as saying that alternate possibilities exist in so far as historical causality is concerned. This would be to say that causality, when man and God are taken into account, has a complexity of meaning which it does not have in so far as it is presupposed in the natural sciences. Man's freedom is such that he can be motivated in fundamentally different ways. Although the religious question is unavoidable and must be answered in some way, the nature of the causal efficacy implicit in these answers also differs basically. This may be what the agape, nomos, and eros motifs are all about. But if this is a possible interpretation of the meaning of these motifs, there are significant implications for historiography and the several disciplines which in one way or another make use of the results of historical research.[46]

There is, finally, an additional relevance of the method of motif research which could be more clearly articulated. If the motifs represent fundamentally different ways of understanding human existence, we are living in a time when these alternatives are constantly before us. What is often called the post-Christian era is rather the period following the discovery that the religious pluralism of the world can no longer be defined geographically, since all of the live faith options coexist in almost every society, and especially in the so-called "free world." In this new situation an earlier Christian strategy of regarding all other faiths as simply various forms of error which could be refuted by a vigorous proclamation of the truth, without the necessity of their being sympathetically understood, no longer seems wholly effective. On the other hand, it seems equally inacceptable from a Christian point of view to regard all of these faiths as partially true, each contributing its unique insights to a more comprehensive world faith. The method of motif research now provides a new approach to this problem. In terms of this method the alternatives to the Christian faith can be understood, not merely as forms of human error, but as alternately possible answers to the categorical religious and ethical questions. At the same time this method suggests that the answer to the problem posed by this pluralism is not an attempted syncretism. Each of these faiths has its own characteristic uniqueness. The significance of the faith decision is that one must choose between them. It is not possible to serve two masters. Yet it is important that the alternatives should be clearly understood. Indeed each motif can be most clearly understood when the other motifs, fairly described, serve as its contrasting background. The method of motif research is consequently an invitation to dialogue, particularly between Christian and non-Christian faiths. Such a dialogue can be the most effective way of testing the validity of the method of motif research. Should it survive this test it could prove to be one of the most effective ways of contributing not only to better understanding among the peoples of the world, but also to the extension of the Christian mission, if indeed Christians believe it is possible by an open statement of the truth, including the truth about other religions, to commend the gospel to every man's conscience (2 Cor. 4:2).

THIS essay has been written to explore the broader historical relevance of the method of motif research. The argument of the essay is that the relevance of motif research as a general historical method can be urged for the following four reasons: 1] Motif research includes as one of its aspects a critical theory of experience whereby useful distinctions can be made with respect to different kinds of validity which are encountered in historical subject matter. 2] Motif research is a method of identifying and describing fundamental structures of meaning which are either implicit or explicit in all human experience. 3] While the method of motif research has most commonly been used to interpret historical texts, this method can also be used by the historian as he himself interprets history-as-actuality, thus producing texts which may become records used in turn by later historians. 4] Motif research makes possible an understanding of the deep roots of the pluralism which characterizes the modern world and could provide a basis for fruitful dialogue between representatives of fundamentally different convictional orientations.

5

LITERARY STUDIES AND THE USE

OF MOTIFS IN NYGREN'S SENSE

Erik M. Christensen

A CADEMICALLY the term "literary studies" signifies "the study of literature." Analytical as it appears, this proposition may nevertheless be regarded as the shibboleth of a university movement which became manifest in and outside university circles during the first decades of this century and which has by now imposed itself everywhere and become almost self-evident: the literary work of art is (or should be) the central concern of any activity named "literary studies." In other words, what you are interested in as a student of literature is the right interpretation, the best possible reading of any given work of literary art. To be sure, this central concern does not preclude your concern with the author's biography, psychology, the current ideas, the period and genre of the work in question, but such areas of knowledge are now considered circumstantial, helpful, perhaps problematic, but above all secondary to your central concern which is, to repeat: the best possible reading of literature itself. Today dissent from this dogma would have to be expressed in the form of explicit agreement accompanied by lower-keyed qualifications such as, "right, but literature is in itself the expression of——and it must therefore be legitimate to read it as such." Thus, controversy over the qualifications made by the different schools of literary scholarship is still possible and frequent. To mention one major confrontation of strident opposites we have the predominantly German-French-Italian "existentialist" factions vis-à-vis "historical" factions everywhere.

In the present essay we shall not pursue, analyse, nor solve conflicts within the literary field. Our intention is much more restricted; we simply want to indicate some possible and actual applications of Anders Nygren's school of thought within the broad field of knowledge called "literary studies," in German "Litteraturwissenschaft." We shall pay special attention to Nygren's well-known main contribution to the structural and historical (genetic) description of central Christian motifs (nomos, eros, and agape) as first developed in his *Agape and Eros, A Study of the Christian Idea of Love.*[1] To begin with we shall ask: What is the general relation between literary studies and the history of ideas?

A famous advocate of the above-mentioned semianalytical proposition ("literary studies" means "the study of literature") is René Wellek, who writes:

> The study of ideas in literature, of literature in relation to philosophy, is old, of course; and, in a technical sense, it was cultivated very strenuously in Germany during the last decades, in violent reaction against philological scholarship. But the German *Geistesgeschichte* had few echoes in this country [the U.S.A.], except among teachers of German: some of these were hostile, as witness Martin Schütze's brilliant attack, in *Academic Illusions* (1933), a book which offered one of the best analyses of the situation of literary scholarship, not only in Germany. As a movement, the "history of ideas," initiated by Arthur O. Lovejoy, made the strongest impression on students of literature in the United States. Lovejoy is a professional philosopher, and his method is that of a philosophical analysis of ideas with close attention to terminology and the contradictions of individual writers. He draws the rather artificial contrast between his method and the ordinary history of philosophy in that he studies "unit-ideas" rather than whole philosophical systems and gives attention to the dissemination of ideas through popular philosophers and poets. His method can be criticized for its excessive intellectualism: Lovejoy conceives of ideological change as a self-subsisting process and pays little attention to historical or psychological contexts. To him poetry is merely a document for intellectual history, and ideas in literature are "philosophical ideas in dilution." [Arthur O. Lovejoy, *The Great Chain of Being* (Cambridge, Mass., 1936), p. 17.] Literature thus becomes the water added to philosophy, and the history of ideas imposes purely philosophical standards on works of imagination. Intellectual history is, of course, a high discipline, with exegetical value for the study of the history of literature. But it is no substitute for literary study. Among American literary scholars there are

actually few historians of ideas in Lovejoy's sense: Louis Bredvold, Marjorie Nicolson, Perry Miller come to mind.[2]

Perhaps what René Wellek has in mind could be illustrated by
recalling the Freudian's conviction that Shakespeare's *Hamlet* should
be read as case history of the Oedipus complex, or the Sunday-school
teacher's insistence on the educational benefits to be derived from his
own reading of literature as *exempli*. Such uses of literature are obviously lopsided misuses to Wellek when he says of Lovejoy, "To him
poetry is merely a document for intellectual history. . . ." In practice
Lovejoy does not consider the reading of literature as literature the
central concern of the historian of ideas. Of course, René Wellek
cannot in all fairness blame the professional historian of ideas for using
literary material as he pleases; what Wellek can and will regret is any
literary study that masquerades as such while in his eyes it might as
well be labelled an essay in the history of ideas. This is not just words.
It does indeed make a distinct difference in discipline whether you
extract from any given work of art (as Lovejoy certainly does) the
state of ideas at the time of conception, or arrive at your preferred
reading of the same work of art from your knowledge of some state of
ideas. This distinction will not be blurred even if you have to maneuver
from the work of art to the state of ideas as long as you remember to
revert to your work of art and show the relevance of your ideas to the
right reading of the whole of the text in question.

Unfortunately, this is exactly what Lovejoy does not do, and since
he and his followers in American scholarship have virtually monopo-
lized the term "history of ideas" it is easy to arrive at the false conclusion that there is something suspect or dangerous if and when literary
studies approach the history of ideas with some confidence.

At this point we may narrow our perspective for a closer look at
the Nygren model of the nomos-eros-agape relationship. It is characteristic of Nygren's presentation that he distinguishes quite clearly and
explicitly between two alternative approaches to the problem of describing the composite phenomenon of "Christian Love" as exemplified
in his source material. One approach is the analysis of the basic
structural possibilities (i.e. the potential interconnections between the
pure forms of nomos, eros, and agape) as they appear to him in the
abstract, so to speak. He arrives at an outline of this structural model,
based on his scrutiny of nomos as exemplified in the Old and New
Testaments, eros as exemplified primarily in Plato, and agape as it is
found in the New Testament, primarily in St. Paul and St. John. Thus

the structural model of nomos-eros-agape may be said to be an abstract which encompasses the possible forms of Christian Love to be found anywhere in reality, i.e., in the sources when you turn to them for an historical description of what did take place. This is, then, the other approach to Nygrens' problem, and he uses his structural model to this purpose in Part II, placing the various realized forms of Christian Love each in its own position within the model.

We may note in passing—as a fact in the history of learning—that Nygren's explicit structuralism is an early instance of the use of structural models in the humanities and in theology. Incidentally, Nygren's Part I was in print in Swedish a couple of years before Professor Lovejoy, in the second half of the academic year 1932–33, gave the William James Lectures at Harvard that became the substance of *The Great Chain of Being*,[3] and the English translation of Nygren's Part I was published in 1932, while as early as 1927 Lovejoy published a chapter of his work in progress in the *Publications of the Modern Language Association of America*. Since then, structural description (i.e., description emphasizing the relations between parts of a whole) [4] has been universally accepted as being in no way in a logical or pragmatic conflict with genetic studies. Rather they are two possible ways of approach to the examination and description of any object, be it an historical event like the battle at Gettysburg (where in the field were the armies deployed, and why?) or an artifact like *Hamlet* (what are the relations between the parts, why and / or with what effect?)

Now, it is evident that Nygren's sharp distinction between his abstract (suprahistorical) structural model and the changing historical embodiments of the given potential inside the (shall we say: triangular) model, gives his way of demonstration an advantage over Lovejoy's, if you wish to compare these two historians of ideas from the viewpoint of literary scholarship. It is unlikely that students of literature would feel it mattered very much, the Great Chain of Being once apprehended, whether a given work of art might be said to embody this or that variation of the well-known contemporary forms of the unit-idea (i.e. the Chain-concept), whereas it would certainly interest those scholars to know in what corner of Nygren's model to place the Christian Love concept in any given—Christian Love implying—work of art. The Nygren model recommends itself because Christianity and Christian Love have for ages been dominant subjective and intersubjective *themes of conflict*, dominating not only part of the individual's outlook but coloring anything he would be able to see and feel. The situation of the Christian Love motif is a situation constantly undergoing changes; the structural model may therefore be regarded as a model of possible tensions in the religious mind; and what you want to be able to do—and will be enabled to do via the nomos-eros-agape model—is to describe with some accuracy what you think is implied of this nature in a given work of art. It is conceivable that most works of art will in this respect hold no significant meaning alien to the dominant theology of its time, but it is, on the other hand, as likely that deviations may be found. If and when such deviations seem to be great, this fact will serve as a fair warning that the work of art in question may perhaps be better understood as a whole if you try to see it either in conflict with its own time or somehow in contact with currents of thought and / or feeling that you did not know to be in play at that particular time and place. After all, what you can do when you read is only to add something to printers ink. This added "something" will be controlled in part by your knowledge or your suspicions, your preparedness to take seriously a hint that touches your sensibility.

Let us exemplify the process, and let us complicate the matter by turning to our own times to have a look at two authors who are obviously preoccupied with Christianity. Everywhere in Isak Dinesen (alias Karen Blixen, 1885–1962) we find suggestions of some special relationship between her characters and the sort of universe in which they live and die. You may say, with H. D. F. Kitto, that this fiction is "religious drama" in which the action seems designed to reveal the universal laws that govern it.[5] The laws in Isak Dinesen's fictional universe are clearly at the center of her characters' interests, they are constantly engaged in clarifying their religious position, their relationship with the God behind their fate. We may here dispense with such clarification—which could presumably be obtained by comparing what happens in these tales with some structural model of all possible relationships between man and God—and limit ourselves to the more immediate, though less satisfying, use of one of Karen Blixen's fundamental declarations which will give us a possibility à la Nygren to shift our perspective and thus sketch out some lines in the structure of the situation in which Isak Dinesen composed her works (and chose her Old Testament pseudonym; christened Karen Christence Dinesen, she married Blixen Finecke in 1914). In *Out of Africa* she says:

> Pride is faith in the idea that God had, when he made us. A proud man is conscious of the idea, and aspires to realize it. He does not strive towards a happiness, or comfort, which may be

irrelevant to God's idea of him. His success is the idea of God, successfully carried through, and he is in love with his destiny. As the good citizen finds his happiness in the fulfilment of his duty to the community, so does the proud man find his happiness in the fulfilment of his fate.

People who have no pride are not aware of any idea of God in the making of them, and sometimes they make you doubt that there has ever been much of an idea, or else it has been lost, and who shall find it again? They have got to accept as success what others warrant to be so, and to take their happiness, and even their own selves, at the quotation of the day. They tremble, with reason, before their fate.

Love the pride of God beyond all things, and the pride of your neighbor as your own.[6]

Whatever this may be, it certainly does not look like agape, but let this limitation suffice for the moment. Again, in tale after tale, the heroes in Dinesen make their religious choice, referring to Old and New Testament commonplaces. Often they seem to think quite clearly or feel remotely that this universe of theirs would have been a better place for them and their neighbor if they had never heard of Incarnation, Crucifixion, Redemption. Further analysis cannot be our concern in this essay. It is, however, reported that Isak Dinesen, alias Karen Blixen, amused herself and a couple of friends by composing anagrams from the names of people they liked or disliked, knew well or had only heard of. During the late 1940's another writer arrived from relative obscurity to prominence on the Danish Parnassian scene. His name was Martin A. Hansen, and Isak Dinesen is said to have composed the anagram "Han er Min sAtan" (i.e. "to me he is the devil") from that name. We need not pay great attention to such rumors unless we are following a track. In the present case the anagram will serve as shorthand in our exposition, for it cannot with reason be doubted that Martin A. Hansen (1909–55) was at the same time as Isak Dinesen at work defining his characters' universe—writing "religious drama" in Kitto's sense of the word—and, as I have tried to demonstrate elsewhere,[7] placing them in a universe governed by agape. We cannot develop this point in a satisfactory way here and now, but a firsthand impression of conflicting tendencies may be obtained by comparing the above quotation from *Out of Africa* with a passage from Hansen's *The Liar;* the hero in the novel is drawing his conclusions at the end of the book:

It was the first time that I had stood here on Western Hill and realized that my fate was bound for always to this hill in the sea: not bound by a root, as are those who are born here, but struck into the island like a spear that is thrown from afar.

I stood on the sacred stone and thought: Here must I choose, here must I sacrifice! More I dare not say. I am grown too old to dare promise more than I know I can do. I can say yes or no; whatever else a man like me says is really nothing but deception. Yes or no. The time for flight is past, the dream is out. I can choose my fate, I can fight, but I cannot grow. I cannot turn back, but that we all know. Only the button-moulder can re-mould. My feebleness and sin are great, for I know God's presence only when He strikes me hard.

But we are not all alike, there is another kind of person. There are those in whom the word, the incident, the emotion bring release; that change, turn green like plants brought out of the shade; that have growth in them, and if they love, they flower and fruit, even though they do not live happily. I believe that she whom I have wronged more than any other is such a person.

I am not like that.

However, (the island) has use for me, I thought, as the darkness gathered.[8]

Given these circumstances it may not be irrelevant to carry with us some understanding of Hansen in order to follow the movements in Dinesen. These things are of a subtle nature, and you will not be able to go all the way with Nygren's structural model as your only guide, of course not, but you may get some help from the model. To begin with, it may open your eyes to shades of meaning you would otherwise have missed (Dinesen's anagram acquires a world of meaning if read as an expression of her awareness that she and Hansen represent motifs in an age-old irreparable conflict). Secondly, you may explicitly compare your reading with the structural model and thereby be able to talk in an understandable and controllable way of what you think and feel is in the text. It is no exaggeration that you may get radically different readings out of Martin A. Hansen's works when you supply one definite opinion (out of several possible) of what it means when Christian Love and religion in general is used, hinted at, or in some way present in his novels and short stories.[9]

We know from Nygren that Christian Love may mean any number of things according to where in the structural model of nomos-eros-agape its realization should be placed, and we know from experience that in order to understand any given person it may be significant to know where in such an abstract model he and / or we would place his particular brand of the central motif. Quite a number of consequences will follow from such localization. Thus, we should not be surprised if it could be demonstrated, beyond doubt that Isak Dinesen's world of fiction is centrally governed by some quite distinct — although perhaps slowly changing — constellation in a model like Nygren's. It may be safely said of Martin A. Hansen that this was the case with what he wrote and what he gave up writing.

Perhaps examples, such as Dinesen and Hansen, are less representative because they have been chosen from a time when Anders Nygren's school of thought may be involved as formative elements. As far as I can see that is no reason why we should give up our examples. We have tried to give an outline, a way of opening the question as far as Dinesen is concerned. A further step would be to try to be more precise, analysing her tales one by one, and then you may proceed to try to determine what she herself knew and felt, thus building up arguments for your reading. In this latter endeavor you would ask: did she ever read Nygren? I suspect you will find evidence that she did.

Examples could have been picked almost at random from any other period and nation within the Christian sphere. Nygren himself has undertaken a holistic analysis of Augustin's *Confessions*,[10] he has indicated a possible reading of Dante's *Divine Comedy*,[11] and we may sum up this essay by mentioning an attempt at reading Rousseau's *Nouvelle Héloïse* as a literary work of art governed by a concept of love, a motif, which is described as an approximation to the eros motif in Nygren's sense.[12]

But, you might say, is it really necessary to know Nygren's structural description of Christian Love in order to find some sort of eros as a motif in the *Nouvelle Héloïse?* By no means! Already in the eighteenth century lexicographers indicated the relationship between Plato, Petrarch, and Rousseau's novel.[13] The relationship is there for everybody to find and study, and everybody may read the novel as a whole with this motif in control; just as the world is there right outside your window, outside your town, your country, your continent — for you to describe! And maps may prove useful.

6

MOTIF RESEARCH

AND THE NEW TESTAMENT

Jacob Heikkinen

FOR Anders Nygren, theological thinking in its deepest and truest sense, is "nothing other than a probing into the secrets of the divine Word." Where the center of Nygren's concern rests remains clear and unquestionable. This center, his personal commitment as a thinker, is the description of the essence of the Gospel of Jesus Christ. This central objective, from his earlier writings of a predominantly philosophic orientation to his later studies on the ecumenical nature of the Church of Christ, has held its firm position.

It would be misleading, however, to infer that he has accomplished it with an uncritical simplicity. On the contrary, he has embraced the fundamental intellectual and historical questions as to the way in which the Gospel ought to be understood. He aspires not to coerce his reader, but only to show lucidly what the Gospel is. He does not thrust his own commitment upon another; one's personal attitude toward eros and agape, for example, is "something entirely outside the province of science. Such a decision is a personal choice which is determined by quite other than scientific considerations." [1] For Nygren himself, we may be sure, the right interpretation of the essence of the Gospel is both a scientific task as well as a personal decision. Biblical interpretation, centering on Jesus Christ, has been for him "the great problem of life." His scientific discipline serves not the end of being a model for methodology, nor a technique, nor a world view, but the indispensable instrument to clarify the meaning of the Gospel.

The scientific discipline exercised by Nygren is called motif research.[2] This essay intends to explore the role of motif research in Nygren's interpretation of the message of the Gospel. The three primary questions which confront such a quest are: 1] What is the technical character of motif research; what elements constitute its basic components? 2] How is it demonstrated in Nygren's biblical exegesis? 3] Is it a viable instrument for biblical interpretation? Are there further frontiers for its practice?

Motif research claims to be a discipline of investigation of a highly organized quality both with regard to its consistency and scientific authenticity. Motif research shuns speculation, places no confidence in any "science of the transcendent," and avoids ambiguous syntheses arising from a mixing of categories. Its temper is to aim at a wholly objective description of the phenomenon under inquiry by means of a sharply drawn projection of *that* idea which conveys the characteristic essence of a problem. It is equally unfriendly to the domination of idealistic and romantic tendencies. It seeks to build its structures of understanding upon empirical and concrete material.

From the very first to his most recent writings Nygren has disclosed certain fundamental philosophic concerns. What he referred to in the twenties and the thirties is expressed equally in the sixties; one need only bring to mind the following, frequent frames of reference: presupposition, logical analysis of presuppositions, context, contexts of meaning, ultimate question, verification, type, power of language, and posing of the right question. To a wrongly stated question there can be no right answer. In his recent discussion of Wittgenstein's *Philosophical Investigations*, Nygren underscores the following points which, in a sense, suggest his own scientific commitments:

> We may say in summary that Wittgenstein's contribution to philosophy is to have focussed attention in new ways and with a new emphasis on those contexts of meaning (the term is equivalent to what Wittgenstein calls "language games") which determine the meaning of words and propositions. In other words he has shown in his philosophy the error of trying to understand a statement in isolation and the necessity of taking account of its "surroundings" and thus of understanding it within and from its context; the statement must be seen in its immediate context, in the "wider context" of which that is part and finally in the comprehensive context (what Wittgenstein calls a "language game"—approximately what we have called a "context of meaning" in the widest sense of the word) which expresses the "sort of context" in which the words stand.[3]

These philosophic accents echo Nygren's own ethos of mind, and suggest the mental milieu for the formulation of the technical structure of motif research. Nygren is not enslaved to it as an iron system, a sort of a public trade mark; through much of his work he hardly makes mention of it. But, its essentials are consistently in operation.

In the strictly technical sense, motif research is carried out within the framework of the following affirmations:

1] It is essential to analyze the underlying presuppositions of ideas, and to question the assumptions that are usually accepted as clear and self-evident. The questions raised require in turn a rigorous examination; for, often enough unexamined questions are received from the past as something fixed, having a once-for-all character and meaning.

2] An understanding of a word, of a belief, or of an idea requires the recognition of the fact that certain limitations attend the techniques of philological and historical-genetic studies. A word-study alone, though an indispensable inquiry, does not explain its actual content in terms of its functions at the point of its observed occurrence. The information of the origins of words does not disclose their total behavior in a particular environment. A study of the historical development of an idea, and the comparison with its parallels, may illumine many things, but, in the end, the question over its characteristic meaning under the point at issue remains unresolved. While the study of ideas and words may be traced with accuracy, it does not follow that this kind of inquiry leads to an accurate explanation of their meanings in their specific functional contexts. The comparison of concepts in their historical forms raises the question of the basic criterion by which such an evaluative determination is made. It could well be that there exists between them no common denominator, and consequently the comparison is drawn by means of answers that belong to quite divergent questions.

3] Motif research concerns itself with problems of meaning that arise out of distinctive attitudes, that is, from "fundamental motifs." Through distinguishing the "different general attitudes to life" expressed by various terms, it is possible to detect their distinctive character and interinvolvement with each other. In this respect, for example, it is to be noted that there exists a genuine relation between eros and agape. This is apparent in their characteristic content, not as constituting identical parallels, but, within their contexts of meaning, as colliding with one another, in tension with each other. Each of these strives to place its total claims upon the whole of life.

4] The task of research is to find through a structural analysis an inner understanding of a term in light of its "fundamental motif." It is false to draw a definitive conclusion from the mere fact that one and the same idea or belief occurs in different religious contexts. Nygren argues as follows:

> The idea or belief may have the same form without having at all the same meaning. . . . What such an idea, or belief, or senti- ment really means, can only be decided in the light of its own natural context. In other words, we must try to see what is the basic idea, or the driving power of the religion concerned, or what it is that gives it its character as a whole and communicates to all its parts their special content and color. It is the attempt to carry out such a structural analysis . . . that we describe as motif-research.[4]

5] The empirical test is of prime importance. Motif research does not rest on unverifiable intuition. Obviously a fundamental motif may be intuitively discerned, but such intuition alone does not consti- tute investigation. That which is obtained through intuition must be subjected to "scientific analysis and verification." Motifs are tested on the ground of history, on their interplay in the course of human experience. Motif research seeks not to collate varieties of data in a particular milieu, but to find out what is characteristic and typical of them.

In summary, motif research seeks to discover that motif which "makes a work of art into a unified whole, determines its structure, and gives it its specific character." A fundamental motif is that which forms the answer given by some particular outlook to a question of a categor- ically fundamental nature. Analysis of questions, thus becomes a crucial issue. A question has an "extraordinary power of suggestion and constraint." [5] Too rarely do we think out the questions themselves. The possible answers may be seriously influenced by the way the question is put. A question indirectly influences the answer.

MOTIF research is not exegesis, i.e., as exegesis is usually understood. To assume, however, that it is something entirely different from or indif- ferent towards exegesis is to miss the mark of its basic intent.

Motif research is inseparable from the exegetical enterprise regard- less of the nature of the texts under study whether they be profane, sacred, or biblical. The texts constitute the proving ground of the fundamental motifs. For this reason the determination of the authenticity of texts and their rendition becomes a matter of first importance.

The interplay between motif research and exegesis (in the philological and historical sense) occurs in several ways within a framework of reciprocity. The roles they play are by means of: 1] interaction, 2] mutual criticism, and 3] hermeneutical judgment, in which the particular responsibility of motif research is to serve as a "perfecter," that is, fulfiller of the purpose of exegesis as an interpretive science.

Interaction

Motif research, in a sense, is dependent on the work of philological and historical sciences for opening up resources, both older and newer. These serve a basic informative purpose. Motif research, on its part, in the course of its labor may render direct exegetical help in particular areas by showing the relative significance of words in their total contextual relationships.

Nygren's interpretation of the well-known passage from the Epistle to the Romans (1:17) on righteousness of faith illustrates abundantly well how he resolves the mutual interaction of exegesis and motif research, and that, in the end, why it is imperative for understanding it to go beyond the specialized exegetical analysis. The total apparatus of motif research is brought to play: analysis of presuppositions, examination of contexts of meanings, and a characterization of the content of the principal terms which disclose the fundamental attitudes of Paul. Out of a complexity of factors a simplicity and a profundity of meaning is won. Consider these points: A] Translation of text, "He who through faith is righteous shall live," might be simply assumed to be a direct borrowing from the new American translation, the Revised Standard Version of the New Testament. This is not the case at all. Nygren's rendition appeared prior to the publication of the American version. Nygren worked out this translation on the basis of the contextual facts of Paul's total outlook spelled out in a most objective way in the Romans epistle. While some professional exegete would insist on making a translation in accord with the Old Testament passage (Habakkuk 2:4), Nygren, quite aware of the original Hebrew text, believes that what Paul said ought to be understood in its most immediate context in the Romans epistle. It is not the words themselves, or their grammar, that produce the final sense. "The very structure of Romans and the letter as a whole are proof that in its theme *ek pisteos* is connected with *ho dikaios* and not with *tsesetai*." [6] In their reach of ideas, Nygren claims, chapters 1–4 constitute an exposition of "he who through faith is righteous," and the theme in chapters 5–8 is "shall live" (where even the word *tsoe*, statistically speaking, occurs twenty-five times). B] The contextual relations with reference to the present-day reader's understanding of this passage as well as the history of the idea of Habakkuk 2:4 in Judaism, are carefully analyzed. A general tendency among numerous modern commentaters is to ascribe to faith a conditional sense, "if you believe . . . or only believe." There prevails a failure to grasp the meaning of faith as being wholly a work of God, even as Paul is speaking of that righteousness which is wholly from God. While the substance of Habakkuk 2:4 is intelligible in terms of its *"Sitz im Leben,"* namely, the imminent Chaldean invasion, it is also to be carefully observed that in the synagogue this memorable declaration had become an expression indicative of righteousness through law. According to the Talmudic tradition, Moses received six hundred and thirteen commandments, which David summed up in eleven (Ps. 15), Micah in three (6:8), Isaiah in two (56:1), and Habakkuk in one, namely, that "the righteous have the right to life because of their fidelity to the law and the covenant. It is by such a faith, by faithfulness, that the just shall live." For Paul, this very expression, familiar to him from his rabbinic background, became an instrument to communicate a meaning which was the direct opposite of salvation by law. "Do not, with the synagogue, understand the prophet to mean that 'the righteous shall live by his faith (i.e., his faithfulness),' but see, with the church, that the affirmation means that 'he who through faith is righteous shall live.' " Thus, it is not Paul as an individual person who borrows an individual phrase changing it at will, but Paul speaking in the context of *his environment, the Church.*

Mutual criticism

It is foreign to the spirit of motif research to interfere with or to lord it over the methods of philology and historical study which are appropriate to their respective fields of inquiry. Tension, and perhaps conflict, may arise between them elsewhere, namely, on the level of interpretive claims. Motif research insists only on pointing out the limitations of philology involving fundamental judgments in interpretive work; equally much, it insists that, in the historical study of ideas, utmost care should be exercised in establishing the objective criteria by which comparative evaluations are arrived at.

The heart of the hermeneutical problem for Nygren, evident in all of his writings involving biblical interpretation, is this: How shall the central concept of biblical interpretation be established? Does the biblical interpretor himself live in two separate periods of history, that is, in two entirely different worlds, in the one working with an ancient text, and in the other making contact with the contemporary mind by means of his personal ingenuity? Is there a disjunction between the biblical record and contemporary historical experience?

The term "biblical research" in modern times (since the enlightenment) is, in Nygren's opinion, largely informed by the assumption that the age-old standpoint of seeing the entire Bible in the light of the gospel and faith in Christ is to be rejected as a guiding principle. It is believed that interpretation of texts can be legitimately made only in comparison with earlier and contemporary texts, but not in relation to later texts, so that the Old Testament is separated from New Testament ideas, and the New Testament from the teaching of the church in later times. Nygren argues for a position which embraces both an objective study of biblical history and the recognition of Jesus Christ as the center of the Bible from whom all understanding of God and man flows to the Christian mind.

> If we are to avoid confusion we must from the very start see clearly that there are two quite distinct, inescapable ways of understanding the Old Testament: the purely historical view and the view that rests on the New Testament. This double meaning is in a certain sense rooted in the very nature of the case. On the one hand, we must not say that, since God meant the prophetic word to say to us Christians that which Paul sets forth, it is therefore wrong to give serious attention to the word's original, historical meaning. But on the other hand, it is quite as unjustifiable to hold that, since the word's historical, original meaning can be shown, it is wrong to follow the example of Paul and Luther, inquiring as to God's further meaning and what the prophetic word has to say to us who view it in the light of its fulfilment. It is improper to inquire what the Old Testament means for those who believe in God's redemptive work in Christ. . . . One must ask what kind of scholarship it is which considers itself able to reject the interpretation of Paul and Luther and to assert that God did *not* mean to say what they understood him to say.[7]

Paul did not think as a modern exegete. His exegesis, as Nygren points out, did not depend on the literal, historical meaning of a passage. "It is safe enough to assert that, in general, he is familiar with the clear, literal meaning of the Old Testament passages. But that is not what interests him. What he looks for are types and references to that which God has done in Christ." [8] Paul's use of allegory is not a free, rhapsodic way of speaking about spiritual reality; his use of allegory is quite unique, in that it is bound to a norm, namely God's action in Jesus Christ.

The decisive issue is: Do we believe that God through Christ actually entered into a completely new relation to humanity? If we believe in the God who sent Christ into the midst of history and thereby gave our race a new beginning, then we cannot keep from looking *at all things without exception* from the central point. Historical study is a necessity to help establish in all its fullness, in a form undistorted and objectively correct, the message of Jesus Christ.

Hermeneutical judgment

In view of the obvious ties between certain leading schools of western philosophy and Biblical interpretation from the Enlightenment of the eighteenth century to the Existentialism of our era, the crucial questions arise: Is the solution of the problem of the communication of the biblical message to be found only within these certain types of associations; and, furthermore, is the search for a culturally congenial philosophic vehicle the perennial task of each new generation of biblical interpreters?

Motif research, while disclaiming to provide a final answer valid for every culture, calls attention, on the one hand, to the all-important obligation of seeking to understand the New Testament message in terms of its distinctive presuppositions, and to determine its concrete message objectively; and, on the other, to examine the fundamental motifs of the philosophic systems which have influenced the history of modern Biblical interpretation. Nygren has sought to bear both of these responsibilities, to explain what is the essence of the New Testament message and to demonstrate the intellectual problems that have arisen in its communication. To clarify the nature of the modern misunderstanding of the Church, Nygren has pinpointed the philosophic and cultural milieu which found an eloquent expression in Adolf von Harnack's *What is Christianity*.[9] Nygren's inquiry into the "history of the Christian idea of love" (the subtitle for *Agape and Eros,* of which too few critics seem to take notice) makes a penetrating probe into the intellectual and spiritual power of Hellenism. Though not always explicitly, yet consistently in all of his writings, Nygren manifests an awareness of the role which intellectual persuasions have performed in the spiritual history of western man. His exposition of the Christian faith does not occur within a vacuum, but always in relation to the crucial contexts of meaning.

What is the Gospel? Nygren's reply to this question is spelled out in a series of questions. He inquires: "What is the content of the Gospel?" "Where lies its unique character?" And, since the content, in terms of its fundamental motif, has taken the form of the message, then it is necessary to inquire: "What are the qualifications which characterize this message?" These interrelated questions involve a two-directional context: the consideration of the New Testament text and the vocation of the contemporary preacher of the Gospel. In this way it becomes possible to perceive the interaction of the objective and the subjective elements in the proclamation of the Gospel. The situation in Nygren's words is as follows:

> That which gives our work as ministers content and meaning is the Gospel, that, and only that. We are but messengers, the passing bearers of the Gospel . . . if one does not hear the Gospel as a message, it is no longer the Gospel which he hears. . . . But just exactly what is meant by saying that the Gospel comes as a message? . . . one day in May, 1945, came the message, "Denmark is free! Norway is free!" When this news went out over these two countries it was indeed a message . . . the presupposition of any news or message is that something has really happened. Nevertheless there is more to it than that. In addition, that which is told must be of vital importance to those who are to hear it. A power stronger than the occupying powers has come, and has deprived them of their dominion. That is the objective thing which has taken place. But—and this is the other no less important side of the matter—at the same time a stupendous transformation of each individual's subjective situation has taken place. They who once had been driven underground by fear of the occupying powers may now venture forth again. . . . One can breathe again, and begin to live . . . an objective and a subjective element here work together . . . both of these two elements constitute a message only when inseparably conjoined.[10]

The content of the Gospel is not identifiable with a state of pure subjectivity. The scope of the Gospel is cosmic. "The Gospel is a power which conquers other opposing powers and frees us from their domination." Man's life is lived under the alien powers of sin and death. What does this mean? "The real and deepest ground of the tragedy of human life lies in the fact that God's own world has become alienated from Him . . . aloof and rebellious against Him." The Gospel is utterly realistic.

> When we read the first pages of the Bible against the background of what our generation has experienced of the godlessness and disintegration of human life, we begin to read them with entirely new eyes. It is the story of man's journey out and away from God. It is not merely a matter of a supposed primeval state, and an event long ago. It is our own story, the history of our own race. The self-centeredness of human life is no myth. The self-seeking individual is no fable. Adam—that is mankind, that is humanity. We are dealing with something of which we are compelled to say to ourselves: "You are the subject under consideration." It is the same with the content of the Gospel. The word about Christ is not just a lovely story, but hard and unavoidable fact. "That which we have heard, that which we have seen with our own eyes, that which we have looked at and put our hands on, that which we preach: of the Word of Life we speak . . ." (I John 1. 1 ff.) . . . When God through Christ snatches us out from the dominion of Sin and Death and sets us down in the new context of Righteousness and Life, that means a totally new creation of the whole of life . . . that newness reach into every phase of our existence.[11]

The central and ever-recurring motif of all Christian proclamation must remain the heralding of our deliverance from the dominion of the powers of destruction.

The all-important question remains: May we conclude, in the interest of sound judgment, that motif research deserves to be considered a viable instrument in the field of biblical interpretation? That is, can it serve as an operable, creatively effective, exegetical discipline? In light of the documented evidence presented in this essay, the answer can be only an affirmative one. Yet, prompted by the spirit of motif research itself, one must hasten to add that certain qualifications attach themselves to this positive answer. These qualifications can best be illumined against the background of certain criticisms that have been directed at Nygren's methodology.

A word about futile criticism. Some would dismiss Nygren's methodology as an example of an arbitrary version of Kantian rationalism applied to theological and exegetical work. Thus he is charged with being a victim of his own intellectual confusions. Nygren's exegesis, to his foes, appears as "consistent in reason but not in actuality." His commentary on the Romans epistle strikes them as "antipsychological, anticritical, antiscientific" to the degree that what he stands against appears as his most distinct characteristic as a scholar. The problem of explaining him has been found very simple to solve by placing him under the general label of a "neo-orthodox continental theologian." He has been roundly condemned for philological and historical deficiency in the handling of Pauline key terms, such as: "faith," "flesh," "body," "in Christ," and so forth.

The criticisms cited here fail to show any awareness of Nygren's investigative discipline. The simple fact remains that little attention has been drawn to the implications of motif research for biblical scholarship.

To deal rightly with motif research, it is well to remember that it is a selective instrument (not a lexical aid) keyed to the interpretation of basic ideas. Motif research is descriptive, not encyclopedic. It is committed to the single purpose of grasping the fundamental idea of a word or of a belief in its functional situation. It seeks to raise the crucial questions about questions which are taken to convey a self-evident significance. It is concerned about the way in which questions are posed. It seeks a clearly defined way of exhibiting the presuppositions of ideas in their organic contexts. Biblical scholarship can ill afford to disregard the sharpness and depth of the critical power of motif research.

Motif research, by its very nature, is "open-ended." On the one hand, strict and unalterable canons prevail, but on the other, there remains an openness to new frontiers, to new questions and to new possibilities. In this respect, criticism inspired by motif research becomes pertinent and purposeful. Two serious concerns present themselves: 1] the articulation of the relationship between *Heilsgeschichte* and the history of ideas, and 2] the exercise of motif research in the analysis of the contemporary cultural situation which has raised the most agonizing questions of human existence in the life of western man. There is reason to fear that motif research may, in the end, escalate the human being out of history, and away from the scene of his actual struggle to a world of clear and untroubled concepts.

To illustrate the first question regarding "holy history" and the study of the history of ideas, it might be asked: Is the tension expressed in the agape-eros-nomos relations an adequate one for placing into the proper contexts the Old Testament meaning of love and the New Testament agape? Is the underscoring of the legalistic interpretation of love in Judaism (although there is a recognition of the basic components of agape in the "steadfast love" of God),[12] the most helpful preparation to recognize the radically new meaning of agape in the New Testament? Does the importance of the Covenant relationship fall into its proper position in the unfolding of the meaning of agape? The Covenant-love found its fulfillment in the disciples' "remembrance" of the words, "This cup is the New Covenant in my blood" (1 Cor. 11:25). One should like to ask Anders Nygren: "If a reformulation of the fundamental attitude expressed by agape were attempted, would it not be in place to focus attention more sharply on its *heilsgeschichtlich* context?"

The second question is: While the criticism of purely "psychological" explanations for the reality of the Christian experience is justified, does not there still remain the obligation to describe the nature and the behavior of the subjective self? What is—or could be—the contribution of motif research to the theory of psychoanalytic thought? The problem of interpreting the New Testament is related to this question, for the New Testament confronts its readers with human crises of a most radical character. What meaning, for example, is there in the cry: "I believe, help my unbelief!" It seems that the untouched frontiers of the discipline of motif-research lie in the effort to understand the nature of human experience. Existentialism in our times claims to be the spokesman for man's question concerning human existence and destiny. Existentialism, however, has shown itself frequently a captive to man's subjectivistic categories, obscuring the objective orders of life with which man himself must come to terms. It seems, therefore, in place, to suggest that Nygren's exposition of the objective-subjective relationships, in his understanding of the proclamation of the Gospel, ought to lead to a searching analysis of the dynamics involved in the subjective life of man, to an examination of the power realities and the power structures of human society. Motif research may well focus its critical acumen upon the study of the symbolic language of the biblical faith.

The Meanings of Love

7

AGAPE IN THE NEW TESTAMENT

Victor Warnach

THERE can be no doubt that Bishop Anders Nygren's theme in his magnificent work *Agape and Eros*,[1] published almost forty years ago, is not only a central but also a very timely subject, which far from losing any of its applicability has rather gained an overwhelming validity and urgency; since the solution of our religious and spiritual, as well as social and political problems depends in the last resort on the true understanding and realization of Christian love. The essence of this theme is naturally the agape in the New Testament, and it is on this particular subject that the author of this article has had the honor to be asked for a contribution.

It is of the utmost importance that this decisive subject be discussed with Bishop Nygren, for it is he who, unlike the authors of other books published on our subject at the same time[2] stresses the significance of the theological "motif," and it is especially from this aspect that these complex problems can be approached and clarified.

Together with other Swedish theologians, such as Gustaf Aulén and Ragnar Bring, Nygren must be considered a champion of "motif research," for it was he who first laid its theoretical foundations and followed up his theory in practice. In his program, Nygren defines motif research as "distinct from historical-genetic research" and "concerned less with the historical connections and origins of motifs than with their characteristic content and typical manifestations" (AE, p.

33).[3] There are certain analogies in the German exegesis, above all in semasiological research.[4] However, Scandinavian theologians are ahead of German exegetes in that they do not content themselves with the philologic-historical approach, but try to penetrate farther into the religious and historical-idea-logical background, at the same time endeavoring to elucidate the true spiritual content of the chief terms.

Nevertheless, the term "motif" is not absolutely clear and carries with it difficulties. By motif, or rather fundamental motif, the Swedes, headed by Nygren, do not mean a subjective (casual) motive of action or behavior, but the basic ideas or the driving power of religion or art or of another field of human culture, in the last instance the more or less historically conditioned answer to a categorically fundamental question, such as the problems of knowledge, ethics, aesthetics, and religion. "A fundamental motif is that which forms the answer given by some particular outlook to a question of such a fundamental nature that it can be described in a categorical sense as a fundamental question" (AE, p. 42). Thus, the fundamental motif serves as a kind of mediator between the general fundamental category and the particular judgment, which thence acquires its precise meaning. But because categories as preliminary to judgment must undergo the critique of philosophers, the attention of the researcher is from the outset focused on certain traits and relations in the historical material or even determined by a concrete philosophical trend of often very relative perspective and outlook. To this "a priori" view must be added the dependence on the inevitable preintelligence of the theme in which, according to Nygren, the fundamental motif lives its reality and manifests itself, in our case on a purely humanistic and cultural-idealistic or a confessional prejudiced Christianity, such as the merely "katabatic" attitude in Protestantism, or the dualistic conception of the unreconcilable cleft between theocentric and egocentric piety, which will prove decisive in our subject.

In spite of these perils (and after all what can be free from risk where human science is concerned?) we consider the transcendental arguments in Nygren's motif research important and even necessary. But this transcendental-critical method should be limited to the justification of this research, and not determine the research itself, otherwise we come to a dead end with apriories and subjectivisms. The motif research as such should rather be inductive, that is historico-critical, determining by exegetic and semasiological work what motifs exist and exercise an influence according to historical sources and, as far as possible fixing their rank and weight in the history of ideas, of culture, and religion, so as to clarify the real meaning of the statements and topics,

Naturally, as Nygren would also agree, one can attempt to find the true interpretation only by using the available conceptions. To this end a phenomenological analysis of the possible motifs must precede the historical interpretation. Such a preview could, however, only have a heuristic function, even if it should be completed by inquiries into metaphysics and anthropology. Thus, a motif-theological research in Scripture and in Tradition can be worked out in order to supplement the dogmatic aspect, but not, as Aulén, following in Nygren's footsteps, does, in order to substitute for it.

This divergence in method, which, after all, depends on previous decisions in the theory of cognition and metaphysics, should on no account conceal the fact that Nygren's fundamental intention is absolutely justifiable and fruitful. The motif theology he initiated has, in fact, brought important results, although certain points may still remain controversial.

Bishop Nygren endeavors to present agape as the commanding fundamental motif of Christianity by contrasting it with Platonic eros. He presumes that it was eros in the Platonic sense which exercised a decisive influence on the spiritual world outside the Bible, especially on the religious environment of the New Testament. Though Nygren follows up his argument through the history of the Platonic eros to its origins in the antique Mystery Religion and also considers its later history from Aristotle to Neoplatonism, nevertheless for him Plato's eros remains the classical peak of the conception of love outside Christianity, and so the main counter-motif to the Christian agape.

In view of the present state of Bible research, important objections could be put forward at this point, for it has been found that it was not so much the "Hellenism" (AE, p. 54), shaped by Greek and particularly by Platonic genius, but Jewish tradition and Oriental Gnosis especially current in the heterodox Jewish world which influenced the nearer environment of the New Testament,[5] so that the Platonic eros can hardly be the essential or at least not the only antipode of the New Testament agape.

However, as it has been already noted, Nygren is not in the first place concerned with the mere historic-genetic aspect, but with clarifying the meaning of the central motif in Christianity. To this end it is at least helpful to compare the structure of agape with that of Platonic eros, even though a better understanding of the character of agape can be expected from its own biblical origin.[6] In point of fact, Nygren also notes the derivation of the agape from its source in the biblical Kerygma, that is to say, especially from the theology of the Cross with the Apostle Paul (AE, pp. 61–159), and only after elaborating the history and the features of the piety of eros as a doctrine of salvation does he point up the fundamental contrast between agape and eros (pp. 200–226) and the possibilities of confusion between the two motifs (pp. 227–32).

Further, it should be mentioned that Nygren does not contrast the ordinary eros with agape, but the higher eros. Already Plato draws a distinction between the "vulgar" ($\pi\acute{\alpha}\nu\delta\eta\mu o s$) and the "heavenly" ($o\dot{\upsilon}\rho\acute{\alpha}\nu\iota o s$) eros, and it is only with this latter that agape is to be compared. The heavenly eros in its most sublimated and spiritualized form is the born rival of the idea of agape.

It could be argued, above all from the phenomenological and historical point of view, that the "heavenly" eros is only a very special kind of love which was not everywhere predominant at the time of the New Testament. Nygren's comparison of motifs therefore seems somewhat one-sided; for by including physical or Dionysian love and its chthonian undercurrent, his exposition would doubtless have gained in depth and fullness, especially since the Platonic eros, as such, is much idealized, or even turned into an abstraction. Nygren, too, would readily admit this, for he says, "undoubtedly there is a connection between sensual and Platonic love" (AE, p. 50). "Yet it is entirely irrelevant for our purposes and we shall do well if we deliberately disregard it; for even apart from it we may very easily be tempted to equate Eros with earthly, sensual love and Agape with heavenly, spiritual love as we seek to compare and contrast them. But if we do that we shall certainly do no justice to Eros. Deep as the sensual roots of Platonic love may be, its whole tendency is to seek deliverance from the merely sensual" (AE, p. 50). It is, indeed, Nygren's special aim to prove the rivalry between eros and agape in connection with the "transvaluation of all ancient values" (Nietzsche) (AE, pp. 30, 57 s; cf., 200–207) and in this not the "lower" love, but only the sublimest eros can have a part.

The antithetical characterization of the New Testament eros and agape as "two general attitudes to life" (AE, p. 209; cf. 47) or "basic conceptions" (AE, pp. 35, 48) must therefore be interpreted with the above-mentioned methodological reservations and limitations. Bishop

Nygren gives us the structural analysis of the two fundamental motifs with great sagacity and admirable clarity. Although he asserts that the difference between the two is so great that they "have originally nothing whatsoever to do with one another" so that they are not really comparable, they have at least "the questions to which they are the answers" in common. We cannot here go into the analysis in detail, it has been done often enough.[7] We will instead limit ourselves to the most important points as tabulated by Nygren himself (AE, p. 210).

Bishop Nygren draws up the first pair of opposites, "Eros is acquisitive desire and longing – Agape is sacrificial giving." These are indeed typical, but not essential points of difference, for it is precisely eros, especially as "benevolent love" (*amor benevolentiae*), and also the Platonic eros which devotes itself "in generating in the beautiful" (cf. Plato, Symposium, 206 B s.) and even spends itself in extravagant outpouring, while the agape, naturally a giver and server, is capable of the highest sacrifice, without necessarily implying it from its own nature. Its essence is like that of every kind of love, a uniting with the beloved, although this union will be very different from that of eros or of sexus. At the same time there subsist in love always desire and devotion, although on two different levels (see below). That agape is also a longing and even desire ($\epsilon\pi\iota\theta\nu\mu\iota\alpha$) may be deduced from an important passage in Luke 22:15: "With great longing have I desired to hold this Pascha with you before my suffering."

The second contrast which Nygren points out between eros and agape is even more open to question. There can be no doubt that eros is in general, and in particular in the Platonic sense "an upward movement," "man's way to God" as the highest good (summum bonum) and that likewise assuredly agape "comes down" and is "God's way to man" (AE, p. 210). Nevertheless it would be a simplification and a falsifying of the concept of history in the New Testament to consider the order of agape only in a katabatic sense. In Saint John the Lord describes his way in the sacrificial agape as a descent, but *also* as an ascent: "I went out from the Father and come into the world; I shall leave the world again and return to the Father" (John 16:28; cf., 3:13; Luke 24:26; Phil. 2:7–9; Eph. 4:9).

When Nygren asserts, "Eros is man's effort: It assumes that man's salvation is his own work – Agape is God's grace; salvation is the work of divine love" (AE, p. 210), that is doubtless correct. But it should not be overlooked that agape emphatically demands individual decision (in faith) and individual activity (in work) (2 Cor. 8:3–9; cf. 1 Cor. 16:2;

Philem. 8, 14). The peculiar dialectical relation between divine and human work makes St. Paul say paradoxically, in writing to the Philippians, "Work out your own salvation in fear and trembling; for it is God who will work in you and your will and its accomplishment according to His pleasure" (2:12).

The next point in Nygren's schema can also be accepted in the main, though not without certain reservations, "Eros is egocentric love, a form of self-assertion of the highest, noblest, sublimest kind – Agape is unselfish love, it 'seeketh not its own,' it gives itself away" (AE, p. 210). Indeed, the true agape is never egoistic, or also egocentric, but this does not exclude an orderly self-assertion and self-love, but rather includes it, as can be seen from the commandment about loving your neighbor: "Thou shalt love thy neighbour as thyself" (Mark 12:31). The reservation, therefore, only applies to the statement in the New Testament, that the agape, in spite of any possible self-sacrifice and self-negation, does imply genuine self-assertion, but only self-assertion in God and in his grace. Thus it is just Nygren's chief witness, St. Paul, who says: "Through the grace of God am I what I am, and the grace that he has given me has not been without effect, for I have done more than them all, though not I, but the grace of God with me" (1 Cor. 15:10). Therefore, the Apostle cries out with confidence: "I am able to do everything in Him who strengthens me" (Phil. 4:13; cf. 4:9). His conscience of the apostolic message and authority are unshakable, above all in the great apology in 2 Cor. (esp. chaps. 10–13). Though man shall not glorify himself before God, he may do so "in the Lord" (Rom. 5:11; see 1 Cor. 13; 2 Cor. 10:12–18). The free man, that is he who has been freed by Christ's redemption may then be the subject of agape and in it he will work out his freedom (Gal. 5, 6, 13 ff).

Nygren's views can, however, be wholeheartedly accepted when he says: "Eros seeks to gain his life, a life divine, immortalised – Agape lives the life of God, therefore dares to 'lose it' " (AE, p. 210), or again: "Eros is the will to get and to possess which depends on want and need – Agape is freedom in giving, which depends on wealth and plenty" (Ibid.). Of course here eros must be interpreted in the strict platonic sense, and benevolent love, which otherwise naturally belongs to eros' phenomenologic and motif spheres, must be excluded.

The following assertion also seems admissable: "Eros is primarily man's love; God is the object of Eros. Even when it is attributed to God, Eros is patterned on human love – Agape is primarily God's love; God is Agape. Even when it is attributed to man, Agape is patterned on Divine love" (Ibid.). It should, however, be emphasized that agape also truly becomes "our love" (1 Thess. 1:3; Phil. 1:9) and thereby demands our personal participation (2 Cor. 8:7). Although the agape can only be realized in coaction (*Mit-Vollzug*) with the love of God, that is with the love with which God loves us on the strength of God's choice and grace, man can become a true subject of the agape, which naturally always reflects the likeness of God.

Nygren assigns the greatest importance to the following difference between the two fundamental motifs: "Eros is determined by the quality, the beauty and worth of its object; it is not spontaneous, but 'evoked,' 'motivated'—Agape is sovereign in relation to its object, it is directed to both 'the evil and the good'; it is spontaneous, 'overflowing,' 'unmotivated'" (AE, p. 210; cf. pp. 75–102). However, this too must be understood with reservations. For the lack of motif, or rather the indifference of value is typical of agape, but not an absolutely necessary characteristic. It is more an obvious accompanying trait than its true substance, because in the New Testament, the motivational character of agape is explicitedly stated: (see Luke 7:42; 2 Cor. 9:7; esp. John 10:17; 14:21–23; 16:27) and the Lord speaks spontaneously of the "reward" ($\mu\iota\sigma\theta$os) of the agape (Matt. 5:46; 10:42; 25:34 ff.; cf., Luke 6:32). Even in Paul, who accepts the supremacy of grace unconditionally, rewards and merits are not excluded (for example, 1 Cor. 3:8–13 f; 2 Cor. 4:17; 5:10; Gal. 6:7–9).

Besides if the agape is essentially without motif and, as Nygren says, all love of God is necessarily motivated, there could be no true agape to God. In fact this is the conclusion that Nygren himself draws when he refers to St. Paul: "If Agape is a love as absolutely spontaneous and entirely unmotivated as the love manifested in the Cross of Jesus, then it is plain that the word Agape can no longer fittingly be used to denote man's attitude to God. In relation to God man is never spontaneous; he is not an independent center of activity. His giving of himself to God is never more than a response. At its best and highest, it is but a reflex of God's love, by which it is 'motivated.' Hence it is the very opposite of spontaneous and creative; it lacks all the essential marks of Agape. Man's devotion to God must therefore be given another name: not $\dot{\alpha}\gamma\dot{\alpha}\pi\eta$, but $\pi\iota\sigma\tau$os" (AE, p. 125 s.). But Paul in several instances speaks very clearly about the Agape to God (Rom. 8:28; I Cor. 2:9; 8:3) or to Christ (1 Cor. 16:22; Eph. 6:24; Philem. 5) and this cannot be considered as an ambiguity in terms or an incidental quotation of former sources. It rather shows us that we should not exaggerate the lack of motivation in the agape.

Nygren makes his problem unnecessarily complex when he holds that the love to God must necessarily be motivated. True, agape presupposes the anticipating love of God because it can only exist in the coaction (*Mit-Vollzug*) of divine love, but this does not mean a motivation or a lack of personal independence, for God's love and his work is so sovereign that it does not remove the free initiative of the individual, but rather makes it possible and fulfills it.

In any case, therefore, any decisive distinction between eros and agape cannot be seen in the lack of motif, even if, as Nygren says, "Eros *recognizes value* in its object, and loves it—Agape loves and *creates value* in its object" (AE, p. 210), for on the one hand also eros, as benevolentia, creates values, and on the other hand agape too recognizes and accepts with gratitude the good which grace effects in others, at least in neighborly love. The true cause of the difference between the two fundamental motifs must be sought elsewhere.

All the points by which Nygren denotes the difference between eros and agape have their relative justification; but as we have seen, none of them is able to signify the essential difference. In the sight of biblical anthropology, this difference emerges in the "psychic" nature of eros and the spiritual or "pneumatic" nature of Agape, according to the distinction between soul ($\psi v \chi \acute{\eta}$) and spirit ($\pi v \epsilon \hat{v} \mu \alpha$), as it occurs especially in the letters of St. Paul. Not only the vital and psychic forces and faculties belong to the psyche, but also the feeling and willing, the mind and intellect ($v o \hat{v} s$) as conscious (reflexive) life and experience, while pneuma is essentially "trans-psychical," an immanent-transcendent, but not necessarily supernatural reality. It is the "other" depth of the soul, the core of man, his "Personkern" (M. Scheler), in which all his faculties and acts unite in a personal and total action. The pneuma is therefore the source of freedom and responsibility in man, and its proper function is the "con-science," as the harmony with God and his will. It is the same as the "heart" (leb, lebab, $\kappa \alpha \rho \delta \acute{\iota} \alpha$, cor) in the Old and New Testament, which is the innermost part of man as a free person and at the same time it is the exposure and the manifestation of his being towards God.

Certainly Nygren and Karl Barth would deny the existence of such a pneuma in man as a fact of nature; but the words of the Apostle Paul leave us in no doubt on this issue (see for example, 1 Cor. 2:11 a; 5:3; 7:34; 14:2; 14–16; Rom. 8:10, 16).[8] Only from this distinction between psyche and pneuma in man can we fathom the depth and understand the implications of the Pauline conception of salvation. It is precisely this pneuma or heart of man that is the specific subject of the agape; for according to St. Paul "the love of God is poured into our hearts by the Holy Spirit which is given to us" (Rom. 5:5). The agape, in its essence and origin, is a "pneumatic" or "spiritual" love because it is generated by the Divine Pneuma in the human pneuma (cf. also Rom. 15:30; Col. 1:8; 2 Tim. 1:7).

As spiritual love agape is essentially distinct from eros which is by nature psychical and depends on emotions and affections, while the agape is a personal and total act in which all the psychic faculties are integrated but also transcended. Moreover, we can derive all the characteristics which we have considered above from the spiritual essence of agape. Whereas the eros as a psychical tendency or trend and also as a benevolence is each time determined by a value, the agape does not depend on any value, for it is no tendency, but a total and personal relation, or better, a personal being—*sein*. It loves the sinner and the poor even though they be unworthy of its love. Since it is not really an act of volition or even a natural inclination, it does not come within the scope of aspiration and that is why it remains outside the field of tension between desire and need. It can be, though it is not necessarily, unmotivated or "groundless" (grundlos), i.e., unfounded, but will rather absorb motifs and motivations in the accomplishment of its total action. It is able to surrender and sacrifice itself unreservedly, without however losing its own identity and freedom. This is the deeper meaning of the Lord's words: "Whoever will save his life ($\psi v\chi\acute{\eta}$) shall lose it; but he who loses his life for me or the Gospel, shall save it" (Mark 8:35; cf. John 12:25). Therefore we have to surrender our individual existence or "ego," if we really want to reach our true inner "self." Here we come up against the fundamental paradox in Christian life and love; the more we surrender ourselves the more we win our true personal being. This is inconceivable to a wordly mind, though everybody should be able to learn from his own everyday experiences; but it is only from the confrontation with revelation and faith that the "secret" of humanity becomes apparent—namely his true "pneumatic" depth which, buried by sin, is liberated, even rediscovered by the grace of Christ.

It is only as a spiritual being or as $\pi\nu\epsilon\nu\mu\alpha\tau\iota\kappa\acute{o}s$ that with agape man can become a lover in the true sense, but he can only be a true spiritual being if he allows himself to be conquered and governed by Christ's agape. So far from being a gnosticism or mysticism, this is the clear teaching of the Apostle Paul, who deliberately placed the hymn of agape (1 Cor. 13) in the context of the two chapters—the gifts and effects of pneuma (2 Cor. 12 and 14).

Now it is precisely the pneuma, even as the basis or depth of the soul open Godwards and susceptible to his grace, which remains the most interior part of man, the center and ground of his personal existence. In the Bible the being is not considered as a universal and abstract idea, much less as a hypostasis in which every being takes part, nor even as a materialistic reality. It is invariably the being of an individual or rather of a personal existence; for only in the free person, ultimately in God who is thought absolutely personal (not anthropomorphical!) can the being arrive at its perfect realization. Therefore it is in his spiritual depth that man achieves his true existence, but then only through God.

On the other hand, the agape also has definite ontological characteristics. Once again St. Paul declares: "If I have not agape, I *am* nothing" (οὐθέν) (1 Cor. 13:2). The agape thus becomes the really decisive factor, the basis and core of our existence. Taken in a different sense agape can also mean an "aeon," a sphere of being, in which we live and walk and have our personal existence (Rom. 8:35–39; 1 Cor. 16:14; Eph. 3:17–19; 5:2; John 15:9, etc.). The ontological function of the agape is very strongly marked in 1 John 3:14: "We know that we have gone from Death to Life, *because* we love our brothers; whoever does not love remains in Death" (cf. 2:10; 4, 12, 16). Thus agape is not only the factor which gives our being its decisive orientation, but it determines it in its innermost nature. It is the sphere of the redeemed existence or the reality of salvation; for unlike eros, which is dependent on transitory values and changing emotions, agape creates a true and permanent (μένειν) community (1 John 4:16) in which the one answers for (ὑπέρ) the other in holy solidarity (2 Cor. 5:14; Rom. 5:6 ff.; Hebr. 2:10–18).

When, finally, St. John says: "God is Agape," to which words Bishop Nygren also gives a special emphasis (AE, p. 164; 210), this should be interpreted in an ontological sense, and even if thereby agape is not immediately identified with God's intimate being and nature, yet it appears as the truest expression, the most relevant manifestation of this same being and nature (Wesenswirklichheit).[9]

No doubt Nygren would have the gravest misgivings because of these pneumatological and ontological interpretations of the agape. These objections would indeed be justifiable, if "ontology" were to be understood in the sense of the late scholastic or rationalistic philosophy, which interpreted being as the same as abstract and, paradoxically enough, as excessively and massively concrete. Such an interpretation of being falls short of and is out of harmony with the sayings in the

Bible. If, however, taking the point of departure in the Bible, one endeavors to think in terms of biblical conceptions, things assume a very different aspect.

With reference to this last point, it is with great satisfaction that the author is able to admit that he is in full agreement with Bishop Nygren. The author takes it as a special honor that it should be from his book *Agape,* among so many written on this subject that Nygren, in the new edition of the German translation of his work (Gütersloh, 1954), should have chosen to quote this sentence in which the common viewpoint is expressed. Nygren remarks (p. 8): "Warnach makes a correct observation when he writes in a note (p. 265), 'the often so critical situation in theology and in exegesis seems to spring from the fact that generally foreign terms originating in profane philosophies should have been adopted instead of those deriving from the infallible sources of revelation of which only exegesis disposes. . . . It is therefore one of the most urgent tasks of our times to free theological thought from this Babylonian word chaos.' " Critically but regretfully Nygren adds: "It is however strange that this should be said in the context of the chapter 'Agape and Being' in which Warnach endeavors to integrate the term Agape into an entirely foreign ontological metaphysical conception of being."

The above critical remark includes a fatal misunderstanding. True, the rejection of ontology, as it was seen in earlier Protestantism is absolutely understandable if we consider the above-mentioned rationalistic conception of being. This at the same time abstract and static or massive conception of being is, indeed, sharply opposed to the historic-dynamic and personal-concrete biblical thinking, let alone the fact that purely philosophically it would be untenable. On the other hand, without a certain philosophical formation the categorical relevance of Bible sayings cannot be observed and analysed. As hinted above, Nygren, too, possesses a philosophical attitude strongly influenced by Kant and German idealism and in no small measure by Søren Kierkegaard, whose influence has been so strikingly felt in modern existence-philosophy. It cannot be denied that these thinkers, especially Hegel and Kierkegaard, were very much inspired by biblical ideas, but, in the author's opinion, they never really succeeded in penetrating into the full biblical conception of reality because the exegesis of that time had not yet established a satisfactory basis for those investigations. Today, especially in connection with the Bible, it seems an urgent task to establish an ontology and anthropology, adequate to the basic motifs of the revelation, and also to meet the demands of modern science. To achieve this, exegetical and biblical theology must furnish the decisive contribution.[10]

If we search the Bible for its opinion of "being," which is naturally not expressed but implied in its statements, we can take as our point of departure the biblical teaching of creation as the word of God setting forth being. This is not meant as an empty metaphor, but as a basic axiom of biblical thinking. This is evident from the great number of such references in both the Old and New Testaments and from the form of the biblical sayings, as well as from the whole conception of the Bible. Our human speech is only a faint echo of God's speech because it does not establish being itself, but only a statement or a postulate concerning it. How seriously the Apostle Paul takes God's creation as an act of speaking can be seen in Rom. 4:17, where he remarks, in a soteriological context incidentally, but all the more relevantly, concerning God: "He who called the not-being as being ($\kappa\alpha\lambda o\hat{v}\nu\tau o\varsigma\ \tau\grave{\alpha}\ \mu\grave{\eta}\ \check{o}\nu\tau\alpha$)." From this it follows that every creature represents a word of God in which the $\mu\grave{\eta}\ \check{o}\nu\tau\alpha$ stands for the undetermined subject (without content) and the $\check{o}\nu$ for the determined predicate which confers the content. Thus, being is an event realized by the union of a determining factor (since filled with content: idea, logos) with an empty but receptive *materia* in the metaphysical sense, and from this we can divine that it is really love—love in the sense of unifying inclination— which brings forth being, as the whole Christian faith and doctrine affirm.

The most fundamental event of ontological constitution can come about in different ways according to the grade of the being on the highest level by the personal-pneumatic realization (Vollzug). In this the content (the idea) or the word spoken by God can best become itself (zu sich kommen) in the "otherness" of its bearer (materia), and since here in the pneumatic sphere all the vital (egocentric) forces and appetites are transcended, it is possible in this connection to speak of "pure" or personal love, that is to say of agape. For the creative word (speech) of God is always a personal act, not enacted as a monologue but, because it springs from the fountain of love, as a dialogue. It is a "call into existence" out of a free decision of love and appeals for personal dignity and commitment. It therefore provokes a free response and this presupposes a true responsibility, which can be implied only in personal existence, and a free correspondence of the personal love, that is to say of agape. Naturally, precisely on account of his presupposed freedom, man can also fail, that is to say, he is free to answer with the love expected of him or to refuse this answer; and, in fact, man has failed. But the merciful love of God has called him back into the original unity with Himself in which man becomes truly one with himself and with others. Thus, all establishing and renewing and achieving of Being takes place in the love which comes from God and returns to him. All is primarily founded in the word of agape and is finally completed in the work of the same agape.

These few hints will confirm what we have said of the ontological character of agape in connection with the New Testament. The agape appears in the general view of the Bible as not merely something ontological, but as the true "essence" of being, or rather as being (existence) in its deepest personal reality and in its "mystery." [11] On this basis an ontology and anthropology can be built, approximately adequate to the Bible and not decayed either into abstract speculation or into materialistic simplification, but with respect for the personally free and responsible accomplishment of the true being. In this personal and full accomplishment of being all other possibilities and values, though only in a positive transcending and fulfillment (Aufhebung), are included, not the least important of which is eros with its teleological dynamics and natural richness of living. In this way is realized the love demanded already in the Old Testament law (Deut. 6:5) and by the Lord (Mark 12:30) as a love "from thy whole heart and from thy whole soul and from thy whole thinking and from all thy forces." [12]

Such a "catholic" synthesis, not in the confessional, but in the etymological sense, may however seem suspicious, if not entirely unacceptable to Nygren and his friends, but this is the way in which the biblical message of salvation represents itself to us and this is the way in which we think it right to interpret it so as to obtain the answer to the pressing problems of our times. Though the author cannot entirely share Bishop Nygren's explanation of the Scripture, because his approach to its unique truth is from a different standpoint and seen from a different angle, he nevertheless is sincerely united with Nygren in a common effort to comprehend the divine fullness hidden therein, having received each one according to his own measure as it has been given him by God, and to listen to the divine word as the life-giving appeal in the Kairos of his own situation.

8

SOME INTERPRETATIONS

OF AGAPE AND EROS

John M. Rist

> Although the poverty of our language is
> such that in both cases it says "love," yet
> the two ideas have nothing to do with one
> another.
>
> —*U. von Wilamowitz-Moellendorff.*[1]

THE great classical scholar Wilamowitz was not the first, even in
more recent times, to contrast agape and eros, to regard them as
direct opposites. As Nygren hardly tires of reminding us,[2] it was
Nietzsche who referred to the coming of Christianity as a "transvaluation of all ancient values." For Wilamowitz, Nietzsche, and Nygren—
and for the whole tradition and view of life which they represent—
agape and eros derive from different worlds, produce different effects,
and, since Christianity began, have been the deadly rivals whose battle
has been fought out generation after generation.

Eros, in Nygren's view,[3] derives in its western manifestations from
the Greek mystery religions, represented best perhaps by what is
commonly called Orphism. According to the Orphic myth of Diony-
sus Zagreus it was the desire of Zeus to give power over the world to
Zagreus. The monstrous Titans, however, captured Zagreus, killed him,
and ate him. In revenge Zeus destroyed the Titans with his thunderbolt
and formed men from their ashes. Since, therefore, all men contain
something of the Titans and something of Zagreus in themselves, they
have a dual nature. They are earthly (Titanic) and yet the possessors
of a divine spark. This divine spark can be liberated from its bodily
"tomb" by purification and can struggle back to its natural divine life.

Man therefore is by nature akin to the divine and through the right kind of effort can restore his compromised divinity.

On this sort of basis Plato, according to Nygren, superimposed his philosophical ideas. For Plato eros is, as the *Symposium* and *Phaedrus* show, the way back to the divine, the way by which man can attain his aim of achieving "likeness to God." Eros is a desire, a drive, yet it is a desire which is capable of varying degrees of sublimation. Vulgar eros will be concerned with the enjoyment of sensual pleasures, whether with women or with boys; its sublimated counterpart will lead the soul of the "true lover" away from the mere enjoyment of particular bodies or even the contemplation of them, up through the joys of the love of all that is beautiful to the ultimate goal of the soul, the vision of the form of Beauty, that form which is the cause of all earthly beauties, and beside which all these earthly beauties pale into insignificance. When the soul of the philosopher has reached such a level, it will resemble the souls of the gods, for it is the vision and knowledge of the forms which makes the gods divine.

For Nygren's Plato, therefore, eros is a self-centered, self-seeking, egotistical drive to recover one's latent divinity. As such it is a way of salvation for man, a rival salvation to that of Christianity. In order to understand this rivalry, the basic features of eros must be described in more detail. That eros is acquisitive we know, for in the *Symposium* it is an intermediary by means of which man-who-has-not becomes man-who-has. The gods are not lovers of wisdom, for they have it already (*Symp.* 203E). Eros enables man also to have wisdom and thus to join the gods. And in what manner can this be achieved? By a flight from the things of this world, the things of sense, to the realm of forms as quickly as possible (*Theaet.* 176AB).

Happiness is the aim of the Platonic lover. All men wish to be happy and eros is the means of attaining this happiness. Hence eros must always be directed towards what is inherently valuable. It does not create value; it recognizes what is valuable and tries to lay hold on it for eternity. The result of this is that eros can be seen as a desire for immortality, a desire for a permanent and abiding vision of all that is permanent and abiding, a grasping by the divine soul of what is divine in the cosmos. Egocentricity, therefore, is in Nygren's view the fundamental and recognizable characteristic of Platonic eros.

Although according to Nygren the classical version of the eros-motif is to be found in Plato, he does not believe that its full historical effects can be understood unless we consider the developments of the theme in Aristotle and the neoplatonists, Plotinus in particular. We can then observe how eros was enabled to enter the Christian world and indeed to corrupt our understanding of the basic truths of Christianity. It is not our purpose, however, to study that "corruption" here, but to consider the ancient formulations of agape and eros, as Nygren finds them, and to examine them in terms of historical and psychological relevance.

According to Nygren the role of Aristotle was to give the Platonic eros a cosmic relevance. In the Aristotelian world we can see all things striving for their own perfection and the Prime Mover moving as a final cause, an object of desire, only. Certainly these ideas did not originate with Aristotle—we may think of the cosmic Philia of Empedocles and the rather comic eros of Eryximachus in the Symposium—but it is beyond question that it was the Aristotelian version of the theory of cosmic desire which conquered the world and contributed to what Nygren has styled "the Alexandrian world-scheme." [4] D'Arcy has summarized Nygren's position admirably: "The divine Being is wrapt up in self-contemplation, but because of his presence he draws all nature by love. He is the magnet, the object which attracts, and so Aristotle can fairly be said to make Eros the driving force of all the world, and the lower is ever striving towards what is higher than itself under the stress of Eros." [5] The world, therefore, in Aristotle's view, is dependent on God and on the power of eros. We should notice, says Nygren, that God is thus understood in a "characteristically Greek" fashion.[6] By this Nygren means that God affects the world not through his activity but through the eros that is in the world.

Although we hear of God as first cause in the Aristotelian world, Nygren is right to notice that eros is not introduced by Aristotle in the context of a doctrine of salvation. Such doctrines, however, as we have seen, were already present in "Orphism" and in Plato; and in Neoplatonism they become dominant. The return of the soul to God under the motivation of Eros is the dominant concern of the philosophy of Plotinus. Yet it is not his only concern, for according to the "Alexandrian world-scheme," of which Plotinus is the best representative, "Eros-piety" sought to explain not only man's ascent but also the necessity for that ascent, and indeed the problem of why man ever descended. Hence Plotinus gives us his "emanation" system, by which all things flow from the One and are then drawn back to him. Here we might wonder how eros, seen hitherto as an upward and acquisitive drive, can be regarded as also concerned with emanation, with outward procession, for Nygren insists that "the doctrine of Eros stands in the center, dominating both those ways," both ascent to and descent from the One.[7] Plotinus accepts from Plato that "the higher cares for the lower and adorns it" (*Enn.* 4.8.8), and it might appear as though something like agape is introduced into his system; but for Nygren "it would be completely wrong to suppose that the 'downward way' of Plotinus bears any real resemblance to the condescending Agape of Christianity." [8] Plotinus is thinking not of salvation here but of a mere cosmological process. Whenever salvation is in question the Platonic acquisitive eros appears in its pure form. Even when Plotinus says that the One (or God) is eros (6.8.15) he must not be misunderstood. The basic idea is that God loves himself because he is worthy of love. He is said to have eros in the same way as all else, namely in a self-regarding way. Nygren summarizes this position as follows: "There is no real departure from the Platonic idea of Eros. The care of the higher for the lower is never related by Plotinus to the idea of Eros, and therefore could not influence it. As regards the statement 'God is Eros,' he makes this a matter of God's love for Himself; the Divine enjoys its own perfection, and such a form of self-love is obviously in the direct line of acquisitive love." [9]

Such then is Nygren's account of Eros, God of Antiquity. What of agape, its Christian rival? Here, as the quotations from Wilamowitz and Nietzsche make clear, everything is changed. The coming of Christianity into the ancient world is seen as a clean break with the past. Agape, the "unmotivated" God of the Christians, reverses all the values established by acquisitive eros-piety. Eros is basically a human desire, and when it is attributed to God by Plotinus he is making God in man's image. Agape, on the other hand, is God's love. When a man can be said to have agape he is allowing God to work through him. Whereas eros seeks its own, agape is the love that "seeketh not its own" (1 Cor. 13:5), and has no care for the self. Above all St. Paul is the exponent of the spirit of agape, though it is St. John who has given the most perfect form to the Christian view with the words "God is Agape" (2 John 4:8, 16). Unlike eros, agape does not look for what is valuable to make it its own; it is itself creative of value. Making one's own is the mark of eros and damnable as such. Agape, on the other hand, is in man a reflection of God's agape. It is in virtue of such agape that man can love God and his neighbor.

There is for Nygren no commandment of self-love. Self-love is selfishness and the inextinguishable mark of eros. "So far is neighborly love from including self-love that it actually excludes and overcomes it." [10] Quoting Luther with obvious approval Nygren remarks that "on the basis of Christ's words in John 12:25 it is a fundamental principle for him that 'To love is the same as to hate oneself.' " [11]

The parables of Jesus, the writings of Paul and John, tell us the nature of agape. Agape leaves the ninety-nine sheep in the wilderness to seek the one which is lost (Luke 15:4). In this respect it is not "the cold reflection of reason but unmotivated love." [12] Agape is seen in the parable of the Prodigal Son (Luke 15:11–32). God's ways and God's agape appear inscrutable to mere human reason. The Prodigal Son receives his reward precisely because God's agape is spontaneous and "unmotivated." It is an example of the fact that human merit does not determine whether God will love. Agape does not respect value; it creates it. The laborer in the vineyard (Matt. 20:1–16) who has worked one hour receives as much as those who have toiled all through the day—to demonstrate that it is not man's merits but God's agape which justifies and leads to salvation.

Nygren has offered a schematic version of his conception of eros and agape which should be reproduced *in toto*, for by such a schematization we can best understand how Nygren sees that his eros and agape motifs are fundamentally opposed.

Eros is acquisitive desire and longing.	Agape is sacrificial giving.
Eros is an upward movement.	Agape comes down.
Eros is man's way to God.	Agape is God's way to man.
Eros is man's effort: it assumes that man's salvation is his own work.	Agape is God's grace: salvation is the work of Divine love.
Eros is egocentric love, a form of self-assertion of the noblest, sublimest kind.	Agape is unselfish love; it seeketh not its own; it gives itself away.
Eros seeks to gain its life, a life divine, immortalized.	Agape lives for the life of God, therefore dares to "lose it."
Eros is the will to get and possess which depends on want and need.	Agape is freedom in giving, which depends on wealth and plenty.
Eros is primarily *man's* love; God is the *object* of Eros. Even when it is attributed to God, Eros is patterned on human love.	Agape is primarily *God's* love; "God *is* Agape." Even when it is attributed to man, Agape is patterned on Divine love.

Eros is determined by the quality, the beauty and worth, of its object; it is not spontaneous, but "evoked," "motivated."	Agape is sovereign in relation to its object, and is directed to both "the evil and the good"; it is spontaneous, "overflowing," "unmotivated."
Eros *recognizes value* in its object—and loves it.	Agape loves—and *creates value* in its object.[13]

Burnaby has observed [14] that Nygren will not be disturbed by a criticism of his analysis on psychological or ethical grounds. That being so, the counterattacks of D'Arcy and of Paul Tillich,[15] and to some extent of Burnaby himself, are doomed to failure as refutations. Speaking of D'Arcy and Burnaby in his preface to the English edition of *Agape and Eros*, Nygren comments that since these writers have started from different premises they have inevitably arrived at different conclusions. What this seems to mean, in the case of D'Arcy at least, is that however much he may argue about the psychology of man, he cannot evade the fact that New Testament agape talks about one thing, Hellenic piety about another. If it seems to D'Arcy, and to Tillich, that what Nygren thinks of as the agape motif is psychologically or ethically extraordinary, that is only a proof that these authors have an inadequate grasp of the true Christian spirit. Their psychological theorizings, though apparently plausible, conflict with the doctrines of agape in the New Testament and thus, for the Christian, must be wrong.

The ground on which Nygren must be approached, therefore, is the text of the New Testament and of the Greek philosophers. If it can be shown that agape in the New Testament is not what Nygren understands it to be, then it can be also objected, and tellingly objected, that Nygren's agape is psychologically and ethically extraordinary. And a corollary to this will be that if eros for the Greeks does not turn out to be exactly what Nygren supposes, and indeed at times bears certain of the features of agape, then the Christian can reject the view that his religion is a transvaluation of all ancient values and draw profit from the theories of love in the writings of the Greek philosophers. Since Christianity holds that the Incarnation is a fact of history, its tenets can thus be seen not as a denial of history but as its fulfilment and culmination.

Such then is the proper procedure. Greek eros and Christian agape must be scrutinized for basic elements which do not correspond to Nygren's schema. If such are found, then the fundamental antagonism of *historical* as opposed to *theoretical* eros and agape can be disregarded. We may reach a point where eros and agape are seen to overlap, and in particular where New Testament agape is seen not to exclude certain features of Greek eros. If we do, then the Christian as well as the non-Christian may recognize that, if modern thinkers find Nygren's theories psychologically and ethically destructive, their views only serve to confirm that the New Testament is right in associating the agape and eros motifs, and that Nygren is wrong in separating them radically. If then we can reject Nygren's reading of the New Testament and of the Greek philosophers, we shall be in a position at least to glance at the question which D'Arcy and Tillich, as Christians, treated prematurely, namely whether Nygren's views are psychologically and ethically misguided.

First then we must consider eros. Since we are limiting our discussion to an evaluation of Nygren's position, we may admit without documentation that the view of eros which he presents is the dominant one in the Greek tradition, and in particular in those parts of that tradition which are strongly influenced by Plato. Our purpose here must be to elucidate those other aspects of Greek eros which do not easily harmonize with Nygren's schematization. First of all, however, we should dismiss a fair-seeming suggestion by which one might avoid Nygren's antithesis, but which in fact is of little value: there are other terms in Greek for love than eros and agape. One of these, much emphasized by Burnaby,[16] is philia. Now philia may, in some thinkers, emphasize aspects of love which those thinkers do not find subsumed under eros or agape. It may be supposed to represent "the personal pole," while eros stands for the "transpersonal," as Tillich suggests,[17] but such distinctions can only be drawn if agape and eros and philia are understood to represent not kinds of love, as Nygren believes, but merely aspects. In Nygren's view Greek philia is essentially subsumed under the eros motif, for, as in Aristotle's *Nicomachean Ethics*,[18] it is essentially self-centered. The "friend," even the ideal friend, is treated as a second self, an extension of the self.[19] Hence in Plato's *Lysis* we find that, although philia is a wider term than eros—for it will include much that is not specifically passionate or sexual—so far as Nygren is concerned we are still in the world of the eros motif.

There is a further preliminary to be considered, namely the relation of eros to desire. According to Tillich,[20] those who attempt to establish an absolute contrast between agape and eros usually identify eros with epithymia (desire). There is obviously a connection between the two. It is clear to everyone, Plato remarks in the *Phaedrus* (237D), that eros is some kind of desire. Yet this desire is not simply a natural drive, a Freudian *libido;*[21] it is the characteristically unfreudian desire for an end, for the achievement of an end, the attainment of a goal outside itself.

Eros then is in the first instance the desire for what is beautiful. In contrast to this, in Nygren's view, agape does not concern itself with the value of its object. Yet this contrast is somewhat curious. Could one have agape for anything, regardless of all value? The Christian God, of course, creates *ex nihilo;* but the Christian is faced with a given world. Within that world he lives, and as Nygren would put it, reflects God's agape. Yet he does not love indiscriminately. He does not show agape for vice. He may love the sinner but hate the sin, yet in his very doing so he is being selective. The objects of his agape are in fact considered. He may differ from Plato in what he loves; he may reject Plato's aristocratic choice of the beautiful as an object of love. Yet even if he says he loves all that is God's and not "the world's," he is still valuing an object, and in this respect his love differs from Plato's more in degree than in kind. The distinction which Nygren wishes to draw between the Christian lover of all God's creatures and the Platonic lover of the beautiful may be accentuated by the use of the words rather than by more substantial considerations.

Platonic eros, says Nygren, is egocentric; agape is theocentric. When Eros is attributed to God, God is made in man's image; when agape is attributed to man, man is made in God's image. Yet we should look at the facts that lie behind this apparent antithesis. The Christian is fortunate enough to start from Revelation. He has some knowledge, from God himself, of what God is like. The Platonic philosopher, on the other hand, must start with his own reason, his own self and his thoughts about the world. Thus, in contrast with the Christian, the Platonist may appear egocentric. Yet this is not because of any inherent selfishness in his character or in his philosophy, but because as a starting point he has no alternative point but the self. Our judgment of the agape qualities of Platonic eros and the eros qualities of biblical Christianity must not be warped by the difficulties (from the Christian point of view) with which Plato began, but be determined by the kind of love he eventually pointed to, whether seen in men or in God. Then we can consider in what significant sense his thought is egocentric.

Let us then look for nonegocentric features in Plato's account of eros. We shall have to consider briefly the Platonic lover in the

Phaedrus and *Symposium*, but before doing so let us clarify our terms. Plato distinguishes, as we must learn to distinguish, self-love from selfishness. He holds self-love to be a legitimate care for one's own soul, for what is divine in oneself; selfishness on the other hand is a vicious greed to be condemned outright. "In truth the cause of all sins is in an excessive love of oneself" (*Laws* 731E). This excess leads to false judgments, false values and ignorant arrogance. Following Plato, therefore, we shall from now on name it "selfishness," keeping the term "self-love" for what Plato regards as a reasoned valuation of one's own self and the laudable desire of improving it.[22] In the passage from the *Laws* Plato goes on to explain that selfishness prevents us from recognizing the good unless we possess it. The truly self-loving man, we shall understand, will both be concerned for his own welfare and be able to recognize, to admire, and to follow the good wherever it is to be found. He must respect anyone who is good but yet *outside himself*, as well as whatever good he himself possesses, and must let no sense of shame hinder him from doing so.[23]

From a consideration of this passage from the *Laws* then we should expect that the Platonic lover both values and desires the Good for himself and values and respects it for itself wherever it is to be found. Bearing this in mind we can consider the *Symposium*. Where in this dialogue is there an eros which is not only concerned with the self? Primarily in the notion that eros involves a desire to "beget and give birth in the beautiful" (107C–212A). Eros leads to an outflowing of the self. But there is a possible objection. In the *Symposium*, it would run, all such "outflowing" is the result of a purely selfish drive to achieve immortality. Consideration of this objection must be deferred for a short space, but let us make one preliminary observation. For Plato man at his highest, man when he sees the forms of Beauty and Goodness, lives a life like that of the gods. But how can the gods desire immortality, for in Greek eyes immortality is their distinguishing mark? Yet the gods, comes back the objector, do not desire. Plato specifically says that they are not "lovers of wisdom" (philosophers), for they already possess wisdom (203E); and if they possess wisdom they no longer desire it. Yet although the gods do not have eros in the sense of acquisitive desire, they appear to act in exactly the same way as the philosophic lovers, for they will be seen to beget in the beautiful. But to consider that we must wait until we reach the *Timaeus*.[24]

Before leaving the *Symposium*, however, we should make a further point. After Socrates has recounted what he has learned from

Diotima about the true nature of eros, Alcibiades bursts in upon the assembled company and insists on giving a speech in praise of Socrates himself. It seems that the purpose of this speech is to depict Socrates as the ideal lover. And what does Alcibiades' account make clear? Not that Socrates is always striving, but that he is a man who displays true virtue; that he is, in fact, creative of beauty through his vision of the beautiful; that his life is a life of love, but not of mere selfish desire in however sublimated a form.[25]

Let us now turn to the *Phaedrus*. Here again we find in the myth that the souls of men resemble those of the gods, but that they are fallen and must return to their fatherland where they will join the train of their kindred divinities. All envy is excluded from the life of the gods (247A) and Zeus "arranges all and cares for all" (246E). How does this affect the loving soul? Each soul is the follower of one or other of the gods (252C). In accordance with this affiliation it chooses an object for its love and "fashions and adorns him like a statue, as though he were a God, to honor and worship him." Love of the forms, of Beauty in particular, once again leads the lover to an overflowing act of goodness. He does not merely "desire" his love-object; he worships him and cares for him. He both reveres him and finds him the sole cure for his greatest troubles (252AB). In short, he is like the gods in that he exhibits no envy (253B) towards his beloved and no meanness, but seeks to make his beloved godlike. There is here a noble blend of the desiring and the self-giving aspects of eros.[26]

We have seen that the soul of the lover, like the souls of the gods, has no envy. Should we assume from this that the gods too have love and show love for what is below them? There are a number of isolated passages in the dialogues which seem to suggest that Plato (or Socrates) had a notion of a nonappetitive down-flowing love of God or the gods for men. These passages may be explained away as metaphorical, or as not in fact concerned with love at all, or as concessions to popular speech and thought, but they deserve a brief mention. In the *Apology* Socrates is made to speak of God's care for the Athenians (31A); in the *Republic* the gods are the source of what is good in the world, but not of what is evil (378C, 380C, 617E); in the *Laws* God in the days of Kronos was a lover of man (713D).[27] But let us disregard these small and vague pieces of evidence and turn to the *Timaeus*. Here we find Plato's myth of the production of an ordered cosmos by the Demiurge. Why does the Demiurge act as he does? For Plato it is because he is good (29E) and has no envy—the theme of the *Phaedrus* once again.

Since he is good, says Plato, he wants all things to be as like himself as possible. In other words to be good means, even in God's case, to do good, to want to do good. And here there is no possibility that this desire to do good is a mere striving for immortality, for the Demiurge is immortal. The fact is that the Demiurge is good, and being good he acts in the way the perfect lover acts. The lover works on his beloved like a statue, to adorn him; the Demiurge works on the world to make it good. Is it not apparent that Plato regards the highest form of love as the equivalent of perfect and creative goodness? The Demiurge in his actions is the prototype of the true lover. Socrates, in the *Symposium*, seems to have modelled himself after him.[28]

It is not possible in the present essay to give details of further "unselfish" features of eros in later writers of antiquity, but a very few indications may be of value. Let us quote two passages from Plutarch's almost forgotten dialogue *Amatorius:* "By means of Eros the goddess (Aphrodite) takes away the satiety of pleasure and produces friendship and fusion" (756E).[29]

"But in the case of lawful wives intercourse is the beginning of friendship, a kind of sharing in great mysteries. Pleasure is short, but the respect and kindness and mutual affection (agapesis) and loyalty that spring from it every day show that the Delphians are far from mad when they call Aphrodite 'Harmony' " (769A).

We cannot linger over Plutarch, but at least a few words should be said about Plotinus and later Neoplatonism. The most important factor to be discussed is the development of what Nygren calls the "Alexandrian world-system." In brief, Plotinus explains the procession of all (including matter) from the One as well as the return of the soul to its source. The first principle, the One, has several names: one of them is "Eros" and "Eros for itself" (6.8.15.1). It is a being infinite in itself and of infinite power; it has some kind of knowledge different from that of other beings; it has its unique kind of will (6.8.21).[30] But what of its eros? This is not appetitive, nor upward seeking, for the One is the king of the universe, is superior to all and lacks nothing. As I have written elsewhere: "The One's love of itself, with its contemplation of itself, must be the cause of the other hypostases. Thus, although the One's Eros is directed neither upwards nor downwards it is the cause of a movement directed downwards, though admittedly indirectly so." [31] And what of the eros in the human soul? It is the aim of all men to return to the One their father. Men must therefore become eros, as Plotinus puts it (6.7.22.10).[32] This eros is not only desire. We

have desire to attain the mystical union, but the eros persists in the
union itself, as the soul comes to share the One's life and as all
appetitiveness disappears.[33]

Even in the ascent of the soul mere grasping is not enough. There
is a most beautiful passage in *Ennead* 5.5.8 where Plotinus tells us that
when in our ascent we have come to the level of the pure forms and
have recognized intellectual beauty we must wait in patience. All
action is taken out of our hands; we are somehow dependent on the
One to bring us to union, not by any new act of salvation, for the One
is always with us (6.9.8.33–35), but because all striving and all self-
seeking must be stilled. The text runs as follows: "We must not pursue
it, but we must wait quietly until it appears, now that we have
prepared ourselves to see it, just as the eye awaits the rising of the
sun." [34]

A few more points should be made before leaving Plotinus. The
first is that for all his great emphasis on the relation of the individual
soul with the One—the alone with the Alone (6.9.11.51 etc.)—we
should not be misled into supposing that lack of concern for others was
any part of his ideal. It is true that such concern does not show itself in
some of the more obvious ways—Plotinus finds the tragedies of earthly
life unimportant—but in his teaching, for he was above all a teacher.
One of his basic anxieties, however, was that in our zeal to help and
respect other people we might come to neglect the value of our own
souls. We are valuable as souls, he urges, and ultimately it is we who
must help ourselves along the road to the One. The most important
acts of any man's life can be performed only by himself. Hence
Plotinus can write: "Since you can respect the soul in another, respect
yourself" (5.1.2.50–51).

Secondly, there is the problem of whether the Plotinian soul, in
union with the One, loses its personality since the One is impersonal. I
have argued against interpreting the One as an impersonal Absolute [35]
elsewhere, and it is possible here to add one text only to that discussion.
Comparing human love with our love for the gods and ultimately for
the One, Plotinus writes in 2.9.16: "The man who loves (philein)
anything is affectionate also to the kin of his beloved. He who loves
(*agapei*) the father loves the children."

Finally we should observe an aspect of the soul which is often
neglected by those who interpret Plotinus. At 6.7.31.17 we read that
the soul loves the One, moved by it to love from the beginning. For
Plotinus the soul is the product of the One, not temporally but in the

metaphysical order. It is made as it is, and given its powers, by the One. These powers include the power of eros. Here the fact that Plotinus derives the whole cosmos and everything in it from the One enables his concept of eros to be an advance on Plato's. The soul's power to love is given, along with its existence, by the One itself. And in the act of loving that power is actualized by the direct inspiration of the One. In a very real sense our eros is caused by God's nature.

There is no need to spend long on nonacquisitive features of eros in Proclus, for Nygren himself admits them to some extent.[36] He is baffled by these features and has to suggest the influence of Christianity. There is no evidence for that; indeed Proclus was hostile to Christianity.[37] The agape features are more naturally explained as a development of certain characteristics already present in the preceding Platonic tradition.[38] And with that we may leave ancient Platonism— having noticed a number of those features which do not fit into Nygren's schema—and pass on to the original texts of Christian agape.

There is little doubt that the word agape, though not the cognate verb, is rare, if not unknown, in pre-Christian times.[39] In itself that means little, for in the Christian view all alternative words had obvious disadvantages. Eros had commonly a sexual association which for a time at least rendered it unsatisfactory to Christians. What matters is not why agape might be used, but what it in fact means when it is used. Has it any eros features? According to Nygren agape is first and foremost God's love and its unique character in the New Testament is that it is freely bestowed, regardless of men's deserts. Nygren quotes the saying "I came not to call the righteous, but sinners" (Mark 2:17); and claims that this turns Jewish values upside down.[40] Yet it is hard to see how this means disregard of the righteous. Clearly in Jesus' view they needed less help than the others. "They that are whole have no need of a physician, but they that are sick" (Mark 2:17).

Nygren thinks he finds confirmation of his view in the parables. Let us consider a few passages. In his interpretation of the Parable of the Prodigal Son, Nygren concentrates on the rewards bestowed on the returning prodigal and forgets the father's words to the son who had remained at home. These are as follows: "My child, you are always with me, and all my goods are yours" (Luke 15:31). The meaning is clear. All that the father can give is already given to the obedient son. And he who has all should not grudge anything to any man, particularly to the man who repents. Heaven rejoices over the return of a sinner (Luke 15:7); but there is no question of the just not receiving their reward. "They shall shine forth like the sun in their Father's kingdom" (Matt. 13:43).

A similar neglect of detail can be seen in Nygren's treatment of the Parable of the Laborers in the Vineyard (Mark 20:1–16).[41] Nygren notices that those who have worked for only one hour receive the same as those who have toiled all day. He comments that in a human framework this seems unfair, but that it indicates that within a religious framework the merits of the laborers are not taken into account. But the point of the story is the same as that of the Prodigal Son. He who comes to work, even at a late hour, receives, in God's eyes, the fullest benefits of His love. Yet even the man who works one hour has done some work. He is paid for his work; those who do no work are not paid at all! "Take away the talent from him and give it to the man who has ten talents. . . . Cast the unprofitable servant into the outer darkness" (Matt. 25:28–30).

Nygren tries to defend his neglect of the notion of man's working with God (2 Cor. 6:1; 1 Cor. 3:9) by the theory that the original agape deposit was weakened and corrupted even within the New Testament. Naturally he has nothing to say about the Epistle of James—the epistle of straw—but he finds that even in John, the apostle who formulates the position "God is Agape" (1 John 4:8), corruption has set in: one especial vice has appeared, namely that agape has become "particularization."[42] The love of the Christian community is to be admired as being directed to its own members (John 13:35). According to Nygren "love in John is limited to the narrower circle of the 'brethren.'" It is extraordinary, however, that he is worried by such passages, for it seems natural and right that the Christians should have loved one another and should have recognized the value they had each attained by their faith. Paul at least urges them to recognize themselves as in some sense a class apart (2 Cor. 6:14).

It is primarily in the Synoptics and in Paul that Nygren claims to find that God's agape is all-important, while man's response is no act of his own but simply a reflection of God's love. Citing Luther with approval, Nygren remarks that "In relation to God and his neighbor the Christian can be likened to a tube, which by faith is open upwards, and by love downwards."[43] Christian agape, in Nygren's view, must be like God's agape, always directed downwards.[44] But men, even if originally made in God's image, are not God; and it would seem natural that God's love would seek to raise them and enable them to raise themselves. Hence we may take the question of self-love as a test case. What Pauline or Synoptic authority has it? Is Nygren scriptural to regard it as unchristian?

Nygren's starting point is Luther's dictum, based on John 12:25 (and perhaps Luke 14:26), that to love is to hate oneself.[45] Let us consider these contexts briefly. In Luke we are told that unless a man hate his father and mother and brothers and sisters and even his own *psyche* he cannot be a disciple. The emphasis here would certainly suggest that the most valuable thing any man possesses is his own psyche. It is implied that it is harder to give this up than all the rest. In man, therefore, concern for others is assumed to be secondary to concern for one's own psyche. Unfortunately, we cannot be too precise about this passage because the meaning of "psyche" ("life" or "soul") is not certain. Let us turn to John. There also, however, the ambiguous "psyche" occurs.

What does this "hating one's *psyche*" mean? The most natural explanation is in terms of, for example, Matthew 10:39: "He who has found his *psyche* ["soul"?] will lose it and he who has lost it for my sake will find it." All worldly values, therefore, are to be counted as nothing when compared with the religious call. It is hard to say that "hating one's *psyche*" means that one should literally hate oneself (*cf.* Eph. 5:29), because, if our interpretation is correct, this would also involve our hating our father and mother and brothers and sisters—and neither Luther nor Nygren would call such hatred the mark of Christianity. In fact "hating one's *psyche*" is probably to be interpreted as the denial of oneself, the giving up of one's earthly concerns that Jesus calls for in Luke 9:23.

The crux of our problem lies in the confrontation of two texts: "Thou shalt love thy neighbour as thyself" (Matt. 22:39) and "Love seeketh not its own" (1 Cor. 13:5). There is no doubt that the second great commandment enjoins love of one's neighbor—there is no question of hating one's neighbor here; the problem is the meaning of "as thyself." The obvious interpretation is that we should love our neighbors in the same way as we love ourselves. Thus we shall love both ourselves and our neighbors equally, because both we and they are children of God. Taking the commandment in this sense we can compare it with the passages about "hating one's *psyche*." In those passages we see that the hardest thing of all to hate is our own psyche; in other words, that in our natural life we put ourselves first. When therefore he makes use of the second great commandment, Jesus takes this fact of natural life as his starting point and commands us to love our neighbor in exactly the same way. A further implication of this, of course, is that we should love our neighbor in the way in which we hope that God (and our neighbors) will love us (Matt. 7:12).

Such an obvious interpretation will not suit Nygren.[46] His view is that the words mean that we must love our neighbor as we *have been* in the habit of loving ourselves. In other words love of neighbor must replace love of self. But there is no evidence in the New Testament that Jesus meant this. In countless passages he implies that although we must love our neighbor we must still hope for heaven. Even John, in the crucial 12:25, writes: "He who hates his *psyche in this world* will guard it for eternal life." Texts like "He who has lost his *psyche* will find it" imply that we ultimately wish to save our psyche, and that we are right to do so. Matthew 6:1 is good evidence here: "Take care not to act justly before men with a view to being seen by them. If you do not obey, you do not gain your reward from your Father in heaven." Hope of Heaven, fear of Hell cannot be left out of the New Testament. And Heaven and Hell are fates laid up for the self.[47] "Be ye perfect, as your Father in Heaven is perfect" (Matt. 5:48).

What then of "Love seeketh not its own"? There is no difficulty in seeing that this passage is in accordance with the interpretation of self-love that we have outlined. In 1 Corinthians Paul is attacking excessive selfishness—which Plato had attacked in the *Laws*. But Plato's condemnation of selfishness did not prevent him from hoping to perfect the self. There is no reason why it should have prevented Paul either. Armstrong has succinctly summarized this conclusion as follows: "I do not quite know where the idea that Christian love is non-eudaimonistic came from—certainly not from the Gospels." [48]

What presumably worries Nygren is that man may be able to contribute to his own justification. But unless man is to be reduced to a creature deprived of any power of choice or free will, a mere puppet, he must be able to contribute to his own salvation in some way. There is no question of man's cooperation with God (2 Cor. 6:1) [49] not itself being a gift from God. As Streiker says: "A man can no more be saved by his own efforts than he can be born by his own efforts." God's initiative and grace are required. But unless man is to be a puppet, he must be free to accept or to reject what is offered. Even if we accept Nygren's language, the language which says that man must simply reflect God's agape, we must admit that only a puppet could reflect without *deciding* to do so.[50] And this decision is some kind of "cooperation," and indeed the cooperation of which Paul speaks and to which

Jesus doubtless refers when he pronounces moral and religious directives like "Love thy neighbor."

As far as concerns the idea that all ultimately comes from God, the
difference between the New Testament and the thought of, for example, Plotinus, is, we can now see, much narrower than Nygren would
have us suppose. In Plotinus everything, even our eros, derives from
the One and is caused by the One; in the New Testament the faith that
justifies is entirely God's gift, as is the life of those to whom it is given.
But both in the *Enneads* and in the New Testament men can reject the
possibility of salvation by a misguided or perverse act of the will.[51]

Nygren says explicitly [52] that "love *in loco iustificationis* cannot be
anything but Eros, or man's way to God." It is not love of God, but
faith which justifies. Yet here again it seems that schematization is what
causes the trouble. Nygren seems to hold that the problem can only be
expressed as *sola fides* versus *fides caritate formata*. What he neglects is
the possibility that we are not concerned with how faith *arises* in a man
but with the fact that it is *indicated* by man's love while still being
caused by God's love for man. If faith can in this sense be *represented*
by agape, then Nygren is released from pressure to misread various
Pauline ideas.[53] Let us observe the following three passages of
Nygren: [54] A] "It has long been observed by commentators how
rarely Paul speaks of Agape in the sense of man's love to God or to
Christ"; B] "It cannot be a mere accident that Paul thus leaves the
term Agape on one side when he is speaking of man's attitude to God";
C] "In point of fact Paul was found to drop the idea of man's Agape
towards God." It is clear that despite the call to "Love the Lord thy
God" reaffirmed by Jesus at Mark 12:30 Nygren is uncomfortable
about man's agape for God. Under the impulsion of his curious separation of agape from faith he would like to speak of God's love of man's
faith, but in fact, as Streiker has observed,[55] Paul is prepared to use
agape of man's love for God on a number of occasions which must not
be forgotten (Rom. 8:28; 1 Cor. 2:9; 8:3; Eph. 6:24).

What Nygren has done to the New Testament, as this very
limited examination has indicated in part, is to select those passages
which might suit the theory that agape and eros are inhabitants of
different worlds and then dragoon other passages into harmony. The
situation in fact is that just as ancient Platonism recognizes that both
the agape and the eros motifs are present in love, so they are also both
recognized in the New Testament. Certainly the New Testament
emphasizes what Nygren calls agape while Plato emphasizes eros, but

the appearance of both motifs in both traditions indicates an agreement between the two that love can only be understood in terms of some kind of balance and relation between them. That Nygren's agape and eros are not *kinds* of love but *aspects* of love has, as we have already observed, been the major point of attack on Nygren's thesis in the writings of Tillich, D'Arcy, and others. And now we see that both the New Testament and the Platonic tradition are in agreement with the psychological theories of Nygren's critics. D'Arcy remarks that "Nygren cuts the knot and sunders love and grace, nature and the supernatural completely. This does not make a peace between the two but only a solitude in which Agape withers." [56]

Much more could be said, but now that we have a clearer notion of Greek eros and biblical agape we can more usefully glance again at contemporary analyses and criticisms of Nygren's position. If Nygren were correct, then Tillich's view that "Love cannot be described as the union of the strange but as the reunion of the estranged" [57] must be wholly irrelevant to Christianity. Tillich holds that by God's grace there is something similar between God and man, that man in fact is an image of God. Nygren apparently rejects this view. Only by God's agape can man do anything; and this means that agape transforms man, at least superficially, from being wholly unlike God to some kind of likeness. Nygren probably would object to this way of putting it, and say that fellowship is by God's descent to man. Yet this cannot mean that God descends to man's moral and religious level, for who would accuse God of becoming a sinner in order to obtain fellowship with man? The Christian view must rather be that God lived a human life in order to help man, to give man the power, to return to Him.

We are back therefore to the question of eudaimonism, to the problem of self-love. And here again we can challenge Nygren that self-love is not only biblical but also demanded by many modern psychological thinkers. According to Erich Fromm,[58] love of self (not selfishness) and love of others are not alternatives. Rather, all those who are capable of loving others will be found to love themselves. We may conveniently close with a quotation from *The Art of Loving:* "If an individual is able to love productively, he loves himself too" (for he "actualizes and concentrates his power to love"); "if he can love only others, he cannot love at all."

9

AMOR IN ST. AUGUSTINE

John Burnaby

I<small>N</small> Nygren's historical study [1] of the "transformations" through
which the idea of love has passed from the New Testament to
Luther, Augustine has a pivotal position, as the creator of that "synthesis" of the motifs of agape and eros which was dominant throughout
the Middle Ages. Augustine's originality lies, not in his understanding
of Christian love as *amor Dei*, the desire for God, but in his ability to
combine this inherited understanding in terms of the eros motif with a
theology rooted in the New Testament doctrine of agape as the act and
essential nature of God. In Nygren's own account of this doctrine, [2]
agape is the pure outflow of divine goodness, "uncaused" or unmotivated" by anything in the character of its human recipients. Its meaning is classically stated in St. Paul's words (Rom. 5:8) "God commend-
eth his love towards us in that while we were yet sinners, Christ died
for us," and in St. John's (1 John 4:10) "Herein is love, not that we
loved God, but that he loved us, and sent his son to be the propitiation
for our sins." The message of the Gospel is that this divine love offers
men fellowship with their Creator, not as a reward for obedience or
amendment of life, nor as the ultimate goal of human efforts to achieve
holiness, but *as they are*, sinners to whom God himself has come down
in forgiveness.

Nygren allows that Augustine, "more than any of the Fathers of
the early Church, has given a central place to Christian love in the

sense of Agape." He finds it unnecessary to do more than refer briefly to the characteristic Augustinian doctrines of Grace and Predestination, in which the agape motif is most evidently at work. Grace is wholly "prevenient," wholly unmerited. It is bestowed on sinners, who have been chosen, as Paul says of Israel's ancestor in Romans 9:11 f. "being not yet born, neither having done any good or evil, that the purpose of God according to election might stand, not of works but of him that calleth." Nygren also acknowledges that the descent of agape in the Incarnation "formed the permanent centre of Augustine's Christian thought"; and that in speaking of God's love he could distinguish it as pure benevolence from the "needy" and unsatisfied love of eros.[3] But this profound understanding of God's love for men has made no alteration in his experience and preaching of love towards God in the Platonist sense of "heavenly Eros." The love of God with the whole heart, soul, and mind enjoined in the First Great Commandment of the Gospel regularly takes for Augustine the form of *desiderium*—the unsatisfied longing for himself which God has implanted in the soul which he has made.

Nygren is aware that Augustine found no difficulty in presenting the divine agape as at once the source and the satisfaction of the human eros. Apart from the Gospel of grace, Augustine sees that the soul's attempt to ascend to God by virtue of its own nature and in its own strength is an act of presumption; and that this fatal *superbia* dooms the attempt to failure. Eros can only reach its goal by humbling itself to accept the grace of "God's humility" in the Incarnation. But Nygren maintains that this, which he calls the Augustinian "synthesis," in spite of its apparent "solidity and coherence," is vitiated by "real inner contradictions": that the true relation between agape and eros is an either-or, and that Augustine's both-and is impossible to carry through.[4]

The contradictions involved are indicated by Nygren in the course of his long and thorough analysis of the central Augustinian concept of *caritas*. *Caritas* in Augustine is of course his Latin equivalent of the New Testament agape. But in the *caritas Dei* which is poured out in our hearts by the Holy Spirit which is given to us (Rom. 5:5), he understands not God's love for us but our love for him: the distinction between agape and eros has disappeared. Nygren accordingly begins his discussion of the *caritas* concept with the unqualified assertion that *all* love in Augustine's view is "acquisitive"—the pursuit of a thing desired for the advantage of the self; and he connects this with the axiom, which Augustine takes as common ground between Christian and pagan, that "all men desire to be happy." [5] In the *Confessions* (x.20) Augustine actually identifies his search for God with the search for happiness (*beata vita*); and Nygren has shown most convincingly [6] that the structure of the *Confessions*, and especially the relation of the last three books to the whole, is only intelligible in the light of Augustine's fundamental metaphysic of creation. The Creator alone in his changeless eternity has the fullness of Being which is also the fullness of Goodness. Man, created "out of nothing" and living in time, is poised between Being and Non-Being, between Goodness and its absence, and is subject to change in either direction: he must continually strive to "be" — continually seek the perfection and security of his own insecure and imperfect being. So Augustine begins the story of his own search with the confession "Thou has made us to be to thee-wards (*fecisti nos ad te*), and our hearts are restless till they find rest in thee." It is therefore perfectly appropriate that having told how the quest led him into the faith of the Church, he should end with a meditation upon the Genesis story of creation and its end in the Sabbath rest of God — the rest in which all men are called to share. Thus, because God only is "self-sufficient," not "needing" his creation, while man is wholly dependent upon his Creator, the love which urges man to seek the satisfaction of his own need is the basic fact of his created nature. "Acquisitive desire" is the mark of the creature; but only when it is rightly directed can it reach its goal.[7] Fallen man seeks to possess himself and the corruptible goods of earth: the same unsatisfied desire which should have fastened him in *caritas* upon God is perverted in *cupiditas* to the things that can never satisfy it. *Caritas* and *cupiditas* differ only in their direction, upwards and downwards, and in their object, the eternal and the temporal; their nature, the pursuit of a good for the self, real or fancied, is the same.[8]

At this point, Nygren pauses to observe that in this psychology of desire — a desire centered in the self and its advantages — there is no place for the agape of the New Testament. Christian love has of necessity been the "losing partner" in the attempted alliance with ethical eudaemonism, simply because "ancient thought has been allowed to put the question": viz. How can man find happiness? What is the *Summum Bonum*, the ultimate good to which all his effort should be directed? [9] God, for man, is the Supreme Good. But God has made all the things he has created good in their degree. What then is the relation of *caritas* to all the lesser goods in which *cupiditas* vainly seeks satisfaction? Augustine's answer to this question is to distinguish a love which "uses" from the love which "enjoys" (*uti* from *frui*). The lesser goods of God's creation have been made "for the use of man": God alone is to be "enjoyed"—he alone is to be loved "for his own sake," as the final end of all man's striving, and not as a means to anything else. The error of *cupiditas* is to seek enjoyment in what ought only to be used. Augustine thus finds sanction for a "relative" love of created things, which can and should be made the means of our ascent to God: our love of them is justified if it is "referred" to God. But he combines his *uti/frui* scheme with the rather different idea of an ordered scale of values in the created world, to which an "ordered love" should properly correspond: it is this scale of values which *caritas* must recognize and observe. If this principle of *ordinata dilectio* be taken as seriously as it is meant, it is not easy to agree with Nygren when he suggests that Augustine's final word is that "if we really loved God as we ought, we should not love anything at all in the world." [10] Nygren argues however that by treating *caritas* as a means to the enjoyment of God, Augustine not only makes *all* love, even the love of God, relative, but ought logically to admit that love, being *ex hypothesi* the desire of attainment, must cease when the *fruitio Dei* is attained; though in fact he frequently speaks of the vision of God as of necessity evoking an increase in the love to which it has been granted. [11] Nygren reaches a similar conclusion in his examination of the Augustinian doctrine of Grace and its relation to *caritas*. The heart of the anti-Pelagian polemic is that the love of God, the love that fulfils the law, must be God-given. For *Deus est caritas*, and we cannot have *Deum sine Deo:* only God can give himself to us. The divine act of grace is in fact that "infusion of love," which is no more "magical" in Augustine than it is in Paul (Rom. 5:5). As Nygren puts it, the love of God revealed in Christ's incarnation "draws us into the magnetic field of the eternal world." [12] Yet he will not allow that this doctrine of grace is more than in appearance a proclamation of God's "uncaused" agape. For the descent of divine grace in Christ is not "unmotivated": its ultimate purpose is the ascent of *caritas* to God, for which it supplies the means by touching the heart with that delight in God and his righteousness (*delectatio justitiae*), which is stronger than all the attractions of the temporal world. And this is to contaminate with a "teleological motivation" the purity, the incomprehensible miracle, of the divine agape. The theocentric antimoralism of Augustine's defense of Grace against Pelagius remains unreconciled with the frank eudaemonism of eros, in which "our gaze is turned unwaveringly upon our self and what can satisfy its needs." Or in Lutheran terms, the *theologia humilitatis* is no more than a means for advancing to a *theologia gloriae*.[13]

Whether this is a fair criticism or not, there can be no doubt that Augustine's treatment of the love of self (*amor sui*) offers at least superficially the most obvious example of the "contradictions" which Nygren detects in his doctrine of love. The central theme of Augustine's most famous work is that "Two cities have been fashioned by two loves: the heavenly City by the love of God extending to contempt of self, the earthly City by the love of self extending to the contempt of God." "Man's primal perdition was the love of self." [14] The cause of the fall of angels and men was their refusal to find their *bonum*, the satisfaction of their desires, in God, and their attempt to be self-sufficient, masters of their own existence. For that is to put self in the place of God: it is the pride which is the primal sin and which is inevitably punished by the subjection of spirit to flesh, the *cupiditas* which is the natural master's shameful obedience to the natural servant. Nygren notes that Augustine specifically rejects the belief (which marks the eros motif) that evil has its source in the flesh. "It is not the corruptible flesh that has made the soul to be sinful, but the sinful soul that has made the flesh to be corruptible. . . . Not by having flesh, which the devil has not, but by living according to himself . . . has man become like the devil" (*De Civ.* xiv.3).

On the other hand, it is (as Nygren says) one of Augustine's favorite ideas that self-love and the love of God must *truly* coincide. For all self-love must seek what is good for the self, and it can only be through self-deception if that good is sought elsewhere than in God. Augustine can even slip into saying that the purpose of the commandment to love God is that we may learn true love of ourselves. The clearest of many statements is that in the *De Trinitate* (xiv.18) — which only echoes the early *De Moribus Ecclesiae* (48): "The man who knows how to love himself, loves God; while the man who does not love God, though he retains the love of self which belongs to his nature, may yet properly be said to hate himself, when he does what is contrary to his own good. . . . It is indeed a fearful delusion, by which, though all men desire their own advantage, so many do what only works their ruin." When Augustine recalls this false self-love, he points the apparent paradox: "In a manner that is inexplicable, whosoever loves himself and not God, does not love himself; and whosoever loves God and not himself, loves himself." Not in the least inexplicable! comments Nygren, if *all* love is acquisitive and therefore egocentric whether its object be God or the self. Man is so made that he cannot help loving himself: self-love is innocent in its *nature*, sin only when it leads in the wrong direction.[15] The various senses which Nygren enumerates as those in which Augustine uses the phrase *amor sui* can more simply be reduced to three; 1] the morally neutral desire for one's own good, for self-fulfilment, 2] the sinful desire to find one's good in oneself and the things of this world (*cupiditas*), 3] the true love of self "in God."

Both the love of self and the love for God can thus be understood by Augustine in the sense of eros. Nygren correctly observes that it is not so easy to apply the Eros motif either to the love of neighbor or to God's own love for sinful men. The love of neighbor was too prominent a theme in the New Testament and in the Christian tradition for Augustine to ignore it. But he could only find a place for it in his eros-dominated scheme of thought by reducing it to the love of God. We are to love both neighbor and enemy, not for what they are in themselves, but for their potential worth—even as Christ loves us for what we may become through him, sons of God. So it is God in our neighbor that we really love; and true self-love is the pattern and measure of true love to neighbor: to love him as ourselves is to desire that he should find his good, where we ourselves find it, in God. And the self-regarding motive is unblushingly stated when love of neighbor is made a "stepping-stone" to the love of God. "We show mercy on one another, that we may attain to the enjoyment of him." [16] Finally, in regard to God's love, however constantly and powerfully Augustine may proclaim the manifestation of that love in Election, Incarnation, and the Cross in terms of agape, it remains the case that this idea of the divine love will not fit into his dominant pattern of thinking. Having applied the scheme of "use" and "enjoyment" to his account of human love, in which God as the Supreme Good is the final object of all love, he assumes (almost without stopping to think) that God's love for us must be either a love of enjoyment—but how can the God who "needs" nothing find his good in any of his creatures?—or a love of use, in which case we can only suppose that God's love "refers" his gifts to men to his own goodness, and so to our advantage, not to his. Even God's love for sinful men is "not so unmotivated and inexplicable as it might appear." He loves us in order to restore his own image in us; "in the last resort it is nothing but himself in us that he loves." And the text of St. John's Epistle—"God is *caritas*"—is taken in the *De Trinitate* to support the representation of God's eternal being on the analogy of self-love: the Holy Spirit as *caritas* is the bond of love in which Father and Son are joined.[17]

The purpose of the foregoing pages has been to summarize as objectively as possible the account which Nygren has given of St. Augustine's doctrine of Christian love. In turning now to a criticism of this account, we are not concerned with the question whether Nygren's own statement of the meaning of agape is either sufficiently true to the New Testament as a whole or theologically satisfactory. We confine ourselves to considering how far he has done justice to St. Augustine: how far, that is to say, by approaching Augustine's work with ready-made definitions of the motifs of agape and eros, he may have condemned himself in advance to failure in understanding the doctrine he is to examine.[18]

"Agape and Eros," in Nygren's words, "are the symbols of two completely opposite attitudes to life, two utterly different religious and ethical types. They represent two streams which run through the whole history of religion, the egocentric and the theocentric outlook." [19] If agape is the essential activity of God the Creator, while eros is the activity which arises from the created nature of man, the activity of agape is of course theocentric in the sense that God is its subject, while the activity of eros is egocentric in the sense that man, the human ego, is its subject. But it is not immediately apparent that "one and the same attitude to life" cannot believe at the same time in the agape of God and in the eros of man. That Augustine did believe in both is quite certain; but Nygren insists that he had no right to do so. He should have chosen the one or the other: he should have seen that if the fellowship with God offered in the Christian Gospel is exclusively the work of divine agape, eros is not only futile but dangerous inasmuch as it encourages confidence in the efforts of the self to attain what only God can give. Augustine would answer that if God wills to give man fellowship with himself, that fellowship must be good for man, and the desire for it can hardly be a bad thing. There is no necessary connection between such desire and the presumptuous belief in man's power to get what he desires by his own efforts.

Augustine's *caritas — amor Dei* is plainly an egocentric desire in the sense that the subject of the desire is the desiring self. It is not plainly egocentric in the sense of being concerned with self, selfish in the ordinary meaning of the word; for while selfishness *is* irreconcilable with agape, hunger and thirst after righteousness are not. There is nothing necessarily un-Christian in an "acquisitive" love: Jesus counsels us to lay up treasures in heaven, Paul to seek the things that are above. But that *all* love is "acquisitive" is no more true for Augustine than it is for the New Testament. It is obviously untrue for Augustine's thought of the divine love; and (as we shall see) it is untrue for his thought of the human love of neighbor.

In what sense is it true for his thought of *amor Dei?* 1] We must not be misled by his occasional use of the language of "possession." In the early discussion of *caritas* in the thirty-fifth and thirty-sixth articles of *De Diversis Quaestionibus* LXXXIII, from which Nygren quotes the general statement that love is *appetitus quidam,* "a kind of impulse," Augustine says that the eternal object of spiritual pursuit or desire is possessed only by being known, and quotes "This is life eternal, to know thee." But he goes on to say that while both the eternal God and the soul can be the objects of love, "the true and supreme interest of the soul is served when God is loved more than the soul, so that a man *would rather belong to God than to himself.*" 2] It is no less important not to be misled by Augustine's identification of the search for God with the search for happiness. The English word "happiness" denotes a state of feeling: the concept of *eudaimonia* in ancient ethics denoted the fulfilment of the purpose of human existence —a fulfilment which one and only one school held to consist in a pleasant feeling-state. When Augustine takes over the axiom that all men desire to be happy (*beati*), the word itself could not fail to recall to him Christ's own promise of "happiness" in the Beatitudes. But for the Neoplatonist, *beata vita* is more than a subjective condition of the human soul. In Plotinus, *eudaimonia* is an objective reality; and it was natural for Augustine to think of *beata vita*, the blessed life, as nothing less than the life of God himself—the eternal life in which the Christian soul is encouraged to hope for participation.[20] 3] *Caritas Dei*, however, is more than the desire for *beata vita:* it is the willing acceptance of the order of creation, the law of the universe which is the will of God. In that universal order, man is set between God and the lower creation over which he has been given a dominion—a dominion which depends on his own submission to God's supreme sovereignty; and the moral order itself, embodied in the commandments of God, is the expression of the *lex aeterna* by which man's life is to be governed. The love of God cannot be separated from the love of God's eternal law. "The pride" (so writes Augustine in *De Moribus Ecclesiae* I. 12:21) "by which man refuses obedience to God's laws, desiring to be as God

in his own power, can only take him further away from that likeness
to God which is realized through submission to him: the love by which
he returns to God is a love that seeks not to be matched with God but
to be subject to him."

All this needs to be borne in mind if we are properly to appreciate
the significance of the term *fruitio Dei* in Augustine's use of it. Because
God *is* both *beata vita* and *lex aeterna*, the participation in the joy of
the divine being is at the same time an embrace of the divine order, an
obedience to the divine law. It is self-surrender to the destiny for
which the goodness of God has created man. Ragnar Holte, in the
book to which reference has been made,[21] entitles his central chapter
"L'Amour de Dieu, don de la vie humaine sous tous ses rapports"—thus
indicating his dissatisfaction with any account of Augustine's doctrine
of the love of God which presents it as the "acquisitive" desire of an
egocentric happiness. Holte's argument is worth noticing. He insists
that it is anachronistic to ascribe to Augustine the notion of an undif-
ferentiated "desire," applicable to this or that object, like the libido of
popularized modern psychology which can be "sublimated" from the
sensual to the spiritual. In fact, Augustine's psychology of love is
governed by the Stoic theory of natural impulses (*hormai*) and the
Platonic theory of "parts" of the soul, to each of which belongs its
own functional virtue. The *appetitus*, the universal movement towards
being, order, and unity which maintains all creatures in existence, takes
in the human soul the form of "a dynamism unifying the soul, yet
differentiated, expressing itself in different ways in the different parts
of the soul." Augustine, in the thirty-fifth article of the *De Diversis
Quaestionibus* LXXXIII, above referred to, grounds upon the existence
of this differentiated *appetitus* in the several parts of the soul the
possibility of a love of God with all the mind, all the heart, and all the
soul. For the "mind" is the contemplative faculty which alone has God
for its immediate object; the "heart" is the "lower reason" which
directs the active life in relation both to the self and to the neighbor;
the "soul" (*anima*) which is common to all living things is the seat of
the animal instincts of self-preservation and propagation. When the
movements of heart and soul are both subject in peace and harmony to
the higher activity of the mind, they become part of the love of God
which is the self-giving of the whole man.[22]

It must be admitted that the texts upon which Holte relies for this
interpretation of the Augustinian *amor Dei* as "don total de la vie" are
few in comparison with those which justify Nygren in his claim that
the identity of "true" self-love with the love of God is a favorite theme

in Augustine. Familiar as he was with the Stoic account of the self-re-garding impulses as an essential part of human nature, Augustine un-derstood the command to love the neighbor as the self as implying sanction and not condemnation of the natural instinct—a sanction reflected in Paul's saying that "no man hateth his own flesh." When he speaks of *amor sui* as the enemy of *amor Dei*, he usually makes it clear that this self-love is a different thing from the natural instincts. In the sketch of the theme of the *City of God* which he gives in the "Commentary on Genesis," the contrast between the two loves which make the two cities is that "the one is social, the other private; the one looking to the common advantage for a supernal fellowship, the other seeking to bring what belongs to the community into its own power for the sake of an arrogant domination." [23] The contrast is depicted in the same way in the famous passage at the end of Book XIV of the *De Civitate*: "The earthly city is dominated by the lust for domination in its kings or in the nations which it overpowers: in the heavenly city, men serve one another in love." Again: "In the fellowship of the free city's eternal peace there is no love of personal and private will, but the obedience of charity, rejoicing in the common and changeless good, making one heart out of many." [24] The Pauline "charity seeketh not her own," which Nygren finds Augustine unable to accept, quoting one text where he adds the gloss "in this present life," is actually expounded in the passage quoted from *De Genesi* xi in the sense of "has no delight in personal superiority (*excellentia*)"; and in a letter to insubordinate monks the same meaning is given to it: "charity sets the common before the private possession, not the private before the common." [25] Nygren takes little account of what is a constant element in Augustine's doctrine of God: that he who is the *Summum Bonum* is also the *bonum commune*, that the supreme good of every man is the common good of all, and therefore can never be possessed as a *bonum privatum*. There can be no such thing as an egocentric enjoyment of God: the sharing in his blessedness cannot be separated from the sharing in the goodness which is his universally extended agape. When this is understood, it should be impossible to maintain that Augustine *subordinates* both love of God and love of neighbor to the love of self, making obedience to the two great commandments no more than a means to the satisfaction of a desire centered in the self. What Augus-tine frankly and thankfully recognizes is that God's goodness has so ordered his creation that the life which gives itself in love to God and neighbor is not and never can be a life lost. "When you love him, you will be where your being is secure (*ibi eris, ubi non peris*)." [26]

It remains to examine more closely the contention that there is "in principle no place in Augustine's scheme of love for the love of neighbor," which he therefore has to treat as a special instance, whether of self-love or of love to God.[27] There is no "unmotivated" love of neighbor. It is either elicited by the presence, actual or potential, of God *in* the neighbor, or is an act which God requires of us in order that we may ourselves attain to the enjoyment of him. Nygren could hardly have presented Augustine's doctrine of *caritas* in the crudely individualistic form which has been imposed upon it by the premise that *all* love is acquisitive desire for the advantage of the self, if he had paid attention to the place which *caritas* occupies in Augustine's doctrine of the Church. In his isolation of the agape motif in the first part of his work, on the basis of the New Testament, he had been obliged to admit that the purity of the motif is "watered down" in the Johannine writings, where Christian love is primarily love of the brethren. He should have admitted that love of the brethren is sufficiently prominent a feature in the ethical teaching of Paul, for whom agape is the bond of unity in the Body of Christ; and it is this Pauline teaching which Augustine develops.[28] The dominant theme of all Augustine's preaching against Donatism is that the very life of the Church is *caritas unitatis*. The Church is not simply an association of individuals united by a common love of God. The Church's unity like the unity of a family is established and preserved by the mutual love of its members; and all schism has its origin in the hatred of brethren. Nygren quotes the Homily on John xiii.34, where Augustine compares Christ's love for his own to the love of a doctor for his patients, a "motivated" love whose object is not the sick as sick, but their health. So Christ has loved us that God may be in us; and we should love one another to the same end. But the preacher continues: "That love is Christ's gift, who by his love for us enables us to be so bound to one another in mutual love that we become the Body of which he is the Head, his members linked together in that lovely bondage." For Augustine as for St. John, the unity of Christians is the image of the divine unity: "that they all may be one, as thou, Father, art in me and I in thee, that they also may be one in us." [29] But this unity can be realized in no other way than by the *mutua dilectio*, the love of Christians for one another, which is the working of the Holy Spirit, God in us. It is not easy to imagine that what Augustine is doing in his impassioned Homilies on the *Epistle of St. John* is no more than exhorting his hearers to cherish an enlightened love of self.

We must take him seriously when he tells us that if we are to know God as he is,

> the first thing for us to learn is the nature of true love—or rather the nature of love; for only that love which is true deserves the name. All other is covetousness (*cupiditas*): it is a misuse of language when the covetous are said to love, as it is when those who love are said to covet (*cupere*). What true love requires of us is a life of righteousness in union with the truth; and this means that nothing in this world should have any weight for us beside the love of men which is the will that they may live righteously.[30]

Nygren would probably dismiss this apparent denial of the identification of love with acquisitive desire, by taking *cupere* as no more than the verbal form of *cupiditas*. He would certainly claim that when the love of men is defined as the will that they may live righteously, love is being "motivated" by a potential value in its object. Yet we have still to ask what exactly Augustine means here by "righteousness."

In the second of his two essays in *Augustin und Luther* [31] Nygren sharply distinguishes between the senses in which these two can speak of the Christian man as *simul justus, simul peccator*. For Augustine, what is meant is that "justification" is a process never perfected in this life, because the struggle between flesh and spirit, between the false and the true loves, is unending: the Christian man as long as he lives needs God's forgiveness for the failure of *caritas* to be always victorious in the fight with *cupiditas*. For Luther, justification is total from the beginning; yet the justified sinner does not cease to be *totaliter peccator*: his most saintly acts considered in themselves are sins. "He must ask for forgiveness, not for a surviving remnant of sin: he must surrender himself wholly as a sinner in God's sight, if Christ is to become his righteousness. In Christ we are wholly justified, that is, wholly pleasing to God." [32] The conflict stems, needless to say, from divergent interpretations of the Pauline words *dikaioun* and *dikaiosis*. No doubt Luther who understands justification as acceptance by God, is nearer to St. Paul than Augustine who takes it to mean "making righteous." In Nygren's account, we are to see here the inescapable clash of eros and agape, the confrontation of "two religious standpoints which differ in principle—that of Catholicism in which fellowship with God is won by our uplifting with the support of divine grace to the level of God's holiness, and that of the Reformation, where fellowship with God comes to pass through God's bringing of himself down in his grace to the level of our humanity and sin." [33] It is plain, however, that the difference is not only, perhaps not chiefly, a difference in regard to the way in which fellowship with God becomes possible for men, but a difference in the meanings attached to that fellowship (Gottesgemeinschaft) itself. For Luther (as expounded by Nygren) fellowship with God is constituted by the fact of God's good will to men in Christ: men's part is limited to faith, trust in the Gospel assurance of that good will. For Augustine and the Catholic tradition, fellowship with God is a communion in which man has been brought through Christ into realization of sonship to the Father, *by conformity of his will to the divine will.* So long as and wherever self-will opposes itself to the will of God, communion with God must be imperfect. For sin *is* separation from God. If *simul justus simul peccator* means that justification is assurance of a fellowship with God which cannot be broken or even touched by sin, we can be sure that Augustine would have found in the paradox not only a dangerous presumption but a monstrous impossibility. For it is impossible that sin should not "grieve the Holy Spirit" who has been given to us; and it is through the Spirit, who is the communion of the Father and the Son, that we are to be "brought together into one," "to have communion with one another and with the Father and the Son." [34] In this communion Augustine finds that "fruition of God" which is for him inseparable from the "fruition of one another in God." So the sin which divides man from man must of necessity deny to men the fullness of that fruition.

The writer of this essay, as will have been seen, cannot but regard Dr. Nygren's treatment of Augustine's doctrine of Christian love as in many respects mistaken. But that does not lessen his admiration for the author of *Agape and Eros,* of his gratitude to him. In a phrase of St. Augustine's, the adversary's questioning has been for him the occasion of learning.

10

CARITAS IN AUGUSTINE
AND MEDIEVAL THEOLOGY

Rudolf Johannesson

THE history of the Christian idea of love is understood, according to Nygren, only if we bear in mind the fact that two disparate views of love, the agape of the New Testament and the Hellenistic eros, contribute to its making.

Nygren describes eros as the central motif of the Hellenistic theory of salvation. Eros is desire, egocentric love, for which man occupies a dominant position as both starting point and goal. The starting point is human need, the goal is the satisfaction of this need. Eros is the homesickness of the soul, its longing for what can give it true satisfaction, at once the mark of its nobility and a symptom of its present humiliation, a testimony both to its belonging to a higher world and to its painful lack in its present situation of what by nature it needs.

Agape has nothing to do with desire and longing, it "seeketh not its own," does not ascend, like eros, to secure advantages for itself, but consists in sacrifice and self-giving. Agape, unlike eros, is not primarily love of man but love of God, a love revealed at its deepest in the Cross of Christ, in His sacrifice of himself for sinners.

In the early church, Nygren points out, the two motifs exist side by side with little inner connection between them.[1] A real synthesis of eros and agape is not realized before Augustine, whose doctrine of *caritas* represents "the classic union of the Christian Agape motif and the Neoplatonic Eros motif, which was decisive for posterity."[2]

The Middle Ages experienced the inner difficulties of the synthesis of the disparate conceptions of love and indirectly prepared for its dissolution. This came through the Reformation and the Renaissance.

> The Renascence brings a renewal of the old Eros motif, in the Reformation the Agape motif breaks powerfully through and the two motifs fall apart. But in spite of the fact that the problem of "Eros and Agape" was solved in principle by the breakdown of the *caritas*-synthesis, this latter continued after the Reformation to be, practically speaking, the dominant idea of love.[3]

In the following discussion we shall study Nygren's analysis of the structure of the *caritas* synthesis in Augustine and his description of how this synthesis is adopted and revised in the theology of the Middle Ages.

An analysis of the view of *caritas* in Augustine must, according to Nygren, start from the assumption, which was fundamental for him, that all love is acquisitive love.[4] To love means to desire an object that will bring happiness. "The idea of love as desire and its connection with the search for happiness betray Augustine's original Eros-attitude and the eudaemonism of the philosophy of late Antiquity."[5] Desire, acquisitive love, is the foundation of all human life. Man's whole life exhausts itself in a ceaseless pursuit of advantages. But in the world there is nothing that is valuable enough to bring about total satisfaction of human desire. Only the highest good (summum bonum), God himself, is capable of bringing it to rest (*quies*). The desire for happiness is typical of human existence. It shows that man is a created being who derives his existence (esse) and value (bonum) not from himself but must receive them from God. "Desire is the mark of the creature."[6]

When man seeks his happiness not in God but in this world, he is dominated by a misdirected desire, a false love, cupiditas or amor mundi, that has taken the place of true love, *caritas* or amor Dei. That cupiditas is a false love is clear from the fact that man does not attain what he seeks, his happiness, the pursuit of which he must continue unrequited. Man is so created that his desire for happiness can be satisfied only by the infinite value of God himself, the summum bonum. "Thou has made us for Thyself and our heart is restless till it finds rest in Thee." (Conf. I:1)

Nygren points out that Augustine, by thinking of Christian love as a form of "acquisitive love" and interpreting it to mean that we seek our own "bonum" in God, obviously has abandoned its theocentric character. "Even though God is described as the *highest* good, this does not alter the fact that He is degraded to the level of a means for the satisfaction of human desire."[7] Nygren characterizes Augustine's *caritas* theory as a continuation of the endless discussion of the ancient philosophy about what is the highest good.[8] His *question* is primarily a link in this discussion, but his *answer* gives expression to Christian thought. So

> Augustine has tried to bring about a fusion of very heterogenous elements in his doctrine of Caritas, a fusion of ancient eudaemonism with Christian love, of the desire of Eros with the devotion of Agape. The meaning of this synthesis is, in brief: *The Christian Commandment of love gives the final answer to the question of ancient philosophy about the highest good.* In this union the Christian idea of love is the losing partner, and that is simply because ancient thought is allowed to put the question.[9]

Nygren's distinction between eros and agape is an ingenious idea which sheds light upon the conception of love not only in Augustine but in all Christian theology. Yet one must raise the question whether Nygren has not overlooked some nuances in the two love motifs. By devoting attention to these it may be possible to carry Nygren's line of thought further. In what follows I shall make an attempt in that direction.

What Nygren signifies as eros is not in my opinion a uniform conception, but includes at least two very different varieties. One of these appears in a rather pure form in Plato, the other in Aristotle.

The platonic eros has a feature of devotion and self-forgetfulness, directed as it is to the good beyond man, the world of ideas. The idea is not a means to anything else. Its value does not depend upon its causing delight or any other effect in the soul of man. Plato thinks, it is true, that the soul benefits by directing itself to ideas, but he never lets the value of the idea rest upon this fact. For it is the nature of the idea to represent a value in itself. The idea is valuable for man not because it is a means for his happiness but because it has an intrinsic value.

Surely all eros, even according to Plato, arises from desire and appetence, from the endeavor to obtain what one lacks—for which reason gods do not love. But this does not imply that the satisfaction of human need is the goal, and the direction to ideas the means. Man's inadequacy consists in his being far from the world of ideas. Because he has not reached his goal he must be striving and longing for it. But it is not decided that his goal must have an egoistic or egocentric note. For, interpreting such words as "desire," "longing," "striving," one must pay regard to the context in which they appear. In a context concerned with man's direction towards values beyond himself, these words have senses different from those which they have in a context concerned with values that are thought to exist, psychologically or ontologically, in man's own essence.

A context of the latter kind we find in Aristotle. In his metaphysics he denies the transcendency of ideas and accordingly in his ethics he denies the transcendency of the highest value: It is a basic principle of Aristotelian ethics that the good for every being consists in the perfection of its own essence. Thus man's striving is not directed in a goal beyond himself but in his own existence and perfection. Man seeks to transfer all the potentialities of his essence into actuality. Every being strives to exist and to exist in as high a state of perfection as possible.

Now it is characteristic of man that he is endowed with reason. The perfection of reason therefore is the highest good for man.[10] When man desires a thing existing beyond himself it is because this thing makes a contribution to his perfection by translating his potentialities into reality. A man who feels cold draws nearer to the fire, because the fire has a power to make available to him the warmth which his body lacks. Values existing beyond the evaluator, "subject-transcendent" values, will thus be used as means of attaining values existing in the subject's own essence, "subject-immanent" values.

The final values, consequently, are subject-immanent. Man's direction to these values, his eros, as it is expressed in Aristotle, is marked by self-assertion and self-perfection. It differs thereby from the Platonic eros, which was principally directed to subject-transcendent values and therefore was marked by devotion and self-forgetfulness.

This difference between Platonic and Aristotelian eros is, in my opinion, decisive. In comparison with that the difference that Nygren points out in his treatment of the eros motif in Aristotle seems to be of less importance. Nygren says that in Aristotle the idea of eros acquires cosmic significance. "In Plato, Eros is the soul's striving after the object of its desire . . . in Aristotle this conception is given a wider reference and applied, in so far as it can be applied, even to the physical world." [11] All things, not only man's soul, are engaged in a cosmic eros movement. But this thought does not give a new significance to the inner structure of eros itself.

The distinction between a Platonic and an Aristotelian variety of the eros motif can help to clarify the structure of the idea of *caritas* in Augustine.

Augustine's opinion that acquisitive love is the basic form of human life may mean nothing else than that man's love is directed to values. Now are these values, according to Augustine, subject-transcendent or subject-immanent? The important part that happiness (felicitas, beatitudo) plays in Augustine's thinking seems to point to the latter alternative. But here one must pay regard to the connection of thoughts in which the word happiness appears. This word may merely denote that the striving for values has not reached its goal, and it is not decided that this goal is subject-immanent, i.e., that it consists of the psychological or ontological well-being of the subject. "Happiness" may rather generally denote the state which prevails when man has *attained* his values, even the subject-transcendent ones. And now Augustine stresses that the highest good, the final goal for man's striving, is in fact, subject-transcendent, God Himself.

It is true that man's love does not have God as its *only* object but that it has him as its only *ultimate* object. This is what is suggested by Augustine's well-known distinction between two sorts of love, *Frui* and *Uti*. Man may love good things in the world, but only with *Uti*-love, i.e. as a means of attaining the highest good. *Frui*-love, the love of something for its own sake must be directed only to God.

Nygren admits that this line of thought in Augustine's theology has an apparent theocentric note. "The idea of Fruitio Dei is an expression of the strongly theocentric tendency which marks Augustine's thought. It has the important task of preventing God from being made into a means to some other end. God must be loved for His own sake, as an end in Himself, a terminus beyond which we do not seek to pass." [12]

But other thoughts, according to Nygren, frustrate the theocentric tendency. One of these is as follows. Augustine says that blessedness consists not in living—i.e., in desiring and longing for the highest good—but in *possessing* it.

> But blessedness does not consist in Caritas directed to God, but in the "Fruitio Dei" to which Caritas is to bring us. But that means that Caritas is made relative and ranked as means—inevitably, since all love, as Augustine thinks, is desire. We possess blessedness "non amando, sed fruendo," says Augustine. [13]

Nygren sums up the result as follows: "The idea of 'Frui' was intended to guarantee the absolute meaning of love to God, but in fact it makes its relativity all the clearer." [14]

Caritas, according to Nygren's interpretation, has only an interim

significance for man, namely, for as long as he lives in this world, far
from his desired goal, separated from his bonum. In the eternal life
there will be no room for love, because man has reached his goal and
possesses his bonum, for which reason he no longer needs to seek it.

It seems to me, however, that the coherence of Augustine's line of
thought will be better understood, if one observes the double sense of
the word *Frui* (*Fruitio*) as used by Augustine. First: *Frui* signifies
man's seeking an object for its own sake, i.e. a thing of absolute value,
as a goal, not only of relative value, as an instrument. Second: *Frui*
signifies that the object intended is actually attained, no longer merely
sought or longed for. Now it is obvious that *Frui always* has the first
sense and that the second sense is only additional. When man attains,
and thereby ceases to seek, a thing of only relative value, Augustine
cannot use the word *frui*. But Augustine sometimes lets this word
designate that man is not only directed towards the highest good but
has also reached it. This, in my opinion, explains sufficiently well why,
as Nygren points out, Augustine, on the one hand, can contrast *frui*
with *amare* and say that we possess blessedness "non amando sed
fruendo," yet, on the other hand, vindicates the opposite idea that love
must increase when at length we meet God face to face.[15] To love is,
according to Augustine, often synonymous with to evaluate – and of
course one evaluates even things which one possesses. Accordingly
Augustine states that in the eternal life, where we come finally to
possess God as our summum bonum, we shall also love him all the
more.[16]

We shall now continue to explicate Nygren's investigation of the
question as to whether Augustine's line of thought is essentially theocentric or egocentric. Nygren's answer is twofold: "1] . . . from the
point of view of the *object*, Augustine's view of love is markedly
theocentric, in so far as no other object may compete with *God* for
our love; 2] with regard to the *nature* of the love, his view is just as
markedly *egocentric*, for even in God I seek *my own* bonum." [17]

Nygren bases his answer upon an ingenious investigation about the
relation between amor Dei and amor sui, love of God and love of self.
To begin with he points out that this problem seems to be one of the
most intricate in Augustine's theology, because here we are faced with
apparent contradictions.

> It is not difficult to find statements which put the two kinds of
> love *in absolute opposition to* one another: amor Dei is the root
> and source of all good, amor sui the essence of sin and the root of

all evil. On the other hand, the thought very frequently occurs, that *love of God and self-love harmonize* in the best possible way.[18]

The line of thought according to which amor Dei and amor sui are opposites we find again in Augustine's view of the dualism of the two realms, the kingdom of God and that of the world. Amor Dei is dominant in the civitas Dei, as amor sui in the civitas terrena.

In the civitas Dei God is "all in all." Inasmuch as he is the "omnium substantiarum auctor et conditor," so must the happiness of every creature depend upon unbroken connection with Him.

The kingdom of the world begins with the fall, first of angels, then of man. They turn away from God into themselves and instead of receiving all from him they live as if they possessed their bonum in themselves. This self-sufficiency of the creature is the principle of amor sui.

According to this line of thought in Augustine, amor Dei and amor sui are in sharp opposition. But there is another line of thought according to which they harmonize in the best possible way. It is, Nygren says, one of Augustine's favorite ideas that self-love and love of God should be entirely reconciled. It follows completely, Nygren continues, that even love of God should be a kind of amor sui, because for Augustine all love is acquisitive love.

> By amor Dei or Caritas, I serve my own best interests; for that love is set upon God, the "highest good," which I thus gain *for myself*. So if I do not love God, it only shows that I do not *rightly* love myself. Amor Dei and amor sui are so much one thing that they grow and decline with one another. The more I love God, the more I love myself too.[19]

Augustine himself, says Nygren, discovers a certain tension between the two lines of thought. He maintains both and sees in their coexistence an inescapable paradox. "For in some *inexplicable* way, it is a fact that he who loves himself and not God, does not love himself; and whoever loves God and not himself, does love himself." [20]

By his analysis Nygren shows that the question is neither so paradoxical nor so inexplicable as Augustine imagines. The difficulty arises because the term "amor sui" is used in two different senses, to indicate the *nature* and to indicate the *object* of love.

> As regards the nature of love, Augustine never doubts that all love is acquisitive love. The whole meaning and content of love is just this that it seeks *its own bonum*. In this widest sense, all

love is amor sui. And "amor sui" so conceived, need naturally not conflict with "amor Dei" as defined by Augustine; or rather they *cannot* conflict, for the simple reason that they have no common denominator, and are not on the same level. "Amore sui" speaks of the nature, "amor Dei" of the object of love. "Amor sui" simply means that love desires its bonum, and so in the nature of the case it finds its fulfillment only when it seeks as its object that which is by nature the highest good, summum bonum.[21]

It is very different when "amor sui" indicates the *object* of love. "Then 'amor sui' and 'amor Dei' are on the same level and are absolutely opposed to each other. There are two rival objects of love. If we seek our bonum in the one, we cannot seek it in the other." [22]

At this point I shall try to bring the discussion a little further by confronting Nygren's analysis with my distinction between subject-transcendent and subject-immanent values, between a Platonic and an Aristotelian view of evaluation.

To begin with, it may seem as if this distinction had bearing upon only the *object* of love and concerned love of similar *nature*, directed to different objects. Even when man directs his love to a subject-transcendent value, love would retain its nature of self-love. But as we have earlier pointed out, desire and appetite need not lend an egocentric note to love. What desire and appetite signify depends upon the context. In Augustine they may denote that the things that are objects of desire and appetite are lost for man, but that they continue nevertheless to bear some relation to him. They are far from him, but they do not cease to appear as values for him and he seeks to regain them. Whether this relation, which exists between man and his values, has an egocentric note or not is not decided.

The same may be said about other terms to which Nygren refers as expressions of the egocentric nature of love in Augustine, e.g. that man seeks his own bonum. The word "his" indicates some sort of relation between man and object, but not necessarily an egocentric one. Whether or not that is the case depends again upon the context. The principle, for example, that every one has to do *his* duty, is obviously not made egocentric by the word "his." In the same way one cannot quite simply read egocentricity in the principle that man seeks *his* own bonum. That man seeks his own bonum may, in Augustinian contexts, mean that man seeks the object of value that is specifically related to him. And it is characteristic for man as a created being that his highest value-object lies not in but beyond himself. In this sense God is man's bonum.

We now come to the question: Is this love of the subject-transcendent or of the subject-immanent type? Thus, is love directed to a component of the essence of man or to an object beyond himself? Is love a form of self-assertion and self-perfection or of devotion and self-forgetfulness?

Augustine stresses that the final object of love must be God. Thus all perfect love is love of God, amor Dei. But in this love of God man also promotes his own existence and perfection. Real self-love, amor sui, therefore is essentially identical with love of God, amor Dei. This fact is comprehensible from the ontological situation of man: his existence is not self-sufficient but depends upon his own origin as a stream upon its own source, cut off from which it dries up and ceases to exist. This ontological fact is psychologically reflected by the structure of human love in so far as man's love must finally be directed not to man himself but to God.

So far there is also a strong emphasis on the subject-transcendent character of evaluation and love in Augustine. But it happens, at least in connection with apologetics, that a subject-immanent trait comes to the fore. It may sometimes seem as if the perfection and happiness of the human subject were the final goal, and love of God only a wisely chosen means to attain this goal. It is sure that Augustine would not approve this view, because, as he always stresses God alone, not man himself, must be the ultimate object of love. But his own statements about the paradoxical connection between amor sui and amor Dei show that this view is not really entirely alien to him.

The result of our investigation will be that Augustine's solution of the problem of the relation between love and love of God may be regarded as a synthesis, in fact a fairly perfect one, of subject-transcendent and subject-immanent evaluation. God is to be loved as the final goal, absolutely, with the love of *frui*, man himself intermediately and relatively, with the love of *uti*. In this synthesis the subject-transcendent component is usually predominant, love as devotion dominates over love as self-assertion. "It is best," Augustine says, "if one totally forgets oneself in love for the Eternal one." [23] On the other hand, this statement shows that Augustine cannot be fully satisfied with his own synthesis.

No doubt with good reason, Nygren regards *caritas* as a synthesis of two components, eros and agape. In my own opinion, however, it will be possible to understand the Augustinian view more clearly if one observes that the first component, eros, already represents a synthesis between two kinds of love, the eros of devotion and the eros of self-assertion, or between subject-transcendent and subject-immanent evaluation. Obviously the former kind of eros has greater affinity to agape than the latter one. Therefore, some traits of *caritas* that Nygren considers as manifestations of agape, may in reality proceed from the eros of devotion. For example, where Augustine regards amor sui as the symmetrical opposite of amor Dei, Nygren sees a trace of the idea of agape. And when amor sui is accepted and preserved, though in a refined and sublimated form, he discovers the influence of eros.[24] To me it seems more natural here to trace the reconciliation of eros in the devotive sense and eros in the self-assertive sense. The banishing of amor sui shows the devotive eros at work, and with the replacement of this amor as a form of *uti*-love the eros of self-assertion comes into its own.

We now come to Nygren's view of the place of the agape motif in Augustine's idea of *caritas*.

The agape motif predominates in the Augustinian theology of grace.[25]

> Grace (gratia) is a key-word-of Augustine's interpretation of Christianity. Everything in our life depends ultimately on God's grace. This is true of the natural as of the Christian life. We have nothing of ourselves, all of God. . . . By God's grace we have been brought into existence, by God's grace we have been justified.[26]

> Augustine may say that by faith and good works we are to merit eternal life as a reward, but he means in no way to detract from Divine grace. Even faith is a gift of God's grace, and if by it we "merit" eternal life, that simply means that we receive "grace for grace." The good works are not really our own but God's, which he works in us by His grace. Above all, the Incarnation is the great evidence of God's grace and love. "If God did not love sinners, He would not have come down from Heaven to earth." (In Ev. Jn., tract, xlix.5.) No rational ground for this grace of God can be found. Grace is the positive expression of God's will; we cannot give it a motif by referring it to anything else.[27]

The proclamation of God's gratia would seem to be the most unreserved proclamation of God's spontaneous and "unmotivated" love. But, according to Nygren, it is not so.

> If God had not condescended to us in his *gratia*, we could never have ascended to Him in *Caritas*. This is what makes grace so extraordinarily important in Augustine, but also limits it. With-

out grace, there is no access to God . . . . Grace "prevents" our
every deed—but as the means precedes the end. *The end is and
remains the ascent of Caritas to God.* This brings us back to
Eros.[28]

Augustine's way of salvation follows, according to Nygren, the scheme
of ascent. Grace has simply been introduced as the indispensable means
of this ascent.

Nygren finds a similar dualism also in other parts of Augustine's
theological views. This combination of gratia and *caritas*, God's descent and our ascent, Nygren considers as a synthesis between the
primitive Christian and the Hellenistic idea of salvation, between agape
and eros. Although essential aspects of Augustine's theology of grace
and predestination were directly rejected by the medieval Church, his
view has set its seal upon the Roman Catholic type of piety, namely as
regards the conception of Christian love.[29]

The eros motif, according to Nygren, had its influence upon
thought in the Middle Ages, not only through Augustine, whose idea
of *caritas* inherited something of this motif, even though considerably
altered. It reached the Middle Ages also unaltered, as evident in writings of Pseudo-Dionysius, which in the course of time acquired considerable importance, and in which Christianity is literally absorbed in
Neoplatonic eros theory.[30] We have no occasion here to trace this line
of thought. We shall rather try to interpret Nygren's conception of
the medieval theology of *caritas*.

Nygren begins with the statement that *caritas* is not merely one
element in Christianity, but the whole of it. In principle there is
nothing that falls outside the sphere of *caritas*. "Medieval Christianity
as a whole is Caritas-religion and Caritas-ethics." [31]

The most moving and influential expression for the medieval conception of Christianity Nygren finds in Dante's *Divina Commedia*.

> Through the whole poem from beginning to end there runs like
> a golden thread the idea of God as love, "the eternal love," "the
> first love," the primal ground of love. It is *Divine love* which has
> created hell from all eternity, which has made possible the prog-
> ress of purification of souls in purgatory, which sets everything
> in the world in motion, and which is the goal of our desire and
> our enjoyment forever in Heaven. Love is the root of all virtues,
> and it is for lack of love we have to atone in purgatory.[32]

The question what kind of love Dante displays is, according to
Nygren, best answered by Dante himself, then questioned (Paradiso

xxvi) by the apostle John as to the nature of love. The answer is as follows:

> It is of the nature of the good always to kindle love and to draw love to itself. The greater the "goodness" is, the greater the love that is awakened by it. Consequently God, who comprises in Himself all reality and all "goodness" so that every other good that exists is merely a reflection of His "goodness," must exercise a greater power of attraction than all else. In theory, human insight alone should bring us to love God, the highest and absolute Good, but in real life this love only comes into being by the help of Divine grace. In this description of love the Augustinian Caritas-synthesis is easily recognized, though the Eros trait in it has been strengthened by the incorporation of the Aristotelian-Dionysian idea of love as the bond of union in the universe, and the idea of God as the ultimate principle of motion. Unquestionably, the most essential traits in this view of love are borrowed from the realm of the Eros motif; but there is also an important element of Agape present, inasmuch that love is regarded as a gift of Divine grace.[33]

Medieval theology, according to Nygren, is not content merely with taking over the Augustinian doctrine of *caritas*. It also brings it further. This theology goes beyond Augustine above all in its discussion of the problem of unselfish love.[34] It felt the inner difficulties of the *caritas* synthesis inherited, and it honestly tried to overcome them. "As a matter of fact, it went as far with the problem as was possible from the starting point Augustine had prescribed. It refined the doctrine of *caritas*, but by doing so made its inner impossibility all the more patent. Thus in a certain way it played into the hands of the Reformation." [35]

The possibility of a pure and unselfish love of God became a burning question for medieval theology. Whether and in what way self-love could co-exist with *caritas* was for it an important problem. This problem is also seriously dealt with by the greatest of the medieval theologians, Thomas Aquinas.

Thomas, Nygren says, starts from the same point and goes a good deal of the way with Augustine. For Thomas also, all love is fundamentally acquisitive. "The reason why we love God at all is that we need Him as our bonum; indeed Thomas does not hesitate to say: 'Assuming what is impossible, that God were not man's bonum, then there would be no reason for man to love Him.' " [36] Thomas's basic idea is summarized by Nygren in two sentences: "1] Everything in Christianity can be traced back to love, and 2] everything in love can be traced back to self-love." [37]

The difficulty of uniting this basic view of love with Christian love, which "seeketh not its own," Thomas tries to overcome by introducing a distinction between acquisitive love, amor concupiscentiae, and the love of friendship, amor amicitiae. This distinction breaks the unity of Thomas's doctrine of love. It is strange, Nygren says, that Thomas immediately after maintaining all love to be acquisitive, gives a new definition of love, based on Aristotle: amare est velle alicui bonum. From this, Nygren continues, it is clear that Thomas felt the tension between the eros motif, on which his thought as a whole is based, and Christian agape–love.[38]

In order fully to understand the structure of Thomas doctrine of love, it seems to me appropriate, as it was concerning the Augustinian doctrine, to introduce the distinction between subject-immanence and subject-transcendence. In Thomas's doctrine of love, are the values to which love is directed of subject-immanent or subject-transcendent character? Do they consist in the existence and perfection of the loving person himself, or in something beyond the subject?

The question is not difficult to answer. The main line of thought in Thomas is obviously of a subject-immanent, Aristotelian character. It is a basic principle for Thomas that every being first of all tries to preserve and complete his own essence.[39] This view is displayed with reference to the Aristotelian metaphysics of potentiality and actuality. The work of each being is to bring its own potentiae into actuality. This self-perfection may often be won by turning to something existing outside the subject, a subject-transcendent value. But the final objective remains the perfection of his own being, the actualizing of his own potentiae. Man may, for example, acquire knowledge by turning to someone who possesses knowledge. For a potentia is actualized not by itself but by some extraneous factor which has an equivalent in actuality.[40] Thus the potentia to warmth of water may be actualized by the influence of fire which holds warmth in actu. This means that subject-transcendent values are sought only as means to subject-immanent perfection.[41]

Thomas therefore insists that man's love is directed to "bonum suum." In Thomistic contexts, "suum" must connote a subject-immanent relation. "Suum bonum" represents a bonum that exists or may exist in the loving subject himself. Man therefore loves only those outer goods, by the influence of which his own potentiae will be actualized. It is completely in line with this thought that Thomas should define amare as *velle alicui bonum*. He insists always that love goes in two directions, namely to the good one desires, and to the person for whom one desires this good.[42] The first is amor concupiscentiae, the latter amor amicitiae.[43] These are consequently not two different forms of love but two tendencies in one and the same act of love.

According to Thomistic-Aristotelian principles, the person to whom one desires the good primarily is oneself. Even in the area of religion man's desire is directed to the existence and perfection of himself.

Thomas maintains however that man's love really can be directed to a person other than the loving person himself. He stresses that human love can be "ecstatic" in the sense that the loving person can strive for something beyond himself and "wish and realize the good totally for the benefit of his friend." [44] This "ecstatic" love has according to Thomas three main directions: 1] to God, 2] to society and 3] to other individuals.

The problem now arises as to how it is possible for Thomas to combine the idea of ecstatic love with the basic principle that man's love is directed always to his own good, suum bonum. In the present space I can do no more than make a few suggestions concerning the solution of this problem.[45]

1] The first kind of love, love of God, Thomas declares as natural by referring to the thought of analogy. God has as Creator, as Causa prima, a relation to effects distinct from causae secundae. A causa secunda can only actualize potentialities that already exist, but Causa prima gives birth to the potentialities themselves. Man therefore by nature loves God more than himself and must, if necessary, be willing to sacrifice his own existence and perfection in order to conserve those of God. Thereby man only renounces the actuality of his perfection while the corresponding potentiality also would disappear with the abolition of its own causa prima.

2] The second kind of love, the love of an individual for the community of which he is a member, Thomas explains by referring to the relation between the part and the whole. Man as a social being (animal sociale) has his existence in society, as the part exists in the whole. A hand severed from the body is no longer a really existing hand. The condition for the existence of the part is the existence of the whole. Therefore the part, e.g. the hand as member of the body, is willing to sacrifice its own existence in order to save the existence of the whole and consequently exposes itself to a blow that otherwise would have brought death to the body. In the same manner man by nature loves his community more than himself.

3] The third kind of love is love of friendship in the more specific sense. That man can love another person whose existence is not a condition for his own, depends, according to Thomas, upon the unitas by which everyone is joined with his neighbor. And because everything loves itself it must also love that with which it is united in to some kind of unitas.[46] Now man is however united in the highest degree of unitas with himself, thus into an *unio substantialis* and not only into an *unio similtudinis* as with other men. Therefore his love is directed primarily towards his own person. He must not love anyone more than himself but prefer his own existence and perfection to those of his neighbors.[47]

The suggestions given above make it clear that in Thomas just as in Augustine the eros component in *caritas* is not a simple motif but a synthesis of two different forms of eros, the self-assertive and the devotive. But while in Augustine the devotive, Platonic eros dominates, the view of Thomas is determined primarily by the self-assertive Aristotelian eros. This fact forms, in my opinion, the main difference between Augustine and Thomas concerning their view of *caritas*, to which fact Nygren has drawn insufficient attention.

Although Nygren regards the eros component in the *caritas* synthesis as a motif on the whole homogeneous, he overlooks some important aspects of the problem of *caritas*.

A further proof of the propriety of my analysis of the eros motif can be derived from the history of *l'amour désintéressé* in Roman theology. The tension between the Aristotelian, subject-immanent and the Platonic subject-transcendent evaluation, between self-assertive and devotive eros, appears already very clearly in the contrast between the view of *caritas* in Thomas Aquinas and in Johannes Duns Scotus.[48] And it is quite obvious that the champions of the real amour désintéressé (e.g. François de Sales and especially Fénelon) postulate the Platonic-Augustinian devotive eros, while their opponents take their arguments from the Aristotelian-Thomistic idea of eros as primarily self-assertion and self-perfection. It would probably be unreasonable to suppose that the difference in question depends upon degree of stress upon the agape motif in the *caritas* synthesis. Nygren, however, has not discussed this question in his writings and we therefore have no reason here to examine it more closely.

Nygren, with his account of the idea of love in Christian thought culminating in the description of the *caritas* synthesis, has made one of the most important contributions to modern theology. It is my conviction that many authors would have been more successful in their work on the history of Christian ideas if they had paid more attention to the investigations of Nygren. That Anders Nygren's results do not form a static and finished whole, but that they are open both to completion and to revision, is in my opinion evidence of the exceptional fruitfulness of his thoughts.

II

AGAPE IN LUTHER

Ernst Kinder

Iɴ Anders Nygren's examination of the Christian idea of love in his now classic work *Agape and Eros*[1] the chapter on Luther is the climax and also the conclusion.[2] Nygren shows here how in Luther the motif of Agape, the basic motif of Christianity,[3] comes in its full purity to an overmastering victory[4] that is to be seen elsewhere only in Paul.[5] In the early church the motif of agape was to some extent overlaid by the Jewish motif of nomos,[6] but its fiercest conflict was with the Hellenistic motif of eros, whose fascination came widely to predominate over it and led to its consequent distortion.[7] The whole of medieval piety and theology was characterized by this synthesis of the agape and eros motifs,[8] the pattern of which was laid down in Augustine's concept of *caritas*."[9] Luther completely shattered this synthesis. Feeling himself to be "the herald of theocentric religion in its struggle against everything that can be called egocentric,"[10] he set up in opposition to "the egocentric attitude which had characterized the Catholic conception of love a thoroughly theocentric idea of love."[11]

It is not our task here to define our attitude with regard to Nygren's views on the New Testament and the history of theology,[12] nor to examine in detail his methods of motif research.[13] Our aim is rather to examine Nygren's train of thought with regard to Luther.

TRANSLATED BY LANCE GARRARD

First we shall outline his sketch of Luther's "theocentric idea of love" in contrast to "everything that can be called egocentric," and then we shall supplement it with some critical additions.

Nygren develops Luther's conception of the nature of Christian love (positively as well as polemically) in close association with his conception of the Christian way of religious salvation, namely, Luther's doctrine of justification (683); [14] in fact, the two are kept parallel throughout. In Luther both are dominated by the same theocentric feeling and the same radical repudiation of every kind of "egocentricity" by which man seeks to make a contribution of his own to his relation with God. Everything, for instance, that Luther says with reference to human righteousness and sin in the famous exposition of his program at the beginning of his Lecture on Romans of 1515/16 [15] can be applied word for word to love.[16] There is a love which claims to be Christian love and yet is built purely on a basis of natural self-love. This must be torn down and destroyed. In its place we must build and implant *the* love which reflects God's selfless, sacrificial love and seeks not its own. True, Christian love is not generated from us but comes to us from God in Jesus Christ. In his full recognition of this, Luther has become the destroyer of everything that Catholicism from the time of Augustine conceives as love,[17] which is really determined more by egocentric eros-love in the Platonic sense than by the agape of the New Testament; he does this in order to restore theocentric agape-love to its place of honor in Christianity.

Love in the Christian sense must, in Luther's view, be understood wholly in terms of that love with which God himself loves, and as it has been manifested in Jesus Christ. In no sense must it be understood in terms of that other love with which man loves God (683), the terms indeed in which it is understood in Augustine and his medieval successors, in fact in Catholicism generally.[18] For this is, in the eyes of Luther, essentially egocentric, selfish, and acquisitive. It is selfishness which is the primal sin, and it is doubly sinful when it seeks to determine our relation to God (682). The relentless struggle that Luther waged in the name of true agape against the Augustinian and medieval concept of *caritas*, was the same struggle that he was waging in his doctrine of justification for a theocentric outlook against every sort of synergism, with its inclusion of justification by works. Because for Luther justification was a matter of fellowship with God not on the level of God's holiness but on our human level, which means on the basis of sin (684), man must not mount up to God, for God in sheer unmotivated love has come down in Christ to sinful man in order to establish fellowship entirely from his side. This rests therefore solely on God's unfathomable love; solely in virtue of this is the sinner justified.

It is for these soteriological reasons that Luther in the various stages of his development completely shattered the *caritas* way of salvation which he had striven to the utmost to attain in his early days (692–716). In its place he put the way of salvation opened solely by the love of God in Christ. In doing so he also rejected the classic Catholic idea of love, which is determined more by the motif of eros than by Christian agape (721). This comes out most clearly in Luther's struggle against the scholastic idea of "fides caritate formata" and his emphasis on the *sola fide* principle in opposition to it (716 ff.).[19] The contrast is not one of love on the one side and faith on the other. It is rather that two fundamentally different conceptions of love confront one another: on the one side it is egocentrically oriented, on the other entirely theocentrically.[20] In conceiving of love as primarily and basically God's agape towards the sinner, Luther produced a complete transformation of the idea of love. When love is consistently understood as coming from beyond, there is no longer a division of spheres between it and faith, but both coincide. Only when love is conceived primarily as love of man do faith and love come into rivalry, so that some sort of balance has to be struck between them.

Since love is commonly understood as love coming from man, Luther was at pains to exclude love altogether from the context of justification and here, where God's love alone is decisive, to speak on man's side only of faith (716 f.).[21] Man's love has no place in the establishment of fellowship with God (717). But in excluding human love from the context of justification, Luther has preserved the purity of the genuine Christian idea of love as well as that of faith; for the doctrine that we are justified before God "fide caritate formata" endangers the purity not only of faith but also of Christian love, because the presupposition of this doctrine is a love quite different from that which is specifically Christian (719). When this kind of love is imported *in loco justificationis* it means in point of fact the rejection and distortion of the true (agape) love. Love, in the sense of God's love, is denied, and in its place love as a human quality is made decisive, and this then acquires a meritorious character (720). So, because love *in loco justificationis* is no longer true agape-love, but human love with an eros tendency, it must at this point be eliminated and give place to genuine agape-love, God's love for us which we can only accept in faith (721).

Luther has been unjustly reproached with destroying the Christian idea of love and leaving only a few remains (717 ff.).[22] It would be truer to say that, in removing man's love from the context of justification, he has reestablished and restored to honor the *true* Christian idea of love in the sense of agape, based on the absolutely sovereign, spontaneous, and unmotivated love of *God* (721).[23] The destruction of eros-love within the framework of Christianity means, for Luther, the establishment of true agape-love. In attacking the scholastic idea of love in connection with justification, he is not setting himself against the idea of love altogether, but only against the particular interpretation of Christian love that finds expression in the idea of *caritas*, an idea determined more by the Greek concept of eros than by the genuine Christian concept of agape. Whereas in the medieval, scholastic, and mystical view of love the acquisitive love of man, in however refined a form, is the unifying thread, Luther's view of love is determined throughout by the selfless, sacrificial agape which has its pattern in God's love for the sinner (739 f.).

The question that now arises is this: Does Christian agape merely provide Luther with a platform for his criticism of the Roman Catholic view of *caritas* and remain otherwise completely empty of content and so abstract, or has he succeeded in establishing in a positive form the idea of agape-love, and that, be it noted, with reference to the Christian man (722)? In the second half of his chapter on Luther, Nygren considers this important question in detail. In his view, it is essential that the inquiry should start from "above," with the divine love, as it has been manifested in Jesus Christ, and in no sense from "beneath," with human love. For in the natural man "love" exists only in an egocentric, acquisitive, and purely self-seeking form.[24] That is why we cannot build love in the Christian sense on this foundation, as scholasticism attempted to do. It is impossible to argue from natural, human "love," which is always basically self-love, to Christian love, which alone is true love (723). On the contrary, love in the Christian sense must find its starting point entirely in God's own love, which he has shown in his unmotivated gift to sinful man, and above all in giving his own Son for him (724). As his answer to the question whether there is any other love than that which is acquisitive and egocentric, Luther points to the love of God for the lost and undeserving which is experienced in Christ. *There* a love is *really* at work which does not seek its own, but gives and sacrifices itself, and so is true love.[25]

Whereas human "love" is always self-seeking, and so is bound up with myself, God's love is spontaneous, unmotivated, and selfless, and therefore creative, because it sacrifices and gives itself and imparts of the fullness of its riches. That is why it is directed par excellence towards the undeserving, sinners, the wicked, fools, the poor and worthless (725). From it Luther draws his criterion and measure of the features of genuine love, Christian love in radical opposition to all human love, *love after the pattern of God's agape in Christ* (726).[26] Nygren sketches this pattern in its characteristic features (726–33), and then shows how it descends from God to man and pervades the man who receives it in faith, as agape in the sense of love for his neighbor (733–41). We shall briefly examine these points in succession.

God's love, as it manifests itself as a pattern in Jesus Christ, is above all spontaneous, in contrast to all eudaemonistically based behavior; it is free from selfish calculation and self-interest, free to render selfless, sacrificial service to others (726). It is, moreover, spontaneous in contrast to every kind of *legalism*. Only when we are free from law, with its external claims and threats of punishment and promises of reward, only when "the imperative of the law . . . is exchanged for the indicative of the Gospel," can we really love—when we no longer feel the Good as compulsion, with our inward wishes working in the opposite direction, but are completely won over for the Good, and do it with inward inclination and desire. This can come about only through faith in Christ or, we may say, through the Holy Spirit (727–29). True, Christian love, moreover, is "overflowing love," it is not moved by any external motives and is not in the least reflective, but is absolutely simple (729 f). It is love "without respect of persons," in no way determined by its object; that is why it shows itself particularly as love of our enemies (730 f.). Finally, it is "a lost love": it belongs to its essence that it is disappointed and betrayed, and it gives itself for the sake of others even when they do not in the least appreciate it (732).

In the end it is clear to Nygren that Luther has succeeded in constructing a theocentric agape-love. Luther has depicted in entirely concrete terms a love which is the exact opposite of the "love" which seeks its own. The marks of this new kind of love are drawn by him from God's love. There remains only the question whether this may not be simply an ideal picture drawn from the divine love and having no connection with actual human life, so that it represents only a postulate. Is such a love possible among men at all, and can it be a reality for them? [27] It is certainly, Nygren says, not a possibility for the natural man (733 f.). But when a man in faith opens his heart to God's activity and his effective love and allows it to work creatively within him, this love receives from above free play to stream into the man, and through him to stream forth to other men and the world at large (737).

In the last section (733–37), Nygren shows how the Christian, according to Luther, becomes a kind of *"tube" for God's love as it streams forth in Christ*, so that through him it passes on to his neighbor. The Christian stands between God and his fellowman. He receives God's love in faith and passes it on to his neighbor in love. The subject, in the case of Christian love of neighbor, is not, therefore, really the man but God, in that *his* love uses the man of faith as the instrument and organ of its own diffusion. Christian love of neighbor is to some extent the continuation and extension of God's love, but is not an independent center of power standing alongside of it; it is a divine work in man and through man (734). Everything that the Christian is and has he has from God, and he gives everything that he receives from God to his neighbor (735). In contrast to Augustine, the stream of love is seen as coming *down from above*. Everything that is rightly called agape comes from God, and it seeks through faith to pass on to our neighbor, and not to lead to any selfish "frui Deo" (736). Christian love is basically always *God's* own love, seeking its way to the neighbor through the Christian. Man can love with genuine agape only when he is "blessed"; i.e., when his egocentric yearnings have been not satisfied but overcome. Luther's ethic is built on our relation with God and, with reference to this, is "not teleological but causal" (737).

IN THE EXPOSITION reproduced above, Nygren has unquestionably given a correct and impressive account of the nature of agape in Luther in its main emphases and characteristic marks, confirming his demonstration at each step with a wealth of characteristic and telling quotations from Luther's works. The novel and peculiar feature of Luther's understanding of the idea of love, strongly emphasized in thesis and antithesis, is really the fundamentally theocentric orientation of agape, in contrast to all egocentrically motivated *caritas*, and, further, the recognition that agape, proceeding from God's nature through his act in Jesus Christ, overcomes the selfish "love" of man and, through the faith which embraces it and lives by it, extends, as it were, to the Christian's neighbor. With regard to the fundamental structure of agape in Luther, there is nothing important to add to the picture drawn by Nygren. His magnificent account needs only to be gratefully accepted as a valuable and fruitful contribution.

The only remaining question is whether this impressive exposition of the central fact is in itself enough, or whether there remain certain *secondary* motifs, overlooked by Nygren, still to be filled in to complete the picture. They will be motifs which were clearly secondary to Luther, but which nevertheless have their place, because without them his view of agape could easily be formalized and might be presented in the form of false alternatives; the life would then depart from it, and it would be wrongly turned into a mere principle. In what follows I shall therefore supplement Nygren's representation from three points of view.

1] First of all, the question has to be asked whether it is really correct, from the point of view of method, that Luther's conception of love should be established as a *motif* of his theology, and accordingly developed, as it is by Nygren, in all possible purity and consistency as a fundamental religious motif. Unquestionably Nygren has correctly penetrated to the uniqueness of agape in Luther's understanding. But surely we must constantly consider *how* Luther came to recognize this agape as the inmost nature of God, and in what manner man becomes aware of it each time afresh. For Luther it is not simply obvious that God's nature is basically agape and his dealings with men fundamentally directed by agape. It is rather an unexpected *miracle*, which can only be constantly apprehended afresh in the "nevertheless" of faith, as *against* our normal experience of God's existence. Our normal experience of God's existence, his activity in law and wrath, judging, terrifying, and slaying man, is for Luther, unlike Albrecht Ritschl, no mere fiction of unreconciled man, but God's inscrutable reality, and God's agape is, for Luther, "concealed" within it; the assurance of his agape comes only in real transcendence of God's real activity in law and wrath.[28] The assurance that God's nature and the meaning of his dealings with men are really agape is not given us by Luther, as it often seems to be by Nygren, in the undialectical simplicity of the claim that it is the fundamental religious motif, but rather in the dialectical "nevertheless" of faith in the sense of the "*theologia crucis,*" standing out in constant relief against God's very real activity in law and wrath. This is not, as it were, eliminated in Luther, but retains for him an abiding validity, and only with this as a foil can we have a correct awareness and understanding of God's agape.

"The reference is to the 'mysterious character' of the opus dei according to Luther's Operationes in Psalmos and his exposition of the Magnificat, how God's work is concealed behind temptation, punishment and wrath, and yet is manifestly saving love." "And indeed here it becomes particularly plain that both sides of the mystery, the fearful, repellent side which hides God's nature, and the gracious, attractive side which reveals God's mercy, altogether overlap each other and do not represent two successive acts. . . . For, according to that saying of the prophet (Isa. 28:21), God works the opus alienum just in order that his own work may be accomplished."— (114) "God's wrath is the side of his reality which must be apprehended first; it must be demonstrated to unbelievers in order that they may come to faith. But where faith has been really aroused it probes behind the appearance and apprehends the whole of God in his merciful love." [29]

This being so, it is inappropriate to speak, as Nygren does, of Luther's understanding of God's agape as a fundamental religious motif which can be worked out in all possible purity and consistency, while all opposing motifs in the picture of God are eliminated. We ought rather to work out Luther's understanding of God's agape with the contrasting motifs, namely, God's activity in law and wrath, *still present and operative*, and to see it as that which really prevails over them.[30] For to Luther the assurance of agape as the deepest factor in God does not rest on an analysis of God's nature but, as Nygren quite rightly brings out, on the experience of the actual unmotivated activity of God in effecting salvation in Jesus Christ. It is in this that God reveals the deepest, the unique aspect of his nature, but there is nothing easy about it, it comes in the *via crucis*, the crossing over his own activity in law and wrath. Faith may indeed recognize this in retrospect as an *opus alienum* of God which in the last resort serves his activity of love as his *opus proprium;* but the one belongs just as truly to God as the other. Experience of it is presupposed in that of God's activity in love, so that the latter is experienced as *God's* agape and as *miracle*, which is nevertheless self-evident. Only in the transcendence, constantly renewed, of God's activity in law and wrath, which is a real and valid part of our experience, is agape experienced as the deepest abyss of his nature. "The ultimate knowledge of God is this, that his love is *contingent*." [31] That is why the concept of the hidden God and his activity in law and wrath are for Luther the constant presupposition and foil for genuine experience of God's agape.

Luther writes in his "Exposition of the Magnificat": "But when God hides himself, and takes away the glory of his goodness, so that they are left alone and in distress, then fail both their love and their praises. They have neither the will nor the ability to love and praise the quite intangible things which lie hidden in God." [32] W. Maurer writes: "So faith recognizes in the work of God at one and the same time his wrath and his grace, i.e., it experiences his kindness only as hidden beneath the outward appearance of its opposite. . . . And to affirm the secret of this double nature of the divine activity, which cannot be rationally apprehended, is the real task of faith in the moment of its temptation." [33] This does not seem to me to have been brought out clearly enough by Nygren. In him God's agape appears too much as a self-evident principle.

It must be pointed out in this connection that, according to Luther, it is precisely as a twofold *commandment* of love as a radical and unremitting demand for completely selfless love for God "super omnia" and as entirely sacrificial love for our fellowmen, that the law of God exercises its function of challenging and judging sinful man. Nygren rightly calls attention to the fact that Luther, in his positive account of agape, adopts a reserved attitude with regard to the commandment of love, just because this is something legal, whereas Christian love is spontaneous and free from all legalism. Only when man is free from the law can he really love, when the imperative of the law is replaced by the indicative of the Gospel. But must we not inquire into the meaning of the fact that one and the same God who gives and renders possible spontaneous love in Christ also demands it of men in his law, so that the twofold commandment of love in its most radical form is the summary of the whole Law?

We know how greatly God's law terrified and challenged Luther in his "monastic struggles" precisely as a radical demand for love. This was not merely a controversy with the Augustinian and medieval way of salvation by eros,[34] but, above all, a feeling of being challenged by the authentic law of God, which "nails" a man to his sin; [35] it is seen as the inward inability to love God and his fellowmen completely unselfishly with his whole heart. Only a man who has been existentially convicted by the law and shattered in his inmost being can ever grasp God's agape in Jesus Christ as a real power, creating anew.[36] Thus the *commandment* of love, at least in the sense of a *law of God* that is still in force, demanding, accusing, and judging, has for Luther a constantly valid significance.

2] In Nygren's positive exposition of the idea of love in Luther, agape plays really only a twofold part. First and foremost, it is seen as

God's love for sinful man; secondly, as a kind of extension of this, "downward from above," as Christian love of our neighbor and of enemies. On the other hand, in Luther, as indeed in Paul, *love for God* (in the Johannine sense) recedes into the background, first because, in the Augustinian and medieval pattern, it is not quite free from egocentric motivation and acquisitive considerations, secondly because, of course, God has no need of it. He does not want to be loved himself directly, but only in my neighbor. So, in Luther as in Paul, the dominant term for man's relation to God must be faith.[37] Nygren is perfectly right in these observations; he has quite correctly reproduced the substance of Luther's thought on the whole and in its dominant features.[38] And yet, in Luther, as again in Paul,[39] the idea of love for God is not completely eliminated. It still plays an important part for Luther, not as an independent capacity of the natural man, but as a response called forth and upheld by God's love.

On this, a few examples will assist us. From the 1515/16 Lectures on Romans: "Can a man who lusts after and loves something else love God? But this lust is always in us; therefore there is never love for God in us, unless it is begun by grace and, by healing what still remains of lust, by which we do not yet 'love God with all our heart,' so that by mercy it is not imputed as sin, until it is wholly taken away and the perfect love of God is granted to those who believe and who resist with perseverance even to the end" (WA 56:275). From the Sermon on Good Works, 1520: "Now it has been said above that such confidence and faith (as the fulfillment of the First Commandment) brings with it love and hope. Indeed, when we see the matter aright, love is the first thing, or simultaneous with faith. For I could not trust God if I did not think that he would be gracious and kind. And so I am kindly towards him and moved to trust him from my heart and to ascribe all good to him" (WA 6:210). In the same sermon: "In whom (Christ) you see that God is so kind to you that he even gives his son for you and so your heart must be sweet and kind towards God in return and nothing but grace and love grow out of it, God's towards you and yours towards God" (WA 6:216). From the "Exposition of the Magnificat," 1520/21: "Where God is recognized as he who looks with mercy into the depths of our being, he arouses a corresponding love in our heart. And this is the spring from which flow our love and praise of God. No man can praise God without first loving him; and, similarly, no one can love him unless God is his best beloved and his nearest friend."[40] When we have experienced God in his merciful action, "then we come to love him with our whole heart. Our heart overflows with joy; it leaps and bounds with the sheer delight which it has found in God." This love loves God *for his own sake;* so in the "Magnificat":

> We ought to love and praise God simply, and in the normal course, without seeking any advantage to ourselves from him. To love and praise God with a pure and upright heart is to praise him just because he is good, and to have nothing else in mind than his perfect goodness, and to have joy and gladness in that fact alone. . . . Those whose love is impure or debased, who are merely self-seeking and eager for benefactions from God, do not love and praise his perfect goodness. With an eye to themselves they look only for the blessings God shows to them; in other words, for the way in which he gives them tangible things and prospers them. Then they exalt him highly and are happy singing his praises as long as the experience lasts. . . . They have neither the will nor the ability to love and praise the quite intangible things which lie hidden in God. This shows that their spirit does not rejoice in God as savior. Nay, rather they take more pleasure in the help than in the Helper, more in the gift than in the Giver, more in the creature than in God.[41]

In this section we shall inquire, in what sense is love for God meaningful in Luther's theology? [42] In doing so, we shall hope to supplement Nygren's conception for the second time.

The most thorough examination of the question of the specific meaning of love for God, with constant reference to Luther, is that undertaken by Werner Elert in his ethics.[43] We cannot do better than reproduce the relevant part of his argument. First, Elert expressly agrees with Nygren's conception of faith as the appropriate attitude of man towards God, and of love, which applies to our neighbor what we have received from God in faith, free from all egocentric desire.[44] He then goes on to ask how far this agape can also have God as its object (364). "What remains . . . of agape towards God when it can give him nothing that does not in any case belong to him? . . . There remains, first, *self-forgetfulness,* the renunciation of all claims for ourselves, of self-love, of our own worth, and so of all merit and claim to reward, the reduction of the self to a cipher because the other is everything. These are precisely the criteria of justifying faith, as it is understood by Paul and Luther. Faith, because it fulfills the first commandment, fulfills also the commandment to love God. It is thus easy to understand that Paul and Luther, comparatively, seldom speak of love for God, because it is included in faith in him; indeed, viewed in this way, it is identical with it. This does not, however, exhaust it" (365).

Elert's second answer runs: "There remains, secondly, love for God . . . the criterion of a *pure personal relationship*" (365). God could easily be viewed as an object, an abstraction, a thing. When Luther here and there speaks of love for God, he is making it plain that our relation to him, directed to God's "fatherly heart," is entirely personal. But this finds expression also in Luther's concept of faith, which consists just in this, "that we place our confidence (fiducia) in him alone and rely entirely upon him" (365). "Here, too, we have once more to ask how far it is still possible to speak of love for God" (365). "At any rate it would not be because God was an object of desire for us. For, to begin with, all objectification of our relationship with God, from his side as well as from ours, is excluded by the attitude of faith. Because faith is assured that we receive all that is good from God, there is no place left for desiring something more from him. Granted that love for God can exist *only within the relationship of faith*, it can only be a relation between subject and subject, not between us as subject and God as object" (366).

What, then, does it mean in positive terms? "In the Gospel of John the love of Christ for his own, his love for the Father, the love of his own for him, the Father's love for him and for his own are inextricably bound up together (John 13:34; 14:21, 23; 15:9, 12; 17:23, 26). Love appears here, taken all in all, not as a predicate attached to individuals, but as an interpersonal relation, always mutual, as an atmosphere in which one abides, loves, and breathes . . . It is not a mere virtue attaching to someone, neither is it an individual act which I resolve to perform, nor again is it a private relationship between myself and God. It is rather an order of things, a new framework of existence in which we are all coordinated with God as both loving and loved, and also with our brethren in a likewise mutual relationship.[45] The man who is in this order is always both loved and loving" (366). "Love is a life without any compulsion." [46] "For this reason love is the perfect fulfillment of the old law which is summed up in the commandment of love, and at the same time its annulment . . . because an order has been established between God and us which is not one of compulsion." [47] "It is clear that this new order is no other than the order of grace, which abrogates the law, and that we can therefore behave as men who love only within the relationship of faith. But the fact that this is now recognized as the order of love, in which we ourselves are not only beloved but also loving, means that the acceptance of divine grace which is fulfilled in faith restores our relationship with God which had been lost through the Fall. Love is the new coordination, the interpersonal order that has its only source in God himself" (367). "To know God means to know love, and therefore to love God means to love the love with which we are loved. Love is the new order that exists between God and us, but through the same order all others whom he loves are coordinated with us" (368). So "love for God with all our heart" always leads inevitably to love for our brethren. But "there is no love for our brethren without whole-hearted love for God. They are not two kinds of love, but one and the same" (369).

I believe Elert has here aptly demonstrated why, and in what sense, according to Luther, our love for God has its necessary and indispensable place between God's love for us and our relationship of faith towards God on the one hand, and, on the other, our love for our neighbor, in which God's love goes out through us to a wider circle. God's love for us loses something of its immediately organic and almost automatic quality when it passes on in our love for our neighbor, since, in passing through us, it is conducted through lifeless "tubes." Our love for God intervenes rather as an expression of our new personal relationship and personal existence in our relation to God. God's love passes on beyond us to our neighbor [48] only through our new personal existence, which constitutes God's love in us, and which receives its vital fulfillment in our love for God directed to him as a person. Here, with reference to the subjective element of Christian love for neighbor, the thought that God's love, which seeks to pass on further through us, is really our own too, is for Luther the idea of the believer's true "conformitas cum Christo" and of great importance. [49]

"Caritas is the principle of good works. . . . It is the fulfillment of the law and the power of obedience. In respect of these functions, the idea of Caritas means 'to love God above all things' and consequently also love for everything that, according to God's will, ought to be loved" (412). "To love God means to keep nothing in view but God, to hate oneself in comparison, to condemn every self-seeking desire, indeed, it means obediently to deliver oneself up as a sinner to God's judgment. Pure love for God is understood by Luther as the conformity of the will with God's will. Thus it is not a feeling-experience, but the obedience of the will itself in the presence of God's will, with its total claim. Our will must be with God's will not only in willing generally, but in all that God wills without exception . . . In perfect harmony with God's will Caritas now loves our neighbor in the same way in which God himself loves us in Christ." [50] Here it is clear that the question cannot be one of how and in what sense our love for God must be *added* to our faith in God; it is rather a matter of asking for the meaning of our love for God *within* the relationship of faith, how it is that there cannot be genuine faith in God without love for God.[51] Faith must not be understood in any coldly abstract sense, nor as a willingness to accept illusion, "as if" it were so. Our whole heart is in it, won over by the love of God and gladly offering itself to him as a person.[52] This finds expression in love for God,[53] and only so can faith be understood as the living fountain which it is in Luther, and from which good works flow forth of their own accord.[54]

My meaning could also be put in this way. The subject in our relation with God is not solely, as in mere faith, the transcendental ego. This, which is undoubtedly the primary and fundamental factor, apprehends, draws in, and interweaves our psychological ego as well.[55] It would, indeed, be a serious misunderstanding to think, whenever Luther speaks of faith, immediately of our empirical, psychical ego. Faith is rooted beyond all empirical experience in a new, transcendental ego, evoked from us by God's call to salvation. But it would be just as perverse to ignore the empirical ego completely in thinking of this transcendental subject in the matter of faith, and to think of the former as entirely unaffected by the latter. We need rather to see how our empirical, psychological ego is more and more drawn by the transcendental ego of faith into itself, and pervaded and transformed by it. This side of our new relationship to God Luther, and the old-Lutheran theology after him, expresses in the imagery of the bridal love-relationship between Christ and the believer, in the first place, and, secondarily, between God and the faithful. "God is for us not only an object of loving thought, but one of the parties in a contract of *mutual* love, which links us with him in an inseparable unity and is present in him as well as in us, though he always remains for us the 'Thou.' " [56] "These notorious operations of the emotions show that Luther does not leave the internus homo, who as such remains always the man of faith, untouched even in his psyche by his fellowship with Christ" (148). Purely in the doctrines of satisfaction and imputation, taken by themselves, Luther does not find the relationship of love towards Christ. This relationship

> means on the side of Christ an act of sacrifice not only for men in general but also for me personally. This is recognized by faith,

which always means its application pro me. But the fellowship of righteousness, which in itself might be misunderstood as a mere sharing of goods, becomes a real personal fellowship only when the believer knows that Christ is thinking of him personally, knows him personally, and loves him personally . . . But the working of God's love is not exhausted in the faith which receives it and refers it to myself. It is not exhausted even in the fact that God's love creates our love for him (WA 10/III:157, 9 ff.), that our love for God expresses itself in keeping his word, his commandments (158,24), and demonstrates in love for our neighbor (157,19) that there is no true obedience to God without love (WA 41:559,5), nor is Christ honored through us without love (WA 20:398 f.).

In all these passages it might appear as if God's love and ours stood in a causal relationship. Indeed, Luther expressly emphasizes in this connection that they do stand in such a relationship. But he also states just as clearly that we are concerned with a real relationship of love, which always remains reciprocal, "a relationship of mutual love between the Thou and the I in the most personal sense." [57]

God's love is received, as everything that comes from God is received, in faith. To this extent there is in all this no overstepping of the bounds of the doctrine of justification. But God's *love* is now understood not merely as God's decree. It calls the believer's *heart* into fellowship with it. It calls the psyche. And it is the believer's psyche, too, which responds. God remains the other. He is not the mystics' "ground of the soul." He remains always the "Thou"—otherwise there could not be a relation of love. But God's Thou and the I of the psyche are united through *love*, which makes "one thing" out of man and God. What we might feel, according to this, to be missing in the idea of faith is supplied in the idea of love; for love is "to feel that God loves us and gives us good gifts" (Tischreden 2:395 f.), in other words, *a living experience* of God's unconditioned kindness. And it is possible to speak of such love here in the Epilogue (to the Ten Commandments) because . . . the term "grace," with which Luther describes the promise, refers to a constant attribute of God's nature, and is only waiting for an opportunity to do good. If eudaemonistic, and so legal, piety is overcome anywhere in the Epilogue, it is in the word "to love." For love can spring up only because, behind the threats and promises of the law-giving and righteous God which belong to the law, man can also detect the grace of the God of kindness, working as the Gospel. . . . Love and trust appear at the side of fear, and because they do not rest on a basis of eudaemonism, they can accomplish more, namely that we "act gladly according to his commandments:"—191 f.: The love that is demanded in the First Commandment is not merely the moral acceptance of God's will, i.e. the amor iustitiae which is bound up with odium peccati and opposed to amor commodi, and which at this stage has not attained to blessedness but is confined to humble obedience . . . , nor again is it a mystical absorption in God, but it is a deep contentment with God, aroused by God's benefactions and the kindness of which they are evidence.[58]

3] Finally, we ought not to dispose of the *commandment* of love, even in its positive meaning,[59] quite so quickly as Nygren does in his allusion to its legal character.[60] Reference has already been made above to its important function (indirectly also for the proper experience and apprehension of God's love) as the summary of the whole law. But the theological meaning of the commandment of love is not exhausted for Luther in this judging, condemning, and death-dealing function of the law. It is for him also God's call to man, inviting him to the life of salvation, to the new relationship to God and his fellowmen. According to Luther, we must also speak of "a commandment aspect of the Gospel, as an aid to faith," [61] an idea which finds expression particularly in his theology of the First Commandment.[62] And God's commandment, which encroaches on "the distinction between law and gospel," [63] besides helping us towards faith, particularly in times of temptation, also continually helps faith itself to transform itself into love,[64] without which it would not be genuine, living faith. This is how we should understand the gracious and helpful character of the commandment of love, which it also had for Luther.

If love, according to Luther, proceeds immediately and spontaneously from our encounter with God's love in faith and keeps entirely within the relationship of faith, this does not mean that it is enough to emphasize faith alone, and to take love for granted as its natural accompaniment. On the contrary, driven to it by the appropriate passages in the New Testament in particular, Luther regarded it as essential, within the *sola fide* and embraced by it, expressly to insist upon the love which faith may be in danger of losing. Even with respect to the believer, it is necessary constantly to *admonish* him to love, and in this sense the twofold commandment of love in the New Testament has a thoroughly positive meaning for Luther.[65] "The real necessity with which for Luther true faith leads to love is not intended, in spite of his illustrations from nature, as something psychologically automatic. The believer must and can be summoned to love as the essential fulfillment of faith, because it is possible for him to stand in faith and yet lack the love which is the law of its being." [66]

In conclusion, perhaps yet another point of view may be emphasized which finds expression for Luther even in the commandment of love, namely that from his first creation man has always been disposed towards agape. God's commandment, especially when it is summarized as the commandment of love, is for Luther always also "lex naturae," i.e. an expression of God's intention in the Creation, of the purpose for which man has really been created by God. The commandment of love as a summary of all God's commandments "unto life" is an assertion that in the very basis of his existence man is willed and intended by God for agape. Seen in this light, Christian agape is the fulfillment of *true* "natural" love.[67] "This [i.e. Christian] love could not arise in the soul if man had not been disposed to it by nature. The disposition towards social activity, with its mutual obligations, given with the law of nature, is the presupposition of the continuance of the fellowship of Christians with one another in love which is sustained by the Spirit." Corresponding to this is the principle that, according to Luther, "the Christian must practise the love that moves him in his ordinary natural life, with its regulations and necessities." [68] "This means that the Christian will not strive to fulfill the duties of his calling under the pressure of outward necessity, but *love* will make him perform aright what his office requires." He will therefore do "what our office or position and love of our neighbor demand" (Luther, WA 36:472). The emphasis on his calling, as the framework within which man is morally active is not intended in any way to neutralize morality, or separate it from the religious life. What Luther means is rather that the moral life of love which is sustained by the Spirit of God is realized, accomplished, and approved in the field of actual creative life, and does not degenerate into an unfruitful, and in the last resort egoistic, devotion to a life of works.[69]

I have now outlined my three points of view: 1] the significance of the law for the interpretation of God's love in man, according to Luther; 2] the significance for him of love towards God; 3] the positive significance for him of the commandment of love. I hope that with these thoughts I have supplemented Anders Nygren's persuasive and magnificent exposition of the heart of the idea of love in Luther, with some not wholly unimportant additions.

Systematic Theology

12

SYSTEMATIC THEOLOGY
AND MOTIF RESEARCH

Philip S. Watson

NEARLY fifty years ago, when Anders Nygren first began his writing and teaching, it seemed to him that theology, and particularly systematic theology or dogmatics, was in a profoundly difficult position.[1] What had once been generally acknowledged as the Queen of the Sciences was now at best the Cinderella, if indeed it was allowed a place among the sciences at all. Even among theologians there was no unanimity or certainty as to the scope and competence of theology, and none of the different, competing schools of thought presented a case which he found convincing. It looked in fact very much as though theology was in the same sort of predicament as metaphysics in the time of Kant. Therefore, just as Kant, observing the confusion in metaphysics and the steady progress of the natural sciences, was led to ask how the acquisition of assured knowledge is possible, and to inquire how it is done in the sciences, so Nygren was led to ask this with regard to theology.

Notice that the question is not *whether* knowledge is possible, but *how* it is possible; for unless we start with the assumption that it is possible, we might as well not start at all. It was with this assumption that Nygren started, setting himself to ask only how, under what terms and conditions, knowledge can be acquired—as in fact it is acquired through the scientific disciplines. His purpose in doing so was, of course, to discover what terms and conditions would have to be fulfilled for theology to be regarded as a scientific discipline, and to see whether these could in fact be fulfilled.

The intellectual journeyings which this inquiry entailed are indicated by the subjects and titles of Nygren's early publications. First there came in 1921 his doctoral dissertation, dealing with "Religious a priori, its philosophical presuppositions and theological implications." In 1922 a condensed version of this appeared in German as *Die Gültigkeit der religiösen Erfahrung* [The Validity of Religious Experience], and a more or less popular, nontechnical account of its conclusions was given to Swedish readers in *Det bestáende i kristendomen* [The Permanent Element in Christianity].[2] Next followed a book on "The Scientific Foundation of Dogmatics, with special attention to the viewpoints of Kant and Schleiermacher," and an important essay on "The Question of Objectivity in Theology." Then in 1923 came a substantial volume dealing with "Philosophical and Christian Ethics," and in 1926 a collection of essays on "Basic Questions in Ethics," as well as a small but significant work on "Religiosity and Christianity." These works, together with a number of occasional essays eventually collected and published (in 1940) under the title of "Philosophy and Motif-research," reveal how thoroughly Nygren has investigated the claim of theology to rank among the sciences. How he has also sought to validate this claim, we shall now attempt to show.

To begin with, Nygren holds with Kant (though he is not himself a Kantian) that there can be no "science of the transcendent." All science must be firmly anchored to the realities of given experience, of which it is its task to gain as clear and accurate an understanding as possible. Every true science has *1*] a given subject matter to investigate; *2*] an interest in that subject matter which is peculiarly its own —otherwise it is merely a duplicate of some other science under a different name; and *3*] a method of inquiry appropriate to its purpose. The question is, therefore, whether theology can meet these requirements.

What, in the first place, is the subject matter theology has to investigate? If we answer either that it is Christianity or religion in general, there are those who will at once tell us that religion is illusion, as any honestly scientific examination of it will show; so that theology as a science can only succeed in putting itself out of business. Others, less drastically, will maintain that religion is in reality only a special form of something else—of morality (Kant), or philosophy (Hegel), or whatever it may be; and in that case theology can at most be a subsidiary branch of some other discipline, to whose norms and procedures it must therefore conform. Others, again, while not disputing the status of religion, will argue that theology merely duplicates the function of the philosophy of religion; and yet others will insist that, since religion is such a highly subjective affair, theology can never be more than a personal confession of faith, entirely lacking in the objectivity which is a hallmark of science.

In order to meet these and similar difficulties, Nygren has recourse to his philosophical studies. And here he insists from the outset, that philosophy itself must fulfill the requirements of scientific inquiry. That is to say, it must abandon metaphysical speculation in favor of a less spectacular "critical" role. Its traditional claim to be the "science of first principles" can be upheld, but only if it is kept in close and constant touch with experience, and if the principles in question are understood to be of a logical, not an ontological nature. Its task is not to discover some "ultimate reality" *beyond* experience, but to inquire into the "validity" that is to be found *in* experience. For this purpose it has to engage first in a "critical analysis of concepts," so that we may be quite clear what we are talking about, and may avoid using concepts which are either confused and therefore confusing, or meaningless because self-contradictory. It must then proceed to a "logical analysis of presuppositions," in order to discover the basic concepts that constitute the "ultimate principles" or fundamental categories of experience. These are concepts which (whether we are consciously aware of them or not) are logically presupposed in all meaningful discourse, and their own validity is demonstrated by showing that it must necessarily be assumed if we are to entertain the idea of any validity at all.

By this method Nygren first reaches the conclusion that there are at least four major "contexts of meaning" or "universes of discourse," namely those of science, art, morality, and religion. He differs here from Kant, as Schleiermacher did, in insisting that religion is an "autonomous" form of experience, and that it cannot rightly be subsumed under any other category. At the same time he differs also from Schleiermacher, although what Schleiermacher was essentially after, he contends, was just the sort of logical presuppositions with which he himself is concerned. Yet by using expressions like "feeling of absolute dependence" or "religious consciousness," and "Christian consciousness," Schleiermacher led both himself and still more his followers astray—admittedly not in an ontological, but in a psychological direction. Both these errors Nygren seeks scrupulously to avoid.

We turn, then, to the four universes of discourse. These are not the only ones that exist, of course, but they are, and have been throughout the history of human thought, outstandingly the most important, and they are quite sufficient for our purpose. Each of them posseses its own peculiar character independent of the rest, so that no one of them can be interpreted in terms of any other without being misinterpreted. Each must be understood on its own terms. In this connection it is fashionable in some quarters today to speak of different "languages," scientific, ethical, aesthetic, religious. But this is misleading. There are only different *uses* of language. If they were really different languages, they would be capable of translation into one another, as in fact they are not. Failure to realize this underlies the popular positivistic notion that religious statements are meaningless because they are incapable of the same kind of verification (or falsification) as scientific statements.

It should, however, be observed, that the different universes of discourse are far from being mutually exclusive. They coexist, and a person can live, move and have his being in all of them at once, as a simple illustration will show. A nuclear physicist, let us suppose, is working in his laboratory. He is investigating an aspect of the physical world with a view to understanding it, discovering the *truth* about it. As he works, he may be admiring the *beauty* of the microcosmic structures he detects, or of the mathematical equations to which he reduces them. At the same time he may be wrestling with a moral problem as to whether it is *good or right* for him to continue his researches, in view of the uses to which he knows his discoveries may be put. He may also be praying to God for help and guidance, both with regard to the work he is doing and the decision he has to make. In other words, he can be engaged in four quite different activities—scientific, aesthetic, ethical, and religious—simultaneously. From a psychological point of view, it is of course obvious that his main attention could be concentrated on only one of them at a time; but we are here concerned with the logical, not the psychological state of affairs. Logically, therefore, it is as clear that none of these various activities could do duty for any other, as that none of them excludes any other.

The chief importance of the distinction thus made, lies in its establishment of religion as an independent form of experience with its own special "context of meaning." But the charge can still be brought that religion is illusion and therefore essentially meaningless. Nygren therefore seeks to demonstrate the validity of religious experience. He seeks to show that the fundamental category of religion—the basic concept which is logically presupposed in all religious experience—is such that its validity must be assumed if we are to accept the validity even of science and morality themselves. He argues that a logical analysis of the fundamental presuppositions of science and morality, namely the validity of the ideas of "truth" and of "the right" and "the good," reveals the necessity of a further concept, that of "the eternal"; and this is the fundamental concept of religion. Not that there is any necessity for the scientist or moralist as such to be aware of this, or in any way to concern himself with it; but if he is (as he may well be) also a religious man, he will have a direct, practical concern with it. For all religion, as a thorough analysis of any aspect of it will show, is essentially a matter of fellowship or communion between man and "the eternal"—a point to which we shall return.

There is, however, a further distinction to be noted which Nygren draws between the various universes of discourse. The first of these, the scientific, he describes as "theoretical," the rest as "atheoretical." In the former, if a statement is described as true or false, its truth or falsity is empirically verifiable. In the latter, if I say (for example) that an action or a person is ethically "good," I naturally intend my statement to be understood as "true," but it is not empirically verifiable. It is true or false only with reference to an ultimate standard or ideal of goodness, which is implied in my making it. Granted that standard, my judgment of a person or action in the light of it may be verifiable by reference to the observable character of the person or action. But the standard is not necessarily granted. For there are diverse ethical ideals, and which of them is the "right" one is a matter, not for empirical verification, but for personal decision and commitment. Consequently there are within the ethical universe of discourse subsidiary contexts of meaning, which are of such a nature that a statement which is true in one of them may be false in another.

The position is similar in religion. Although religion forms an independent universe of discourse, *sui generis*, there are within it also subsidiary contexts of meaning. There are different "religions," each with its own understanding of the religious relationship, the nature of communion between man and the eternal, and the way in which it is realized—everything depending ultimately on how the nature of the eternal itself is conceived. Hence, although a religious statement is meant to be understood as true by the one who makes it, its truth is no more empirically verifiable than that of an ethical statement. Within the religious universe of discourse it is entirely meaningful, but what precisely it means, and whether it is "true" or "false," depends on its relation to the subsidiary context in which it is placed.

To illustrate this point we may recall that both the philosopher Plotinus and the Apostle John say that "God is love." Admittedly, the former uses the Greek word *eros* for "love," while the latter uses *agape;* but that in itself is not important, since different words can sometimes mean the same thing, just as the same word can mean different things. But when Plotinus explains that God is "love of *Himself*," because God alone is worthy to be loved by God, he is clearly poles apart from St. John, who declares that "God so loved *the world*" and "so loved *us*," as to give His Son to be the propitiation for our sins. What Plotinus says may be true within the context of Neoplatonism, and of Hellenistic religiosity generally, but from a Christian point of view it is simply false. As to whether Plotinus or St. John is "right" about the nature of God—whether what either of them says is "true" in that sense—this again is a matter for personal decision and commitment, not for any kind of theoretical demonstration.

A final point in Nygren's philosophical prolegomena, and a point on which he strongly insists, is that all real religion involves vastly more than any abstract notion of the eternal or of man's relation to it. It is concrete experience of the eternal, an actual, living relationship with it. This relationship, moreover, can be shown to possess universally a distinct fourfold character, involving 1] an awareness of being confronted by the eternal, 2] a sense of estrangement from it, 3] some means of coming to terms with it, and 4] an intimate communion with it, or participation in it. Of these various aspects, some may be more, some less, prominent in the different religions, but all belong to the essential structure of religious experience. They are, however, like the concept of the eternal itself, nothing but abstractions—"concepts" which "without percepts are empty"—until with them in mind we approach the concrete realities of this or that historically given religion, and inquire what content it gives to them.

These concepts have, of course, been derived by a process of scientific abstraction from the concreteness of actual religion. They do not represent a preconceived pattern to which religion is supposed to conform, but rather the common skeletal structure (so to speak) which is discernible beneath the flesh and blood diversity of the religions. This is as true of the concept of the eternal as of the rest, although from what has hitherto been said it might seem to have been reached by means of a philosophical analysis of nonreligious presuppositions.

The purpose of the analysis, however, was not to demonstrate the existence of the concept, but its necessity. Its existence was known already, for the idea of eternity is familiar enough in religion. It could be argued, of course, that the idea of "God" or "the gods" is even more familiar; but Nygren has nevertheless preferred the idea of the eternal in order to avoid unduly limiting his definition of religion. There are, after all, religions in which the gods are not eternal (Hinduism), and there is the possibility of an atheistic religion (classical Buddhism). For the Christian theologian, admittedly, it is more natural to speak of "God," and in his theological work this is precisely what Nygren does.

In the light of all that has now been said, we should be the better able to understand Nygren's conception of systematic theology as a scientific discipline. Clearly it cannot be the traditional "science of God and divine things" since there cannot be any "science of the transcendent." Instead, just as it is the task of any other science to understand and expound a given subject matter, so it is the task of systematic theology to understand and expound the Christian faith. It is not concerned with religion in general, which can never be more than an abstraction, but with this particular religion. Its business is to demonstrate the essential meaning and content of the Christian faith, showing what makes it specifically Christian and different from all others. It has to place the various articles and affirmations of faith—and this is what makes it "systematic"—where they severally belong in the total context of Christianity, relating them to one another around their common center. In other words, it has to exhibit the inner, organic unity of the faith, while giving as clear, comprehensive and coherent an exposition of it as possible.

But this is much more easily said than done. It is not too difficult to give an account of Christianity "according to" a whole series of very diverse exponents (such as St. Paul, St. John, Origen, Tertullian, Augustine, Aquinas, Luther, the Wesleys), or even of the Catholic or the Reformed "conception of Christianity," and so forth; and the accuracy of these accounts is open to objective discussion, since the material on which they are based is available for public inspection. But what we want is an account of Christianity *sans phrase*, not "according to" anyone in particular; and where is this available for public inspection? Where in objective reality, as observable fact, can we find it in order to give an account of it? And if we could find it, would not our account be simply *ours*, and so yet another example of "Christianity according to"?

The solution for these problems Nygren finds in what he usually calls "motif-research." He is not wedded to this term, and if we prefer to speak of "typological research" or "structural research," or to call it by some other name, he will not object. The name is less important than the aim and method of the inquiry. What these are, he has described quite fully in his Introduction to *Agape and Eros*, his Introduction to *Urkristendom och reformation*, and several essays in *Filosofi och motivforskning*. In brief, however, we may say that the aim is quite simply to discover the *differentia* of Christianity—that which makes it specifically Christian and uniquely different, and that which therefore must necessarily find expression in one way or another in everything that can rightly be called Christian. The method is to start from the plain fact that Christianity is a religion, and that religion is essentially a matter of communion with the eternal, or God, and then to inquire where and how this communion is actually realized in the Christian scheme of things. That is to say, we take what has already been established as the fundamental concept of all religion, and ask with what content this particular religion fills it.

This procedure has been criticized on the ground that it allows philosophy to put the question which theology is required to answer. But that is not in fact the case. What philosophy—the philosophy of religion—has done for us, is to establish the idea of the eternal as the fundamental, and fundamentally valid, "category" of all religion. If this is a highly general and abstract idea, lacking any particular content, that is as it should be, for it is beyond the competence of philosophy to give it any particular content. But we have the right to ask about its content. We have the right to raise what Nygren calls the "categorical question" regarding the nature of the eternal and the terms and conditions of fellowship or communion with it. When we do so, however, we are not raising a philosophical but a religious question, and one which of all questions is the most fundamental in all religion. No doubt the different religions will give different answers to it, and neither philosophy nor science nor theology can determine which of them is "right"; but with this the Christian theologian is not primarily concerned. His aim, as a systematic theologian at any rate, is simply to gain as clear an understanding as possible of the Christian answer. This point should be stressed: systematic theology is not an attempt to answer the "categorical question," but simply to understand an answer already given.

In seeking to fulfill this aim, Nygren proceeds as follows. Christianity has from the beginning been a "gospel," good news, about the love of God shown towards men in Christ, who has sacrificed himself in order to save the lost. There is nothing in man to call forth such a love, and God's love is in that sense "unmotivated." God loves because it is His nature to love, because He "is love," not because of anything that man is or does or leaves undone. (In His love, God no doubt deals variously with men according to what they are or do, comforting or chastising them as He sees they need; but that is here beside the point.) What is more, it is God's loving of man, as this is brought home to men through Christ, that brings about Christian communion with God and determines its nature. It is through Christ that the bare bones of religion which we described above, become clothed with Christian flesh and blood. The confrontation of man by the eternal God, the disclosure of man's sin and estrangement from God, the means of overcoming the estrangement and reconciling man to God, and the way for man to share in God's eternal life—all these are found by the Christian faith in and through Jesus Christ, and all as the gift and work of divine love.

This love, which the New Testament calls *agape*, is what makes Christian everything that can rightly be called Christian, and it sets its mark in one way or another on every aspect of Christian faith and life. The idea of Agape, therefore, as representing the answer that Christianity gives to the "fundamental question" of religion, can very well be said to be the "fundamental motif" of Christianity. This is not to say that it is the only motif, but that it is the one to which all others are necessarily subordinate. We might speak, for example, of the ideas of holiness or judgment or atonement or sacrifice as motifs. They are both familiar and important enough in the world of religion generally, as well as in Christianity. But they have in Christianity a distinctive meaning and content not found in other religions, and it is the Agape motif that makes the difference. How it does so, and what kind of a difference it makes, is admirably illustrated in Nygren's essay on the Atonement in his *Essence of Christianity*.

The idea of Agape is, of course, essentially an abstraction from the concrete realities of which the Christian faith normally speaks. Of this we are reminded when Nygren in *Agape and Eros* shows how the dogmas of Creation, Incarnation, and Resurrection—the "Three Fundamental Dogmas of the Early Church" as he calls them—are expressions of Agape. The Christian faith always expresses itself in terms of concrete, dynamic images and symbols, rather than in the static, abstract terms of formal definition. In the course of Christian history a multitude of such images and symbols has been used for the confession and communication of the faith—not all of them drawn from Christian sources. Their origin, however, is quite unimportant beside the question whether they are genuinely capable of expressing the idea of Agape, and whether they are so used that they do in fact express it. The Agape motif, therefore, furnishes us with a criterion by which we can judge what is and what is not a genuine expression of the faith.

The Agape motif also furnishes us with an organizing principle for our exposition of the faith. In the light of it we can expound the different articles and affirmations of faith, demonstrating their significance by relating them to it and to one another in a systematic way. For example, it makes a great deal of difference to our understanding of the problem of "faith and works," whether we interpret it in terms of the Agape motif or, let us say, the Nomos motif. The meaning of the terms "faith" and "works" and the nature of the relation between them is quite different in the two cases. Similarly, it makes a great deal of difference to our understanding of the doctrine of the Virgin Birth and its relation to the Incarnation, whether we interpret it in terms of the Agape motif or the Eros motif. Nygren himself, it is true, has never attempted a full-scale treatment of dogmatics, or systematic theology, though he has given us a great deal of material towards one, especially in *Agape and Eros*—for this is essentially the work of a systematic rather than a historical theologian. If we wish, however, to see the kind of thing that can be done in dogmatics when the Agape motif is taken seriously, we cannot do better than turn to *The Faith of the Christian Church* by Nygren's old friend and colleague, Gustav Aulén.

Now it may, of course, be objected that in all of this we have nothing more than another individual interpretation of Christianity— "Christianity according to Nygren." But this objection will not hold. For when the idea of Agape (or any other idea) is proposed as the fundamental motif of Christianity, this is a theory, a hypothesis, which can be verified or falsified by reference to the historically given material. Not every theory will fit the facts, and that theory is clearly to be preferred which does most justice to them and makes the best sense of them. This is excellently illustrated in *Agape and Eros*. Here it is shown how the Agape motif, finding expression in very diverse ways through a long period of history, does in fact represent that which is specifically Christian; and its essential character is all the more clearly exhibited by contrast with the fundamental motifs of Judaism and Hellenism, namely the Nomos motif and the Eros motif.

Nygren's thesis in *Agape and Eros* has been subjected to distinguished criticism, but this has generally been quite wide of the mark. The critics have been interested in something other than what Nygren is doing, and they have paid scant attention to the explanations given both in his own introduction and in the translator's preface. None of them has even begun to show that Nygren has mishandled his material from the point of view with which he approaches it, or that that point of view is either illegitimate or irrelevant; and until one or other of these things is done, his thesis stands unshaken.

The method of motif research is thoroughly scientific, in that it enables and indeed requires us to observe our material about it, and to put the hypothesis to the test. For example, when Nygren was working on Neoplatonism in connection with the writing of *Agape and Eros*, he came to the conclusion—or formed the hypothesis—that Plotinus must have said somewhere that "God is *eros*." He therefore sat down and read through the *Enneads* till he found a passage where Plotinus says precisely that. This did not in itself prove that the idea of Eros was Plotinus' fundamental motif, but it did suggest that his interpreter was on the right lines; and when he could go on to show by analysis of different aspects of Plotinus' thought, that Eros was its constant presupposition, he might well be taken to have proved his point. In this connection it is perhaps important to observe that the method of motif research is applicable to other outlooks as well as Christianity, and we can have a "systematic theology" of other religions also if we wish. When Nygren defines the subject matter of theology as the Christian faith, that is chiefly because for all ordinary purposes, when we speak of theology, we mean Christian theology.

We are now in a position to substantiate the claim of systematic theology to a place among the sciences. To begin with, it possesses like every other science a given subject matter which it has to investigate and seek to understand, namely the Christian faith. This exists in a considerable variety of forms in which it has found expression through the centuries, and which are available for public inspection. Secondly, it possesses, like every other science, an interest in its subject matter which is peculiarly its own. It differs from biblical and historical theology, for example, and from the history and comparative study of religions, in that it is not concerned with what Christianity once was, or with the origins and development of Christian ideas, or with their possible connections with other faiths and philosophies. Its interest centers rather in the question what Christianity essentially *is*, always and everywhere, no matter how diverse the garb in which from time to time and place to place it appears. Thirdly, it possesses, like every other science, a method of inquiry appropriate to its purpose, namely, that of motif research. With this the theologian can penetrate beneath the surface to the inner meaning of the phenomena he has to interpret, as he must if he is to fulfill his task. He cannot assume that similar or even identical modes of expression necessarily mean the same thing, or that dissimilar ones necessarily mean different things. Everything depends on the underlying motif.

There is one point here that should be specially emphasized. The task of systematic theology, we have said, is to understand and give an account of the Christian faith; that is to say, it has simply to tell us *what Christianity is*. It is not its business to prove to us that Christianity *is true*. That is quite another question, and one that we cannot even begin to answer intelligently before we know exactly what Christianity is. These two questions have all too often been mixed up with one another in the history of theology, sometimes with disastrous consequences. Unless they are kept clearly distinct, it is all too easy for the theologian (or anyone else) to let his account of Christianity be shaped by current trends of thought and what they will allow him to accept as true. It is therefore not the least of Nygren's merits that he keeps these questions strictly apart. Systematic theology, as he conceives it, can give us a demonstrably correct answer to the first of them; it can give us *a true account of Christianity*. But scientific proof of the "truth of Christianity," or of any other faith is in the nature of the case unobtainable. Whether we accept Christianity as true or not, is a matter for personal decision and commitment; and while we may be able to give excellent reasons for accepting it, these cannot and ought not to amount to coercive demonstration. They belong, moreover, within the province of apologetics, not of systematic theology.

Even so, there may still be those who would dismiss theology as a pseudoscience, on the ground that it lacks the "objectivity" that characterizes genuine science. It requires us to *assume* what it admits it cannot prove, namely the "truth of Christianity," which is in no sense an objectively given reality, but an intensely personal and subjective conviction by no means universally shared. This objection, however, rests on a confusion of thought. Admittedly, theologians are as a rule Christians, who as such believe Christianity to be true. But there is no rule to say that theologians must be Christians, or that only Christians can be theologians. Lack of interest may prevent the non-Christian from being a theologian, and lack of empathy might prevent his being a good one; but there is nothing in the nature of theological inquiry itself to prevent his engaging successfully in it. After all, Anders Nygren is not a Neoplatonist, yet he has given us an excellent and an an objectively verifiable account of Neoplatonism; so why should not a non-Christian who has the taste and talent for research in the field of religion, be able to show similar insight into the nature of Christianity? Practically this may be extremely improbable, but theoretically there is nothing to prevent it.

What ensures scientific objectivity is not the personal attitude of the scientist towards his subject matter, nor even the nature of the subject matter itself, but rather the method of inquiry that is employed. Scientific method is never arbitrary but always necessitated by the character of the investigation. It does not reflect the scientist's personal preferences or prejudices, but demands precisely that these should be set aside. Consequently, systematic theology as a science no more requires us to assume the truth of Christianity than to prove it. It requires us to recognize that Christianity exists, that it merits serious attention, and that it can be scientifically investigated—by the appropriate method, which Nygren calls "motif-research." And who can deny that Christianity merits attention, when about a third of the world's population is at least nominally Christian, or that it urgently calls for scientific investigation, when the variegated multitude of churches, sects, and parties testifies to the confusion even among Christians themselves as to what Christianity really is?

It will no doubt have been noticed that the present writer shares Anders Nygren's point of view and would rather reply to his critics than join their ranks. Yet it must be confessed that his work displays certain weaknesses which are the almost inevitable defects of its virtues. To begin with, Nygren is a cobbler who sticks so closely to his last that relatively few of his readers are capable of the same sustained and concentrated attention. They want answers to all kinds of questions that arise from their own points of view as they read, and because he does not turn aside to deal with these they are apt to jump to erroneous conclusions and attribute to him views he would never dream of holding. It has been alleged, for example, that with his idea of Agape he excludes not merely selfishness but even human selfhood, and that by his refusal to make room for the Eros motif in Christianity he fails to take the doctrine of Creation seriously. Such mistaken notions illustrate the desirability of his spelling out in more elementary detail some of the implications of his teaching.

Part of the difficulty is due perhaps to the very sharp distinctions he draws between the logical, ontological, theological, and psychological standpoints, and his rigorous exclusion of the ontological and psychological from his own consideration. These are undoubtedly necessary distinctions, and he undoubtedly has the right to decide which of the various standpoints he will or will not adopt. Yet other people cannot be forbidden to raise questions concerning the possible implications of his position when it is viewed from other standpoints. For example: how can the logical necessity of the idea of the eternal be held to guarantee the validity of religious experience, unless it implies the ontological reality of the eternal as that which is religiously experienced? Or how can we maintain theologically that salvation is wholly God's work, to the exclusion of all man's working, without landing ourselves psychologically in sheer determinism? Clearly there is need for elucidation of the relationships between the different standpoints.

Something similar is true with regard to the different universes of discourse—science, art, morality, and religion—and perhaps also with regard to the subsidiary contexts of meaning within each of the last three. The essential distinctions between all of these have been made sufficiently plain, but it is much less clear what connections, if any, there may be between them, beyond the fact that they all in one way or another presuppose the concept of the eternal. Possibly this is the only logically necessary connection, so that we must look in other directions for any further relationships between them, and possibly then we must be prepared to find very variable relationships. But whether that is so or not, the whole matter calls for much fuller exposition than Nygren has yet given it in print.

Finally, the question of the "truth of Christianity" must be faced. The systematic theologian may properly disclaim responsibility for it, but the Christian certainly cannot. For the Christian accepts Christianity's own claim to be true, yet finds this claim disputed, not only by the counterclaims of non-Christians, but by the doubts and questionings that arise even in his own mind. Unless, therefore, the matter is to be settled by sheer dogmatic assertion or denial, he must be prepared to discuss and give reasons for his position, and to require his opponents likewise to give their reasons. No doubt the critical philosopher will very rightly remind us that scientific demonstration is here impossible, and that everyone must make up his own mind on this issue. But can it be denied that there is both need and possibility of reasonable discussion to assist us in making up our minds?

The need is clearly undeniable, and as to the possibility, Nygren himself seems to offer us some very promising clues. His discussion of the nature and validity of religious experience, for example, is in part at least a defense of religion against its detractors, and a plea that it be taken seriously. Then his contention (in *Essence of Christianity*, for instance) that the radically theocentric character of Christianity does justice to the nature of religion in a way unparalleled elsewhere, looks very like an argument for the superior claim of Christianity on our attention. Again, his insistence on the principle that the theory is to be preferred which makes most sense of the facts, points to the possibility of arguing that the Christian way of looking at things makes the best sense of human and indeed of cosmic existence. Nygren may have had no apologetic intention in all this, but at least it suggests apologetic possibilities.

Admittedly, apologetics is a risky business, exposing us as it does to the constant temptation to accommodate the faith to the tastes of our readers or hearers, and to the danger of subtle metaphysical snares. Yet its widespread neglect in recent years—due partly to the general and almost panic flight from metaphysics, partly to the exciting preoccupations of neo-orthodox, biblical, and ecumenical theology—has not made the communication of the faith conspicuously easier or more successful. We need the systematic theologian to tell us what Christianity is before we begin to discuss its truth, and we need the critical philosopher to warn us against false methods of argumentation; but we need no less the apologist who, taking full account of the work of the theologian and the philosopher, will show us how to engage in a reasoned advocacy of the faith. It may very well be true that apologetics can lay no claim to rank among the sciences at the university, but it deserves a place of high importance among the arts in the seminary and the Church.

13

NYGREN'S THEOLOGY OF AGAPE

Nels F. S. Ferré

THEOLOGY of agape is basic Christianity. Such and no less is Nygren's claim. The scope of this chapter is the investigation of this claim. Can it be substantiated theologically? In order to perform this task responsibly it is necessary to delimit the undertaking. We shall not discuss the background of Nygren's theology of agape in Swedish theology, nor Nygren's use of the Bible, nor his employment of historical theology, nor his understanding of the history of philosophy, nor his approach to history through motif research, nor Nygren's own history in the use of terms, nor the history of the literature which has dealt with his theology of agape. We are even foregoing almost entirely the privilege of discussing the many possible relations between his philosophical and his theological methods. The definite focus of this study, rather, will be the question whether Nygren has used agape in the fullest possible Christian sense, thus releasing its inmost truth and putting it to its most effective theological use.

Every topic that we have purposely excluded from our discussion is of both major importance and major complexity. The problem in each instance is not only technical correctness but the basic "feel" of the subject. For the sake of sharpness of focus for concise, but central discussion we shall further limit our investigation to Nygren's standard work *Agape and Eros* in its basic intention. In support of such choice we have Nygren's own testimony to the consistency of his basic use of the agape motif throughout the several publications of this work. Any discussion, moreover, of possible shades of differences, for instance, in his use of "creative love" inside and outside his main work, directly or indirectly, through his long life would be both wasteful of space and basically unnecessary. Because the center of Nygren's theology of agape is emulably clear and consistent, it lends itself readily to effective appraisal.

In fairness to the readers of this chapter the writer should state that his own theological history was basically altered by reading *Agape and Eros,* that Nygren has always impressed him as a great human being as well as a scholar of the first order, that Nygren's development of the theology of agape has already proved itself epoch-making, but that he also believes that Nygren has never made the fullest possible use of his own theology because he has not let agape itself become central either to his theological method or to his interpretation of Christian faith. The writer is convinced, rather, that Nygren's service to theology will become qualitatively enhanced and enriched if he will deliver it not only from its confining Lutheran frame but also from its traditionalistic Christian outlook. His definitive identification of the Christian center as agape may involve a theological revolution of different dimensions and proportions from those envisaged by Bishop Nygren. The importance of his work may be far greater than he has himself seen. The aim of this chapter is to state Nygren's theology of agape at its own center, to appraise the validity and vitality of his position, and only then to suggest where he may have failed to take full advantage of his own findings.

Nygren's theology of agape is, first of all, through and through God-centered. Agape as the fundamental motif of Christianity means God is agape. To be sure God is so completely agape that the proposition is unequivocally reversible: agape is God. But in either way of putting the case, God as agape is ultimate. There is no God in the Christian faith who in any sense is more than, or other than, agape nor is there any agape that is not entirely God, or of God. Within authentic Christian faith, to say God is to say agape and to say agape is to say God. Nygren is clear and consistent on the point: God is the only source of agape because agape and God are synonymous. There is no agape apart from God. Nor is there any aspect of God that is not agape. All of God is agape and all agape is God. There is no independent agape in man or nature. Thus Nygren's theology of agape is unexceptionally God-centered.

This affirmation of God-centered agape as central to the Christian faith depends upon a competent analysis of the Christian faith, naturally of the Bible, and primarily of the New Testament, but then also of the history of Christian thought. Such analysis is not merely historic in the sense of detailed, disparate investigation of thought. Certainly it is not mostly etymological. Nor is it a matter of semantic analysis. Nygren cannot be unseated by any unearthing of the use of words in biblical or classical times, inside or outside the Bible. Nor is he primarily concerned with the use of concepts. His method is no merely propositional analysis, concerned with minute internal consistency of meaning. Even though we are not discussing method as such, it is well to be aware that Nygren has devoted his life's loyalty to the understanding of agape as an attitude of life. He deals not with value judgments in the merely personal, subjective sense, nor with merely judgments of value in the objective sense, but with the main attitudes of life, objectively reflected in the historic religions. He holds that there are total attitudes of life exhibited by these religions at their very centers, whatever then be the historic compromises that can be found in the history of these religions and whatever shades of understanding and acceptance may be exhibited in the concrete faith judgments of individual believers.

Thus the Christian faith can be established as objectively witnessing to agape just as Judaism testifies to nomos and Greek religions to eros. Nygren's fundamental motifs are normative, historic descriptions of the governing centers of religions. They aim at being factual descriptions of historic faiths, but his method does not deal with the question of the normative truth of these religions. The motifs, or attitudes of life, are *coram deo*. Religion deals with the category of eternity. In this basic methodological sense, not only concerned with the Christian faith but with religion in general, agape is God-centered. Other religions, from the Christian point of view, put law or self-centered love, for instance, in the place of God. But in the Christian faith, when it is genuine, nothing is put in God's place or made into God, for agape is God-centered both methodologically and analytically. God is agape.

Such God-centered love can be indicated by terms that point toward it without ever taking the place of, or fully describing, the living God of Christian faith. Agape is spontaneous. It needs no motivation outside its own nature. Therefore it is unmotivated. Nor is it caused by anything. Since God is his own cause, agape is uncaused. In the same manner agape can be called groundless or ungrounded in the sense that there is no ground for agape that is not God. Similarly agape is uncalculating in that it never acts out of prudential considerations. Agape motivation never calculates the value of the object it loves. Nor does agape arise out of community experience, but is rather itself the sole cause of the community it creates. Agape is thus love creative of fellowship. It is beyond reason and justice if either term is considered to have content of its own. Agape is through and through its own ground, its own motivation, its own calculation, its own power of creation, its own reason, and its own justice. Nygren is thoroughly consistent in his understanding of the ultimate nature of agape that can be defined only in terms of itself. He means precisely that God is agape and agape, God, and that is the end of the matter. Agape is completely God-centered. Let us look further at his delineation of the fundamental motif of agape.

Agape is then, God's love. Agape is God himself who by nature is love and who always acts in accordance with his nature. Agape is personal love, creative of community in terms of personal relations, especially by the forgiveness of sin. Agape is not love of God in the sense of man's loving God within any reality and power of his own. In this sense agape is unequivocally and unexceptionally God-centered.

But agape is also Christ-centered. God does not love by nature in any rational sense in such a way that man can find him and attain to him by reason, as he traces God's thoughts or evidences of his love in some general manner. Rather, God showed his love concretely by himself coming into the world. He showed it personally. God demonstrated his love for us in the Incarnation. By loving the world all the way to the sending of his Son to die for our sins, God revealed his love. Thus God-centeredness means Christ-centeredness, not of some essence or way of life, nor merely teaching, but supremely in the Cross. God showed his agape particularly by Christ's dying for his enemies. Not that God loves the enemies more than others, of course, for such discrimination would obviously motivate love in inverse proportion or ratio to the object of love, but that the nature of agape is peculiarly demonstrated in the love of enemies.

Christ-centered agape, moreover, is no substantive love from which deductive judgments can be made. It is no metaphysical, cosmological kind of love. For this reason Nygren glories in Saint Paul's understanding of Christ's love through the Cross. No wonder Paul's Letter to the Romans finds such favor with Nygren where acted agape, the Cross-crowned agape, dominates the discussion. In the Johannine writings, however, Nygren insists, agape has already been compromised. To be sure the Johannine author reached the summit of agapaic love when he actually defined God as agape propositionally. But John had already compromised agape by suggesting that the Father loved the world for the sake of the Son, that he loves the Son peculiarly, and that love of the brethren is superior to love of the world. Indeed, John even went so far in limiting agape as to say that the Son does not pray for the world and that neither should the disciples love the world. Such qualifications, however, rend asunder the seamless robe of agape. Agape is no longer completely God-centered and unexceptionally for the whole world. On the contrary, it is now motivated and therefore no longer the pure agape of the Christian faith. In Paul's letters, however, agape is based on the historic manifestation of Christ and especially the Christ of the Cross. Here is no speculative, substantive, metaphysical understanding of love, but the direct confrontation of God in history. Nor is agape's judgment, moreover, other than the concrete confrontation of the Christ. It is no rationalized judgment, no inferential rational appraisal, but precisely the result inherently and inevitably of man's rejection of God's concrete revelation in Christ as agape.

Agape, then, according to Nygren's analysis, is entirely God-centered and Christ-centered. As such it is completely for the world. It is for men. It is from God, never from men or of men. Love of enemies is the test. All must be loved not only equally but fully. A specialized love of the brethren, as we have seen, denies the reality of agape. Not to love the world, in the ingroup sense of limiting love to the circle of disciples, is glaringly an alteration in the meaning and power of agape. In agape God's love is full and free, the only reality and source of love. No "horizontal" love, therefore, some love in terms of man's mutuality, or conditional love within man's power, can be classified as agape. And so much the more, in agape there can be no self-love. In agape all self-love is excluded, for all love is from God and of God. Self-love cannot be outgoing love either in origin or in direction. Self-love is thus a double contradiction of agape.

Indeed, self-seeking love, the Greek eros, is at its very heart the rival of agape throughout the history of the Christian faith. Eros is love from the self to the self. No matter how high such love seeks or how worthy its objects, eros is still the love of self, for it is the self seeking satisfaction from and in its objects. Especially indicative of the meaning of eros is the Platonic exposition of "the heavenly eros" which is man's seeking the eternal, the supreme good, but still seeking it for self. Another outstanding illustration of eros we find in the Neoplatonic understanding of God wherein God can love only himself because he alone is a worthy object of love, whereas God's love of the world, an inferior object, would indeed be a violation of the nature of true love. In these classical instances eros is seen at its highest and truest nature. No matter how high eros strives it never escapes being the seeking love of the self for the self. Thus eros is centrally, categorically, analytically self-love. Such love stands at the opposite pole of agape.

The main problem in the history of Christian thought, however, has not been the direct opposition of eros to agape, but rather the subtle way that it has become insinuated into the agape motif so as to dilute it. To be sure, the eros attitude to life is so naturally human that apart from some kind of adjustment to it the proclamation of agape would have seemed irrelevant. Therefore, both proclamation and apologetics related agape to the thought of the classical Greek world which was fundamentally saturated with eros. Such synthesis may have been historically unavoidable, but it is always analytically illegitimate. The tapestry which was fashioned from the confrontation of the Gospel with the Platonic and the Neoplatonic thought worlds, however, could not be allowed to remain unrent. If it had, the reality and power of the Christian message would have been lost. Therefore, great periods of reformation were necessary to restore the original message of the Christ as interpreted by Paul. Some major reformers were Marcion, Irenaeus, Athanasius, and finally Luther.

But Luther had in fact to contend with the mightiest compromise, or with the stateliest synthesis of all, Augustine's fashioning of the *caritas* motif. Within the true Christian faith, Nygren holds, love of God is mostly the reflection of God's love. It is not at all the same as love to God within the Jewish nomos motif, or within the Greek eros motif. Since man possesses no love in himself in the agape sense and since agape is never seeking love, agape to God is only linguistically legitimate within the full New Testament or Gospel context, where it really means faith, or man's receiving love, rather than man's outgoing love to God, spontaneous and creative of fellowship. In Augustine, however, self-love is accepted as necessary and basic. Such love of self, nevertheless, can be attained by nothing less than man's love of God. Augustine passionately insisted that man is made for God and cannot rest until God become the total object of his quest. All other loves,

moreover, whether of others or of the created world, must in essence
be the love of God. Man loves God in and through all these, for finally
only God can satisfy man's basic drive for satisfaction. Thus, in Augustine's writings, we have a God-centered love that is really for the
satisfaction of the self who can never rest except in God. If Augustine
had stopped at this point, he would definitely have been within the eros
motif of most of his early devotion both before and after becoming a
Christian, but Augustine was equally insistent that man could not by
himself manage to find such satisfaction. The pagan philosophers could
by their natural insight see the goal of the Christian religion, but they
could not attain to it. They perceived the end, but they had no way of
getting there.

Therefore Augustine was eloquent in his Christian insistence that
there was no way to salvation except through Christ. God in his eternal
love had sent us his Son to die for us that we might see in the light of
Christ's humility in being crucified for us our own natural pride and
thereby also find the means to overcome such pride by entering
wholeheartedly into the love of God from which natural man is ever
kept by his pride. Thus apart from God's agape there is and can be no
salvation for man. The Christian faith is the only way to God; it is
God's way to man. But in Augustine's theology, as Nygren interprets
it, God does not in Christ kill the natural man in order to give him new
life only within the grace that lives in utter gratitude and obedience
within God's love for him and within God's love within his life for all.
Rather, love of God is made possible only in the eros sense of satisfying
the self by God's acting in agape to make such love possible. This
august wedding of the agape and the eros motifs Augustine called
caritas. The Christian church up to the Reformation, Nygren develops,
was mostly conquered by this *caritas* interpretation of the Christian
faith.

Luther, however, dissolved the *caritas* synthesis by his full-blown
return to the original Pauline Gospel. The Reformation, especially in
Luther, is therefore critical for the purity of the Christian faith. In
Luther we reach a summit not only of the original interpretation of the
meaning and saving power of Christ but also of the peak of Christian
theology that has by now resisted not only the nomos motif of the Old
Testament but also both the eros and the *caritas* motifs, and discriminat-
ingly and effectively caused the downfall of them all. Unfortunately,
however, the history after Luther is not one of theological consumma-
tion, but is, rather, one which changes the nature of the conflict
between agape and its adversaries. The historic eros and *caritas* motifs

as such are now exchanged for other forms of the same problem, and Nygren feels that it is not his own problem to continue his historic analysis.

We have thus put Nygren's case for the theology of agape as directly and simply as we can, believing that our stating it within the space allowed involves no basic distortion or diminution of his epoch-making analysis. Naturally we can in no way even suggest the care and competence, yes, the analytical brilliance his writings display. We can only point to the results in a concentrated summary for the sake of weighing them in the theological balance. Before so doing, however, we repeat that our task is in no way to discuss our attitudes toward the niceties of historic analysis or Nygren's empathy in rendering the deepest intention of the historic writers, Christian or non-Christian. In general Nygren has made out a case that stands both strong and steady.

BOTH THE validity and the vitality of Nygren's theology of agape are striking. Naturally the following appraisal, creatively and critically, is the writer's, not Nygren's.

Historically agape is the distinctive and determinative motif of the Christian faith. The author of this chapter spent several years resisting Nygren's thesis that agape was peculiar to the Christian faith. He read and asked experts continually, hoping to prove Nygren wrong. He found many approximations in several religions, but his final conclusion after arduous seeking to deliver himself from what seemed ignorance or prejudice, yes, almost an insult to God the Creator, was that agape is indeed not only characteristic but distinctive to the Christian faith. After capitulating, he has continued to seek with open eyes, and has in truth been impressed by what may seem to break the seamless robe of agape, such facts as the life and teaching of Mo Ti, or of Shinran, instances in the Old Testament which for him have a "feel" closer to agape than to mere election and covenant love, or aspects of Amida Buddhism or Caiva Siddhanta. As a matter of fact, if agape is confined to forgiving love, or grace, rather than released for the total nature and work of God, Nygren's claim that agape came only in Christ seems even more vulnerable. We shall see later that God the Creator who is agape may be the main distinction between the Christian and some non-Christian understandings of love or grace, but our task is not to make a historical investigation, but only to admit in general the validity of Nygren's claim.

Again to look at the historical validity, the fact seems ever more impregnable that agape is the determinative motif of the Christian faith. Certainly Christ is the central authority for Christianity. The Scriptures are authoritative, in the final analysis, because they speak of him. Christ is not only the founder of the faith but the abiding heart of its meaning. The meaning of Christ, however, is precisely the Cross and the Resurrection. Christ means the eternal Love who came to us from God "for us men and our salvation." Christ means God ultimately and Jesus Christ historically. Christ means agape, the sovereign Lord who is saving Love, who is seen in a concrete life, an historic event, but who made the meaning of his own life clear by his teachings in parables and sayings that press agape upon any open and receptive spirit. We may, of course, come to the New Testament with stubborn convictions based on our ordinary world which may keep us from receiving the strong claim of the truth of agape, but once we enter into the Christian perspective, the New Testament and the deepest core of genuine Christianity fairly shout the determinativeness of agape at us.

We need an organizing context both for thought and for history. The life of Christ, his death and resurrection, are most adequately understood in terms of the meaning of agape. This life, with this kind of meaning, is our ultimate and permanent model for God. It cannot be exhausted by propositional definitions. Even the true sentence, "God is love," does not fill in concretely the meaning of this love, nor can it do so, for the free God, the living God of agape, the creative love, can never be confined by being defined. Yet for thought and for historic identity we have to have guide lines, correct pointers, reliable indicators, for faith and worship, for study and life; and such indicators are exactly the motif of agape, which is more than conceptual, more than analytical, more even than a faith judgment or Nygren's favorite "attitude to life," for agape is an open pattern beyond all verbal renderings of it and beyond all human believings and feelings toward it. To call agape "it," although linguistically expedient, betrays its meaning. For that matter, even to call agape "he" distorts the truth that the living God can none the less be pointed to by means of a motif. Thus the Bible, under the creative authority of the fundamental motif of agape, becomes source book for faith and not textbook for belief. Even though some of us cannot follow Nygren in believing that the whole New Testament witnesses to agape in the way and to the extent that he holds, nevertheless, after decades of careful study, the writer owns that Nygren is right in claiming agape to be valid as the determinative motif of the Christian faith. Thus, although we have not here made a separate study of the question, the writer can affirm that Nygren's position has at least central validity in its main intentions.

For some of us, however, the historical validity of agape would mean little unless it also proved itself more theologically adequate than any other motif. It does so. The doctrine of God, becoming transformed by it, loses its inherent frustrations. If God is understood as primarily holiness, for instance, there is no intrinsic reason for either creation or incarnation. From within the meaning of agape, however, God's very nature is to be outgoing, creative. God who created the world out of love eternally loves his world and comes to save it for no other reason than that he is agape. At the same time, there is no forfeiting or diminution of holiness. Agape is eternally self-consistent in its nature, eternally separate in itself from all that is not agape, therefore repudiating from within totally and always all that is unholy, while at the same time moving in love toward men, toward the world, to redeem it, to transform it, to perfect it by the overcoming of all that is sinful and wrong. Refusing any basis except its own perfectly holy agape, it holds off all finally unacceptable relationships while yet going out to sinful men to claim them for the love for which they are made. Agape perfects holiness in the fear of God because it is complete concern for all men according to its own eternal, inviolate perfection. There is thus functional tension both in God and in the world between holiness and love, never to be minimized, requiring even God's own self-giving in the world for the world to save men for himself and for themselves (a situation which makes the Atonement a historic necessity), but there is no permanent dualism between love and holiness nor an arbitrary paradox due merely to a false starting point in theology.

In the same way, just as Christian theology cannot make holiness central, so it cannot make power central to the nature of God. If God is basically power, Calvary cannot be central. Nor can the distinctive teachings of Jesus. But, even more, systematically, if power be central to the reality of God, God must surely be limited, for he has then become finite by giving us power. Power is capacity to choose, to control and to direct. Theologians who make power to have independent meaning in God rather than the power of agape often deny human freedom and magnify the doctrine of election, but the whole reason for creation as well as the genuine fact of responsible human freedom must be denied in order thus to think of God. Some theologians, to be sure, have fallen prey to such a fateful choice. When, however, God is understood systematically as agape, God does not limit but expresses his nature by giving the children of his creation responsible choice. Love gives freedom to the other. Love craves to have the other real and responsible, and only then to transcend the duties of freedom within the love of community. Thus God, by bestowing power on his creation, expresses his nature, agape, by the self-limiting of his power. God who has the power of agape shares his power for the purposes of agape. In published works the writer has long stressed this kind of creative criticism. Nygren may not always be in full sympathy with some of these developments of theological adequacy in terms of agape as the fundamental motif of the Christian faith for reasons that we shall discuss in the next section, but undoubtedly agape has unrivaled validity and adequacy for systematic interpretation within the theological needs of the Christian faith.

Sometimes, moreover, the Christian faith is rendered within the framework of alien philosophies, thus losing its power and creating inauthentic problems. One main alien framework is that of being. When God is defined within the ultimate presupposition of being, or in terms of such a substrate, he is in fact effectively bowed out of his universe. The absolute cannot be related without becoming relative. The unconditioned cannot be related without becoming conditioned. The infinite cannot be a separate being in any sense without becoming one among beings and therefore finite. Thus God, within the framework of being, cannot be consistently defined in terms of anything we know, but only negatively. Agnosticism should result or some contrived superimposition of revelation which is illicit according to the critical analysis of the consequences of defining God in terms of being. But when God is understood as agape and Christian theology purged of its false dependence upon extraneous philosophies, the very nature of God is understood to be such as indirectly to create relations, to be the living God within relations, and to perfect relations within his constant and unconditional concern. Such use of agape is, in fact, not to philosophize the Christian faith, but to let its intrinsic truth illumine and help men solve their real intellectual problems which otherwise, directly or indirectly, unconsciously or deliberately, believers will take to philosophies which are in fact rivals of the Christian faith in their claim to truth.

Or to take one more example, for illustrations are all we have the opportunity to develop, sometimes God is interpreted in terms of process philosophy. Philosophies of being, it is claimed, cannot account for change, for becoming, perhaps even for non-being, whereas an entire new range of solution is introduced when these matters are understood within the perspective of process. The fact is, however, that such philosophies when made consistently ultimate fail to account for the eternal Purpose beyond cosmic process. Alfred North White-head, for instance, affirmed the need for metaphysical beyond cosmo-logical universals, but admitted his inability to deal with the subject. God and his eternal destiny for man usually get short shrift, therefore, in modern theologies that transpose the Christian faith into process philosophy. When God is understood as agape, however, he can be eternally changeless and create the eternal community within the conditions of his love while participating continually not only in and with all change, but for the highest quality of change. He can direct and control all at the highest and ultimate level even while allowing his teaching process of created experience to develop. We shall develop this topic further in our third section, but here we can see that he who is the changeless Love is also by that fact the most inclusive participant in the process of change.

Instead of the illustrations above, we could have shown how theology forced into the strait-jacket of being cannot admit the reality of the Incarnation without violating its inner nature, for not only can the infinite not exist as transcendent being but it can never participate or exist within the world of the finite. Therefore the heart of the Christian faith is denied by a theology working within the framework of being. On the other side of the ledger, moreover, process theologies cannot adequately deal with the meaning of suffering in terms of God's permanent victory through and over it. Process itself is the category of final explanation and suffering is ingredient to it. Within a philosophy of perfect being, of course, suffering is deficiency and a scandal. Thus the very center of the Christian faith is denied when theology is transposed into philosophies either of being or of process, whereas the same problems consistently give depth to the Christian faith when rightly understood in terms of agape, for love by its nature enters into relations and suffers in the face of sorrow.

The validity of agape as the fundamental motif of the Christian faith thus possesses both historical and systematic validity. The most searching requirement of any faith, however, is neither its historical correctness nor its ability to solve intellectual problems. Christianity, although it accepts intellectual tasks and contains explanatory sugges-tiveness, is no philosophy. It is a Gospel with the power of salvation. The final test, therefore, must be the vitality of agape as the "basic attitude of life." We must accordingly examine the existential qualifications of agape as the fundamental motif of Christianity.

First of all, agape as a fundamental motif allows for no ready made faith, but requires continual rethinking. It puts a premium on creativity. It provides a steady context for thought but repudiates all systems as Christian. Thought can never be finished nor take the place of life. Personal relations are not only primary but ultimate. Thus agape is the basis for the fullest possible legitimate existentialism. Similarly agape never allows for moralism or legalism in ethics. All attainment is by the grace of God and therefore the basis for all boasting, inwardly or outwardly, is excluded. So is all prestation, or man's seeking security in God or his acceptance by means of good works. Legalism is done to death by the fact that man lives not by law but by love. Within love there must be right relations and therefore agape is the royal law fulfilling the demands of ethics without reducing morality to rules and regulations, to principles, or to social conformity. Agape outstrips both the ethics of principles and of contextual and situational ethics. It uses both relatively but lives only by the love of God.

Then, too, agape provides the motivation that is pure. It is nothing less than God's own presence in the believer. There can be no more legitimate motivation for thought or conduct than the work of the Holy Spirit. The Spirit never compels but only constrains. He moves but never pushes. He comes only into man, co-operates only as man opens up his own inner self to God's presence and lives the love of God as his own. Man is created for God's presence which none the less makes man more man by fulfilling his deepest nature. Agape is thus never heteronomuous, but neither is it autonomous. Theonomy in ethics means rather man's full freedom within his own nature as made for the presence of God, working not externally but in perfect coincidence with man's true self. Therefore agape provides the solution for the kind of motivation that is neither man's isolated freedom nor determinism in ethics. Agape as motivation is God's presence in man releasing his true freedom within the kind of fulfillment that unites freedom of choice and freedom of life, or metaphysical and moral freedom.

Moreover, agape provides the right relation not only receptively and responsibly to God but also to others. Agape is creative, outgoing concern. It centers in the other. Or, as some of us should prefer to put the case, it centers in God and is focused in the other. The nature of love is to bestow freedom on the other while still having complete concern for him. Merely to let live is not love. Always to do for the other, oppositely, is not love. Agape is complete concern for the other while allowing him to be genuinely free. Therefore agape acts or refrains from acting according to the need of the other.

Nor can love act or not act without responsible knowledge. God has such knowledge in himself. But for man study becomes encumbent. Concern, or good intentions, if agape be genuine, can be no substitute for either study or action. But neither can study or deed take the place of being and living together. Agape has thus an inborn pedagogical principle where needed. It has, indeed, a cybernetic feed-back device. With such concern to help rightly stressed, we must re-emphasize the fact that our relation to our neighbor is not basically one of teaching or of helping but of accepting, of sharing, of becoming involved, of communing together. The fundamental relation of man to man is precisely love, outgoing creative love in fellowship, from, under, and with God, but insofar as study or help is needed agape is perfectly suited for assuming such service without condescension or servility. Thus agape also provides the locus of solution to motivation and relation with regard to the other.

But finally agape is based on faith in God. Nygren is even hesitant to speak of man's love to God in order to prevent altogether the misunderstanding that man can live agape in any way apart from the motivation that comes from God, who is the only source of agape. Such stress on faith is needed. No matter how much light man is given to see or how much responsibility he is allowed to carry, God is the only source of truth and right. Man cannot fully live by philosophy based on any other illumination than the true light that shines on all who come into the world. Man cannot ever act rightly except with regard to that Love which is the final ground and goal of reality and the only final standard of holiness. Thus man ultimately must live by grace alone and by faith alone. Such is the truth of man's situation. Therefore agape remains sovereignly a matter of faith for man. Only those who are made right through faith shall live the life of agape. Thus the validity and the vitality of agape as the fundamental motif of Christianity come right from God.

Finally, since agape is unconditional and universal, the community that results authentically from the living of agape is ever open, creative, concerned, and inclusive. Only those who reject such fulfilling community become excluded. But they judge themselves. Such judgment, too, is unconditional and unequivocal. There is no compromise of the source and standard of personal or community relations. All the while, however, the community of agape is ever open, seeking, redemptive. None of its members could ever live by his own righteousness. Each and all must live by God's grace in forgiveness and motivating presence. Here, then, is a doctrine of the Christian community which is through and through rooted in God, centered in history on the Incarnate Love, open to all who accept God's inclusive love for all, and who in worship and work, in faith and witness, are focused on sharing the Gospel with the world. Here is worship, witness, and work on the part of a community the reality of which centers in its continual living in the Holy Spirit, and which therefore lives through the love of God with and for others. Agape is thus from God in personal and corporate life for the world. Here is full Christian validity and adequacy as existentially vital as its appropriation.

IF THE preceding section mostly points at, rather than points out, some of the inherent strengths in Nygren's theology of agape, what seem to be some of its weaknesses? The critical reason should match the creative. Only so does theology perform its task. Possibly it is best to treat what seem the shortcomings of Nygren's position under three headings, even though basically they come down to one major deficiency: *Mirabile dictu*, Nygren appears not to take full interpretative advantage of the nature of agape.

Theologically Nygren comes short in his understanding of outgoing, creative love. Love, we have already suggested, bestows freedom on the other. The other must be real to live a genuine life of his own. Therefore, love to God cannot be merely or mostly faith. It cannot be a matter of the reflection of God's love through man back to God. Such love would indeed be neoplatonic, not Christian. It would in effect be God's love for himself, even though through the other. Nygren's failure comes at the point of having no genuine, fully developed love of man to God. If man is real, he must be capable of loving God in himself. His love must be his own. But if agape is the fundamental motif, man's love to God cannot be other than agape. It, too, must be outgoing, creative *for its part* of fellowship. Man must be and do *his part* in the divine-human relation.

The reason for Nygren's lack at this point we shall observe almost directly, but if God be love he must need man's love. God must be capable by nature to be loved as well as to love. God must have receptive as well as outgoing love. God's need for love, furthermore, cannot be a deficiency but a sovereign sign of the perfection of his love. Perfect love is never one-directional. It is always a matter of loving and being loved. Love is a two-way affair. Can such fullness and genuineness of love be described in terms of agape? It certainly cannot be real in any love that is primarily self-centered or eros. Can it be true of agape that is through and through God-centered? We shall shortly propose a solution.

Then, too, Nygren fails to have any horizontal love. In his theology brother loves brother, neighbor, and enemy with the same kind of love, agape's downreaching from God, reflected in man through faith, or working through the Holy Spirit in man. If man is genuine and free, however, cannot he not only love God from within his own true self, with agape, but also love his neighbor horizontally? If there can be horizontal love within the Trinity, so to speak, can there not be genuine love from within man that is not mostly God's love working in man? Can God's love be transmuted in man, still be the motivating power, but not, so to speak, be God present in man doing the loving?

For that matter, if man is free and genuine and not merely a qualification of God, must not man love even himself horizontally? Can man have agape for himself? Or can there be a self-love that is not eros? Can man acquire from God, from agape, a self-acceptance in creative, reflexive concern that is not curved in selfishly on himself, but which transcends self in grace and gratitude, in obedience and creative concern? If philia is a term for love of others that is too far associated with conditional, covenant love, if *caritas*, in the second place, the love to God and through God, is too far involved with a mixed motif of agape and eros, and if self-love, in the third place, generally is tied up with eros, is there yet another way in which the fundamental motif of agape can be carried through unexceptionally from God out while genuinely allowing for true love to God, real love to others, and a genuine love of self? Must not agape in order to be wholly God-centered as an all-inclusive ultimate in some manner do full justice to love for all? Can anyone, or any truly needed relationship of love, be excluded from this universal agape, even one's own self? Is not every self part of the total community? Is there not a solution that will do even fuller justice to the fundamental motif of agape?

When agape is taken with complete seriousness as the nature of the ultimate, it becomes apparent that Nygren, not fully following through the way love works, has not grasped the reason for creation or its function in the divine plan. Nygren has no strong doctrine of creation and history. No wonder that he appreciates Marcion! Creation is the means of God's indirect work in rearing his children. As a teacher, the God of agape works mostly indirectly in order to bestow and foster freedom. God created responsibly. Therefore he gave man a real measure of responsible freedom, a genuine portion of control over his choices, but gave this freedom within the controls of man's nature and the kind of universe in which he must mature. Thus man becomes responsibly free within the way he has to decide and live, personally and together, in nature and history. God's indirect relation both in man, by means of his nature, and for man, by means of the kind of nature God prepared, is love's way of making and setting the other free but within a context of responsible concern and wisdom. Beside such indirect work God also reveals himself in a genuine measure directly to prophets and pray-ers and climactically in his Son. God works not only in general but also in special providence. Especially he meets his children in prayer which at its highest reaches involves in a large sense direct communion.

Inside man, moreover, God not only encounters man in his experience but also interpenetrates his inmost spirit. God is both for us and in us, as we let him. The work of the Spirit, however, is carried on in different forms according to man's readiness and spiritual maturity. The Spirit operates on the level of fear, frustrating man's self-seeking ambitions and coveted self-sufficiency; he operates on the level of duty, pricking man's conscience and urging him to the right; but finally he works on the level of love, not only in but with man's willing spirit. Thus man matures into responsible selfhood and community under the tutelage of the Spirit in several manners. How God works in creation, indirectly and passively, and also directly and actively; and how similarly God works in man indirectly and operatively as well as directly and co-operatively, has been suggested in the author's *The Christian Understanding of God* and *The Universal Word*, but generations of scholars are needed to carry through these beginnings of exploring the implications of agape for a fuller Christian theology. In any case, Nygren has not sufficiently developed the Christian understanding of nature or of man in terms of agape.

Possibly the reason for this failure to have a vital understanding of the function of creation within the fundamental motif of agape is Nygren's Lutheran stress on justification at the expense of a full-orbed Christian theology. The perspective *in loco iustificationis* dominates

Nygren's thinking throughout. Such a distorted *Einstellung* is, of course, all too often characteristic of Lutheran theology. It has been centrally concerned with the meaning and reality of the forgiveness of sin through the Cross of Christ, and not in the same sense or degree with the total truth of the Christian Gospel. Such at least has been its general concern, whatever the exceptions. But Christ is not only the power for salvation and not only power for newness of life; his life is also the central light of truth for man's knowledge. Nygren is afraid that the acceptance and use of such light will turn the Christian faith into a philosophy; he feels that already in the Johannine writings, as we have seen, such a danger is present. For him "metaphysics" is mostly a swear word.

Man as a whole, however, has to think in relation to his experience as a whole. If the Christian faith does not inform his thinking, he will simply borrow his thinking from non-Christian philosophies. To be sure, such has unfortunately been the procedure of those who have officially tried to express the light of Christ in terms of world views. They have fallen prey theologically to alien and distorting philosophies. Better have none of it, exclaims Nygren.

But, since thinking about the world is not optional for man but situationally unavoidable, we offer another choice. The right choice is surely to take every thought into obedience for Christ, thus letting him be the light that lights not only every one who comes into the world but everywhere that light is needed by man. The answer is to let God work in us to create for man the true framework for thought, the true understanding of creation, where reason can rest in revelation even while continually carrying out the responsibility of shaping ever new regions of man's growing understanding of his world. Nygren can make his own theology far more important and helpful if he will grant and help further the deeper understanding of love in creation as well as in redemption, in God's indirect, preparatory as well as in his direct, consummating work. We need to develop a Christian framework of knowledge as well as Christian tools for thought.

Our second main critical suggestion is to the effect that Nygren needs to widen his understanding of method. As it is, he stresses revelation and faith exclusively in his theology. In his philosophy of religion he has worked out the rightful claim of religion to be not only a category but the category of categories. Religion is categorically necessary to human experience and sovereignly demands its rights in the realm of human reason. But the claim Nygren stakes pertains only to the form of religion. The content must be had by faith and only by faith. This chapter is not the place for the description or appraisal of his methodological position with regard to its philosophical adequacy, but even theologically his position could be strengthened if he bridged this gaping gulf between faith and reason. He can do so also without in any way lessening his stress on the centrality and finality of faith.

Faith must be fully faith and yet also live in creative tension with, and fulfillment of, reason. In the final analysis faith must be either / or, for it is decision concerning ultimates. But such final decision need not be a completely arbitrary leap. If Christ is truth, and if truth judges and directs as well as points to the source of salvation, there can be no other candidate for knowing the ultimate that so fully illumines, so severely judges and so radically saves man as agape. It must possess explanatory adequacy as well as redemptive power. For the New Testament this question is not a live issue, but the Christian faith has had to encounter it ever since. For modern man the problem of meaning is critical. Not to address man genuinely at this point is to fail him. To be sure all such light is partial and cannot attain the status of attained or provable knowledge. It is at best probable, or preferable to other views of the ultimate. At best it searches our experience the most deeply while still leaving us in deep existential mystery. After a lifetime of careful, deliberate study of this subject this writer is convinced that there issues from agape more light than we had dared hope, if only we truly seek to explore without fear or compromise where it leads, and this light pertains to all areas of knowledge and life relevant to man's meaning and destiny. As a result of long and searching inquiry the author is convinced that Nygren can strengthen even his own theological case by putting in its proper place the secondary methodological use of reason.

Such positive and proper appreciation of reason honors God in man's creation. Man can become authentic and responsible because he can reason. He can transcend nature and history enough to interpret and evaluate both, relate himself to both meaningfully, and become a free agent in relation to his world. Thus love endowed man with reason in order for him to use it in his growth, personally and corporately. Even the abuse of reason in partiality and distortion calls for correction and maturation. Yes, even man's sinning by the abuse of reason in falsifying his situation, in fighting God or fleeing him, in constructing systems of thought under which to hide from him, even in denying him under the pretense of coming of age or of not distinguishing the spiritual from the secular—all these false uses of reason secure man's freedom from God in order that man might become real, so that when he finally accepts God it is not only willingly but understandingly. Reason becomes right, in the last analysis, only when it is cleansed and directed by faith. Such salvaged reason can competently and continually be applied to its proper work. Such reason becomes part of the new being who receives the eyes of faith as a total person. God shows his love by his humility in letting us thus become real, free and finally fulfilled.

Nygren, however, has an all-or-none analysis of agape wherein he never makes use of God's preparatory work in creation. He never relates God's preliminary work in creation to his final work in redemption. The writer is convinced, however, that we must understand agape in its relation to eros as our destined relation to God on our way to God. If eros means simply receptive love, of course, then God himself has eros and man has basic need of it always. But if eros means self-centered love in the sense of selfish search or drive for satisfaction, then there is obviously no eros in God and should be none in the saint except as sin remains. Eros, however, can also be understood as that stubborn drive of self created by God to make man real. As such, eros has a preparatory meaning as a means of creation, a means of natural grace, but not a place as a final end in the Christian life. If eros be of such nature, for such a purpose, man must seek his own way in order to become real and in freedom find through his frustrations that he can be fulfilled only within the will and presence of God's agape in his life. Eros is then replaced and destroyed by agape, even as frustration is done to death by fulfillment, even while it can also be clearly seen that God's purpose in creation is through and through agape.

Only when Christ the truth is allowed to confront the problem of evil, man's only problem, in the full scope of its meaning, can the truth of the Cross and the Resurrection in relation to all of life and history be seen in their own distinctive meanings. Nygren has failed to find the fuller meaning of his own fundamental motif of agape by limiting his basic search to a historic and doctrinal analysis in terms of basically opposed motifs or compromised motifs rather than by opening up to a stage of understanding where even the meaning of nomos and eros, or gnosis and *caritas* are seen for what they are on the preliminary or preparatory level of God's work. The final absoluteness of agape remains; nevertheless, the place and meaning of creation is made clear and agape truly seen not only in the place of redemption but throughout the whole scope of God's purpose for the world. Creation is honored as of God without in any way being excused for its sinfulness and relative attainments.

Besides Nygren's theological and methodological failures to do justice to his own findings, there are practical shortcomings, in the view of this writer, that need not be if Nygren took agape at its own inner and fuller meaning. In refusing to let agape be defined from within its own self solely as unconditional, universal love, unmotivated by the worth of the object, spontaneous, outgoing, and creative of fellowship, but trying instead to make out that the New Testament as a whole expresses agape, as does the basic history of Christian thought, Nygren has become victimized by his own allegiance to traditionalistic theology. There is no chance at all that sovereign agape and eternal hell, for instance, are consistent notions. Theological paradox cannot legitimately protect such an intellectual contradiction. If God is sovereign agape, love creates and must win the final victory in terms of agape. Otherwise agape is limited either in nature or in competence. But Nygren opts for neither a finite God nor for God's final, supreme victory. Certainly such refusal to let agape have inferential power for central doctrines is due to a limiting traditionalistic loyalty to established dogma rather than to the inner requirements of agape. But such clinging to traditionalism is listed as a practical deficiency as well, because today the Christian faith will meet not only an enlightened, generally educated Western man, but the other great world religions with their deep wisdom and strong appeal for empty and confused man. Christian ideology most likely will have to be thoroughly refurbished as a whole, but the case of eternal hell is a conspicuous example of a practical lack due to Nygren's emotional involvement with traditionalistic Christianity. Many are the hours during which the writer challenged Nygren personally at this point, but as far as he has been able to ascertain Nygren has never renounced this kind of commitment.

Nor has Nygren worked to capture general education for the Christian faith. In spite of his recognition of the problem of relevance and the need for a powerful way to relate the Christian faith to the modern world, Nygren has clung to his own chosen task of disentangling the Christian faith from its false rivals. Honor and power to him for such a life of loyalty! He will now, we hope, also support the work of those who have learned from him what ultimate Christianity is distinctively and determinatively, but who see the need to be radically revolutionary in the proper use of this final truth in its reworking of theology and in its becoming properly related to the world at every level of call. Without destroying the final meaning of revelation and without minimizing the realm of redemption, we need bridges from both to the whole gamut of modern man's life and thought.

With all these suggestions, however, as to how, as the writer sees it, Nygren can take even fuller advantage of his life work, the indisputable fact remains that Nygren has helped immeasurably to change our entire theological situation by his insistent stress on what is genuinely Christian—by his biblical studies, by his philosophical method, yet to be completed, by his historical investigations, including the historical method itself, and by his total impact on the ecumenical thinking of our age.

Ethics

14

NYGREN'S ETHICS

Thor Hall

As a systematic theologian, Anders Nygren has taken it upon him-self not to develop a theological system, but to deal with matters which influence Christian thought both in its understanding of itself and in its relationship to other forms of thought. He is, in other words, first and foremost a methodologian. As such, his interests are inclusive rather than exclusive. He does not limit himself to the "theological circle," laying a methodological foundation upon the special presuppo-sitions which belong within the household of faith. Instead he ventures boldly into the field of philosophy, attempting to find a way to establish theology as a discipline fully acceptable on the presupposi-tions of logical reflection. Again, his method does not only encompass theological reflection per se, it includes also a systematic interest in the practical aspects of the Christian faith, such as ecclesiastical concerns and Christian ethics.

To understand Nygren's approach to Christian ethics, therefore, one must consider it against the backdrop of his entire philosophical and theological methodology. Nygren himself has built the framework of his ethical thought this way. His two basic works in this field, *Filosofisk och kristen etik*[1] and *Etiska grundfrågor*[2] are both heavily loaded on the side of philosophical and methodological matters. For Nygren this is both natural and necessary, for two reasons. First, Christian ethics must find a way to remain true to its own characteristic nature. It must, therefore, seek a clear and conscious recognition of its proper place and role, its orientation and center. Secondly, it must develop an ability to relate itself with intellectual respectability to its surroundings. For that reason it must take up the challenge of the contemporary thoughtworld and prove its justification as an autonomous thoughtform in relation to this thoughtworld as a whole. Nygren's double aim or dual concern is, in a sentence, to secure for the discipline of Christian ethics the quality of being both genuinely Christian and thoroughly scientific.[3]

We shall abstain from the temptation to expand upon the virtues of this dual undertaking here. We shall also guard against premature judgments as to the success of the undertaking. In comparison with the theological situation as a whole, however, one could say that Nygren has wanted to take hold of both horns of the theological dilemma which we inherited from the nineteenth century. He recognizes the requirements of the modern mind and desires to speak intelligently and relevantly to it, but he acknowledges also the demands of the Christian tradition and hopes to represent it responsibly and honestly. Not all the contributors to twentieth-century theology have managed to keep both these concerns together. Not many who have tried have been able to penetrate so deeply into the methodological problems involved. Very few have succeeded in relating their thought with equal honesty to the interests of the philosophical community as to the theological circle.

At the point where Nygren starts his consideration of Christian ethics, one basic methodological problem appears to him. It is derived from the logical requirement that no duplication of purpose can be allowed within the total spectrum of the scientific disciplines, nor can any unnecessary and arbitrary questions be made the rationale for a scientific discipline.[4] Before Christian ethics can be acceptable as an autonomous discipline among the sciences, it must be shown that "even science from its perspective must demand such an undertaking," [5] and that without it there would open up a disturbing gap in the scientific spectrum. Furthermore, Christian ethics must be able to show that its purpose is not already taken up by another scientific discipline, leaving no room for its particular approach to it. For Nygren this situation crystallizes itself in the relationship between ethics in general ("philosophical ethics") and Christian ethics. He finds no ground on which to deny the rights of philosophy to deal with ethical questions. Such questions have been part and parcel of philosophical study ever since

Plato. The burden of proof, rather, "rests exclusively on theological ethics" when it presents itself with the claim to have a contribution to make to the consideration of ethical questions.[6] Thus it becomes Nygren's concern at the outset to clarify what specific contribution Christian ethics can make, and how it must relate itself to the discipline of philosophical ethics.

He begins by exploding the simple notion that the two disciplines might meet in a friendly compromise. The outcome of such a combination would be suspect from both sides. It would neither be acceptable as a philosophical science, nor would it truly represent the Christian ethical ideals.

> If the philosophical problem which is involved in ethical experience is to receive a satisfactory treatment, this seems possible only if the philosophical consideration is kept free from all foreign intervention. And if the Christian ethos is to have influence on the discussion of the ethical problem, this can seemingly only happen in a theological ethics which already at its starting-point lets the Christian point of view be decisive.[7]

The problem is thereby set. A dualism of philosophical and Christian ethics seems unavoidable, but it is not at all clear how the two can be held together in harmonious relationship. This becomes the main subject of Nygren's *Filosofisk och kristen etik*. Among ethicists one may find all sorts of approaches to this problem, the various alternatives taking their color from—and in turn also revealing—the individual author's general point of view. Nygren discusses these various theories at length, relating his own alternatives to the philosophical/theological debate at large. His main reaction to much of the debate is that most of the participants enter into it with vague, unanalyzed concepts of theological as well as of philosophical ethics.[8] They take them as given, defined, and posited entities and do not see that, since the problem is methodological, one must approach the two disciplines rather in terms of their particular scientific purpose and in view of their individual contribution to the spectrum of scientific disciplines as a whole.

It is obvious, then, that Nygren must reject the tendencies toward mutual exclusiveness as well as the attempts to claim inclusiveness in the relation between philosophical and Christian ethics. The philosophical rejection of Christian ethics, represented by Schopenhauer, for example, who argues that philosophical ethics must be left free to seek ethical norms by its own light, since it is illegitimately circular to hold that ethics must necessarily be religiously grounded, is countered by

Nygren's double-sided insistence that Schopenhauer misunderstands both disciplines. Philosophical ethics cannot long remain acceptable from a scientific point of view if it assumes the function of formulating normative ethics. Nor does all theological ethics argue for the necessity of a religious legitimation of ethics as a whole. Rightly understood, then, the two disciplines are not mutually exclusive. This is why Nygren has little patience with the tendency among theologians, notably Herrmann and Mandel, to counter the attitude expressed by Schopenhauer by simply giving up the claim to a specifically Christian ethics. In making ethics a part of man's natural experience and explaining that it is possible therefore to establish the concept of the good on an objective scientific basis, these men give up the claims of Christianity in the realms of ethics only in order to concentrate on the theological claim that ethics by itself is not capable of completion; it needs religion "to give (the) answer to a question which the ethical mind of necessity must ask but cannot itself answer," [9] partly because of the inner tension and conflict which inevitably settles on the philosophical ethicist (Herrmann), and partly because of the twistedness of man's natural will (Mandel). In defining the relationship of philosophical and religious ethics in this manner these men have, in Nygren's view, compromised both of the elementary requirements of scientific respectability and theological responsibility.

The most common method of solving the issues in relating philosophical and Christian ethics which prevails among the theologians, however, is to claim that only theological ethics is capable of dealing with the ethical questions and that ethics without religion is an impossibility in itself. To support such a view the theologian will have to pull two tricks out of his bag: He must expand the borders of Christian faith and give the handshake of brotherhood to anyone who fights a good fight, but he must also narrow the ethical concept and show that only that form of goodness measures up which is the direct expression of a Christian spirit. The assumption behind it all is, quite simply, that of all the ethical systems in the world, none has the potential for grasping the essential nature of the ethical good which is given to the Christian faith. And that, to Nygren, is not an assumption that can be the foundation of a discipline which claims to be scientific.

There are, however, other ways of approaching the problem. Instead of reducing two disciplines, philosophical and Christian ethics, to one, philosophical *or* Christian ethics, one can give to both a different task so that each is shown as a necessary contributor to the field of ethics as a whole. Nygren is obligated by his own premises to seek his answer this way. But even here he must warn against several pitfalls. The delineation of the relationship between philosophical and Christian ethics in terms of a two-storey structure of "innerworldly" and "overworldly" orientation such as Troeltsch sets up, for example,[10] immediately excludes the possibility for Christian ethics to finds its place among the sciences. So also, on the other hand, does the designation of one (philosophical ethics) as the truly scientific discipline while the other (Christian ethics) remains a "science" of a secondary sort, valuable only as a catalyst within one particular context for the grand ethical principles which are defined by the science of ethics itself. Most significantly, for Nygren, this way of structuring the relationship between the two disciplines compromises the *Christian* character of Christian ethics and falls for that reason short of the goal. A different way must be found.

Nygren finds it intimated in Schleiermacher, although Schleiermacher himself did not manage to follow his own methodological guidelines consistently. When Schleiermacher distinguishes the two disciplines in terms of "form" and "method" (or "interest"), Nygren sees in it the key to their mutual complementation.[11] No two forms of ethics can impinge upon each other's place within the spectrum of scientific disciplines if they are seen to be different in presuppositions and purpose, and move, as it were, on different planes. However, when Nygren discovers that Schleiermacher goes on to claim that the two are alike also in content, object, and results, he is afraid that the sound parallelism of scientific philosophical ethics and scientific Christian ethics has been compromised.[12] As for himself, Nygren proposes that the two disciplines are not only different in task and purpose, they are also different in content and result. For that reason they can enter into a true relationship of methodological complementation. If the *one* is seen to represent a "universal" philosophical discipline, having the task of investigating ethical experience in general, and the *other* has the character of a "specific" theological discipline, explicating the particular Christian ethical ideal, then the relationship between them can be defined as follows:

> When philosophical ethics is to set up in a formal way the scheme of ethical categories so to speak, then it has room within its framework for all sorts of content-defined ethical viewpoints. The relation of Christian ethics to philosophical ethics, then, is evidently that it represents one of the possibilities for which philo-

sophical ethics leaves room and in which it finds its concrete content determined.[13]

This, actually, is Nygren's own way. This is the kind of philosophy with which he operates, and this is the type of theology which he has been working to establish throughout his career: two parallel, necessary, and autonomous disciplines, each with its own purpose and object, each thoroughly scientific in approach and method. And this is the kind of relationship between them that he has consistently sought to establish: mutual respect and acceptance, individual autonomy and freedom; in short, two distinct disciplines in necessary methodological complementation. How he has done it and whether he has succeeded shall be the subject for the balance of this essay.

NYGREN'S APPROACH to philosophical ethics parallels closely his philosophy of religion, and both emerge from his concept of philosophy in general. In an admirably clear delineation of the philosophical situation, included in *Filosofisk och kristen etik*,[14] Nygren describes how philosophy has responded to the rise of the special or "positive" sciences and their frontal attack on the traditional status of philosophy as the "universal science." Three responses are outlined, each related to one of the three factors determining the nature of philosophy as such: its universality, its scientific character, and its relation to experience. First, philosophy can give up its claim to universality and be reduced in the process to a "special" science along with the other positive sciences. This, of course, would not solve the issue; it would only sharpen it. Secondly, philosophy can give up its scientific character and assume the task of defining by rational procedures a metaphysical essence in which all things are said ultimately to converge. In Nygren's view, this would lead not only to a clash between philosophy and *some* sciences; it would set it in insoluble tension to *all* science. The third and only acceptable alternative is for philosophy to retain its claim to universality and remain within the framework of science, but change its relation to experience so as to accommodate both. It must keep its double position as a *universal science*, but relate itself to experience in such a way that neither its universality nor its scientific character would be made void. And this, to Nygren, is only possible in a consistently *critical* philosophy.

As Nygren comes to pose the direct question "How is Philosophy as a Science Possible?"[15] the first answer is that it cannot be scientific in the same way as the positive sciences are. It is not a "science of particulars" but a "science of universals," not a "science of experience" but a "science of principles." [16] Its relation to experience is close, yet it does not fall within the bounds of empiricism. It represents, rather, "a general theory of experience" or an analysis of "how and on what conditions experience is at all possible." [17]

If the relation between philosophy and the positive sciences is clarified by such delimitations, there is yet need for further explication of the philosophical task. For as a "science of universals" philosophy must not fall back into metaphysical speculations about ontological "essences" or "substances," i.e., rational definitions of objective entities of a transcendent sort. Nygren has no qualms about accepting Kant's refutation of such metaphysics. His own encounter with Axel Hägerström and Adolf Phalén, the two most "dangerous" Swedish philosophers whose merciless criticism of subjectivity and arbitrariness became the reef on which no Scandinavian thinker could avoid wrecking a speculative or unscientific craft, had convinced him that ontological metaphysics of this sort is an illegitimate form of thought.[18] For it ignores the epistemological problem, and epistemology, to Nygren, in the sense of "analysis of logical presuppositions," is the primary—perhaps the only—task of scientific or critical philosophy. Philosophy is most uniquely itself when it functions as "presuppositional analysis," searching for the universal principles which operate as presuppositions for human knowledge and experience as a whole.

There is in Nygren's thought, then, a certain distinction between the empirical reality of our experience and a transcendent realm of universals or presuppositional principles. But this distinction is not thought of in the way of idealism, as a separation of one reality from another more essential and *real* reality. The distinction is rather between reality as we experience it and a logical abstraction of the formal categorical presuppositions which govern the various areas of our experience. The critical philosopher is not concerned with an ultimate reality. He is concerned, instead, with the validity of experience [19] and the ultimate presuppositions for its understanding.

Before we narrow our concern here to Nygren's view of the nature and task of philosophical ethics as such, two further notes must be made regarding his philosophical stance as a whole. The first has to do with his method. In approaching the task of presuppositional analysis, Nygren finds himself forced to reject as untenable both what he calls the "empirical" method and what could be described as the "rational" method. In the first place, logical presuppositions are not present within experience and reality as something "given" or factual, so the empirical method of induction will not be capable of getting to them. But neither can they be identified by rational deduction, for that method simply assumes that we already know the presuppositions from which to start, which in this case is just what we are out to seek. The only adequate method, to Nygren, is what he calls the "transcendental method," [20] divided for clarity into two parts: A] the preliminary ordering of experience within a variety of basic conceptual frameworks or "areas of meaning" (the "conceptual analysis"), and   B] the main task of delimiting the fundamental categories within which experience as a whole and each area of experience is to be understood, and on the basis of which its validity rests [21] (the "transcendental deduction").[22] Nygren's philosophy is thus primarily an analysis of experience. "Experience and nothing but experience is its problem." [23] But philosophy as Nygren sees it is not to be thought of as empiricism or rationalism; his analysis, rather, leads to what he calls an *"allmän erfarenhetsteori"* (general theory of experience) or—what is really the same to Nygren—*"allmän giltighetsteori"* (general theory of validity). The term *"allmän,"* which Nygren stresses particularly, distinguishes his "theory" both from the particularity of empiricism and the arbitrariness of rationalism. Against particularity it sets universality, and against arbitrariness it puts formal analysis.

A second note must be added regarding the purpose of analytic criticism as defined by Nygren. As a general theory of validity, critical philosophy aims at a logical deduction of the universal categories forming the presuppositions for valid experience. These categories are defined as principles of which it can be demonstrated that only as they are accepted can one understand experience in its wholeness and variety at all.[24] When the critical philosopher looks over experience as a whole, he finds himself confronted by "great and different areas of meaning, each ruled by their specific categories." [25] It is his task to sort out this experiential material, to find what answers belong to what questions, and "to perform a presuppositional analysis in each of these areas and thus *open the way to an inclusive theory of the categories."* [26] Nygren has explained in several connections which areas of meaning he is thinking about. They are four in particular, namely the area of theoretical knowledge (ruled by the category of "truth"), aesthetics (presupposing the category of the "beautiful"), ethics (answering to the category of the "good"),[27] and religion (governed by the category of the "eternal").[28] Within each of these areas, critical philosophy seeks to show, by its analysis of presuppositions, what a priori categories are basic to each. However, philosophy has not been able to reach very far in this endeavor. Nygren has repeatedly pointed out that the task of presuppositional analysis has only begun.[29] There are signs of a certain hesitancy on Nygren's own part with regard to the actual transcendental deductions required of a critical philosopher. And the development of an "inclusive theory of the categories," which he called for, is still only a prophetic dream.[30]

Recognizing, then, that one does not, in Nygren's philosophy, have a completed system, one may nevertheless find in it the rudiments of what might become a philosophical system of considerable importance on the contemporary scene. These may be summarized as follows: Philosophy must be a critical discipline, with experience as its object of investigation, aiming for a theory of universal presuppositions rather than knowledge of experiential facts. Its method is the conceptual analysis of experience, leading to a transcendental deduction of certain a priori categorical presuppositions within the various areas of experience. Its aim is to delimit these categories both in their autonomous nature and in relation to each other. However, in order to remain critical, philosophy must not define the categories in a material or normative way. Material considerations are for the positive sciences, and normative claims are possible only as expressions of subjective value judgments. It must, rather, keep its categories "open," capable of accommodating any and all experience which properly falls within their domain. The transcendental deductions result in "abstractions," not definitive content. But the abstractions have form.

Against the backdrop of this description of Nygren's philosophical stance, we come now to the task of delineating his philosophical ethics and his Christian ethics separately. Since man's total field of experience includes experiences which can only be understood on the basis of autonomous ethical categories, a philosophy which claims to represent a general theory of experience must, of necessity, include an analysis of the presuppositions for ethical validity. Critical ethics has thereby been shown to have a rightful place among the sciences. In the same manner, since the commitmental orientation of life which is characteristic of the Christian faith clearly includes a particular ethical ideal, any scientific discipline of theology which claims to express the essential and characteristic nature of this faith must, of necessity, also explicate the ethical implications springing from it. Christian ethics is thereby justified as an autonomous scientific discipline.

But there is more to it. Each of these disciplines must be defined methodologically so as to make sure they are cleansed of all elements that might compromise their scientific status. Nygren devotes much of his effort to these methodological concerns.

In thorough and careful analyses, Nygren seeks to define the nature of critical ethics. First, he distinguishes it sharply from what he calls "descriptive ethics." [31] The latter presents descriptive summaries of the ethical experiences at hand. It is interested in what *is*, while critical ethics is interested in what is *valid*.[32] The one is a descriptive science concerned with facts; the other is a universal science, analyzing the presuppositions for factual validity. Again, in clear argumentation, Nygren differentiates critical ethics from metaphysical ethics.[33] Metaphysics represents a projection of subjective and arbitrary convictions into a total view of the universally ethical. It is not interested in the ethical phenomenon, but only in the establishment of its own preconceived world view. Thus it falls short both scientifically and ethically. Critical ethics, on the other hand, takes ethical experience for what it is and approaches it not with a prejudicial theory, but with the question "Where does ethical experience ground its claim to validity?" [34] It seeks only the formal presuppositions for experiential validity. The difference between critical, descriptive, and metaphysical ethics can be expressed this way: There are two spheres in which ethics is being considered, the scientific and the philosophical. Descriptive ethics belongs solidly within the scientific sphere, while metaphysical ethics is purely philosophical. "Critical ethics falls within both spheres. It gains thereby a double determination: within the sphere of scientific ethics it distinguishes itself from descriptive ethics in that it is philosophical; within the sphere of philosophical ethics it differentiates itself from metaphysical ethics by being scientific." [35]

In a third facet of his delimitation of critical ethics, Nygren is careful to point out that it must also be clearly distinguished from all sorts of normative ethics.[36] The latter attempts to formulate a rule by which ethical experience must be tested and in accordance with which it finds absolute legitimation. The former is guided, rather, by its triple intention to be truly scientific, genuinely ethical, and honestly philosophical. It must abstain from defining an ultimate ethical ideal. This definition is not a task for a discipline desiring to be scientific. Again, it must refrain from all tendencies to casuistry. Where ethics is reduced to an intellectual acceptance of and an outward conformity to a predefined "good," it actually ceases to be ethical. Furthermore, critical ethics must not allow its philosophical universality to become a tool for special interests. To claim that the ultimate ethical norm has been reduced to a definitive doctrine is philosophically illegitimate.[37]

Most immediately, then, critical ethics is concerned with the validity of ethical experience and with the transcendental deduction of the formal category (or categories) underlying this experience as presupposition(s) for its validity. If one should ask, however, how critical ethics goes about its task, Nygren's answers might be seen to grow disappointingly thin. There is no need to look for the transcendental deduction of the ethical categories anywhere in Nygren's writings. It is simply not there. But, if one looks for indications of his thinking on the matter, one can find important clues in several separate places.

The first is an essay on "The Concept of the 'Good' According to Evangelical and Catholic Points of View," reprinted in *Etiska grund-frågor*.[38] In what he calls some "general reflections" on the concept of the "good," Nygren makes a strikingly modern reference to the linguistic difference between the two statements "this is good" and "this is black." The "is" obviously does not mean the same in the two instances. The latter describes a property as belonging to the object itself; the former expresses an evaluation of, or a response to, the object on the part of a subject. "This is black" is an "objectivistic" kind of statement; "this is good" is "subjectivistic." Against this background, Nygren goes on to say that ethical experience is of such a nature that an ethical system developed in an objectivistic way is "ohållbar" (indefensible).[39] However, despite the fact that ethical evaluation is possible only by reference to an evaluating subject, one must be careful to guard the subjectivistic approach against all foreign considerations. For example, when utilitarianism insists that the "good" must be good "for someone" and eudaemonism claims that the "good" must be good "for something," the purity of the concept "good" is immediately compromised by extra-ethical references. The "good" in utilitarian perspective is actually changed into the "useful"; in eudaemonistic interpretations, it has simply come to mean the "enjoyable." The subjective ethical evaluation has thereby been intermingled with other interests (or egocentric interests, as the case may be). It has become *relative*. Nygren argues that ethical evaluation, even though it is subjectivistic in an epistemological sense, can be absolute in a critical-presuppositional sense, i.e., subjective value judgment may hold something for good "in and of itself and as such." [40] In fact, only that which is good in and of itself is ethically acceptable.

Nygren has thereby drastically limited the area of experience within which ethical validity can legitimately be claimed. This represents an important step in his progress toward the definition of ethical validity proper. However, the question may already be legitimately asked whether the presuppositional formalism of critical ethics has been properly assured when it appears that the concept of the good, even in its most elementary delimitation, is actually taken to exclude two systems of thought which have influenced ethical ideals of various kinds throughout the history of ethical consciousness. It may be granted, that, from a certain point of view, a good which is good "in and of itself and as such" seems more genuinely good than something which is good in respect to something else. But the point of view from which it is so evaluated must be openly confessed, or else one is guilty of not differentiating clearly enough between a formal category and an ethical ideal. One may suspect that Nygren's particular point of view in distinguishing between an *absolute* and a *relative* concept of the good is informed by the prior commitment that something which is good relative to itself ("absolutely") is more truly good than that which is good relative to something else. Such an arbitrary assumption would naturally force the definition of the ethical category so as to make it a criterion of validity imposed upon man's ethical experience rather than a presuppositional form underlying all such ethical experience.

That Nygren himself is aware of this danger is evident in his penetrating discussion of Kant's approach to the ethical category.[41] Nygren uncovers two parallel lines in Kant's thought. The main line is his philosophical criticism, in accordance with which Kant is seen to search for a concept of the "good" which is "good in and of itself," i.e., the "unconditionally good." Kant defines the category formally as the "categorical imperative" and proceeds to show how it manifests itself in man's ethical experience, namely in "the good will" ("im Prinzip des Willens"), and most uniquely in man's sense of "Pflicht." However, at this point Nygren finds the second line in Kant's thought becoming evident, namely a normative element which tends to compromise his criticism. Kant is actually making the concept of the good cover an equivocation of ethical category and ethical ideal, thus identifying the question "What do we mean by describing something as good?" with the question "What is it that we must describe as good?"[42] As a consequence, Nygren says, the "categorical imperative," which should simply be the formal foundation for ethical validity, becomes a psychological concept of "Pflicht," serving at the same time as Kant's definition of the essence of ethics (his ideal) and as criterion for his rigorous rejection of all ethics of inclination. Thus Kant's critical formalism has broken down and has become "formalistic." His categories are no longer "empty." Kant attempts to deduce the essential ethical content from his concept of the categorical imperative.[43]

If this development represents Kant's downfall as a critical ethicist, Nygren is ready to accept this fact as a challenge to his own thought.[44] He seeks conscientiously to cleanse his own conception of the ethical category from all "external" considerations, for example, the question of its psychological locus or point of contact within the inborn capacities of man. The ethical a priori must be retained as a formal category, not defined as a factual reality.[45] It is an abstraction, not an ethical norm.[46] However, as one follows the development of Nygren's argument, one is apt to find further evidence of a second line of thought, one that tends to compromise his primary critical intentions.

This is most clearly apparent in a chapter entitled "Teleological, Legalistic, and Attitudinal Ethics," first included in *Filosofisk och kristen etick*, and later condensed (but not changed) for *Etiska grundfrågor*.[47] Here Nygren continues to narrow the experiential area within which critical ethics asks the question concerning the presuppositions for ethical validity. In the first place, only human ethical experience qualifies. Secondly, considering that the human ethical condition is composed of several different elements ("moments"), Nygren goes on to ask what particular element within the human ethical condition must be considered decisive for its evaluation. The elements are, specifically, the mind or *attitude* of the subject making the ethical judgment, the behavior or *act* in which the subject expresses his decision, and the goal or *aim* which is being pursued. These are not, to Nygren, exclusive elements. They are closely related in any ethical experience, but the nature of their relationship is not always the same. In fact, the different ethical systems can be analyzed and characterized by reference to their differing emphasis on the primacy of one or the other of these elements.

So far, one can probably follow Nygren without compromising the critical method. His pronouncement that the nature of the relationship between attitude, act, and aim within the ethical condition of man is decisive for the nature of ethical validity itself, is perhaps formal enough. Even though he speaks at times of a certain ethical condition as "unethical" or as a condition which "from an ethical point of view" must be rejected,[48] it may still be possible to accept it as a critical statement.[49] He might simply mean that the condition in question does not represent a response to reality which involves an attitude, act, or aim that can be considered under the viewpoint of good / evil. But it soon becomes apparent that Nygren desires to go beyond this point. The three elements in the ethical condition—attitude, act, and aim—are not permitted to remain as three formal elements within an "open" category, capable of being combined in a variety of ways so that each alternative would correspond to a potential ethical system, but incapable of being used as a criterion for judging the individual ethical systems. On the contrary, Nygren makes the arbitrary judgment that, among the three elements, "only the attitude has primary ethical significance, and both the act and the aim receive a secondary ethical meaning by the fact that they stand in a causal relationship (of dependence) to the attitude." [50] He simply rejects the idea that the ethical condition can have "more than one center." [51] Says Nygren:

> There is no contradiction in evaluating the ethical from the standpoint of attitude, act, and aim. But one of these must be the ultimately decisive point of view. Ethics must, in other words, be either attitudinal ethics, legalistic ethics, or teleological ethics; a choice between these possibilities cannot be avoided.[52]

Whereupon he proceeds boldly to make his choice. He dismisses summarily two unacceptable ways of combining attitude, act, and aim within ethical experience, namely "legalistic ethics," in which the act has predominance, and "teleological ethics," in which the aim is the primary element. His method is simply to discredit these forms of ethics by showing that they give only secondary importance to that element which is primary or central in the ethical condition itself, namely the attitude.[53] Clear references are made to the categorical qualification that the "good" must by definition be "good in and of itself," and the end result is that only an attitudinal ethics, in which acts and aims are in necessary causal dependence upon the attitude, is judged acceptable from the ethical point of view.

At one point, Nygren indicates that his restriction of ethical validity to that ethical experience which is centered around the attitude forms a useful basis "for limiting the area which in the first analysis becomes the object of ethical evaluation" (i.e. validation as ethical).[54] He even suggests that it is fully legitimate from a scientific point of view to make such a restriction.[55] This may well be so. It may be easier to perform the transcendental deduction of the formal category when one's starting point is less inclusive and the experiential material less varied. But the restriction of the material must be made, not in terms of a predefined judgment as to what constitutes valid ethical experience, but rather in such a way as to have all important facets of the experiential material represented. This Nygren has not done. His principle of selection is a biased one, tending to prejudice the matter even prior to the transcendental deduction of the ethical category itself. He has, therefore, precluded the possibility of finding a formal category which can serve as a common presupposition for a variety of actual ethical ideals. In short, Nygren's critical stance is compromised.

The notion is perhaps an unworthy one, but one can hardly avoid the thought that this may be the reason why Nygren has never reached the point of actually performing the transcendental deduction of the ethical category.

Going on, at this point, to consider Nygren's approach to Christian ethics specifically, we are not surprised at finding that he changes his perspective and enters upon what he calls "exclusively theological considerations." [56] What may be somewhat surprising, particularly in view of Nygren's stress on the scientific nature of systematic theology and theological ethics, is that he does not propose or perform an exercise in motif research in which all the material expressing some form of Christian ethical reflection is taken into account and from which the hypothetical ground-motif would arise and become self-evident, but establishes instead, rather arbitrarily, that what characterizes Christian ethics and gives it a distinctive form in comparison with all other types of ethics is that it is "attitudinal" and not "teleological" or "legalistic." [57] Nygren suggests, in fact, that the question whether Christian ethics is oriented around aim or act or attitude is a redundant one, particularly since the philosophical analyses that he has made already "prove" that only the latter "measures up" as ethically valid.[58] Furthermore, he proposes that, since Christian ethics is a religious type of ethics, its character is thereby necessarily attitudinal.[59]

Nygren has apparently carried the philosophical assumptions which we have noted above over into his theological considerations. As a consequence, he can settle the question of the nature of Christian ethics by logical definition. Theology, including Christian ethics, after all does not need to go to the given experiential or historical material to find out in a scientifically responsible way what actually characterizes the Christian ethical consciousness in its many explications; it can simply hold together the philosophical definitions of essential religion and valid ethics and play with the assumption that Christian ethics fulfills both. Nygren does, of course, make references to the historic tradition of Christian faith and ethics. However, his references are not only very selective and perfunctory,[60] they are clearly biased, on the one hand by reference to Nygren's particular philosophical definitions, and on the other hand in the direction of his particular theological tradition.

The upshot of what is said here could constitute some rather devastating criticisms against Nygren's use of the scientific method. The end result, however, is not as bad as all that. This is due partly to the soundness of Nygren's theological instinct, and partly to the tendency of most of his readers to forget the methodological presuppositions upon which Nygren professes to work. His delineations of the nature of Christian ethics do, in fact, sound very convincing. He advances his argument in direct reference to Luther and in sharp opposition to all legalistic or teleological emphases within Roman Catholic thought, within the spirit of the so-called left-wing Reformation, and within the idealistic liberalism of the Ritschlian Kingdom-of-God tradition. Genuine Christian ethics, he claims, makes everything dependent on the attitude and motivation of the believer, while acts and aims come into play only as "secondary considerations," and simply as fruits causally rooted in the attitude.[61] Only one type of ethics can be considered true to essential Christianity, then, and that is the "evangelical" ethics.[62] For most readers, this result seems adequate. It fits the contemporary theological orientation, it parallels the basic emphases of Reformation doctrine, and it has clear foundations in certain New Testament texts. What more can one desire? What else could Nygren have done?

Perhaps just two things: First, perhaps the investigation into the essential and characteristic emphases of the Christian faith should be made from a point of view which serves not as a filter, letting only acceptable material through, but rather as a prism, open to all the light which is there within all the traditions within the faith, and functioning only in its own "reflections" to order the various light rays into a recognizable spectrum. Secondly, perhaps the three elements of the genuinely ethical condition in man, the attitude, the aim, and the act, should be allowed to remain a unity, so that, *if the total personal religious orientation of a man's life is genuinely Christian, then his ethical condition would also be genuinely Christian, regardless of whether it is explicated in terms of the priority of attitude, act, or aim.* Perhaps it should be taken more clearly into account, even as it is recognized by Nygren himself, that the "attitude" which is given such emphasis in his thought, though it points to something central in man's total life, signifies only one of the elements in the ethical condition. If a man makes an ethical commitment, it is this commitment which becomes the basis of his new orientation, a center of ethical unity inwardly as well as outwardly. If a man is ethically committed, then the total person is involved, and it does not make sense to speak of the part of the experience as primary and other aspects of it as secondary. For, if a man is totally committed to an ethical ideal, then this commitment of the total man represents a total orientation of his total life, influencing every facet, aim, act, and attitude, equally.

This, apparently, Nygren has not seen. What we have described here as "commitment" or "total personal orientation" is for him primarily a matter of "attitude." This is how he defines the essential element of ethical experience, as well as religious life. At this point, one is tempted to ask whether Nygren has slipped into the same error which he has uncovered so consistently in others, namely the definition and localization of a religious or ethical essence within man's own life, i.e., in one part of man's life, his attitude. How different is Nygren's use of the concept "attitude" from Kant's use of the concept "Pflicht"? That Kant's procedure necessarily leads to an explication of the ethical category which is arbitrary and partial and one-sided, Nygren is the first to acknowledge. Whether he would agree that this is really what has happened to himself, philosophically as well as theologically, is another question altogether.

When Nygren reaches the point where an explication of the characteristic motifs within the Christian ethical ideal is called for, he is quick to point out that such an explication must be grounded in the essential nature of the Christian faith itself.[63] Since Christian ethics, by definition, is the explication of the ethical implications that are integral to the Christian faith, the problem of the relationship between ethics and religion comes into view. Traditionally, this problem is posed in terms of the double question "Is the 'good' good because God wills it, or does God will it because it is good?" Or, to pose the problem principally, "Is ethics to be validated by reference to religion, or is religion dependent upon ethics for its validation?" Nygren approaches the problem initially in terms of the autonomy of the categories. Religion and ethics are two categorically different, independent, and autonomous frameworks of experience. They do not, therefore, find their validation by reference to each other. The traditional question, then, is obviously wrongly asked.

However, Nygren does feel obligated to explain "the connection" between the two autonomous categories, particularly since they can both be connected with the predication "Christian." At one point, he defines the relationship as a "causal" one, indicating that from this standpoint there is, in fact, "identity" between ethics and religion.[64] Recognizing that such a formulation might jeopardize the autonomy of the two categories, Nygren seeks to clarify the matter by explaining that the causality he refers to is "not direct." [65] A new-found depth in religious experience does not *eo ipso* entail a revision in ethical judgments. Religious experience must be made "ethically legitimate," i.e., the believer must consciously re-evaluate his ethical ideal in the light of his enlarged vision of his relationship to God. A new decision is called for if the relationship between the religious and the ethical categories of experience is to be causally consistent.

One might say, therefore, that the relationship between ethics and religion is a relationship of two autonomous categories of experience, each of which revolves, although in different orbits, around one common center. This center is, in the case of Christian faith and Christian ethics, God. But, in the ultimate orientation of life around God as center, Christian faith and Christian ethics do not represent the same category. We have observed above [66] that Nygren chooses the concept "eternity" as his description of the religious category. Furthermore, we have found that he prefers to operate with the term "fellowship" as his basic description of the ethical category.[67] Nygren refers to these concepts once more while dealing with the problem of relating ethics and religion. However, all that he manages to do with them is to define "ethical religion" on the one hand and "religious ethics" on the other: the first is present when the relationship between God and man is seen in terms of "fellowship," the latter when the relationship between people is being included under the category of "eternity." [68] One soon discovers that these definitions do not really answer the principal question regarding the interrelationship of ethics and religion. They only show how the one may come to influence certain considerations belonging to the other, and this is perhaps the limit of what one can do when the prior problem of developing an "inclusive theory of the categories" has not yet been solved.[69]

This does not mean, however, that Nygren can say nothing about the actual content of the Christian ethical ideal. Regardless of the elusiveness of the problem of *relating* ethics and religion, Nygren has shown no hesitation in affirming the inner *consistency* between the content of the Christian faith and the ideals of Christian ethics. "So indissoluble is the connection between the Christian God-relationship and the Christian ethical ideal that he who hails another ideal is thereby proving that he does not have a real experience of the Christian God-relationship." [70] The "indissoluble connection" Nygren speaks about is established by the central concept in Christian faith, as well as in Christian ethics: love, agape. The Christian God-relationship is characterized by love, i.e., by spontaneous, "unmotivated" love. So, also, is the Christian ethical relationship. Only *that* is truly "good" which has its source and beginning in the spontaneous Christian attitude of love.[71] To understand the Christian faith and to live the Christian life is, therefore, identical with understanding the nature of *agape* and living the life of love.

Here, then, we have reached the point where Nygren's explication of ethics reverts into the framework of his systematic theology, and where we must leave it. Only two further notes are needed. First, there is absolutely nothing in Nygren's theology which could form the platform for producing ethical casuistics. The Christian attitude of love cannot possibly be formalized in a set of statutes or reduced to a scheme of laws. On the contrary, it must be free to express itself in the fullest variety of ways. This does not soften the character of the ethical demands; it actually increases the challenge to decision und expands the individual's responsibility. Secondly and finally, Nygren is careful to point out that "a generally valid ethical relationship . . . cannot be determined with a point of departure in the Christian attitude." [72] One cannot possibly expect the Christian ideal of love to be accepted outside of the Christian community itself. On the contrary, its close ties with the particular character of the Christian religious commitment must be recognized and respected. This does not weaken its impact in the world; it actually strengthens its influence and enhances its reforming power. For, it does not impose itself upon the world in the form of laws, statutes, rules, and regulations designed to restrict and govern man and his situation. Rather the Christian ethical ideal shows itself as the free and open-ended principle which finds its content defined, not in general, not once and for all, but in particular and at every moment, namely in that dynamic interplay of human situation and divine orientation in which ethical decision is cast. And it is cast most uniquely, says Nygren, as an expression of love.

Few Christian ethicists on the contemporary scene would disagree.

15

INTERPRETATION AND

CRITICISM OF NYGREN'S ETHICS

FROM A PHILOSOPHICAL

STANDPOINT

Charles W. Kegley

A NYONE who examines the lively discussions of ethics today is impressed with at least three features of the scene. One is this: developments within the field of ethics in the last decade have occurred at such a rapid pace, due largely to the appearance of language analysis, that even many recent discussions of ethical issues seem almost outdated. Another is that religious ethics, or, more generally and correctly, questions turning on the relation between morality and religion, have come to the fore. A third fact which becomes increasingly clear is that most of the discussion among advocates of religious, as contrasted with philosophical, ethics, is infected with a lack of clarity and a deficiency of rational argumentation. Concerning the last observation, which may sound arrogant and even arbitrary and unwarranted, it should be pointed out that deeply committed religious scholars, on the one hand, and philosophers who are far from hostile to religion, on the other hand, have repeatedly written to this effect of late. Thus, H. D. Lewis states that religious thinkers have been curiously and regrettably indifferent to the progress that has been made in contemporary ethics. William Frankena, in not one but in three recent publications, has spelled out the ways in which Christian ethicists especially have failed to define their issues and to state and argue their claims with rigor and cogency.[1] The harshest statement of all came more recently from within the household of Christian ethicists, when James M. Gustafson, speaking of their deference to traditional philosophies, wrote: "Theological ethics is always out of date, because it takes at least thirty years for the Christian thinkers really to absorb what is going on in secular philosophy." [2]

I record these three observations because they help to identify the context in which any fruitful discussion of ethics and religion, such as this dialogue with Anders Nygren, must occur. Although it would be grossly unfair to make Anders Nygren responsible for the explication and defense of the position of religious ethicists in general, and of Christian ethicists in particular, the more so because of the very ambiguity and contradictoriness encountered in the literature, it is a deserved tribute to address certain of the more crucial questions to him. The propriety of this rests on the fact that he is one of the very few creative minds in the field capable of engaging in depth in philosophico-theological discussion. With this encouragement, we can engage in the following study which has two parts. In the first, I shall identify the formative elements in the ethics of Anders Nygren and show how these informed and gave content to his resulting individual and social ethics. In the second part, I shall discuss several questions concerning the nature and claims of religious and Christian ethics, and especially of the possible justification of these claims. By means of the latter, metaethical, discussion, I hope to engage Nygren in the type of clarification philosophers would like to elicit from Christian ethicists.[3]

Formative and Constitutive Elements

Three main influences appear to be at work in Nygren's ethics. Two of these—and they are mutually supporting factors—are Christian agapism and the Kantian critical approach. In addition to these two formative factors, which he shares with several other contemporary religious and Christian ethicists, Nygren has the distinction of being one of the few such ethicists who has been influenced by and contributed to the employment of the methods of linguistic analysis. Although he is almost unique among Christian ethicists in engaging in the exploration of the implications of linguistic analysis for ethical study, he has not either subscribed without reservations to that "way of doing philosophy," nor to any one of the particular approaches advocated by the analysts in their ethical writing, for example, the emotivists, the intuitionists, and the like. About all three of these formative features it should be noted that I name, and shall treat them, in what I take to be a relative order of importance, not in the chronological order in which they developed in his writing.

Because adequate documentation of the first, the role of agapism in Nygren's ethics, would require at least an essay if not a book, we can here simply identify it and proceed to raise questions which seek clarification, explication, and defense. The first point to be made is that few contemporary thinkers have exhibited greater originality, combined with historical and biblical erudition, than has Nygren in exploring the core *meaning* in the noun "love" and its relation to the adjective "Christian." Whereas many others have employed these terms with reckless abandon, and usually with emotional overtones, Nygren, whatever one concludes in final judgment of his thought, has at least striven to clarify the meaning of the terms. Other interpreters, more competent in these areas than I am, have discussed and criticized Nygren's concept and use of agape. This job having been done, we are concerned here to show the determining role of agape in his ethics.

The primary way in which "love" is determinative of Nygren's ethical thinking is in his opting for a dispositional and motivational type of ethics as contrasted with those types of ethics which emphasize act and consequences, for example, utilitarianism. Nygren rejects all the varieties of ethics which fix exclusively upon this or that goal or set of consequences at which ethical action should aim and in the light of which it is to be judged. Thus, he examines and repudiates various teleological theories—hedonism, utilitarianism, eudaemonism, self-realization, and power ethics, all of which seek to bring some nonmoral value into existence. The reasons for which he rejects these teleological theories vary, depending in part on which theory he is examining. One reason, however, applies to all of them, namely that they ignore or deny that there is an integral relation between ends and dispositions. Thus, he believes a person employing the standard of power or of utility may do so with a disposition or motive which is at best ethically neutral, at most evil. A fairly clear-cut example is available in the case of refraining from an action—e.g., taking a life, committing adultery— but from a "wrong" motive, say fear of social and religious disapproval. The other ground, deriving from Kant, is that whereas a disposition may be "good," in itself, an end or consequence of an action, even when it is the result of a good motive, may not be good. Thus, though an action motivated by love is always and everywhere good, in a sense, the results or consequences are not necessarily so, as is illustrated in the giving of financial assistance to a person who proceeds to use the money for "evil" or destructive actions. Criticisms such as these, of course, invite answer and rebuttal from teleological ethicists. They are stated here not for the sake of argument, but to show why Nygren's ethics is essentially attitudinal or dispositional. He believes ethics properly is dispositional, and, although he is well aware that the nature of that disposition varies from one ethical theory to another, in *his* ethics there is no doubt but the ultimate disposition should be love.

A second formative influence in Nygren's thought is the Kantian. This is best illustrated in Nygren's identification of the various kinds of ethics, that is, descriptive, normative, metaphysical, critical, and scientific, and his understanding of their relationships to each other.

The fundamental distinction which Nygren makes is between scientific and philosophical ethics. The former—remembering always that he uses the term "science" in the broad, continental sense of any systematic study, not the narrower sense of the inductive method of the empirical sciences—includes descriptive ethics and critical ethics. Descriptive ethics seeks to identify and classify past and present ethical systems. "Critical" is used in the Kantian sense of inquiring into the presuppositions and action-guiding norms of any ethical system. In contrast to those theological ethicists who would deny either the existence of ethics or its validity or both when ethics is independent of theological presuppositions, Nygren emphatically asserts the autonomy of descriptive and critical ethics. He does deny, however, that either descriptive or critical ethics, qua scientific, can establish valid norms, i.e., establish as valid a particular standard or "good." A *normative science* (of ethics) he calls "a contradicition in terms." [4]

Philosophical ethics, on the other hand, like philosophy in general, is a study (a science, in the broad sense) of universals, not of particulars, like a natural science, it studies man's ethical experience to discover the principal and universal character of ethical thought and life, e.g., the role of value(s), of alternatives, and of any serious consequences of certain kinds of action. However, it is most instructive for our present purposes, and to prepare for questions which will arise later, to observe that Nygren holds a very low opinion of one type of philosophical ethics, namely, the metaphysical.[5] Metaphysics, according to Nygren, is a subjective attempt to arrive at a world view. Most metaphysical systems, at least precontemporary, have been speculative. It is for this reason that, in Nygren's judgment, metaphysics is more an aesthetic than a scientific enterprise.[6] The metaphysician is, in fact, he holds, incapable of achieving the objectivity of the scientist, and his conclusions do not (could they in principle?) achieve the universal validity of a science. Even if they could, however, Nygren has another objection to metaphysics, and by implication, to any metaphysical ethics. He holds that these systems "do not do justice to the uniquely ethical phenomena." I am not clear precisely what this phrase "uniquely ethical phenomena" designates. One hopes that Nygren is not identifying himself with what Henry Aiken perceptively described as the "decision is king" philosophy. I say "hopes," because there is a strong strain in the writing of Christian ethicists today which dwells on the subjective character of ethical decision. It usually speaks vaguely of faith responding in love to love, of love which is more than an ethical principle, of shapes of response, and the like. Nygren may have something entirely different in mind when he writes about uniquely ethical phenomena. If so, one wishes to know what it is.

What is clear, however, is that he rejects totally the massive and amorphous knowledge claims of speculative metaphysicians, and of the ethical systems which, built on these metaphysical systems, involved normative claims. Contemporary philosophy generally agrees with this rejection.

There are two questions concerning metaphysics vis-à-vis ethics, however, which demand to be asked, because the answer to them which is implied in Nygren's thought has considerable importance. One is this: granted his commendable rejection of old-fashioned, speculative metaphysics, and, further, recognizing the surprisingly frequent points of affinity with linguistic analysis and its implied "elimination of metaphysics," is there any logical reason why exponents of Nygren's philosophical stance could not welcome and cultivate the newer views of metaphysics? One has in mind, of course, the view of metaphysics as the attempt to identify and interpret the generic traits of empirical reality, that is, of whatever can be known by the empirical method. Instead of condemning any and all metaphysics, are there not compelling reasons why Nygren should leave himself open, nay, explore carefully the present-day efforts of John Findlay, P. F. Strawson, Paul Weiss, Charles Hartshorne, Justus Buchler, and other metaphysicians to interpret the actual structure of the universe? I must admit, however, that it is just here that metaphysics, as Gilbert Ryle once said, reveals its basis in ontology. A statement of his which is relevant reads: "If he (the philosopher) is not an ontologist he is not a metaphysician." [7] Further, it is partly because of the *theological* involvement of ontological efforts, as well as the alleged inability to establish their knowledge-claims, which leads Nygren to reject them in principle, not merely in their particular historical forms. Still, one is suspicious of so universal and final a repudiation as Nygren's of any and all possible efforts at metaphysics—with or without ontologies. After all, if one engages in talk about things and their relations one is talking metaphysics. Better a criticized and "good" one than a hidden and unexamined one if there is to be any at all.[8]

There is another closely related question. If, as is well known, Nygren's is an ethics which says that the ground and source of all existence is a god of creative love, does this affirmation not involve metaphysical presuppositions, indeed, a particular *kind* of metaphysics, that is, a theistic one? If Nygren agrees, for example, even with minor reservations, with Emil Brunner's central claim, that the Christian view of man and of the good is that man's source, ground, and goal is a god of love, is he not committed to some kind of metaphysics? Faced with this kind of question, another Lutheran philosopher-theologian, Paul Tillich, it is instructive to observe, insisted on the centrality of the ontological grounding of ethics (and of Christian theology) but without ever choosing, so far as I know, from among the traditionally contending positions, such as idealism, realism, naturalism. It is well known that he did reject supernaturalism.[9] Where, if anywhere in this maze, does Nygren stand?

Returning to the examination of formative influences and to their expression in Nygren's ethical writing, another illustration of *critical* Kantian influence is encountered in his deduction of the basic types of human experience, and the fundamental categories of each of these. The types are: A] the theoretical; B] aesthetic; C] ethical; D] religious. Nygren speaks of the "validity" of ethical experience, for instance, and of religious and aesthetic experience. This phrasing has a strange, indeed, jarring ring to English-speaking philosophers, but what he appears to mean is that the theoretical, aesthetic, religious, and ethical are at once autonomous and necessary kinds of human experience. Furthermore, this validity (uniqueness and necessity) is exhibited in part by their capacity to explain and render meaningful other kinds of experience. It is the task of philosophy, Nygren holds, not only to *identify* the fundamental types of human thought and experience, but also to furnish a broad deduction of the categories of these types. Thus, philosophical ethics establishes the *formal* category valid for ethical experience. A category is "formal" precisely because it is devoid of content, that is, of "matter." The category of the ethical is fellowship, of religious experience the eternal, of aesthetic the beautiful, of science, the true. *What* each of these is, or how the matter or content is described, depends on factual and scientific considerations. For example, how "the eternal" is described depends on the particular historical religion examined. We shall have more to say about this use of the term "formal" shortly.

This way of analyzing the basic types of human experience poses several interesting problems, one of which is that Nygren reserves "truth" for the theoretical, that is, the scientific sphere. The implication of this is that Nygren consistently and boldly draws the conclusion that it is inappropriate and impossible rationally to demonstrate the "truth" and superiority of one particular ethical, religious, and aesthetic system over another. Accordingly, *alla Kant*, one may demonstrate the uniqueness, for example, of the Christian ethic of love, but not its superiority. Thus, in a spirit which Nygren holds is both soundly empirical and evangelical, the "truths" or insights which cannot be demonstrated rationally or scientifically, may, under certain conditions, be embraced by faith.

In addition to agapism and Kantian influences, there is a third formative element in Nygren's ethics. We have already said that Nygren's major and lifelong concern was with an analysis and clarification of the linguistic uses and various concepts of love. That neither his facility nor belief in the value of linguistic analysis has slackened is evident not only in a recent and brilliant essay "From Atomism to Contexts of Meaning in Philosophy," but also in his forthcoming book: "Meaning and Method: Prolegomena to a Scientific Philosophy of Religion." [10] In the former, in connection with an interpretation of Wittgenstein, he re-emphasized his view that a statement can never be understood in isolation, but only in context, indeed in the wider contexts of languages and their use. What has this to do with ethics? So much that it calls for another essay, but at least this much can be said here. If meaning is necessarily in contexts, is meaningful ethical decision also contextual and in what sense? Presuming (safely, I believe) that in some sense it is, does this place Nygren in the camp of present-day contextualist ethics? Not necessarily, and in one sense definitely not. That is, he clearly rejects one type of contextualist ethics, namely, one which, repudiating all principles and rules, has a built-in relativism which is fatal. As we have seen, he considers principles or values necessary, but he does not deny that their meaning, and the way in which they should be applied, depends on the ethical context or the situation. It may be, according, that Nygren has the advantages of contextualism epistemologically without its disadvantages in ethics.

Nygren is quite able, as the reader must be when the debate between the contextualists and the situationists occurs, to distinguish between the two. While not for a moment denying that ethical decisions should be relevant to the concrete situation in which the agent finds himself, he certainly denies the usual situationists' rejection of principles or of action-guiding norms. Further, his use of "context" is clear and cautious, as most "contextualist" ethical discussion is not. For, unlike Nygren, the latter use "context" to denote two quite different things, first, in a neutral sense, an interrelation of the parts, or a milieu, and, second, as a set of values or as a philosophy of life, e.g., the biblical.

Summing up, when one combines the Kantian, the Christian, and analytical elements, there emerges an ethic which is agapistic, dispositional, and faith-ful. Ethical experience is autonomous and necessary, although it is intimately related to religious experience. In fact, Nygren has said that "the Christian ethos is an ethos determined from first to last by religious considerations: that is, the ethical behavior of the Christian must derive its character from Christian fellowship with God . . . [It] is theocentric: it is primarily obedience to the will of God. But what the will of God is the Christian knows through Christ . . . the whole content of Christian ethics can be expressed by the single word 'love.' . . . God's will is one and consistent in all the relationships of life it requires one and the same thing – love." [11]

Although the content of the divine imperative, to use both Kant's and Brunner's phrase, is love, and although love constitutes the primary answer to the question "What is God's will, and how are we to know what to do?" Nygren holds that there are additional ethical guides available to man in his quest for the good life. In one context, the principle, if one may with reservations call love a principle, is said to be supplemented by the principle of service – "he who would be great among you, let him be your servant" – and by the will to forgive. He appears to take the principle of service to one's fellow man and of willingness to forgive as distinctive, but subordinate, ethical principles. The main drift of this thinking appears to be that they are derivative from love and thus not fully autonomous. At any rate they are both derived from the New Testament. He is also of the opinion that a person may gain a special or distinctive kind of guidance in addition to love and its subordinate principles. Thus he writes, "alongside love there appear the 'ordinances of creation' as a second source for the knowledge of God's will." [12] This presumably refers to the familiar "orders of creation" as Luther described them, i.e., to the family, the economic order, and the like. We shall not here press the point, but a critic surely would like to know how the person asking: "What ought I to do?" can receive information—if that is what is meant by "knowledge"—by being told that there are certain orders of society.

There is no sharp distinction in Nygren's ethics, so far as I am aware, between individual and social ethics. This does not mean that Nygren does not distinguish between the kinds of problems characteristic of so-called personal or individual ethics and those which characterize man as he relates himself to his fellow men in the social, economic, and political realms. As a matter of fact, Nygren has said that the goal of social ethics is the creation of "community." Presumably this is used in the sense of the German word *gemeinde*, and refers to the complex set of relationships spoken of in religious terminology as the kingdom of God. The more the emphasis falls upon the term "community," and the more one recalls at the same time Nygren's fundamental ethical category, "fellowship," the more English speaking readers will be reminded of the description of this ethical ideal by a major American philosopher, Josiah Royce, and of his extended discussion of what he called the "beloved community." In making this comparison, we do not mean to approve or disapprove either of Nygren's nor of Royce's social ethics, but simply to point to an extremely interesting parallel, meriting further exploration.

In another context, at any rate, Nygren's emphasis is constantly upon the will directed toward the establishment of community, on the one hand, and upon that kind of community which is characterized by Christian love, on the other hand. This distinguishes his social ethics from two other classically familiar types, namely, the Nietzschean power ethics, and the Stoic-Kantian ethic. In the latter, Nygren holds, the emphasis falls far too strongly upon rights and duties rather than upon love, and furthermore upon a community in which individuals are too abstractly considered in terms of their equality and their relationships, atomistic-like, one to the other. But it is the difference between these ethics, not the demonstrable superiority of the Christian over the others, which needs stressing. Finally, on the question of the content of Christian social ethics, Nygren clearly states that, "No Christian social order exists which as such can rightly be described as a

'Christian social order.'" He cites the example from the economic order that neither capitalism nor socialism is to be considered the sole economic system demanded by the ethic of love. His statement is that "everything depends on the spirit whose ends such a system is made to serve." [13] His concern is that the Christian ethicist or theologian never absolutize any particular and historic political, economic, or social order. In this context, as in others, he agrees with Tillich's stress on the Protestant principle.

Some contemporary ethicists will be quick to attack this position, of course, not primarily for what it affirms, but for what it fails to say. Thus, it may be urged that the various competing systems in the political order, for example, are not as neutral as is here implied, and that they are not equally competent to serve as the framework in which the spirit of love of their members is expressed. More important, some critics will allege that an ethical relativism is implied in what Nygren has said, resulting in the view, for example, that there is no ground of choice among the contending political, economic, and social philosophies. Now it is doubtful whether Nygren actually does hold, to cite a contemporary debate, that as between democracy and dictatorship there is no ground of preference for one or the other from the point of view of the ethics of love. One may agree that neither democracy nor dictatorship is to be absolutized anymore than is any other particular political system. Surely each of these sysems, and any other candidate for our adoption, not only can, but must be analyzed and criticized in terms of what it holds concerning the nature of man, the methods it advocates, and its theory of the structure and function of the state. Once such an analysis is conducted, it would appear to many social and political philosophers that, at a very minimum, one may decide that certain political systems—for example, dictatorship, absolute or divine right monarchy, totalitarianism—fail in all three of these categories to meet either the requirement of support by empirical fact and / or the criterion by which one estimates their capacity to serve as the framework for the expression of the Christian philosophy of love. Nygren may reasonably be expected to defend himself, within the structure of his philosophy, against these criticisms. But some clarification on his part seems necessary. Whatever avenues his response pursues, his fundamental stance is clear: The Christian ethos and the religious content of Christianity, as he has written, are "two sides of the same thing." Philosophically, what this comes to is that the good life is the religious life of love.

From this sketch of the formative and constitutive elements in Nygren's ethics we turn to a statement of certain crucial but generally unstated questions which philosophers believe are either unrecognized or ignored by religious ethicists today. Others, closely related, concern Nygren's own system.

Questions

The first and most general question is: where does Nygren's ethics fit into the present-day categorizing of ethical systems? In attempting to answer this question—and there are reasons for doubting it can be answered with any specificity—we also hope to shed some light on the confused state of religious ethics today.

A very useful scheme of classification of contemporary ethical theories is that of William Frankena's, referred to earlier. It divides all theories into teleological and deontological. The former assert that the ultimate criterion of what is "good," right, our duty, and the like, is the nonmoral value which any ethical action brings into existence. Teleological ethicists may hold any one of a variety of views, even contradictory, concerning *what* that nonmoral good is. The clearest examples of these kinds of ethics, to cite only three, are hedonism, the ethics of power, and of self-realization. We may omit subsidiary divisions among these theories, e.g., the question of whether it is the individual ethical agent's good or the good of all men or of the universe as a whole which one ought to promote, because Nygren, like all religious and Christian ethicists so far as I know, is clearly universalistic rather than egoistic. It was also stated earlier that he has gone on record as rejecting in principle the *above named* kinds of teleological theories. It is by no means as clear, however, whether his agapism is, in the end, a teleological ethics or not, but more on this tricky question in a moment.

Deontological theories, in contrast with teleological ones, hold that an action is good, right, or obligatory when and to the degree that it promotes a surplus of good over evil in the individual, in society, or even in the universe; its goodness inheres in itself. It is not the consequences of an action, as in utilitarianism, for example, which makes it good, nor is it the nonmoral (or even moral) value it brings into existence. It is rather that it is expressive of a duty—e.g., telling the truth, keeping promises, or of obeying a command of God, or of being just. The deontological theories may be better understood by observing that they subdivide, as do teleological theories, into *act* and *rule* theories. Ethicists who emphasize ethical acts also emphasize the role of decision and the relevance of the situation, as we said in another connection. Ethical judgments, they contend, are always particular: they must be made in this situation, here and now. This kind of ethics is the joy of existentialists who never tire of insisting upon the anxiety and urgency with which the Christian is required to decide what to do. What alarms many critics is that these act-deontologists often claim that this and this alone is the biblical, i.e., New Testament way of interpreting ethical issues. It is especially instructive that Nygren, who stands in the main line of the evangelical and Lutheran tradition, and who therefore might be expected to adopt this Kierkegaardian stance, does not in fact do so. It would be valuable to elicit his criticism of this now-so-popular ethical viewpoint. I should imagine that his rejection would rest on two grounds. One is that the knowledge of what one ought to do in any specific situation appears to most act-deontologists to be intuitionistic—a notoriously objectionable epistemological position—or at best, to ask us to make decisions in the light of our knowledge of "the God who is the Father of our Lord Jesus." [14] The ambiguities growing out of this are so glaring and numerous as to put a philosopher in a state of shock. The other reason for rejecting this form of act-deontological ethics is that it seems not merely to invite, but often to glory in contradictoriness. I am not talking about any contradictoriness which may arise between a disposition and an action, but about contradictoriness between judgments concerning a particular action. Thus, in a specified ethical situation, many Kierkegaardian existentialists seem to be quite prepared to allow flatly contradictory ethical judgments to be described as equally "true" or justified providing each ethical agent renders a conscientious judgment in the light of the given facts. Because such particular judgments are determinative, no criterion is available to pure act-ethicists for arbitrating between these judgments. If it be countered that there is the will of God, or acting in response to and in light of one's knowledge of God's saving grace, and the like, no help is afforded, because each agent claims to be doing that. Is not this the ethical night in which all good and evil is confused and mere assertion reigns?

Fortunately, another form of deontology is available, i.e., one which employs principles, action-guiding norms, or what religious ethicists like to call "creative guides." Ethicists of this type assert that the principles are valid whether or not (though in fact they usually do) promote the good. They also hold, against the exponents of act-ethics, that the principles are not derived by empirical induction. What, then, is their source? That depends on the particular theory we examine. Thus, it may be reason, it may be revelation, it may be natural law, it may be inductive generalization from very wide religious experience. Whatever its derivation, it must be susceptible of universalization, that is, the proposition that everyone in a specified situation should act in the light of it. In the case of Nygren's ethics we have what Frankena would classify as a mixed agapism as distinguished from a pure agapism. That is to say, it is not love and love alone which is the guide for ethical living (pure agapism) but love supplemented by at least two subsidiary principles, service and the will-to-forgiveness. The very term "principle" is awkward, and Nygren, like many Christian ethicists, no doubt is uneasy with its use in ethics. He is so on the grounds that "principle" suggests something abstract, purely conceptual, propositional, whereas "love" is concrete, alive, active, and a creative power ("God is love"), even though the word "love" can be conceptualized. The fact remains, however, that ethics is concerned with the good life and with finite creatures who are wrestling with the question "What ought I (or we) to do?" And Nygren, following the New Testament, and believing, as he does, in the centrality of disposition and motive in ethics, says that the basic guide is love. Recognizing that this often fails, of itself, to give sufficient specific guidance, he adds the two subsidiary guides or principles named above.

On this whole issue of motivation vis-à-vis principles, the alleged hostility may be more imagined than real. Thus, the disposition and attitude of love (as an ethical trait of character) has its counterpart in actions guided by the principles of love and willingness to forgive and to serve. So seen, an agapastic ethics is not without principled guidance, as an act-ethics may be.

The aspects of Nygren's ethics which are the most interesting and puzzling, however, are probably those in which he relates the ethical and the religious categories and, accordingly, ethical and religious thought and life. These categories, it will be recalled, are described usually as "fellowship" and "the eternal" respectively, although the ethical often seems to be described by the term "duty" or, in Kant's phrase, the categorical imperative. So one might say in excessive brevity: the good life is one which universalizes fellowship in the light of eternity. There are some questions, however, which must be asked about all this.

First, what is the source of these formal terms, "fellowship" and "eternal"? They are startling because we would expect Nygren to follow the standard terminology, deriving originally from Plato, of the true (for the theoretical sciences), the beautiful (for aesthetics), and the good (for ethics), and thus far, at least, they would be purely formal and serve, separately and in juxtaposition, the purposes of each of these inquiries or areas of experience. But "fellowship" and "the eternal" are puzzling as transcendental deductions. Wingren, among others, has alleged that they are not, as Nygren claims, purely formal, but rather that they distort, force, and intrude upon the empirically or the historically "given" content and on the answers we give to ethical questions. If a category *is* purely formal, then it is A] devoid of content and B] does not prohibit or distort any content. The categories of the sciences and of aesthetics clearly meet these criteria, as Nygren describes their formal intent, that is, the true and the beautiful. To designate "fellowship" as the category of the ethical, however, surely seems tantamount to giving it content and determining a priori what it is, as, for instance "the good" would not. Similarly, the "eternal" is at least ambiguous, at worst, also content-filled. Are there not historical religions, for example, which are devoid of the concept of the eternal? How then are they handled in this categorical schema?

There appears to me to be an ineradicable ambiguity here in the employment of the term "formal" in Nygren's philosophy. To unpack this would be to embark on a separate essay. Ths following observations may suffice. The term "formal" has a primary use in logic, as when we talk about X, Y, and Z and of their relations. Clearly, "X," "Y," and "Z" do not have any meaning; they refer to nothing until we specify, for example, "Men," "Socrates," and "Mortality." But "true," "beautiful," "good," and "religious" are *not* thus devoid of meaning. It appears to be misleading, accordingly, to say, as I did earlier, that these are devoid of "content," because we have already spedified or indicated a concept whose content is the formal characteristic of an area of discourse and of experience. Perhaps the best that can be said here is that, as Nygren envisions it, the concepts of the true, beautiful, good, and the religious do not in themselves afford criteria for their empirical use.

Related to this is a question which comes to the fore in several connections as one ponders Nygren's thought. In more than one context Nygren says that in a sense all the other categories, the theoretical, the aesthetic, and the ethical, depend upon the religious. Thus, in the work, "The Christian Ethos," he states, "the great fundamental questions are the True, the Beautiful, and the Good, and—to crown them all—the Eternal," and in his, *Essence of Christianity*, he writes that "none of these essential pillars of the spiritual life (i.e., the categories of knowledge, ethics, aesthetics) is able to stand by itself, but each must rest on the foundation of the question of the eternal." [15] These are rich but ambiguous figures of speech. Exactly how do the other three categories depend upon the religious? One thing that is involved for our present purpose, of course is the old question of the sense in which the ethical is alleged to depend upon or be an expression of the religious. In the long and instructive history of the relation between ethics and religion, at least four main steps are discernible. A] The ethical and the religious are identified. B] The ethical is held to be distinguishable from and in a sense independent of religion, yet to sustain a special relation to religion, as in Kant who saw ethical imperatives as divine commands. C] Religion is seen as a mere aspect of morality, as in Huxley's definition of religion as "morality tinged with emotion." D] Ethics is not only autonomous and independent of religion, it performs the functions formerly assigned to religion, as in John Dewey, Nygren, as a highly sophisticated philosopher-theologian, is well aware of these positions in the history of thought, and as a liberal Christian he has stoutly affirmed the autonomy of the ethical. He still takes the position, however, that the other categories are dependent upon the religious, and hence that a normative ethics depends on religion, still more specifically, that the ethics more worthy of our rational commitment is the agapism of the New Testament. One question the philosophical ethicist must press is: What does this *mean* ("depends upon," is "informed by," etc.) and on what grounds is this claim justified? Most Christian ethicists have been hopelessly vague, or unaware of, this question. In addressing it to Nygren, we are complimenting him by saying that he is one of the very few who are aware of the issues and could clear up several basic metaethical confusions.

The fact is that most religious and Christian ethicists have failed to make clear A] what is claimed and B] the *grounds* of their claim that a religious (e.g., Christian) ethics is superior to the allegedly inadequate nonreligious ethics, if, indeed, they make that claim. Tillich, in *Beyond Morality*, graciously, and several others, less graciously, have asserted that religious ethics has this superiority. Their assertions about love as commanded by God, about response to and living in accordance with God's will is fraught, however, with ambiguity. Do they mean, for example, that A] the commands of God are good per se; B] that being "willed by God" *means*, by definition, being obligatory on man; c] that God, as *the* good, contains and discloses the nature of ultimate reality, that God is or furnishes the ontological foundations on which ethical directives are grounded?

The first contains a hidden premise and postulates an ambiguous answer to the ethical question "What, if anything, is good?" For its fuller form reads, God, who commands what is good, commands love, and finite creatures, who ought to obey God, ought therefore to love him and each other. In this grounding of ethics, not love but God's commands or his will is ultimate. We shall skip here all the epistemological difficulties concerning how, e.g., by revelation, God's will is to be surely known—and we are left with God's will or commands. At this point Plato's question presses: Is X good because God commands it, or does he command it because it is good? Nygren surely opts for the former, which means that the basic ethical affirmation is a disguised religious assertion. If so, then, as with nearly all religious and Christian ethicists, normative ethics depends on religious affirmation. If it be retorted, "Why not?" there are two comments. One is: what then has become of the alleged autonomy of *normative* ethics? Or is the claim of the Christian ethicist that his is the best of all thus far proposed ethics? The latter, unlike most Christian ethicists, Nygren has wisely refrained from doing. But then his position is compromised.

Another comment is this: it will not do to "solve" the root claim of religious ethics by definition—which is what one suspects most religious ethicists do. For, as A. C. Ewing has pointed out, if "being obligatory" simply *means* "willed by God," it becomes meaningless to ask why God wills one thing rather than another.[16] Ewing continues: "If it were said in reply that God's commands determined what we ought to do but that these commands were only issued because it was good that they should be or because obedience to them did good, this would still make judgments about the good, at least, independent of the will of God, and we should not have given a definition of all fundamental ethical concepts in terms of God or made ethics dependent on God." [17]

It is apparent that most religious ethicists confuse the *content* of ethical judgment with its justification, i.e., the grounds on which it is held. In essence their position contains a hidden premise, namely, that we ought to imitate and obey God, or "love what we are at one with." This premise, however, is itself not derived from religious presuppositions, and, further, it is loaded with epistemological difficulties.

I turn to another critical question addressed to Nygren and to religious ethicists generally. This concerns the constantly recurring claim that theological ethics alone affords the *motivation* for the good life. With this claim, as with previously considered problems, Nygren should not be required to answer for all Christian ethicists. At the same time, his view of the integral relation between the ethical and the religious life makes it apparent that, in his own distinctive way, he views the "good life" as fundamentally motivated by a grateful and service-ful response to God's creative love. What, then, is to be said about this claim?

One is that, like all general claims, it charms with a deceptive vagueness. It sounds "Christian" in its emphasis on love, Kantian in its stress on motive, and existentially "right" in making central the role of decision. Exactly what, however, does it mean, and on what grounds may it be justified?

Does this claim mean that people are not really "good" unless and until they act in the light of belief in God? Even in this way of expressing it two subclaims are evident, which are not contradictory, in fact, but mutually supporting. They are often encountered together or voiced as if they amounted to the same thing. The first places the emphasis on the "insights," the principles, the divine imperatives which allegedly the nonreligious (usually this has meant the nonsupernatural-istic) [18] oriented person lacks or cannot have. The second is existential in import, and says in effect that in the absence of certain beliefs in and experiences of a transcendent God, the good life, in any adequately and religiously appropriate sense, will not and cannot appear.

With reference to the former, one wishes to ask Nygren on what grounds the principle(s) and goals—one takes these to be love and eternal fellowship respectively—are justified. Assuming that the defense does not rest on the timeworn claims such as ecclesiastical and / or biblical authoritarianism, nor on intuition and / or mystical insight, is there any rational and empirical defense? In other words, if the basic religious claim rests on faith (in a noncognitive sense) rather than on rational and empirical claims, is not the alleged basis of morality in religion no more rationally justifiable than the characteris-tically ethical claim? One suspects that when the issue is put this way, representative defenders of religious ethics almost unconsciously shift the argument to the existentialist type of claim, mentioned above. That is to say, they have the embarrassing, but unconfused awareness that the religious beliefs and principles to which they appeal have no stronger and no other justification than faith, and so they shift from the logical to the psychological argument stated above, namely, that the only adequate motivation for the ethical life is religious.

Here, however, we encounter at least two extremely dubious assertions which require examination. One is whether it can be shown that any specific sets of religious beliefs, when existentially held, do generate the life of love. The other is whether it can be demonstrated that when these religious beliefs are not existentially held, the life of love is not generated. What gives one very serious pause about the former is the degree and extent to which precisely those persons and institutions acting in the name of the theistic god were not only the most deficient in the ethical realm, but the arch practitioners of cruelty and injustice. Still more disconcerting is the very considerable evidence of the practice and advancement of benevolence, justice, and equality on the part of persons and groups who either disavowed traditional supernaturalistic beliefs or who held them to be an impediment and an obstacle to virile ethical action.

Pondering these and other questions not voiced here, the philosophical student of theological ethics feels urged to ask the following question. After patiently analyzing the various claims of religious ethics, is one not compelled to choose his ethical stance on grounds of reason and experience, in the light, to be sure, of the teaching and life of no less a one than the founder of Christianity?

Cultural
and Ecumenical Concerns

16

THE ROLE OF CULTURE IN

THE THOUGHT OF

ANDERS NYGREN

Søren Holm

THE problem of the place of culture in the theology of Anders Nygren is a difficult one. He himself has not dealt with the problem collectively, and the question can therefore not be taken up for discussion without being related to his thinking as a whole.[1] This is necessary even though it means that several thoughts must be included here which have been dealt with elsewhere in the present book. The place of culture in Nygren's theology is a question which must be answered by a study of Nygren's thinking as a whole. The answer is not to be found collectively in any one of his writings.

Nygren's theology claims to be historical and not speculative. In contrast to the usual natural theology prevalent during the period of Enlightenment, it is a concrete theology. It is Schleiermacher's close influence on Nygren which forbids him to accept any other forms of religion than the historical, which was exactly what the young Schleiermacher had maintained in his *Reden über die Religion* of 1799. Nygren's dogmatics, therefore, derives its content from something he considers to be a historical fact, and he accepts it as the truth on the strength of a personal value judgment which can neither be proved nor disproved by reason. It is otherwise with the religious attitude. This is not merely an actual attitude to life, but it is a *valid* attitude to life and thereby it also becomes *necessary*. While Christianity is thus a historical and sociological religion, which is the "truth" for multitudes of people, including Nygren himself, "religion as such," i.e., the religious attitude to life is something that demands a philosophical justification. When talking of Christianity alone, our approach is theological; but when we are talking of the validity and truth of the religious attitude to life as such, then we are approaching the problem from a philosophical or, more exactly, a religious philosophical point of view.

More or less parallel with his rejection of a natural religion or a universal religious attitude, is Nygren's rejection of the theory that *humanism* has any independent justification outside the specifically Christian revelation which has found its ethical expression in the concept of love. Two as different personalities as the famous classical scholar Ulrich von Wilamowitz-Moellendorff from Berlin, and his compatriot, the theologian and philosopher Max Scheler, have pointed out, independently of each other, the fundamental difference between the Platonic eros, which seeks its values in fellowship with the gods and the heavenly ideas, and the New Testament agape which, in contrast to the value-seeking eros is indifferent to values and is addressed to all men without exception. This appearance of the divine agape is identical with the revelation in Christianity, and it is through this revelation alone that the link can be established between God and man. Agape is in a sense the divine analogy to the "schenken Tugend" of the superman in Nietzsche, and where it appears it must produce an effect which also becomes visible through the given *forms of culture.*

Thus Nygren has rejected pietism in all its forms and has also repudiated any form of sectarian theology which shuts itself off from the world. However, this repudiation of humanism and of the intrinsic value of man indicates that Nygren's theology is parallel to the conception of man in the Barthian theology, and we can therefore say both that his theology has no relation to culture at all, and that cultural life in all its forms derives its ultimate validity and truth from the necessity of a religious attitude to life or from the religious a priori which is a purely categorical term of validity and truth. This is transcendental and not material, and therefore Nygren also refuses to discuss the *existence* of the religious a priori. In a meaningful way, we can only say that the religious a priori *is valid.*

If this transcendental principle is applied to religion, it becomes Nygren's task to prove that there is a certain element in religion, and if this element has no validity, no knowledge and experience is possible at all. The result of this is that the problem of religious philosophy becomes the problem of religious experience; but because this experience should not be understood psychologically as an expression of spiritual experiences, it is better to say that it is the task of religious philosophy to demonstrate the validity and truth of the religious a priori. On the other hand, philosophy of religion should not be understood as something which in itself is an expression of religion, as was the case in the pre-Kantian philosophy and particularly so in Hegel's philosophy. The post-Kantian–nontheological–philosophy of religion, which was introduced by Schleiermacher, does not set out to be religion, and therefore does not compete with any given positive form of religion.

According to Nygren it should thus be possible in this way to combine a critical philosophy of religion with "orthodox" dogmatics or the dogmatic content of a given historical religion, in this case Christianity, if only this is defined in the right methodological way. Religious philosophy should thus not be critical in the sense that it eliminates the unscientific and unphilosophical aspects of theology by rationalistic means; but it should be critical in the Kantian sense. Religion exists as a given historical and empirical quantity which religious philosophy must attempt to understand from a cognitive point of view, just as it is the ubiquitous task of science to interpret what is given and not to create something new.

Religion may be studied through three different disciplines. From the historical and genetic perspective it may be studied through the history of religion, the psychology of religion, and through the three usual historical disciplines viz. Old Testament history, New Testament history, and Church History. To understand religion as a whole, and in its logical context, it should be studied through dogmatics and ethics, which are the two main disciplines of systematic theology. But this does not suffice. Religion claims to have objective validity, and this claim must be investigated by the philosopher of religion, who must ask whether religious value has any validity at all, and on what conditions this claim to validity can be recognized as legitimate. This validity cannot be sought in anything transcendent or supernatural, as was done in ancient dogmatics, for in that case the philosophy of religion would not be philosophy; but the validity must be transcendental or a priori, which thus leads us to the concept of the religious a priori.

This means, however, that the philosophy of religion must investigate whether the religious phenomena manifest any element which can prove that religion as such is a necessary and unavoidable way of life. It must ask whether religious value is a fundamental value or a derivative value, and again, what is the place of religion in the realm of consciousness and cultural life. But this leads precisely to the question of whether religion is an a priori way of life. For only in this way can religion come into true contact with general philosophy and become related to the existing forms of culture.

The religious a priori must show us religion as an essential and universal way of life. In order that it shall not become an isolated or incidental psychological factor, the religious a priori must be related to the other spiritual a priori; but however closely it may be connected with these forms and values it does not become identical with any one of them. The religious a priori is neither culture in general nor philosophy in particular; but the existence of the relationship does mean that there can be no religion without knowledge, morals, and art; for through worship, religion bears a special relationship to the aesthetic, or as the present author has expressed it in an aphorism: the moral expression of religion is ethos, the aesthetic expression is cult. The special nature of religion is shown in the fact that philosophy of religion is concentrated on the specifically religious a priori—it asks about "the religious element in religion."

If we are to prove that a cognition is a priori, we must first prove that without the validity of this cognition no cognition whatsoever is possible. If religious experience itself claims to be valid, we commit no violation of this experience by ranging it under the a priori point of view, and it does in fact make this claim of validity and truth because it does not wish to be a subjective experience only, but an objective and universal experience as well. It claims to be a true experience of something extramental because it takes its origin in the divine revelation; this is not incompatible with its universality, however. The a priori concept is merely the philosophical formulation of the claim of religious experience to transsubjective validity. The transcendental method apparently does not guarantee the claim of religion that its objects must have a transcendent reality, however, and this very reality must therefore be secured by other means, for transcendence claims to be real. Transcendentality is, however, merely formal.

But the religious a priori would merely be an empty form if religion did not exist, just as the epistemological a priori would be empty if there were no universal experience. The religious a priori must therefore be *actualized*, and it is actualized if the possibility it opens is realized in the existing forms of religion. Whether religion is real or not, i.e., merely possible, is not determined through philosophy but through experience, for only through experience is the religious a priori realized. The fact of religion is empirically ascertainable, but its validity is deduced transcendentally, and this happens when we are able to point out an element in religious experience without which no experience would be possible at all—or, in other words—this element must be valid in order that anything can be valid at all.

The transcendental method of deduction need not "prove" religious experience in its entirety, but merely the element of validity as such in this experience. The question is of the fundamental category or fundamental value of religion; but this is no isolated factor as are the a priori conditions of possibility of cognition, morals, and art. In religion, the transcendental deduction must consist in proving that if religious experience was not valid there would be no validity at all. It is here and precisely here that the *relation between religion and culture* lies. If religious experience as such was not valid there would be no question whatsoever of any validity within the sphere of art at all. Any attempt to differentiate between valid and nonvalid, between ideal and false forms of culture would have to cease.

The object must be to prove either that not only is there no religious cognition but that there is no cognition whatever without the fundamental religious category—or that validity exists solely on a religious basis. If the validity of the forms of culture rest on the validity and truth of religion, then religious validity must rest upon an even deeper foundation than the epistemological, ethical, and aesthetic a priori. Cognition has no transcendent criteria and consequently its acceptance of the universality and necessity of religion can only be based on the influence and importance accorded to religion as an empirical and sociological factor in the context of the cultural system, and this influence and importance could be proved in two different ways. It could either be proved that a hiatus or lacuna would arise in the entire cultural system if religion were lacking, or it could be proved that the entire cultural system was founded on religion.

The first of these alternatives must be rejected, however, for religion, even in its empirical form, would protest against being considered as a form of culture on a par with art, science, and morals, and it is therefore necessary to prove that the cultural system as a whole rests on something which is realized only in religion. This does not imply that the autonomy of religion is limited in any way, for this concept merely means that religion does not entirely integrate with the different cultural forms to which, according to Nygren, it does not belong.

The object now becomes to investigate on what the *validity* of the different cultural forms is based, in order that their content may be accepted as true, good, or beautiful according to whether we are dealing with science, morals, or art. We then understand that when we attribute validity to something, be it knowledge, an act, or the standards of a work of art, we raise it up above the conditions of sensual experience, above the limits of time and space; for such a transcendental validity must be unrelated to time and space. The condition underlying the validity of anything is thus that we are entitled to raise it up above the spheres of time and space. It is this condition that cultural life must build upon if its empirical forms of appearance are to be considered valid, for the different forms of culture cannot confer this validity upon each other either singly or collectively, however good their intentions, for this validity is of a *religious* nature.

This means, in other words, that religion claims to raise human nature up above the finite spheres of sensual experience and lead it into the *eternal*. The different forms of culture are thus founded in the eternal; but the category of eternity is *not* a form of culture, it is *religious* in the deepest sense of the word. The category of eternity is therefore the fundamental form of religion, within which all religious experience exists and on which all cultural validity ultimately depends. From a philosophical point of view, the eternal can only be defined negatively as something which is raised above the bounds of time and space, from a religious aspect, however, it can be defined positively as that something which shares in the life of God himself. It is "out of this world." Our cognition is thus ranged under this category of eternity inasmuch as it seeks for the mark of eternity in all that exists, and the more fervent it is, the fewer temporal things are allowed to fall outside the realm of eternity – or, more positively expressed, the more every single element of life also becomes a religious element – for the more all is seen *sub specie aeternitatis*.

But all this is expressed in purely formal terms. Nothing has been said about the content of religion, for the category of eternity is a purely formal category, equally as formal as the other a priori which are the foundation of the sciences, morals, and art. But the category of eternity is more *universal*, for it underlies all the others. Whatever is to have religious validity and truth must be *sub specie aeternitatis*, and whatever claims to have validity at all must be ultimately anchored in this religious a priori.

It was thus Nygren's aim to prove, solely on philosophical

grounds, that religion constitutes a valid attitude to life, but from this follows nothing about the truth of *Christianity* specifically, for this is a theological and not a philosophical problem. In agreement with Schleiermacher, Nygren claims that the philosophy of religion is able to show us that the fundamental value of religion can only be *realized* in a concrete religious form. Whether the different concrete, historical forms of religion are true or not cannot be determined by religious philosophy, but can only be settled by theology, and each theology only recognizes one single historical form of religion, that is to say, its own. The Christian theology must therefore ask about the truth of Christianity, and the answer can only be given on the basis of the Christian experience of values. The claim to truth merely means that a theology accounts for the foundation on which a Christian builds his certainty, that is to say, that when he experiences faith he stands face to face with a transcendent and actual reality—and not a transcendental or formally a priori reality. The roles are thus divided between the philosophy of religion and theology in such a way that while religious philosophy determines the question of the objective validity of religious value as such, theology answers the question of the objective reality of a given religion or of the truth of that religion's demand that its dogmatic objects must have a transcendent reality. In both cases Nygren's answer is in the affirmative.

We are here concerned with systematic theology and not historical theology, and Nygren considers systematic theology an objective, neutral discipline. There is no question of proving anything, it is merely the question of *understanding*, and it is therefore the object of systematic theology to understand the Christian concepts of faith and Christian moral life from their very core and as a whole. This core is the condition and is neither to be sought for or to be proved or, in other words, it is the actual form of religion which is a positively given fact. As systematic theology deals both with concepts of faith and with moral life it is only natural that it should be divided into two disciplines, i.e., dogmatics and Christian ethics, and Nygren has written a prolegomena to both these disciplines in *Dogmatikens vetenskapliga grundläggning* in 1922, and *Filosofisk och kristen etik* in 1923. As a science, dogmatics must be classifiable in the scientific order; but this is not possible if it is to be a speculative and metaphysical discipline. It must take its starting point in the given positive religion, as in the case of Christianity, but it can only do so, if a truth-value is attributed to Christianity, and this is the result of a personal act of will.

In this way it becomes the task of dogmatics by theoretical-cognitive means to describe what is contained in the Christian faith, but it can never be the task of dogmatics to give an apologetic proof of the truth of Christianity. This rests upon a value judgment. It cannot be denied here that Nygren's theology is an extension of the Ritschlean evaluation-theology, but whereas Ritschl used evaluation to remove alien elements from historical and sociological Christianity, Nygren's evaluation concerns Christianity as a whole. Nygren's aim was to remove alien elements through motive research, which he considered objective. According to Nygren, Christianity is the only realization of the religious value which is acceptable to us; but thereby the objective basis for dogmatics should also be given. Christianity is the one religion in which the consciousness of God is awakened and strengthened through the influence of the person of Jesus, and it is a religion of redemption, redemption coming from Jesus. The need for redemption, and redemption itself, belong together, and in the Christian terminology handed down to us they are known as sin and grace.

The same is true of *Ethics*. Philosophical ethics, whose relationship to concrete Christian ethics corresponds, roughly speaking, to the relation between religious philosophy and dogmatics, proves the validity of ethics as such, whereas Christian ethics is characterized by a positive historical fact. Philosophical ethics provides the a priori and formal element of validity in the ethical philosophy of life, while Christian ethics provides an empirical and real element of fact. Just as religious philosophy can say nothing about the content of a concrete religion, neither can philosophical ethics say anything about the content of concrete ethics, in this case Christian ethics, and, in Nygren's opinion, it was Kant's great fallacy that he wished to derive moral content from the universal form of the law of morals. By reason of its religious validity the ethical content belongs under the category of eternity, but its ethical content places it under the category of society; the latter, however, must also be realized in a given content. According to Nygren, in Christian ethics this content is determined by love or the *agape motive*, and it is precisely this motive which Nygren has called the fundamental motive of Christianity.

For Nygren, to study a religion is identical with finding and investigating the fundamental motive of that religion. In relation to the entire complexity of beliefs and deeds the fundamental motive is the "lapis Lydius" of the religion in question, the touchstone of all the different elements to discover whether they are true or false, integral parts or alien elements to be removed by a reformation of the religion in question. This is a case of motive research which admittedly takes its starting point in philosophy; but the answer can only be found in historical facts, and the usual historical method is essential and unavoidable if this fundamental motive is to be discovered. The importance of this research to systematic theology lies herein, that it indicates an objective means of determining the special nature of the Christian faith, which again means that it differentiates between what is peripheral and what is essential or central. Nygren considers agape to be the fundamental motive of Christianity, while in Platonism the fundamental motive is eros and in Judaism it is nomos. Full certainty of the special nature of Christianity is never reached, for then faith itself, which is a question of faith, would coincide with the knowledge about the faith. Full certainty is something inherent in faith itself. It is not to be sought in any form of science or scholarship.

This motive research is not entirely historical, but is more accurately a special systematical and theological method, characterized by being applicable to a given historical material. In itself it is part of systematic theology, and is, in effect, the most important aspect of systematic theology. If it succeeds in explaining the fundamental motive of Christianity then it will *eo ipse* have solved the problem of systematic theology, for this problem is in reality solved when the special nature of the Christian faith is demonstrated. But this solution is precisely the main object of systematic theology.

If the theoretical-cognitive, the ethical, the aesthetic, and religious experience are all a priori forms of experience, it follows that they are also independent, *autonomous* ways of life. This autonomy implies that none of the a priori forms of experience can be evaluated on the basis of the others, and this applies likewise to religion, which cannot sit in judgment on science, ethics, and art. Truth, goodness, and beauty must be accepted for themselves and not by reason of their importance to religion. The question is then whether cultural life in its entirety can be maintained except on a religious basis. Critical philosophy confines itself to purely formal laws, while the teaching of the philosophy of life, which is not purely formal, is not based on experience to such an extent that it is able to point out anything that necessitates its points of view being elevated to meanings. Religious perception rests on experience, however, and is able to unite theoretical and practical experience, whereby we obtain a complete and conclusive survey, which is just what a philosophy of life demands.

The fact that religion provides the foundation of ethics does not mean, as many have thought, a violation of the ethical autonomy, because this autonomy only applies to the form and not the content of moral conduct, for the content must always be fetched from the concrete empirical world. Religious ethics has an advantage over non-religious ethics, namely that the philosophy of life on which it is based rests upon a broader and firmer foundation. The possibility of a nonreligious culture is excluded by the concept of the transcendental necessity of religion. The fact that the religious a priori is, so to speak, the foundation of the other spiritual a priori means that it is the ultimate basis of any validity in the sphere of culture, and a nonreligious culture must therefore be rejected because its different forms cannot be accepted as valid.

As any form of experience which is part of the cultural system must ultimately obtain its validity from its relationship with the fundamental value of universal religion, every single empirical element of culture is in itself a refutation of the assertion that cultural life is indifferent towards religion, and for this reason religion is no more a "private matter" than culture is. This knowledge gains theological content, however, if it is borne in mind that the fundamental value of religion is always realized in the shape of a concrete historical religion. The result of this relation between religion and culture therefore becomes a "duty to believe," though this should not be taken in the legal sense as something which precedes the introduction of religious freedom. It should be understood from a transcendental point of view, and in the sense that a person who lives a spiritual and cultural life may rightly form an objective point of view, be expected to have a positive attitude to religion.

Nygren understands this duty to be analogous to the intellectual duty of every man to accept what he considers to be the truth. If religion is of such essential importance in the life of man that transcendentally it forms the basis of all experience, then it is every man's absolute duty to reflect upon this the profoundest truth of his life. From this starting point it becomes the task of theology, as far as is possible, to continue along this line and to prove that reflection on the deepest reason and meaning of life, which is imposed upon us by our religious duty, necessarily leads to Christianity.

The logical conclusion of the thought of the transcendentality of religion ought, strictly speaking, to be the recognition of religious idealism or of a universal revelation which should have manifested itself in the different historical forms of religion and in intellectual studies. As the years passed, Nygren apparently became increasingly loath to draw this thought to its logical conclusion, and the reason is presumably to be found in the failure to appreciate human nature and human ideals which followed in the wake of the victory of the agape theology over the eros cult. In a lecture given in 1937, "Kristendom og Idealisme," published in the book *Filosofi och motivforskning* in 1940, Nygren totally rejects the alleged value of idealism for Christianity, repudiating, in principle, the thought of a reconciliation of the two factors. He chooses to consider a "synthesis of culture" as a legitimate conclusion, but he will under no circumstances accept a "synthesis of religion."

The problem of culture has always given rise to difficulties in Protestant theology. It is as if the problem solves itself in Catholic theology. For Luther this problem did not exist at all, and in fact it did not arise until the Age of Enlightenment in the eighteenth century. The Age of Enlightenment demanded that cultural life should be set free from the tutelage of the Church. The secularization of knowledge that took place during this epoch was an act of emancipation, but it was not intended to be a profanation. There were later developments which made cultural life profane. To the enlightened age before 1750, when practically everyone believed in revelation and natural religion, culture in itself was "religious." The pietists and the puritans, however, did not accept this. To them culture was "worldly" or secular.

In New Testament Christianity there is no particular cultural ideal, and consequently there is no special cultural problem. Through the whole of its history Christianity has formed one cultural synthesis after the other with the intellectual life of different epochs, and no "motive research" has therefore been able to demonstrate how this synthesis was made up of "religion" and "culture." To the Romantic Age and the liberal theology of the nineteenth century it was obvious that Christianity could not be unrelated to culture, and the most exuberant representative of Protestant theology before and after the turn of the century, Ernst Troeltsch, spoke of "Cultural Protestantism," and of a "Church Type" which was open to culture, in contrast to the "Sect Type" which was introverted and held itself isolated from culture, which to him was an expression of "worldliness."

Anders Nygren is himself a distinguished representative of culture, which is clear merely from the fact that he is both a theologian and a philosopher, and by no means in the narrowest sense of these words.

His philosophy is representative of a Kantianism which is more Kantian than Kant himself in that he seeks to apply the transcendental
point of view to religion, while Kant's own religious philosophy was
"pre-Kantian," for it did not ask what had to exist that religion might
exist. Like the so-called dialectic theology, however, Nygren's theology represents an antihumanistic and anti-idealistic attitude, which
again means that he represents an anthropology which denies human
value as such. Agape, which is God's universal love for man, is described as being indifferent to values. While eros seeks values, agape
aims at creating values when it meets an object.

This object is man, who, being valueless, can create nothing himself. There is nothing in man that counts for anything in the face of
God, and therefore man cannot create valid cultural values either. The
validity and truth of these cultural values must be ensured through the
religious a priori, which is valid from a purely philosophical point of
view, and their causality must spring from the divine agape, which
should be valid if the thought is followed to its logical conclusion.
Thus, on the one hand, Nygren asserts that the value of natural man is
equal to nothing, and on the other hand he asserts the validity of the
cultural forms. This forms the starting point of an attempt to answer
the problem of Anders Nygren's view of the relationship between
theology and culture. On the face of it a positive and affirmative
answer seems difficult to give. But it is no solution to give up straighta-
way and say that Nygren's theology has no relation to culture at all.
Even though he is a distinguished representative of culture, his theology need not necessarily have any relationship to culture. Luther's
theology was devoid of such a relationship, although he was one of the
foremost representatives of culture in his century, and the same applies
in an even higher degree to Calvin and his theology.

We shall now attempt to investigate the problem of the place of
culture in Nygren's thought, which may be divided into his views on
the philosophy of religion and his theological views, beginning with his
philosophical theories. We are indebted to Nygren for having stressed
the purely transcendental nature of the religious a priori. On this point
he differs from Rudolf Otto who, from the time he published his book
Das Heilige in 1917, described the religious a priori as emotional and
consequently also as empirical, which in Kant's terminology must be a
contradictio in adjecto, because transcendental in Kant is synonomous
with a priori. Furthermore, Nygren opposes Ernst Troeltsch's theory
of the religious a priori, which is described as a both-and, both as
something transcendental and as something real. Because Nygren

thought that the religious a priori must underlie the empirical, the ethical, and the aesthetic a priori, the forms in which these three a priori are realized, viz. science, morals, and art respectively, must indirectly be ranged under the category of the religious a priori, but this again means that in their inmost core they must be religious. Nygren expresses precisely this by saying that he who desires culture has also a duty to believe, and consequently he must have religion too. The forms of culture are thus religious—but this must not be taken to mean that they must necessarily be Christian forms of culture, for this is not so. They are religious in the universal sense, not the confessional sense. It is neither Christianity nor Buddhism, for example, that endows them with validity.

We shall now deal with Christianity as a positive form of religion and with the theology which is to deal with Christianity. It is quite obvious that a positive form of religion in a cultural society must be full of cultural elements. However fallacious the whole doctrine of the Roman Catholic Church may be, it does not affect the fact that Roman Catholic thought, the Roman Catholic churches, and Roman Catholic art are expressions of a high culture, and the same naturally applies to the Protestant Churches. Where we find these Churches and their theology we find, *eo ipse*, culture as well. But this does not necessarily mean to say that there is an organic relationship between theology, on the one hand, and the forms of culture, on the other hand, and even less need there be any organic relation between these theologies and the universal forms of culture outside of the churches. We shall now see how Nygren understands this problem. The answer is by no means easy to find.

Nygren differentiates very clearly between a priori as a value category of a formal nature and the realization of this a priori in the empirical world. The empirical a priori is realized in science, the ethical a priori in moral codes, e.g., in Christian ethics, and the aesthetic a priori in art. Correspondingly, the religious a priori is realized in certain positive forms of religion such as Christianity and Islam, and thus religion as a historical and sociological factor becomes the fourth form of realization next to and on line with science, art, and ethics,—all four being autonomous. This seems, however, to produce a certain maladjustment in the system,[2] for hereby religion becomes parallel with science, morals, and art, while the religious a priori itself is the foundation on which the a priori of these three forms of culture are based.

Thus, while these three forms of culture are ranged under the religious a priori, the realization of the religious a priori, i.e., a positive religion, does not range above science, ethics, and art, and can therefore not dictate their content to them; but on the other hand, neither can these autonomous forms of culture prescribe the content of religion. In other words, the religious a priori ultimately gives these forms of culture their validity and truth, but it is not realized in any of them, but only in a positive religion. However, a possible explanation might be that the religious a priori, religion being indeed autonomous, might be able to give validity to sociological forms which science, ethics, and art must declare invalid even though they are found in a given positive religion, and consequently stamp them as being illegitimate. This seems to be inconsistent, and it is this very inconsistency that I have tried to avoid in my own religious philosophy by insisting that all phenomena in a positive religion must justify their existence by their correspondence with the cultural standards.

Nygren seems to be aware that there really is a problem here. In his article in German, *Die Gültigkeit der religiösen Erfahrung* he states that two different things are involved: whether a proposition in regard to its content itself is religious or whether it rests upon a religious foundation. If this is applied to the universal forms of culture it is obvious that according to Nygren's a priori theory they must have a religious basis, viz. a transcendental basis, while in accordance with their content, which is empirical, they need not be religious. They may also be worldly. The transcendental a priori of religion is not realized in them, and therefore something else must be, for in truth they cannot be empty.

If the forms of culture must perforce be religious in accordance with the basis of their validity, though not according to their content, a difficulty arises in regard to the *extent* of the religious revelation, and this difficulty—which Schleiermacher also deals with in his *Reden*—appears once again when we consider the truth of the different historical forms of religion which should all be justified through the religious a priori which was realized in them, but which according to Nygren nonetheless cannot all be called ture in the same sense and in the same degree.

We will take the forms of culture first. Having been endowed with their ultimate religious validity and truth through the religious a priori, the question, then, is why they have not also received it through a revelation. Why is the revelation limited to the positive forms of religion, indeed perhaps not to all of them? Why does the revelation not also apply to the universally valid forms of culture when these are basically religious? Nygren would probably reply that we are here faced with an empirical and historical fact which we must simply accept, and that Schleiermacher was right when he denied the historical existence of a universal natural religion. We then turn to the problem of the relation between the various historical forms of religion which all claim to be realization of the religious a priori. Nygren seems here to think both that a concrete form of religion must be chosen by means of a value judgment, which in its turn is the result of an act of will, and also that reflection on the profoundest reason and meaning of life imposed upon us by our religious duty necessarily must lead us ultimately to Christianity.

What influence has this on our understanding of revelation in other religions? Does revelation in the true sense of the word only exist in Christianity? Nygren's answer would presumably be "yes," but the result must then be that the other religions may lose their validity in regard to their "religious" content and only retain their validity in regard to the universal forms of culture which are related to them. It seems to be almost self-contradictory to say that the religious a priori has realized itself in these forms of religion but that despite this fact they contain no revelation, that in reality, as religions alone and apart from their inherent forms of culture, they are false. The ambiguity is undeniable and it seems to stand uncontradicted.

The result of the present study might be expressed as follows: All forms of culture are religious by virtue of the religious a priori on which they are indirectly based, because it is a condition of the special empirical, ethical, and aesthetic a priori of the forms of culture that the forms of culture must be religious if they are *valid* forms of culture at all, and if they are not valid, then they are not expressions of culture, but of "unculture." This is what Nygren believes as a philosopher. As a theologian he must restrict himself to speaking of the concrete historical forms of realization of the religious a priori, and these positive forms of religion may be imbued with culture. This may be true whether these elements of culture are integral parts of the religion in question or not. However, their validity lies directly in the historical religion, owing to the religious a priori and / or on the basis of a divine revelation; but how the relation between this a priori and revelation is to be imagined is not revealed—possibly because one cannot speak of revelation in philosophy and because theology, by virtue of its claim to be an empirical cognitive discipline, cannot recognize revelation but must leave its acceptance to faith.

In Nygren's theology, culture is a fact, while in his philosophy and his religious philosophy, culture is accepted as a valid realization of the transcendental a priori. In theology, we may say with equal right that all is culture or that nothing is culture. The fact that Nygren's theology as such is itself a brilliant cultural product is beyond doubt. It stands *in confesso*.

17

CHRIST'S CHURCH AND

THE CHURCHES IN

NYGREN'S THEOLOGY

Vilmos Vajta

GUSTAF Aulén tells a little anecdote in his book about the discussion of the church in Sweden during the last century.[1] The story aptly characterizes the theological situation at the turn of the century. A well-known liberal German theologian, during a visit in Uppsala in 1910, asked Aulén with what he was working. Aulén was then in the process of publishing a book on "the Lutheran concept of the church."[2] Upon receiving this information the famous visitor made the following remark: "I congratulate the Swedish theologians that they can find time also to busy themselves with such questions." Aulén comments, "He, like the old liberal theology itself, regarded them (i.e., questions about the church) as belonging to the utmost periphery of theology."[3] Naturally the situation was soon to change both in Germany and in theology more generally.

In Sweden theological discussion of the church belonged to the order of the day. When the conversation recounted above occurred in Uppsala, the discussion on the concept of the folk church was in full course. The so-called free-churchly churchmen had carried out an attack against "the state church," and "the religiously motivated folk church" became accordingly the watchword of the official church theology.[4] The idea of an "association-church" was thereby rejected. It

TRANSLATED BY BERNHARD ERLING

must be noted, however, that this contrast cannot be identified with the contrast between the "state church" and the "free church." Those who represented the concept of the folk church maintained that the Church of Sweden should in principle remain a "folk church," even if the bond between the state and the church were to be severed.

Nygren received his basic theological education in this theological and ecclesiastical atmosphere.[5] Interestingly enough this discussion did not exercise any influence on his theological orientation. "The church discussion" at the turn of the century did not catch his interest. The discussion referred to above took place, of course, mainly in Uppsala, while Nygren studied in Lund. But he also came from a strong churchly tradition on the Swedish west coast,[6] and in addition to this Lund had a theological tradition closely related to the discussion of the concept of the church in the German confessional theology during the previous century.[7] In the period just before the First World War there were several representatives of this theological orientation in Lund. Despite all this Nygren remained remarkably untouched by the theological questions that were thereby raised. His interest was given wholly to the philosophy of religion, which determined both his choice of a topic for his doctoral dissertation and to which he also devoted the first years of his teaching at the University of Lund.[8]

As one goes through Nygren's writings, one can make this interesting observation: The concept of the church is lacking in Nygren's theology up until 1942, when in the well-known collection of essays, *En bok om kyrkan*, he published his first contribution to the discussion about the church with the title "Corpus Christi." [9] This naturally does not mean that Nygren was inactive in the life of the church for more than two decades. At an early stage he engaged himself in the ecumenical movement, as well as in the work of his own church.[10] But his theology remains in the main untouched by the question of the church for a long time.

If one is to examine Nygren's concept of the church, one cannot, however, neglect this first period, for theologically interesting questions can be raised precisely from the viewpoint of the concept of the church already during this first period of Nygren's theological activity. If one can thus divide an examination of Nygren's writings into two periods (before and after 1942), it will also be advisable in the second period to separate somewhat the question of the christological foundation of the church from the ecumenical application of this concept of the church.

IT IS understandable that Nygren's first writings, which deal with the basic religio-philosophical question of the validity of religion in general, would not discuss the problem of the church. Even if many of the early writings continue to be dominated by this question, however, they nonetheless in addition to this discuss questions relating to the content of Christian theology. It is the content of the Christian faith which dominates his great work on the Christian concept of love.[11] It is in these works that one also has a right to expect an answer to the question of what the church is. Yet one finds here an ecclesiological vacuum. Some specific references will support this assertion.

Fellowship with God without the Church?

In the little monograph, *Det bestáende i kristendomen* (1922), Nygren analyzes the basic religious question, aspects of which thereafter become the categories for Christianity. Naturally one might put the question, not least in view of the well-developed concept of the church in Nygren's later writings, as to how it is possible in this analysis wholly to leave out reference to the church as that reality where "vital fellowship with God" is realized.[12] As we shall see farther on, according to Nygren a reference to Jesus Christ is unthinkable apart from the messianic people of God. But this presupposition is one of Nygren's later ideas, and it can hardly be implied in the exposition in which Jesus Christ is introduced as the answer to and the fulfillment of the basic religious question.[13] Only on the general level, where "the life of the spirit" and its various domains of experience are described, does one find a reference to the fact that "these questions of the spiritual life have shown themselves capable of creating enduring social forms." The questions of the spiritual life "embody themselves in very tangible, objective, outward forms of organization." Among such "forms of organization of the spiritual life" religion also as an answer to the question of the eternal is able to create "religious societies and cult-communities." [14] The word "church" does not appear in this connection. The main viewpoint is the existence of community as a purely sociological (and even religio-philosophical) necessity. As a community, "Christianity" is one among other "forms of organization." From this line of thought it follows that the church thus far lacks a theological justification. It belongs to human experience, but it has no theological basis.

If we take another little monograph, written ten years later, which deals with the atonement, we can discover that the ecclesiological vacuum still exists.[15] The monograph deals, to be sure, only with certain aspects of the Christian doctrine of atonement, namely, the atonement viewed as God's own deed and consisting in the fact that God establishes fellowship "on the basis of sin" instead of "on the basis of holiness." The atonement is here interpreted as an implication of the idea of agape, which does not make the atonement superfluous, but instead necessary, and thereby qualifies the atonement as God's descending love to sinful men. What Nygren says here is related not only to his great work on the Christian idea of love, but also to a main emphasis in contemporary Swedish theology.[16] One who is acquainted with Nygren's later writings will be surprised that the idea of the church is not even mentioned. The connection between the atonement and the church is not even suggested, despite the fact that this is one of the most essential ideas in the ecclesiology which Nygren later develops. The matter is even more remarkable, since the monograph on the atonement, despite its limited scope, is written as reflections on 2 Cor. 5:18 f.[17] As is well known, "the ministry of reconciliation" and "the message of reconciliation" play a central role in this text. But Nygren is not yet concerned with the question of the church, but only with the description of the distinctive character of fellowship with God through the atoning activity of God's self-giving love. Not until later does Nygren deal also with the question of "the spiritual ministry." [18] Here we find the statements we missed in the previous writings, also related to the above-mentioned text. "The reconciliation in Christ and the ministry of reconciliation in the congregation both belong inseparably together." [19] This still, however, is not related to the concept of the church. It is the question of fellowship with God that continues to be determinative.[20] Nygren's suggestion is, nonetheless, sufficient to indicate that he already has developed certain ideas with respect to the concept of the church, although they remain thus far implicit and unexpressed. "The gospel requires a ministry, which brings forth the divine message to each and every one. . . . How shall we have any notion at all of the righteousness from God if the message about it does not come to us from outside ourselves?" [21] In contrast to a sociologically based concept of the church (see above), a more evidently theological justification of the church is already emerging. "The spiritual ministry does not only have a practical and a social significance, but it also has a significance which is constitutive, based in the gospel itself." [22] The concept of the church is thereby implicitly given, and when it later appears, the concepts described above can be used without this representing any radical transition in Nygren's systematic writings.

Before we move on to Nygren's development of the concept of the church, however, let us look briefly at his work which dominated the decade of the 1930's, and which at the same time characterizes one epoch in his theological activity. We are thinking of *Den kristna kärlekstanken genom tiderna*, which even in a methodological sense represents the high point in the so-called Lundensian theology. [23]

In this great biblical and historico-theological investigation, Nygren continues to be engaged in finding the Christian answer to the basic religious categorical question, namely, the question of fellowship with God. In the Christian context agape provides the answer to this question, just as eros is the answer in the Greek-Platonic doctrine of salvation. But as in the idea of atonement, as indicated above, so also in the Christian idea of love, the church is still absent from the picture. This applies both to the biblical and the historico-theological presentation. The church is not mentioned. The concept of agape describes God's love descending in Christ to achieve the salvation of mankind. It describes the great divine activity in Christ's death and resurrection. Love to God and even neighbor love are characterized by this divine agape. But Nygren's concept of agape does not go further than this. The question of how this agape comes to mankind through the ministry of the church, through the word, baptism, and holy communion is not discussed.

Critical Questions

Now one can naturally ask oneself whether this is at all necessary. Is not God's agape in Christ described in and through telling of the reconciling activity occurring in Christ's death and resurrection and through the deeds of love which in response to it extend from individual to individual? In other words, must the biblical concept of agape and its historico-dogmatic interpretation be bound to the church and its activity? This question must be answered with an unconditional affirmative. This positive answer cannot be defended in detail at this point. Reference to two biblical citations must suffice. In Eph. 5:25 there is meditation on the love of the husband to the wife with this

reference: "as Christ loved the church and gave himself up for her."
Of this same love Paul also says that it has constrained him to enter
upon his apostolic ministry: "For the love of Christ controls us,
because we are convinced that one has died for all; therefore all have
died" (2 Cor. 5:14). *The concept of agape and the concept of the
church are thus even literally bound together in the New Testament.* If
in addition to this we were to consider all of the passages which tell of
Christ giving his life (though without mentioning that this is the
meaning of agape), we should here get a perspective on the concept of
agape—one might call it "the church perspective"—which in any case
is not mentioned by Nygren during the thirties. Not only is exegesis of
the biblical citations referred to absent,[24] but even the church, the
ministry of the word, baptism and holy communion [25] are left out of
the presentation.

Nygren's writings before 1942 thus lack the concept of the church
even at those points where he, in his later writings, with inescapable
necessity came to introduce it. In the period we have thus far investigated his writings are dominated by the concept of "fellowship with
God." One may therefore ask how this concept is related to the
concept of the church. A significant observation indicates that the
question is justified: To the extent that the concept of "the church" is
absent until 1942, Nygren's writings during this period are dominated
by the concept of "fellowship with God." To the extent that the
concept of "the church" dominates his writings after 1942, the concept
of "fellowship with God" is absent during the same period. Are these
concepts perhaps synonomous? Can the one concept suddenly replace
the other?

We would be led too far afield were we to analyze Nygren's
concept of "fellowship with God." [26] Instead we can here only select
one test question from the wealth of the material available. In *Agape
and Eros* Nygren presents the agape motif through relating it with
fellowship with God.[27] He shows "that we find here . . . an intimate
connection between Christian life and the Christian relationship to
God, Agape and fellowship with God" (p. 66). Jesus' achievement is
characterized in this manner: "What Jesus seeks to bring about is not a
new conception of God, or new ideas about God, but a new fellowship
with God" (p. 68). In what follows this relationship is characterized as
a "love fellowship" in contrast to a "law fellowship." Thus it becomes
also consistent to summarize by pointing out that agape establishes
fellowship with God (p. 61).

The test question is now as follows: Could one in the context referred to above exchange "fellowship with God" with "church"? Could Nygren in 1930 when these words were written have said that agape establishes the church? In terms of biblical theology such an expression would be fully justified. Nygren has himself after 1942 developed such ideas, as I shall shortly point out. But before 1942? Perhaps the question cannot be answered unequivocably. There is much to indicate, however, that the concepts cannot be synonomous. "Fellowship with God" reveals strong individualistic tendencies. In the relationship between God and man, man hardly represents a type but is rather an individual. The universal religious question which Nygren analyzes has to do with fellowship between God and the separate individual.

That his analysis reveals individualistic features is by no means surprising. The theological situation in Sweden during the 1930's, despite the continuing discussion of the church, was characterized by individualism.[28] Nygren has not separated himself from this individualism, even if he can hardly be regarded as its representative. His concept of "fellowship with God" thus stands open to individualistic interpretation during the thirties, at the same time that it can contribute much to an understanding of the concept of the church.

What can be said with respect to the ecclesiological development that follows is that Nygren's theology in its first period was in principle open to receive the concept of the church, and it was possible within this context to draw heavily on the material already at hand, which thus far came under the concept of fellowship with God. But the transition from the one to the other is clearly not merely the interchange of synonomous concepts. It is evident that a new theological influence must here make itself felt. It will be our task to discover from whence it comes.

THE CONCEPT of the church first appears in Nygren's theology in the essay "Corpus Christi" (1942).[29] This essay consists of a lecture which Nygren presented at a conference of Swedish theologians. Exegetes, historians, and systematicians met at the conference in order to discuss the concept of the church from various theological viewpoints. Especially significant at this occasion was the meeting between the exegetes and the systematicians. They entered into a mutually enriching collaboration, which however did not last very long. Swedish exegetical theology and systematic theology soon went their separate ways.[30]

At what point, then, does Nygren begin as he presents his concept of the church? He begins by examining the question characteristic of the liberal theology: "Did Christ establish the church, or not?" [31] He puts aside this question, since it leads only to viewing the church as an organizational structure. One must instead begin with the concept of the body of Christ. "The truth can be most simply expressed by saying that in the fact that Christ exists, the church exists as his body." [32] In this way a theological rather than a sociological point of orientation is introduced. With this statement one finds oneself already in the area of christology, "inasmuch as Christ is what he is only in relation to the church." [33] Nygren also delimits his view as over against an individualistic understanding of Christ: "What it [christology] has to say about Christ is not to be said about him merely as an individual, but as the One who unites and embraces all Christians on earth." [34] In delimiting his view of the church as over against both a sociological and an individualistic understanding of the church, Nygren thus shows that the foundation of the church is to be christologically understood. Thus, his basic principle is: "He who would know what the church is . . . must begin with the relation between Christ and Christ's body." [35] This christological orientation with respect to the concept of the church has been steadfastly retained by Nygren ever since these first utterances: the connection between christology and ecclesiology is the basis for Nygren's understanding of the church.

> A Christology that does not include an ecclesiology is false. In such a case Christology passes over into a "Christ-idea," or a theory of divinization or the like. At the same time an ecclesiology whose content is not fixed by Christology goes astray, in so far as the Church is then made into something external, into a merely sociological form. If Christ is to be considered rightly, then his Church also must be included in this consideration.[36]

These words from Nygren's most recent discussion of ecclesiology are characteristic and can provide the point of orientation in terms of which the concept of the church of the second period of Nygren's writings can be summarized.

Adam — Christ

For an understanding of Nygren's new approach to the concept of the church the parallelism between Adam and Christ (Rom. 5 and 1 Cor. 15) is of basic significance. This Pauline train of thought is later identified with the idea of Christ as the head of the church (Eph. and Col.).[37] This identification is a thesis with which Nygren works, without, however, giving it any further exegetical explanation. It is also important to note that the train of thought about Christ as the head of the church is interpreted wholly in terms of the Adam-Christ parallelism in the Letter to the Romans.

Here we have the first answer as to what the new impulse is that leads Nygren to the concept of the church. It is his work in interpreting the Letter to the Romans. His *Commentary on Romans* was completed in 1944, and one can find there more fully set forth the viewpoints suggested in "Corpus Christi." [38]

For Nygren, the Adam-Christ parallelism and with it the concept of the two aeons is "the high point of the epistle, in the light of which the whole is best to be understood." [39] Adam stands for the old age, where sin and death reign, while Christ stands for the new age, where righteousness and life reign. Two different existential contexts are therefore involved, which have objective reality for mankind. Characteristic for the commentary on Romans is the fact that the identification of this train of thought with the other about Christ as the head of the church is silently presupposed and terminologically as well as theologically consistently carried out. "Adam is the head of the old aeon . . . Christ is the head of the new aeon." [40] Nygren is, to be sure, careful to examine the difference between Christ and Adam. The latter "is mentioned only as antitype for Christ." [41] This does not, however, prevent Nygren from also transferring the *corpus-Christi* concept to Adam. "Adam is not merely a single individual who lived long ago. Adam is significant as the head of the 'old' humanity, as the head of the present aeon (*ho aion houtos*). That which happened to the head involves the body also." [42] This train of thought concludes with a thesis, which is expressed in the essay "Corpus Christi" but only suggested in the commentary on Romans. This is the identification of Christ as the head of the church and as "the first fruits" (*aparche*, 1 Cor. 15:20).[43] In the commentary on Romans this appears as if in the margin, when the message of the two aeons is summed up "in Adam" and "in Christ" (see 1 Cor. 15:22).

The train of thought here set forth is not isolated in Nygren's writings. It appears at all the points that he describes the church and its activity. We see here how in a manner characteristic for Nygren christological expressions, as it were, immediately receive ecclesiological relevance. The development of the basic thesis therefore occurs throughout in relation to the Adam-Christ conception. Yet this influence is only the one branch. We can also observe another stimulus which enriches Nygren's train of thought.[44]

The Atonement and the Church

The contact with exegetical theology gave Nygren the stimulus to relate Christ's atoning activity with the concept of the church. The suggestion came especially from Anton Fridrichsen, professor of New Testament exegesis at Uppsala. In an essay published in 1945 he develops the following thesis: "Atonement, christology, and the concept of the church form in the New Testament an organic unity and cannot be separated or isolated from one another." [45] He closes his presentation with a critique of the concept of the atonement as it had been developed by Einar Billing and Gustaf Aulén.[46] He maintains that the systematic line

> must issue in the church and the means of grace. The line must be drawn to that point as soon as one sees clearly the meaning and the implications of the New Testament concept of the church. It becomes impossible to stop with a *regnum gratiae* as the fruit of the atonement without placing the Risen One's dominion in connection with the church of the new covenant, the new people of God with its common life in the sacramental fellowship with Christ.[47]

Nygren has, as it were, tacitly accepted this exegetical advice, which well-suited his basic theological outlook regarding the close relation between christology and ecclesiology. The biblical passages about the solidarity between the Messiah and the messianic people of God, about the Messiah and "the remnant," about the Suffering Servant of the Lord as the only righteous one for "the many," about Christ's atonement and "ransom for many" through his broken body and shed blood, are a brief summary of the ideas through which this main thesis is developed. These insights are known from the exegetical theology of the period also outside of Sweden,[48] and fecundate during the following years Nygren's understanding of the church. In this way he can illustrate the thesis that Christ is not to be found apart from his church, just as the church is nothing apart from Christ. He can summarize in this pointed way: "Each assertion bears not only on Christ, but also on his people and his Church. In order to emphasize this we can say that Christ and his Church are inseparable entities. . . .

The Savior has certainly not come into the world to appropriate and use this lofty name for his own benefit; he came for the sake of those he wished to save. It is this relationship that characterizes both his work and his name." [49] The purpose of Christ's giving of himself is thus the church, through which man may participate in Christ's saving deed.

We can recognize in the emphasis on these ideas the basic Reformation teachings about Christ and the *pro nobis* character of his saving deed. Nygren can, therefore, even on the basis of his Reformation orientation, well introduce these ideas in his theology. For in this way it is emphasized that the church is by no means a human activity (not an organizational problem), but God's own activity in Christ. [50] The continuity with the agape concept is thus preserved, while the eros piety of mysticism is rejected. Fellowship with God, to use a concept from an earlier period, becomes concrete in the church, where we become participants in Christ and his atonement for many. The ideas which we missed earlier now appear in full bloom in Nygren's writings due to the stimulus received from exegetical research. But one can hardly say that these ideas were already earlier implicitly present. Instead, the biblical word draws forth new viewpoints and explicates things which in any case did not have this significance in Nygren's earlier writings.

The Word and the Sacraments

With the ideas last presented we have already come to the question of participation in what Christ has done for us. "Christ is present in a real way through his Word and sacrament, and by means of these the Church participates in a real way in all that belongs to Christ; it is participant in a real sense in his death and resurrection." [51] The solidarity between Christ and his church is here clearly expressed. "That which happened in Christ was that Christ, the One, the 'Suffering Servant of the Lord,' gave himself for 'the many.' That which takes place in the Church is that 'the many' are incorporated into him and participate in his fullness." [52] Between Christ's incarnation, death and resurrection, and exaltation at the right hand of the Father, on the one hand, and his *parousia*, on the other, the church has its period, when it as the body of Christ enables men to participate in all that the Head has and wills to share. "Through the work of Christ, a new body has emerged, into which 'the many' will be incorporated as members." [53]

Nygren on one occasion has answered an objection which might easily arise, not least due to his argument about the dawning of a new age in Christ, who creates a new humanity in which he himself is its head and Lord. One might reason in this manner: "If deliverance from the powers of destruction is won, nothing more is needed. Then the conditions of human existence are changed, and we as members of humanity also share in this transformation." [54] But Nygren rejects such a conclusion. He refers instead to the fact that this objective drama does not occur "apart from us." Through a message of the redemptive act in Christ God approaches each individual *personally*. Through this message, which itself is "an act of God," God "continues and fulfills his work in us. When the gospel is at work God frees men from the dominion of the powers of destruction and places them in the new humanity, whose head and Lord is Christ." [55] An objective and a subjective element are involved in that the benefits of the divine act in Christ are given through a message (the word), through incorporation in the body of Christ (baptism), and through the edification and the feeding of the body (holy communion). [56] "Something *did* happen when Christ became man and died and rose again: the life was manifested. Something *does* happen in the Church by virtue of Christ's living presence in Word and Sacrament: the life is given to us. Something also *will* happen. The life was manifested and given to us, but so far only as a beginning, or as an introductory gift." [57]

Nygren often uses also the figure of an occupied land to illustrate what deliverance through Christ from the powers of destruction means. [58] But to the decisive victory, the deliverance, the message about it also belongs here, so that those who live under oppression might be able in their own situations to draw the implications of the objective victory. It could appear as if the message according to Nygren is a mediation of knowledge of such a character, that at the same time that it announces the objective change it would also bring with it a subjective change. [59] Against this supposition, however, stands the fact that Nygren emphasizes the personal character of the message, which requires faith of the one who hears it. "If I believe, I have it, if I do not believe, I do not have it; then it does not exist for me." [60] With these words, partially borrowed from Luther, Nygren points, however, to a relationship which he does not discuss in greater detail. The interpretation of the word and the sacraments stands as an independent thought complex, without a clear theological connection with the christological foundation of the church.

Critical Questions

With this suggestion we have already prepared the way for some critical questions which may be raised with respect to Nygren's christological ecclesiology.

The first questions have to do with *biblical theology*. We have noted the identification of the Adam-Christ conception with the concept of Christ as the head of the church. The question however, is whether this is biblically justified. It is to be noted that the concept of the church as the body of Christ does not appear at any of the points where the Adam-Christ parallelism is discussed in the New Testament. In Rom. 5 the consequences which Adam's fall had for all mankind are described, and also the transformation of the conditions of human life through the righteousness of Christ. Is not the title which Christ receives in this passage to be "Lord" rather than "head"? In their biblical sense these two titles of Christ must be carefully distinguished. Christ has, through his work of justification, through the cross and the resurrection, become the *Lord of all*. But he is not head of humanity in its totality, but only in and through his church. As the head he stands as the giver of life, as the one who through faith grants salvation and participation in the gift of grace. Where the relation of faith does not exist, Christ to be sure is Lord, but not the head, from which the body receives its life. When no distinction is made between these two biblical contexts, *are not christology and ecclesiology improperly mixed together?* Christ is the Lord of the entire humanity and not only where he is so confessed. Therefore christology is broader than ecclesiology, even if the latter receives its entire existence from the former. It is not humanity which is the body of Christ, but the church (*ecclesia*), i.e., that humanity which has been called out through grace and faith.

In Rom. 5 is described not only the basis of the existence of the church, but that of all humanity, even that humanity which, following in Adam's footsteps, also stands under the dominion of death. This Christ, who through his resurrection from the dead has become "the first fruits," inaugurates the new history of humanity. He is, furthermore, "the first fruits" for all of humanity, for following him all are to rise—but to life or to death. To be "the first fruits" corresponds thus with the title of Lord, but not with "the head" of the church. When this one who is "first fruits" of those who have fallen "asleep" (1 Cor. 15:20) shall return in the *parousia*, this will be certainly in order to save his church, but also in order "to judge the living and the dead." Would it not therefore be necessary carefully to distinguish these two biblical trains of thought instead of identifying them. One could naturally be of the opinion that this is a distinctively exegetical question, which does not have systematic significance. But this is by no means the case. This situation can best be illustrated by pointing out *the systematic consequences,* which follow by reason of Nygren's exegetical freedom described above.

The most comprehensive and apparent consequence is that Nygren can describe the church on the basis of christology without bringing pneumatology into the picture. Is it at all possible "for practical reasons" to limit an interpretation of the church to its "christological foundation"? [61] What is decisive is not that one thereby departs from the universal dogmatic tradition of presenting the church of Christ. The problem is deeper in its significance. One could suggest it in relation to the critique by Fridrichsen of a certain concept of the atonement, cited above, which remains with the *regnum gratiae* without breaking through to the concept of the church. We may, after all, ask whether this critique does not also touch Nygren himself. If it does, this is certainly surprising, for, as we have indicated, Nygren has dealt with all the material which exegetical theology offered to illuminate the relationship between the atonement and the church. But the question is whether Nygren, through the dominant role which the Adam-Christ conception has received in his ecclesiology, and through the identification of this thought complex with the thought of Christ as the head of the church, has not transferred the ecclesiological prescriptions to the *regnum Christi.* The terminology and the train of thought for Nygren is ecclesiological. He describes, nonetheless, the *regnum Christi* without arriving at the *ecclesia Christi.* It is at this point that the absence of statements about pneumatology becomes decisive.

There is justification for all that Nygren says about the connection between christology and ecclesiology only on the basis of one presupposition: that this has to do with the gift of the Holy Spirit, the presence of the exalted Christ in the word now being preached and the sacraments now being administered in the church. The Holy Spirit, according to Christ's promise, is himself sent out in order to carry out this work until the *parousia.* For, until that day, the possibility of falling away remains for that humanity to which Christ has come as the only one, as "the first fruits" in order to proclaim God's rule, his kingdom. The Holy Spirit is thus God's new deed after the exaltation of Christ, a deed through which Christ's own reconciling activity now becomes active among men. Therefore the church is given in and through the receiving of the Holy Spirit according to the promise of Christ. He takes Christ and gives him to a humanity for which Christ has become man, suffered, and died. The new life of humanity is, to be sure, given in and through Christ—but it is distributed, applied, and realized through the activity of the Holy Spirit. The Spirit is Christ as he is present in his church to give her life and keep her holy and undefiled. *This work of the Holy Spirit is a new act of God in the sequence of saving acts which he carries out for his people.* It has however continuity with the historical Christ event. It is in this way that pneumatology and ecclesiology are connected with christology. But ecclesiology is not wholly equivalent to christology, which itself promises something more, namely the coming last day with the people of God going into eternal rest and the rejection of the godless. The Holy Spirit is an "earnest" in this age of the coming age, while he carries out his work in and through the church. Only he who has received the gift of the Holy Spirit, through which Christ as head of the church grants participation in his holiness and righteousness, truly belongs to the church.

We need not go further, for the question of *the necessary distinction between christology and pneumatology in so far as ecclesiology is concerned* has in this way been indicated. If this distinction had been carried through by Nygren, it would not have been necessary to speak of the "subjective" appropriation of an "objective" reality. The ministry of the word and the sacraments could instead have been placed in its proper context in the history of salvation, if the Holy Spirit had been given its—certainly relatively, but nonetheless—independent status. Then it would have been possible for both the difference between the *regnum Christi* and the *ecclesia Christi*, as well as their essential internal continuity to become evident. Then ecclesiology could have retained its christological foundation, but also its pneumatological realization. Only if such an ecclesiology was clearly developed would it be possible to get a new view of humanity, "in Adam" given over to the dominion of death, but now "in Christ" gathered through the work of the Holy Spirit, waiting for the Lord's return and thereby salvation's fulfillment.

The problem is not that Nygren has neglected to speak of the ministry of the word and the sacraments in the church. About this he has said many instructive things. But the problem is the relation between this ministry and the Adam-Christ conception. It is this relation which it is impossible to explain without introducing pneumatology. As long as this doesn't happen, the two thought complexes stand side by side without systematic connection. Our question to Nygren is *whether he will ever be able to clarify this basic ecclesiological question without including a description of the situation conditioned by the saving history to which the third article of the creed refers.*

WE HAVE already indicated that Nygren, at an early stage, began to participate in the ecumenical conversation among the churches. This occurred even before he began to discuss the concept of the church in his theology. Thus his theological confrontation with the problem of the unity of the church is not necessarily contemporary with the appearance of the concept of the church in his theology. "Christian fellowship" must have been of interest for Nygren beginning with the Lausanne Conference on Faith and Order (1927), where he for the first time participated as a delegate of the Church of Sweden. From that conference a direct line can be drawn to the conferences in Oxford and Edinburgh (1937), to his election as president of the Lutheran World Federation (1947), and, finally, to his latest position as chairman of the Faith and Order study commission on "Christ and the Church" (a result of the 1952 conference in Lund). Nygren is to be found in the first ranks of those who in our time are determining what is being done in the area of church unity.[62] In confrontation with the multiplicity of the churches and the many problems occasioned by the fragmentation of the body of Christ as it manifests itself in the world, Nygren must obviously take a position also with respect to the concrete theological problems which are raised by Christian efforts to achieve unity in our time.

If the church is regarded as the body of Christ, the unity of the church is also thereby given. For Christ can only have *one* body, of which he is the head.[63] To be sure there is a variety of gifts, but they are all to edify one and the same body. Each member has thus its own task within the given unity.[64] This prior given unity prevents the unity of the church from being regarded as the result of human efforts. If the unity of the church manifests itself here and there, this does not mean that men have succeeded in achieving unity, but that the unity given in Christ has found an expression. "We can never effect any unity in the Church if it has not been already given from the very beginning." [65]

In contrast to this unity of the church given in Christ stands, on the other hand, the actual division of the Christian churches. Alongside of the indicative about the given unity there must therefore also be the imperative, which states that no division may occur in the body of Christ. "The actualization of unity which exists in Christ and into which we as Christians have been introduced, must be allowed to set its imprint upon our lives. The Church of Christ is a unity in Christ; accordingly, in its life the Church must become one and remain one. *It must constantly become anew what it is already in Christ.*" [66] Nygren is certainly here thinking of the unity of the church in terms parallel to those used by Paul in Rom. 6, where he describes baptism as the given righteousness for the Christian (thus as an indicative), but at the same time sets forth the requirement of a ministry of righteousness (thus the imperative) as the necessary consequence of that which was given in baptism. [67]

Here the question arises as to what the actual division among "the churches" signifies. The variety of gifts cannot justify division. Nor can Nygren conceive of the various formulations of the gospel as necessarily resulting in different church communions. The liberal idea, which has received new currency, to the effect that the different "theologies" of the evangelists and the apostles could explain the division of the church, is for Nygren an absurd idea. He has even (at the second general assembly of the Lutheran World Federation in Hannover in 1952) warned against regarding Lutheranism as a manifestation of a specially Pauline theology—a point of view which not infrequently is expressed. Instead he emphasized the necessity that Lutheranism must also be able to express its message in Johannine terms. [68]

But what, then, are "the churches" in the light of the unity of the church given and thus unalterable in Christ? One answer is that the different churches represent questions to one another "if they really have understood the gospel in its deepest meaning and in its fullest content." [69] God's activity in Christ retains its continuity, that is to say, the church retains its unity in the midst of the many churches. The question of the different churches to one another can therefore be formulated in this way: Do you intend that your proclamation of the gospel is to represent the universal gospel, or do you intend only to defend a particular tradition, a special teaching? [70] In this connection Nygren points to the division which the Reformation has brought. Luther's activity was related to the universal church. It is a tragedy in the life of the church that this achievment was rejected by a part of Christendom. The consequence now is "that that which should belong to the whole church, temporarily must be administered by a part of the church." [71]

What, then, is the reason for the actual division of the churches? Nygren answers: "That the one Church of Christ appears in such a shattered form, so that one must speak of several different Churches, is, from one standpoint, an indication of the power of sin within the church." [72] This had occurred already in the New Testament period. The congregations in Corinth, in Galatia, etc., were divided because one did not consider the given unity in Christ, but instead emphasized human factors (the bond with one or another apostle, ritualistic prescriptions, etc.). Their division was thus actually not a division of the church. Nygren's argument is important and also characteristic for his theology: "Despite all the division that exists in the Church of Christ, yet it is one in Christ. Schism—no matter how deplorable and harmful it is in itself—cannot break down the unity that is in the body of Christ." [73]

Two questions here arise. The one has to do with *heresy*. What happens in case a false gospel is proclaimed and a part of the church does stray from Christ? Nygren's answer is to refer to the congregation in Galatia. Paul expresses his *anathema* over the false proclamation but retains fellowship with "the brethren." The church of God continues to exist in Galatia.[74]

The other question has to do with altar fellowship. It is of course a fact that the churches have separated themselves from one another just with respect to the sacrament, which is called the sacrament of unity. How does Nygren evaluate this division? He emphasizes that "we must not exaggerate the extent of this division." And the explanation at this point is: "Even where two Church communions refuse the fellowship of the Lord's Supper to one another and believe themselves unable to meet with one another at the Lord's Table, they yet cannot dissolve the fellowship that exists in the fact that both—each for itself—partake of the one loaf: 'Because there is one loaf, we who are many are one body, for we all partake of the same loaf' (1 Cor. 10:17). To meet together at the same table—which ought to be the *Lord's* Table and not that of an individual Communion—this the Church Communions can refuse to do with one another, but they cannot refuse to participate in the same one bread. The given unity can never be nullified by any external division." [75]

We have here a unified point of view: The church's unity is given. The sin among men, which even leads to division among the churches, cannot destroy this unity of the body of Christ. Nygren's position, which has here been outlined, harmonizes with his basic understanding of the church's christological foundation.

The Ecumenical Task

We must now seek to determine how Nygren, on the basis of this basic conception of the unity of the church, understands the ecumenical task of the actually divided churches. That he has to this day actively participated in this work, we have already noted. The given unity of the church as the body of Christ thus by no means implies complacency with the divisions that actually exist. On the contrary, the given unity drives forward the imperative, which consists in the fact that the church "must constantly become anew what she already is," namely, *one* in Christ, in his body.[76]

What we must first note is that the ecumenical task is not an organizational problem.[77] One must not therefore interpret the given unity in the church as though only external organizational questions remained, while the essential unity was already achieved. Instead one must penetrate to the bottom of what is meant in the fact that this unity is already given, and then draw the inescapable practical consequences which follow therefrom.[78] This implies, as compared with the earlier stages of the ecumenical movement, that one cannot stop with just coming together with others in brotherly love";[79] nor that one can be satisfied only with factual confessional comparisons. Neither a fraternal compromise nor the willingness to learn to know each other as we are in agreements and disagreements can be a sufficient definition of what the ecumenical task actually is. "The way to the unity of the Church runs not merely through brotherly love, but also through fidelity to the Gospel which has been entrusted to us by God."[80] Only to such seeking for the truth is the promise given. Ever since 1952 in Lund, Nygren has made this new ecumenical method function through his own participation in it.[81]

The method as such is not new as far as Nygren is concerned. He has been pleading for it for almost three decades. This orientation can most simply be expressed in Nygren's own words, namely, that the ecumenical activity must free itself from the influence of internationalism and the tendency to find the least common denominator, and instead move into "the stage of seeking greater depth," [82] which takes seriously the gospel which has been entrusted to us as "the church's true treasure." [83] Instead of consisting of mere comparisons, the conversation between the churches then becomes an expression of their striving for unity.

Nygren has always seen this ecumenical program as the continuing contribution and responsibility of Lutheranism. In this connection he has also defended the significance of the Christian confessions for the ecumenical enterprise. Until there is an ecumenical confession, all so-called ecumenical advances have reached only the externals. Therefore, confessional loyalty fructifies the ecumenical enterprise. Actually, the "confessional" and the "ecumenical" strivings are by no means in competition with each other. "A correctly understood faithfulness to the confessions has a tendency in the ecumenical direction, toward Christian fellowship, and the correctly understood ecumenical idea has a tendency toward faithfulness to the confessions." [84]

Nygren, accordingly, opposes the suspicions which often exist between the confessional and the ecumenical contenders. "An opposition between the two could only exist if Lutheranism were something other than it is, and if the ecumenical enterprise were something other than it is." [85] Nygren certainly does not close his eyes to the concrete experiences of those who see "the confessional" and "the ecumenical" as mutually opposed to one another. But he refuses to accept them as justified and sees instead a theologically based possibility of reconciliation between the two.[86] The ecumenical enterprise is bound to the truth of the Christian faith, if it rightly seeks to make world-wide (ecumenical) claims.

These considerations have, ever since the Edinburgh conference in 1937, confirmed Nygren's conviction "that unity can be reached at the center and not in the first place with respect to practical questions." [87] Or in another context: "The way to the center is the way to unity. If one seeks the unity of the Church, then one must pursue the relevant questions to their central issues." [88]

What is the meaning of this principle for the ecumenical task? With all probability it is this: The way to the unity of the church does not bypass the many churches which we now find in Christendom, but instead goes straight through them. If the ecumenical movement were to depreciate the existing divergencies in the confession of the gospel, the unity already given by Christ would not be manifested, but instead the result would be the formation of a new church communion, arising alongside of the others, and thereby the problem of the division of the church would be complicated instead of solved.

Nygren's "Edinburgh-thesis" for the method to be used in ecumenical work was based upon concrete experience at that Faith and Order conference.[89] The doctrine of justification by faith had been presented in a preliminary report, which was to introduce the sectional discussions on grace, in a somewhat false light. It seemed that the conference, for this reason, was not going to come any nearer to unity between—as the report put it—the Orthodox-Anglican and the Reformation conceptions. In this situation Nygren himself received the opportunity to explain the "troublesome" doctrine of justification by faith, to emphasize its ecumenical importance, and to reject the conception that this had to do with "a Lutheran specialty." He was supported by another Lutheran, Professor Nörregaard from Copenhagen, who gave a historical presentation of the influence of the doctrine of justification by faith in other church communions. The result became a sectional report on grace. This became the only unanimously approved report during the whole conference. "The way to the center is the way to unity."

What has been said above leads by no means to any confessionalistic self-sufficiency. Nygren has the whole time been on watch against such tendencies, not least within Lutheranism.[90] No church can build on its advantages as over against other church communions. This would be a denial of the *sola gratia-sola fide* message. A church which builds exclusively on God's grace in Christ will itself always be ready to test itself. It will also be properly afraid of the "risk connected with the passing of judgment." [91] Therefore, according to Nygren, the denial of church fellowship becomes "a very serious matter," an "abnormal case," which "must be done by other 'churches' only 'with fear and trembling' in remembrance of Rom. 14:4." [92] This does not imply, however, indifference with respect to the Christian truth question. The requirement of love and the requirement of truth must not be set against each other. "There have always existed and there ought always to exist serious discussions within the Church so that the gospel, the true treasure of the Church, may not be lost. But these discussions of differences should result, not in judgments of one another, but in a common struggle to help each other as much as possible toward the whole truth. In this way controversy within the Church becomes a means of building up the body of Christ and confirming its unity." [93]

Thus, Nygren's ecclesiology concludes with a consistent train of thought: *The church's given unity is the ecumenical task, which is to lead the divided churches to unity in the body of Christ.* This ecumenical train of thought well corresponds with Nygren's whole theological program. The material for his theology can have changed during different periods. But during the whole time he was en route to find and solve the Christian truth question, by which the unity of the church itself stands or falls.[94]

Critical Questions

Nygren's basic ecumenical ideas reveal an imposing thought structure. They have demonstrated their fruitfulness in the recent ecumenical enterprise. Nonetheless certain critical questions can be raised when one considers the problem of the given unity of the church and the ecumenical task that is bound up with it.

We have already suggested that these ideas are systematically related to Nygren's christological foundation of the concept of the church. The critique we have directed against the foundation will accordingly also apply to the application of this concept. We recall one main objection, namely, Nygren's identification of the Adam-Christ conception with the concept of Christ as the head of the church. As a result of this identification we found that the dominion of Christ and the church of Christ were not distinguished from one another.

This critique also is applicable to the question of the unity of the church. Nygren speaks of the *given* unity of the church. This retains its validity only in the sense that the church has Christ as its head. In other words, the church's unity is given in and through the fact that the Holy Spirit unites together the parts of the body with the head, granting them participation in the work of Christ, whose real presence is mediated and applied among men in the Spirit. Yet the realization of the unity of the church through the Holy Spirit encounters opposition in a world, which yet lives under the old age. Against this opposition the Holy Spirit carries out his work in that he separates the body of Christ through the word and the sacraments. He builds the spiritual temple, the new Israel, while at the same time he creates "division" in the world and delimits the church as the gathered people of the new age. The church shares in this struggle of the Spirit as it proclaims Christ's dominion in the world and calls men to repentance and amendment of life through incorporation in Christ's death and resurrection.

On the basis of what we have just said we must raise the question as to whether Nygren's ecclesiology is capable of theologically mastering the problem of division among the churches. Does not Nygren's foundation of the "given unity" actually lack a dialectical element so completely, that it is unable to take into itself the motif of struggle, which applies to the church just as well as to her Savior? Is not the unity realized only and exclusively in that it creates disunity, an incurable division, which will remain until the last day? With gratitude one must note Nygren's emphasis on the fact that the body of Christ cannot be divided. But does not this unity actually stand out only against the background of the fact that "there must be factions among you in order that those who are genuine among you may be recognized" (1 Cor. 11:19)? What place is there in Nygren's ecclesiology for this necessary division, which until the last day runs alongside of the manifestation of the unity of the body of Christ? Nygren naturally cannot ignore the fact that there are several different churches, which also refuse to have church fellowship with each other. But can he do justice to this empirical fact of division simply through putting in opposition to it the given unity of the body of Christ? A strange embarrassment arises in Nygren's theology the very moment he begins to speak of the actual divisions. One has the feeling that this phenomenon quite simply does not fit into his basic theological outlook. It is abnormal (and not only in the same sense as sin); it should really not be permitted to occur. But this irritating fact is there in the church's life and should therefore also be given theological significance. For Nygren only the *unity* in the church exists, that is to say, Christ as the head of the church. But does not Christ exist also as the Lord of the church, or as Lord over all of humanity, who shall return to judge the living and the dead? Will not this Lord's judgment begin precisely with the church? For the church in its earthly existence lives at the boundary between the old age and the new. Therefore she can fall and be delivered over to the antichrist, who also builds his "church" in order to destroy the church of Christ.

It is necessary to remind ourselves of these relationships in order to be able to discover that such trains of thought are lacking in Nygren's ecclesiology. The division which he takes into account is the division possible and permissible within the church. That we live in a time when one can make a valuable theological contribution by showing that an existing division is in fact by no means necessary is here not to be denied. Nygren's special charisma would seem also to lie in this direction. He has certainly helped to bring together churches which, for irrelevant reasons, have broken off fellowship with each other.[95] But the question is whether all divisions which have arisen and which continue to arise in the church can be healed in this manner. Or to use Nygren's own terminology: What happens when the way to unity is blocked, in that the chosen way is not permitted to be the way to the center? To speak more concretely, in all of Nygren's writings there are very few passages where this problem is at all mentioned.[96] Where this happens the problem is partially neutralized with a rejection of "the passing of judgment" on other churches. No matter how valid this warning is, it should also be granted that a denial of church fellowship in certain cases is directly necessary in order to preserve the unity of the body of Christ. Nygren, on the other hand, speaks only of "difficulties which obstruct the way for . . . ecclesiastical and sacramental fellowship." [97] For him the problem is dissolved in the phenomenon of that division which can be tolerated *within* the church.

Two examples will briefly be touched upon in order to illustrate our question. The first is the situation of the congregation in Galatia.[98] Nygren seems to maintain that Paul pronounces his *anathema* only over the false teaching, while he retains fellowship with "the brethren." But can one ignore the fact that at the same time the apostle's *anathema* has abrogated church fellowship with concrete individuals? It is not only a proclamation which is rejected, but also those individuals who have put themselves in its service (Gal. 1:7, 9). The misled "brethren" are retained in fellowship with the self-evident presupposition that they follow the apostle's gospel and not some "new gospel."

The other example is the passage cited above about churches which have broken off altar fellowship with each other.[99] With reference to 1 Cor. 10:17, Nygren maintains that church communions can refuse to meet together at the same table, "but they cannot refuse to participate in the same one bread. The given unity can never be nullified by any external division." This is true with some modifications. In our day's confused ecclesiastical situation there are certainly many churches which deny each other altar fellowship without actually being divided in Christ. At this point the Bible passage cited is in order. But may not the presence of the "one bread" be legitimately questioned in those communions, which claim to celebrate the Lord's Supper, while they actually intend only to celebrate a fellowship meal or a meal of remembrance? In any case, when the Reformers put this question they were not satisfied with the answer that the other group thought that it was celebrating the Lord's Supper. In other words, one concretely denied altar fellowship because one questioned whether the *one* bread, which according to the promise is Christ's own body, and the *one* cup, which is Christ's own shed blood, were really distributed at that "Lord's table." This denial is still to be found today. It is self-evident that a historical denial can be declared antiquated since conditions have changed. But is it actually in principle impossible to deny altar fellowship with other "church communions" which appear in the name of Christ?

We may stop at this point. The question is sufficiently indicated. We may summarize in the following manner: *Is not the reference to the church's given unity altogether too one-sidedly determined by the concept of Christ as the head of the church? Is not Christ also the Lord of the church, who shall call us to account for the service which the church has carried out until the last day?* For it is only this last judgment of the Lord which can take away the self-sufficiency of the churches and their tendency to judge one another. But the coming judgment must not paralyze the church. Already here and now in obedience to Christ and under the guidance of the Holy Spirit the church must carry out a division as over against that which is not the church. For even if this must happen "with fear and trembling," it is at the same time required by the Lord himself in order that it might serve as a sign pointing to the coming judgment.

At the close of our presentation of the first part about the christo-logical foundation of the church we found that Nygren's identification of Christ as Lord and head meant that the church of Christ was interpreted in terms of the dominion of Christ, and thereby Christ as head of the church was not clearly seen. Now, on the other hand, we can ask whether the church of Christ and its unity has not received an interpretation where the dominion of Christ has been neglected.

Nygren's ecclesiology, in a wholesome way, reminds us that the dominion of Christ cannot be ignored in the theological determination of the church. Though not giving any attention to the difference between the two christological aspects of headship and lordship, how-ever, Nygren has defined a concept of the church, which — despite its undeniable merits in a certain theological and ecumenical situation — yet lacks essential biblically legitimate features.

We mentioned that Nygren, during his early years, was not influenced by the discussion then going on in Sweden about the church. After having surveyed Nygren's doctrine of the church, the question can now be asked as to how in principle it relates itself to current Swedish thinking about the church. Such a confrontation cannot here be undertaken. Only a surmise can be expressed. Nygren's ecclesiology contributed much new material to the Swedish discussion of the church and also to the ecumenical discussion. But it has not freed itself from a pattern of thinking about the church which in its presuppositions still lives in terms of a corpus christianum, which not least in the present has shown itself to be a fiction, and even a burden. Yet intensive work with Nygren's doctrine of the church and the problems internal to it could lead to new impulses, which in turn could lead to a concept of the church which is based on the New Testament —yet in quite a different way than the "free church" critics of the "religiously motivated folk church idea" could conceive.

In this perspective Nygren's ecclesiology represents a fascinating study with inspiring implications for the future. Nygren's great theological contribution probably lies in the fact that he had the humility to carry out his own work in the context of the worldwide wrestling with the ecumenical problem of the church. This gives his work abiding value.

Reply to Interpreters
and Critics

REPLY TO INTERPRETERS

AND CRITICS

Anders Nygren

IT IS something extraordinarily fascinating for a scholar to see the problems with which he has been engaged for decades interpreted and critically examined by several scholars, who have dealt with the same or similar problems, and who therefore can give them a really competent examination. Nothing can compare with this as a way of making the problems come alive and of displaying them in a new perspective. We all see in part, and it is therefore extremely important to bring about intellectual co-operation and exchange, whereby different scholars may make their contributions, and wherein instances of onesidedness are polished away through the friction of mutual give and take. Not least is the fact that each one approaches the matter from his own special starting point, and, considering it against his own background, contributes to the richness of the whole. When one has come upon a clearing in the thick forest of the material and seen the light from it play over the surroundings and thus contribute toward orientation, one may see, through the many different contributions, the rays of light which one has seen break into a whole spectrum of different colors, which give life to the landscape in its entirety. I need not say how thankful I am to the different contributors that they have been willing to make themselves available for this purpose. One would

---

TRANSLATED BY BERNHARD ERLING

preferably, in this situation, let these contributions stand there and speak for themselves, without one's own comments.

For several reasons, however, this may not be done. First of all, the plan for this volume requires a reply from me. In addition to this, dialogue—and continued dialogue—is a vital requirement for the scientific enterprise. In this enterprise it is not essential that a position once taken be maintained at any cost, but that the *matter* be discussed and illuminated from different angles. This is what makes it so important that different viewpoints meet each other, be weighed against each other, and thus through this mutual argumentation contribute to the factual clarification of the question. It is not merely by chance that critique plays such a large role in the scientific realm. Instead it belongs to the indispensable conditions of science that every theory presented be submitted to the purging fires of criticism. Theory and critique are both equally necessary, and it is in this way that science is able to make progress. It is thus a misunderstanding when, as often happens, one regards critique as something solely negative. Actually critique, when properly done, is one of the more positive elements in the scientific world. And even if at times it happens to miss the mark, it has even then a positive function, insofar as it reveals where further clarification is needed. In the scientific context the rule holds without exception, that one can never achieve too high a degree of clarity. I will therefore make use of the critical questions which have been directed at me as an occasion further to clarify and make precise my position.

Philosophy of Religion

As introductory essay in this volume there is Professor Ragnar Bring's inclusive and penetrating treatment of my works in the philosophy of religion. This is entirely in order, for it is above all in the philosophy of religion that the great decisions are finally made. Thus it was during the first decades of the century, and so it is now during the 1960's and will be in the 1970's. As long as one permits the unclarity and confusion that have reigned in philosophy of religion as a result of a heritage taken over unexamined from past centuries—especially from the Enlightenment—to remain, this has desolating consequences for the understanding of philosophy and theology and of their mutual relations, and also for theology itself in its concrete task. One can certainly successfully carry on theological research with respect to special problems without first having gained clarity with respect to the fundamental theological-philosophical questions. But as soon as the larger perspective and the systematic total outlook are involved, the consequences of religio-philosophical unclarity are immediately apparent. As a concrete example, the question of Christianity's "demythologizing," which has so vitally concerned the theology of the last decades, can be mentioned. Actually this "problem" arises out of a deeper religio-philosophical confusion. Thus it has become apparent that this "problem's" solution—or rather its dissolution—is not possible on the basis of concrete exegetical-theological observations, but can only be achieved through religio-philosophical analysis and clarification. I am therefore grateful that in his essay Ragnar Bring has not simply given an account of my religio-philosophical position, but has placed it in its larger historical context, and made apparent its implications for an understanding of the task and significance of theology.

There are two questions to which I am to respond. *The first question* can briefly be summarized as follows: When I, in my book *Religiöst a priori* (1921), characterized the basic religious category with the designation "the category of eternity" and emphasized its inseparable relation with the concept of validity, and in that connection pointed out that *all* experience (this could be any domain of experience whatsoever, theoretical, ethical, aesthetic, or religious) in the final analysis points to the basic religious category—does this mean that there exists a more intimate relationship between "the category of eternity" and "validity," and that the other basic categories as lower forms of validity are to be placed under the basic religious category and, so to speak, derived from it? Or, to put the question in Bring's own words: Does it mean "that above everything there was a general a priori, from which could be derived the a prioris of the different domains of experience, and that the religious domain stood closer to the highest a priori than the a prioris of the other domains?" To this question the answer must definitely be: *No, not at all.* Bring correctly characterizes the idea which lies behind this question as a "radical misunderstanding" and "a view completely opposite to Nygren's." I am extraordinarily grateful that Bring has brought forth and so extensively dealt with this misunderstanding. For actually this has to do with a point where misunderstanding can easily occur and where it is of the greatest importance that such misunderstanding be effectively prevented. I am here aware that to a certain extent I have given occasion for this misunderstanding—less through what I have said than *through what I have not said.* It was for me so self-evident that such a conception was unreasonable, that I never for a moment reflected about the fact that such a misunderstanding could arise, and that it would be necessary for me to do something to prevent it. After I answered the question, in *Religiöst a priori* "Is there a religious a priori?" with a clear *no,* I believed that a misunderstanding of the kind indicated above should be excluded. My whole analysis was designed to show that to speak of anything a priori could be meaningful only if one excluded every thought of something ontological. If one speaks of several different a prioris, among them "*a* religious a priori" or "*the* religious a priori," it can become a question of deriving the one from the other. If, on the other hand, one rejects this whole question, as I have done (see, for example, the italicized passage in *Religiöst a priori,* p. 200: "*since there is no logical a priori, and equally no ethical or aesthetic a priori, there is also no religious a priori*"), this possibility of derivation disappears, for the simple reason that it is here not a question of any metaphysical principles valid in themselves, from which all other validity could be derived. It is here not a question of ontological concepts, not even of universal concepts, but of *presuppositional* concepts. The "transcendental analysis" or "presuppositional analysis"—in whatever domain of experience or context of meaning it is put to use—has one and the same meaning: it shows what is implied in all experience and first makes this "possible" (to use Kant's language), or, as I have expressed it, "*it shows* what must be valid if anything at all is to be valid." [1] If the theoretical, the ethical, the aesthetic, and the religious basic categories in just the same way "must be valid if anything at all is to be valid," it is clearly meaningless to say that one of them is placed above the others. If with respect to each and every one of them it can be said that it is a necessary presupposition for all experience, this means that they mutually condition each other and stand and fall together. Which of them becomes the "last and ultimate presupposition" depends on what the actual research deals with. In epistemology this clearly becomes the presuppositions of knowledge, in ethics the ethical, and in the philosophy of religion the religious presuppositions.

As soon as I encountered this misunderstanding, I used the first convenient opportunity to correct this matter in the manner indicated above. I shall here only cite a passage from the year 1923:

> Only that presupposition, without which no experience and no validity at all is possible, is basic and fundamental enough to be characterized as philosophical . . . When thus the question is put:

"It certainly can't be the author's meaning, that every particular deduction strictly builds on experience in general in a strict sense?" it should be sufficiently clear from what has been said that this is precisely what I mean . . . Just because philosophy . . . is one and systematic, there is no *particular* deduction in the actual meaning of the word, but *one and the same* process of deduction in the several domains. But for this reason also, none of the "particular deductions" is fully carried out, until all of the "particular deductions" are carried out and united in one systematic whole of *mutually dependent* presuppositions.[2]

It is here, thus, not a question of any "shift in my way of thinking," but only of a correction of an elementary misunderstanding. Indeed the idea of several mutually dependent presuppositions, where no one of them stands above the other, represents *the actual core of the original conception*. This idea includes two elements: 1] The different domains of experience or contexts of meaning must be clearly distinguished. Each and every one of them stands under its own meaning-determined basic presupposition. They are *autonomous* in relation to each other, and any tendency to confuse them leads inevitably to meaninglessness. 2] Yet they are not separated from each other, so to speak, by watertight compartments. There is a problem of integration which here faces us; experience does not fall apart. But that which holds it together is not the fact that one context of meaning is added to another. This is not possible, in that they are not commensurable, and thus when taken together do not give a unified meaning. The connection must occur via the presuppositions, which stand in a necessary connection with each other and mutually condition each other. Thus at the same time each context of meaning's autonomy is preserved and their integration in a total context is guaranteed.

With respect to the second main question—to what extent "the category of eternity" can rightly be designated as the basic presupposition of religion—I can express myself more briefly. Bring points out "that the concept 'eternity' in my later writings is less markedly used as a characteristic of the religious context of meaning." This, however, has been brought about by more external circumstances. When it is a matter of analyzing the transcendental presupposition of religion, it still seems to me that "the category of eternity" is the only one available. It is doubtless connected with the risk of misunderstanding, above all through the philosophical tradition's Platonizing concept of eternity, something which of course must be excluded from the category context. But every other conceivable presuppositional concept is connected with even greater risks of slipping in a psychological or ontological-metaphysical direction. That which makes "the category of eternity" especially well suited for this purpose is, on the one hand, that it clearly distinguishes the religious context of meaning from other contexts of meaning, and, on the other hand, that, as a purely formal, categorical question, it provides room for the different content of the answers (basic motifs) given by the several religions, thus, e.g., for such different outlooks as the Greek-Platonic concept of eternity, the Christian faith in God (agape), or for Buddhistic atheism. The category of eternity, in other words, fills just those demands which must be placed on a basic presupposition. When it has sometimes been argued that "the category of eternity," which in its content is not religiously determined therefore cannot be the religious basic category, this indicates that one has not gained clarity as to what is meant by the idea of a "category." The difference between true and false is not itself true, the category of causality is the *presupposition* of knowledge, but not itself knowledge. Take away the aspect of eternity—easier said than done!—and religion disappears, every religious judgment loses its meaning.

If one has only gained clarity as to what is meant by the idea of a category, the ambiguity of the concept of eternity disappears. The concept remains with two distinct meanings, as a category or a presuppositional concept, and as the content-determined answer of an individual religion. This is no more strange than that we talk of cause sometimes as a category or an epistemological presupposition, sometimes as an individual concrete factual relationship. It is no more strange than that we speak of "good" both to clarify categorically what we *mean* when we make ethical judgments, and to designate what a certain outlook values as ethically good. This double meaning does not have to lead to confusion; no more does the double meaning of "the concept of eternity," as a category, and as the individual religion's basic answer, give occasion for any confusion.

Two characteristic features of a significant part of contemporary philosophy are its *analytic* approach and its concern with the problems of *meaning*. To this can be added a certain antimetaphysical tendency. In all of these respects I feel myself closely related to it. My view of philosophy and its task has always involved the requirement of *analysis*, concept analysis, presuppositional analysis, structural analysis. The question of *meaning* and "contexts of meaning" has always stood in the center, and the rejection of every form of metaphysics has been a constantly recurring theme. Even if this modern philosophy comes far from fulfilling all the requirements which I would like to see taken care of by philosophy, there is nonetheless here a marked affinity. It has therefore been a great satisfaction to me that an articulate representative of this new philosophy, Professor Paul Holmer, has been willing to make a critical contribution to this volume.

In order to do full justice to the important problems dealt with would require a discussion which would go far beyond the space available. Precisely these problems shall receive more extensive treatment in a new book which I hope soon to publish under the title "Meaning and Method: Prolegomena to a Scientific Philosophy of Religion." I shall add here a few reflections in the interests of further clarification.

Actually, our positions would seem to be much closer to each other than would at first appear. When Holmer holds that there is no one concept, "truth," under which the many kinds of theoretical statements could be subsumed, also no common concept, "good," under which the many kinds of ethical statements could be subsumed, I am also wholly of the same opinion. "Truth" is *not a universal concept, but a presuppositional concept,* and this means that one cannot define the concept of truth in the customary manner through giving its proximate genus and its specific differentia—possibly placed under a common concept "validity" and differentiated from other kinds of validity. Such a procedure would lead straight into metaphysics, which I, together with Holmer, reject. What is meant by the fact that we designate something as *true* is "defined" through the use we make of this concept and through its inescapability.

There is nothing which can be called "the scientific method," but several different methods, adapted to the different objects which the various sciences investigate. So also there is not a common concept "validity," which would stand as the genus, under which several different things were "subsumed." But there are several different judgments which can be designated as "valid." That something is "valid" is about equivalent to saying that it has meaning. That which is "meaningless" cannot be "valid." Two scientific judgments, which mutually exclude each other, can both be meaningful even though they cannot both be true. Often, at first, one cannot determine which of them is true, but there can be an objective argumentation between them, and thus they are both "valid" as scientific theories. Science includes both parts: true and false judgments, correct and incorrect observations, etc., and science has to carry out the sifting between them. It makes progress through testing the different theories against each other.

Here a word must be added about the meaning of speaking of "questions." It can be simply expressed in this way: What is *in question?* This is a very meaningful use of "question." I illustrate with an example: If someone conceives a prayer in a service as if a scientific statement were "in question," I say to him: This is not at all "in question." The "question" is not scientifically but religiously intended. Another time it is perhaps an ethical judgment which is confused with a scientific statement. Here one can say precisely the same as in the former case. Two altogether separate "questions" have been mixed together. And now it is philosophy's, i.e., the critical-analytical philosophy's task to prevent such mixing of categories and the consequent confusion in the individual judgments.

If one has seen the significance of this critical-analytical task of philosophy, it is no longer possible to regard it as only a substitute for the rejected metaphysics. It has an altogether independent and indispensible task. With respect to metaphysics Wittgenstein's words, "no problem" can be applied, but absolutely not with respect to the critical-analytical philosophy. For here there is a real problem, and a problem of huge dimensions: *the problem of implications.* Wittgenstein has made a great contribution to philosophy. Even if, perhaps, he never accepted without reservations Russell's metaphysics, and in *Tractatus Logico-Philosophicus* somewhat removed himself from it, it is nonetheless a feat to have made one's way from *Tractatus* to *Philosophical Investigations.* But Wittgenstein does not represent a philosophical halting point. His thought can yield other important things. Thus it can give good help in clarifying the different contexts of meanings and the "problem of implication" inseparably bound up with them.

Implication is an excellent and extraordinarily effective instrument. With implication one catches the criminal in the net of his contradictions. With implication one catches the scientist, when he has made a mistake, due to the fact that without closer thought he has presupposed a great deal—some of it correct and other things less correct. That which is implied lies there hidden, but can be brought forth through analysis. Even correct thinking builds on its—often unconscious—presuppositions. That we can at all carry on a scientific debate presupposes infinitely much. It is, to be sure, no small matters that here are in question, even if one generally makes one's presuppositions covertly. Here philosophy as analysis of presuppositions has its great task, namely, to make the implicit categorical presuppositions explicit.

It is interesting to see how Holmer, who otherwise wants to push to one side talk of contexts of meanings, cannot himself escape making use of it. He, too, must speak of different "kinds of discourse." With approval he points out that I have shown "why moral expressions and behavior are not the places where several distinctively Christian words derive their meanings." But this is only another expression for the fact that here two different contexts of meaning are in question, which may not be confused. And this also is the case when he asserts that it is impossible to "put together incommensurate components." When he speaks of different "games" or "grammars," he reveals here actually the same concern as when I speak of "contexts of meaning." When Holmer closes his essay with the words: "the grammar of the faith is quite enough," I can therefore wholly agree. For it is just in order to bring forth its meaning and liberate "the religious language" from the confusion to which it is so often exposed through being mixed with other "languages"—just this concern lies back of speaking of a "religious context of meaning." And here one makes no progress without a philosophical analysis of presuppositions. Some think that one can without loss avoid such a philosophical investigation. For my part I want to agree with a statement by the well-known natural scientist and philosopher, C. F. von Weizsäcker. In his book, *Die Tragweite der Wissenschaft* (1964), p. vi, he writes: "Philosophy, however, is indispensable, where we, who have expert knowledge in any domain, seek to achieve clarity about our own prejudices"—to which I only want to add the remark that instead of "prejudices" I would put "presuppositions." Even the research scholar in a special area certainly does well to take into account the presuppositions with which he works, even if this in the final analysis is a philosophical concern.

Motif Research

We have discussed rather fully the problems related to the philosophy of religion. The reason has been that it is in this area that the major decisions are made, also it is here that we see that the idea of contexts of meaning is the presupposition for an understanding of the meaning of speaking of motif contexts. From now on we must express ourselves much more briefly. This is also possible, especially with reference to this section on "Motif Research." The four essays which are put under this rubric, taken together give the best conceivable introduction to the subject of motif research, what it involves and what it can accomplish. In general there isn't much that must be added beyond that which is already said in the essays.

First, and as an introduction, stands Dean Valter Lindström's very initiated and objective orientation regarding the problem of motif research in its entirety. With respect to his concluding question I want only briefly to express my agreement "that the basic motif of Christianity must not necessarily be summed up in a single concept," whereby, however, it is to be noted that this does not change the fact that in the constellation Agape-Eros, only agape, but not eros, nor any kind of synthesis of the two, can be recognized as the Christian basic motif.

Professor Bernhard Erling has already, in his dissertation, *Nature and History: A Study in Theological Methodology with Special Attention to Motif Research* (1960), directed his interest toward widening motif research into a general historical method. To this question he returns in the essay before us. This is also an altogether legitimate interest. For it lies in the character of the method itself that it does not want to be a special theological method. Even if it at the outset became developed in a theological context and was used on religious motifs with reference to the contributions these could give toward an understanding of different religious formulations, it is to the same extent usable also in other areas, wherever historical interpretation of any kind is involved.

In my investigations I have restricted myself to bringing forth motifs from history. Erling correctly underlines these motifs' *alternative* character. However he does not want to stop with the mere factual affirmation that such is the case. And in a certain respect this is entirely correct, insofar as the basic motifs do not appear in this form in history, but rather could be compared with ideal structural models. It is thus a question of "possible" alternatives. It is here he would go a step further and present these alternatives as an interpretation of what he calls "historical causality." But thereby the motif concept receives, if only slightly, in some measure an ontological coloration. Here I hesitate to take this further step with him. Yet, in any case the fact remains that he, through his powerful emphasis, on motif research as a general historical method, and on the alternative character of the motifs, has contributed to a high degree further to clarify the meaning of motif research.

The Danish literature historian, Dr. Erik M. Christensen, has in his book, *Ex auditorio: Kunst og Ideer hos Martin A. Hansen* (1965), in a sharp-sighted and persuasive manner provided an example of how motif analysis can open the way toward otherwise hidden depths in a literary authorship. He there has shown how the famous Danish author, Martin A. Hansen, in several of his works, certainly without using the terms, has operated with the tension between the agape, eros, and nomos motifs, and how a motif or structural analysis can spread light over points which would otherwise remain in darkness.

In his essay, "Literary Studies and the Use of Motifs," Christensen follows this line of thought further and shows how motif analysis is one of the necessary instruments, which the literature historian may use in order to come to terms with his often obscure and subtle material. It is thus here a question of an essential broadening of the utilization radius of motif analysis.

If Christensen thus has shown what motif analysis can mean for "the right interpretation, the best possible reading of any given work of art," what he, on the other hand, has done through his essay to spread further light over the meaning of motif research should be pointed out. Through his appropriation of the field of the history of literature for motif analytical examination, through his demonstration of the richness in ore which thereby can be obtained, through his use of the motif analytical method on relevant contemporary material, and not least through his placing of the program of motif research in the contemporary American discussion, Christensen has made an essential contribution to motif research.

With Professor Jacob W. Heikkinen's essay, "Motif Research and the New Testament," we return to the theological domain and the actual point of departure there. For when one seeks the Christian basic motif the point of departure must clearly be taken in the New Testament. There it must, first of all, be determined whether there is anything which may rightly be regarded as the Christian basic motif, and if motif analysis is at all usable in this area. If it should appear that the New Testament were only a conglomerate of contradictory conceptions which mutually canceled out each other, if there were not coherence or unity to be found there, then it would clearly be a hopeless task to seek to find a basic motif there. One cannot speak of a Christian basic motif, if it were wholly absent at the very starting point.

I am therefore grateful and happy that a practicing exegete has been willing to give the question of motif research and the New

Testament a thoroughgoing examination. And I am doubly grateful that he thereby has proceeded in a manner so congenial to my own approach to this question. I can only say: this is just what is meant by speaking of motif research. Motif research is not the same as exegesis. It does not dispense with the usual historical-exegetical, philological, genetical, psychological investigations; rather it presupposes them and builds on them, but it has in addition to this its own structural-analytical question to put to the material, and it emphasizes that also this question is of essential significance for the interpretation. The hermeneutical problem has different aspects, and among them motif research is not of least importance. This Heikkinen shows in his essay, which represents a generous welcome to the method of motif research in the exegetical working fellowship. And when he finally puts a few critical questions to me, I can essentially agree with him both when he wishes a clearer determination of agape in its "salvation historical" context, and when he wishes that the analysis given in motif research of the gospel's content were, to a greater extent, balanced by an analysis of the nature of human experience. In both cases it is evident that motif research is not the whole, and that my carrying out of it in many respects is fragmentary.

The Meanings of Love

In the introductory chapter of my work, *Agape and Eros*, I (1930), I wrote that the problem dealt with there, despite its central significance, belonged to "the most neglected in the theological field." So it was at that time; but now the situation is the complete opposite. A stream of investigations have appeared during the past decades. Foremost among these is the Roman Catholic scholar, Professor Victor Warnach's large and extraordinarily basic work with the title, *Agape* (1951). Its subtitle, *Die Liebe als Grundmotiv der neutestamentlichen Theologie*, already reveals a close relationship with my approach. Warnach thus reckons with a Christian, a New Testament basic motif —which many do not—and he finds this basic motif in "der Liebe." Furthermore he is clearly aware that there is an essential difference between the New Testament's "Agape" and the extra-biblical "Eros." When it is further required to distinguish these two from each other, our paths partially separate, and Warnach has in his book given extensive space to a critical discussion of my presentation.

Under such conditions it is particularly satisfying to me that Warnach has been willing to cooperate in this volume with an essay, "Agape in the New Testament," and thus permitted his viewpoints to be expressed just at the central point which constitutes the theme of his large standard work.

If one thinks of how different the traditions are which lie behind our presentations, it is quite surprising to note the extent to which we have been able to agree. It is a beautiful example of how biblical studies are suited to unite. At various points where there can seem to be a decided difference, it would not seem difficult through further clarification to arrive at full agreement. As an example I would name Warnach's objection, that it is not Plato's Eros, but "Jewish tradition and Oriental Gnosis, especially current in the heterodox Jewish world, which influences the nearer environment of the New Testament." This is precisely my opinion. When I have used the contrast between agape and eros, this has not been done primarily to bring forth the Christian meaning of agape. As Warnach very rightly points out, I have derived agape "from its source in the Biblical Kerygma, that is to say, especially from the theology of the Cross of the Apostle Paul." This I have done without any side views at other concepts of love, and this I believe is the only scientifically correct procedure. If agape had not during its later history been exposed to a constant confusion with eros, there would have been no reason for this contrast. But if one goes to the history of theology one finds there a mixing together of agape — and this precisely with the Platonizing eros-idea. It is this knot which must be untied, and this can happen only through a distinct motif analysis, where the "motifs" are gotten from the historical-empirical reality and distilled to form clear and usable structural models. That which could appear to be a difference of opinion between Warnach and me is thus actually only a difference in our approaches to the problem.

If we go to the individual points, we find there also at the same time agreements and certain disagreements — to express it in Warnach's words: "accepted in the main, though not without certain reservations." Actually we are quite agreed that there is an essential difference between agape and eros, and even to a considerable extent about where this difference is to be found.

But even if it often is more a question of differences of accent or of different explanations for a commonly acknowledged fact, yet the general difference in outlook which is in the background should not be trivialized. In brief it consists in the fact that Warnach seeks to trace everything back to certain metaphysical, ontological, or anthropological concepts, while I—just because of the tendency of these metaphysical concepts to promote the mixing of motifs and thereby a blurring of the Christian basic motif, something of which the Christian history of ideas bears eloquent witness—take a negative position with respect to such externally derived explanatory concepts. Warnach himself has expressed this matter decisively: "We must attempt to comprehend the Bible in terms of its own conceptuality" (*Agape*, p. 6). It is this principle which I should like to see yet more consistently applied. God's saving work in Christ is a sufficient foundation, sufficient also to clarify the divine love, the meaning of "agape." Here "the biblical conceptuality" suffices. No further ontological or anthropological foundations are needed.

One must always reckon with such differences in starting point and outlook. But not least in this respect Warnach's essay is an excellent example of how far one can come in mutual understanding and cooperation "across the boundaries."

Professor John M. Rist in his essay proceeds from the citation from U. von Wilamowitz-Moellendorff, which I set as a motto for the first part of *Agape and Eros*, and which reads as follows: "Although the poverty of our language is such that it in both cases says 'love,' yet these two ideas have nothing to do with one another"—and his presentation in its entirety seeks to refute this statement. The essay includes many interesting observations, but as a totality it presents a strange ambivalence, if not to say contradiction. On the one hand, Rist at the outset can say: "The Christian is fortunate enough to start from Revelation. He has some knowledge, from God himself, of what God is like. The Platonic philosopher, on the other hand, must start with his own reason, his own self and his thoughts about the world. Thus, in contrast with the Christian, the Platonist may appear egocentric. Yet this is not because of any inherent selfishness in his character or in his philosophy, but because as starting-point he has no alternative point but the self." Now my presentation deals precisely with this starting point and its implications. When Paul speaks of agape, he means thereby the love which he has experienced at the Cross of Christ. Plato had not experienced this, therefore he could not also speak of agape, and this he does not do. If one is not wholly to lose the perspective of historical reality, one must here unreservedly agree with Wilamowitz: "Of eros the one (Paul) knew nothing, of agape the other (Plato) knew nothing; they could then have learned from each other; however, given the way they were, they would also not have done so."

Rist has clearly been misled by my expression "egocentric"—and then naturally also by Paul Tillich. Now I have directly stated: "In order to remove every misunderstanding it must expressly be stated, that 'egocentric' here is not used as a value term, but as characteristic of the type." For some inexplicable reason this statement happens to have disappeared in the English translation. (It should come at the beginning of n. 3, p. 181, *Agape and Eros* [1953].) Rist therefore cannot be charged for not having seen it; yet my book in its totality bears witness to the same thing (see, for example, pp 209 f.). Plato needs no excuse or any defense because his outlook is centered as it is. "Egocentric" is not the same as "selfish," and even less does Plato's eros have anything in common with "a Freudian libido"—there I am wholly agreed with Rist, and this is the actual starting point for my interpretation of the eros concept. Generally I can accept what Rist presents from the Platonic-Neoplatonic position. It contributes to make the picture I have given more complete. On the other hand, I must reject a number of strange interpretations of New Testament passages. There is a tendency for Rist to blur out as much as possible the characteristic differences between the Greek and the biblical points of view, and thus he at last reaches this conclusion: "Just as ancient Platonism recognizes that both the Agape and the Eros motifs are present in love, so they are both recognized in the New Testament." It is difficult fully to understand the meaning of these words. The opposition to Wilamowitz has clearly had an unfavorable effect on the formulation. He made the point that two things, for which there are two Greek words, can easily be mixed together, by virtue of the fact that we have only one word in this connection. Now instead we are told that both Platonism and the New Testament have *one* concept, namely the concept of "love," and that in this concept there are included two motifs, the agape and the eros motifs—whatever this can mean. Have the motifs or the structural models, which are to make possible a structural analysis, here been conceived as separate psychological elements, which through appropriate alloying or fusion can be used for the purpose of obliterating given structures?

If one wishes a synthesis of agape and eros, one may seek to build one. There is nothing that hinders; this has happened many times before. But to maintain for this reason that Paul, in speaking of God's agape or of Christ's agape, should mean about the same as Plato means with eros, only that he develops another *aspect* or lets the accent fall at a different point—this it would seem is to force the meaning of the texts far beyond what any useful purpose requires. Why is one eager that great men should think in about the same way? Actually they think quite *differently*—and it is just in this that the richness of the history of humanity consists. Plato thought out the eros idea to its ultimate conclusion: this is a part of *his* greatness. Paul thought something wholly different. He thought out the agape idea to its conclusion: this is a part of *his* greatness. When Paul says: "God shows his agape for us in that while we were yet sinners Christ died for us" (Rom. 5:8), this has actually nothing to do with the Platonic eros. Wilamowitz is correct. He who says that it is love of the same kind, only under a different aspect, is in error. When all is said and done the little respect to the expression "egocentric" was probably downright advantageous, to the extent that it contributed toward showing the necessity of a distinct motif analysis. For only such an analysis can make it certain that while we are engaged in straining out gnats, we do not happen without noticing it to swallow camels.

That Augustine's *caritas*-doctrine represents a decisive juncture in the history of the Christian idea of love is wholly apparent. It is equally apparent that an understanding of his conception of love requires taking into consideration the double influence under which it has been formed, Neoplatonism and the New Testament, in brief, eros and agape. When an attempt is made to define more exactly the roles of these different influences, it immediately becomes more difficult to achieve full unity, especially because this does not have to do with a simple quantitative evaluation, but with recognition that a transformation has occurred.

It is a great advantage that two so distinguished Augustine scholars as John Burnaby and Rudolf Johannesson have been willing to make contributions regarding the interpretation of Augustine. Both have published penetrating investigations in this area and given important contributions to the understanding of Augustine. These two scholars deviate considerably from each other, however, in their interpretations. While Burnaby finds that I, in my presentation, have underestimated the agape element in Augustine, Johannesson's position would rather be that of certain of Augustine's ideas, which I have characterized as agape elements, could receive their adequate explanation if one recognized that the eros motif "already represents a synthesis between two kinds of love, the eros of devotion and the eros of self-assertion."

Johannesson adds: "Therefore, some traits of Caritas that Nygren considers as manifestations of Agape, may in reality proceed from the Eros of devotion."

First, with respect to Johannesson's presentation, I appreciate both what he here and in earlier writings has presented as a welcome complement to and a significant further development of what I have achieved in my Augustine investigations. Especially the distinction he makes between the eros of devotion and the eros of self-assertion is of importance for an understanding of the medieval conception of love in its dependence on Augustine, and reveals itself thereby as constituting a refining complement to the method which I have used. One should note, however, that this distinction does not in any way alter the general relationship between eros and agape. This is clear even from Johannesson's own description of Augustine's view: "It is characteristic for man as a created being that his highest value-object lies not in but beyond himself. In this sense God is man's bonum." This is perfectly correct. But at the same time it is clear that an outlook so designed cannot attain to the deepest meaning of the New Testament agape. The value perspective itself, applied to God, constitutes a hindrance—something which Johannesson more than anyone else has emphasized. From this viewpoint there is no decisive difference, whether one begins with a Platonic or an Aristotelian basic outlook. Many difficulties disappear, however, if only one constantly bears in mind the distinction between "egocentric" and "selfish," and that these mean two widely different things.

This distinction is also important in connection with Burnaby. It is correct that I have permitted the two concepts, *bonum privatum* and *bonum commune*, in Augustine to move into the background. This has happened because what is decisive is not the different specifications within the *bonum* concept, but this concept itself and its implications. As has been indicated above, the consideration of God as a "value object," as *bonum*, does not offer any approach to agape in the New Testament sense. On the other hand, I want in this connection to indicate it as an omission on my part, that with reference to agape features in Augustine I have, to be sure, indicated, but not sufficiently discussed, the significance of the idea of the church (see *Agape and Eros* (1953), pp. 455, 559). One can often in the history of Christianity make the observation that a polemical situation sharpens the awareness of that which is uniquely Christian. For Augustine such a polemical attitude has sharpened the agape element. This applies not only to the polemic against Pelagius in the doctrine of grace, but in the same way to the polemic against the Donatists in the doctrine of the church. I cannot, however, accept the—certainly tentative—viewpoints, which Burnaby presents with reference to R. Holte. Burnaby also states: "It must be admitted that the texts upon which Holte relies . . . are few in comparison with those which justify Nygren in his claim." Naturally, Stoic conceptions have also influenced Augustine, but this makes no difference with respect to the main question. In general Burnaby and I do not stand as far apart as it could appear. In that which for me is the main point, namely the question of the great main line, Burnaby can reveal a considerable measure of agreement. With respect to the question of justification, so central to the Christian concept of love, Burnaby can say: "No doubt Luther, who understands justification as acceptance by God, is nearer to St. Paul than Augustine." Finally I want to recommend Burnaby's excellent book, *Amor Dei*, as worthy of careful study. It includes much of polemic encounter with my interpretation of Augustine. But—as was said above—just the polemical attitude can contribute toward opening one's eyes to essential things, which must not be overlooked. There is much in this book which I regard as a valuable supplement.

If Augustine represents the first great juncture in the history of the Christian idea of love, insofar as he in his *caritas* doctrine, in a manner decisive for the future, bound together the eros and the agape motifs, Luther represents the other great juncture, but in the opposite direction, insofar as he more than any other disconnected the juncture, dissolved the synthesis, and in a reforming manner restored the agape motif in its purity. I am happy that this main point has been the object of a special essay and that the editor has succeeded in obtaining such an eminent Luther scholar as Professor Ernst Kinder. With genuine German thoroughness he has supported his presentation with an extensive note apparatus, which includes a great deal of what has been thought and worked out in these questions. I find myself here in the unique situation, that I can accept nearly all that Kinder himself presents as *supplementary* to my presentation, but that I am far from being able always to accept the viewpoints, which are maintained by other authors which he cites. This selection from the Luther literature gives many examples of how Luther's outlook has been pressed into thought structures foreign to it—but it would wholly burst the bounds of this presentation, if I were in detail to demonstrate this. I limit myself therefore only to accepting gratefully what Kinder himself has presented as a supplementation to my interpretation of Luther. All of it is such as should be included in a more comprehensive presentation of Luther's theology and doctrine of love. And it is all such as without constraint can be fit into the total outlook which I have presented. Actually it is all included in the Christian basic motif. What would agape be, for example, if God's law had no place in this context? This it also has in Luther's theology. But this, on the other hand, does not change the fact that love, and not law, is the actual basic motif.

There is a difficulty which easily arises when there is discussion of "basic motifs," that one tends to think that the basic motif is the whole and excludes all other elements. No, the basic motif is in this respect not exclusive, but inclusive. It is, to be sure, exclusive over against competing basic motifs, but inclusive with respect to the different elements in the religious life. Let me illustrate the function of the basic motif with the help of a metaphor. It is as when one sets a signature before a series of notes, a melody. If one changes the signature, the whole melody is changed, but this does not mean that the individual notes are taken away; they remain, but they receive another meaning. The law remains, but it receives a different meaning, when it is placed under agape's basic motif as compared to when it is placed under nomos' basic motif. Therefore, when Kinder says that Luther brings together several different religious motifs (power, justice, love) in a tense "dynamic synthesis," which centers on the motif of love, this is just the same as what I have intended—only that I prefer to avoid the term "motif" for these elements, since it easily can be confused with "basic motif." That all of these elements are present, but are concentrated on, ordered under, and receive their character from agape, is what is meant by asserting that this is the "basic motif." If these elements were instead ordered under "law" or under "power," as the basic motif, they would receive a wholly different meaning—but then also no one would any longer in this recognize Luther's outlook.

Systematic Theology

The two tasks which have been assigned for this collection of essays—that they are to provide an interpretation, and that they are to represent a critical stance—generally interpenetrate each other to such an extent that it is difficult to say where the one begins and the other ends. As a rule this does not cause any difficulty. When the question now becomes systematic theology, however, it is of the greatest importance to be able to proceed from a clear and correct interpretation. My understanding of the task of systematic theology and the method required for its accomplishment differs so essentially from approaches that have been generally accepted, that if one were, without such interpretation, to go directly to the traditional questions, one would fall into helpless confusion.

Professor Philip S. Watson, whom I have to thank for perfect translation into English of several of my works, above all *Agape and Eros*, has in his essay given an interpretation of my position which is at the same time easily grasped and in every respect adequate and authentic. At no point have I found occasion to insert a question mark. Here there is nothing to add and nothing to subtract. I can therefore immediately go over to his critical observations. Both of the points he raises have to do with important problems, which I have dealt with in a very scant manner.

The first problem could be called *the problem of translation*. When one follows strictly a scientific line, one must be prepared for the fact that many who approach the matter from another starting point have questions, which do not all correspond with the orientation which one has argued is the only meaningful one. It is an awkward situation, when one becomes misunderstood, as if a statement made should provide an answer to a wholly different question from the one raised—through which the statement then also receives a wholly different meaning from the one intended. What one in such a situation ought to do is, so to speak, to translate what one says into the language of the other, to the extent that this is possible. In this case I have rather done too little than too much. Often I have neglected to discuss misunderstandings that were near at hand, and this in order to avoid deviation from my own line of thought, and in the confidence that the context would sufficiently provide the right meaning. This omission thus does not mean that I underestimate the importance of "the problem of translation." On the contrary I agree wholly with Watson's observation.

Also the other reminder, that the question of "the truth of Christianity" simply must not be ignored, is altogether in order. The affirmation that no scientific proof can be given for the truth of Christianity (just as no scientific proof can be given that it is not true) must not be taken to mean that the Christian may be indifferent with respect to the question of truth, or that he should lack arguments for his faith. The

Christian has the very strongest arguments—only they are not of the scientific type. But what use would he make of arguments of this latter type? He does not build his faith on any historical or natural scientific or quasi-philosophical theories! Here is a broad field for further cultivation. Unfortunately, I have had much too little occasion to deal with these problems, which does not mean that I depreciate the task or deny its pressing necessity. Also here I wholly agree with Watson's observation.

The point of departure for Professor Nels Ferré's essay is a clear affirmation of agape as the Christian basic motif and in the main an acceptance of the definition of its meaning which I have given: "Agape as the fundamental motif of Christian faith thus possesses both historical and systematic validity." Thereby every form of theology which has its basis in a "philosophy of being" or "philosophy of process" is rejected. Ferré's essay brings to lively remembrance the first time I met him, when for him, the battle was hot between agape and the philosophy of process. It became agape which gained the victory. And since this, Ferré has devoted all his energies to maintain agape and in every way draw out the implications of this, so that his theology can rightly be characterized as a "Theology of Agape." It is thus in his very own domain that he moves in this essay. The starting point is agape as "God-centered" and "Christ-centered," as creative, outgoing agape, or, in order to use yet another expressive formulation of Ferré's, "It centers in God and is focussed in the other." In all this we are wholly agreed.

To this Ferré now adds his critique, which is that I never made the fullest possible use of agape, and that the implications to a much higher degree should be drawn theologically, methodologically, and practically. Now I am the first to acknowledge how limited and fragmentary my presentation of agape is. Who would be able to exhaust its richness or even suggest all of its implications, which extend to every point of the Christian faith and the Christian life? Here I can make Ferré's words my own: "Generations of scholars are needed to carry through these beginnings of the implications of agape for a fuller Christian theology." And I naturally subscribe without reservation to the statement that follows: "In any case, Nygren has not sufficiently developed the Christian understanding of nature or of man in terms of agape."

The reason for this limitation is not, however, the one that Ferré surmises, namely, that it should be due to a limiting traditionalistic loyalty to established dogma rather than to the inner requirement of agape. The limitation has wholly different reasons. I have always found that altogether too little attention is given to the very starting point of an argument. It is *there* that the clarification must begin. But this often means that too little is done with respect to the detailed development of the argument. Here one can only hope for the contributions of fellow workers and subsequent generations. Without this every beginning remains a torso. But one thing more: If without sufficient clarification at the center one devotes oneself to drawing implications in various directions, one can all too easily find oneself engaged in doubtful metaphysical speculations. It is this which has hindered me from taking as my starting point "the inner requirement of agape." For only a slight displacement at the center is sufficient for the implications to become doubtful or erroneous. This has to do with how strict the requirements are which one is to place on a science, in this case the theological science. There is nothing of which I am more afraid than to draw tempting as well as bold conclusions, leaving the material far behind. Upon closer examination the conclusions often reveal themselves to be premature. This is the reason for my self-chosen limitation.

Ethics

We have now come to the problem of ethics. Here Professor Thor Hall has given an excellent presentation of the especially intricate and difficultly mastered questions which have to do with the problem of philosophical ethics. Whoever would have a certain and dependable view of my understanding of these questions will receive it from Thor Hall. Only at one point must a correction occur. This is essential because it has to do with the fundamental relationship between philosophical and Christian ethics, and unclarity at this point can have far-reaching implications for the understanding of the whole. The point in question is marked by the statement: "Nygren suggests, in fact, that the question whether Christian ethics is oriented around aim or act or attitude is *a redundant one*." And further: "Nygren has apparently carried the philosophical assumptions . . . over into his theological considerations. As a consequence, he can settle the question of the nature of Christian ethics by logical definition. Theology, including Christian ethics, obviously does not need to go to the given experiential and historic materials." Now this is precisely the complete opposite of my understanding, the complete opposite of what I have constantly said. What can have happened? Professor Hall's interpretation is otherwise extraordinarily dependable. Filled with ill forebodings I began to suspect that perhaps an error of translation had played a role in causing this distortion. In this connection I remembered a discussion which I had with Professor Ferré decades ago. He cited one of my ideas which I refused to acknowledge as my own. But so it stands plain and clear in *Agape and Eros*, Ferré replied. Upon closer examination it became apparent that an error in translation had crept into G. Hebert's translation of 1932. In this case, however, I found no such error. Instead Hall has happened in reading the text to make a small error, but an error extremely misleading in its consequences. A position *which I argue against* has been conceived as if it were my own position. In the passage in question I *reject* the notion that the meaning of Christianity could be derived from any philosophical deliberations, and I maintain instead that this question "must be decided in a theological context. We must therefore *let Christianity itself answer the question*"—thus it stands plainly in the lines immediately after the words cited by Hall. *If* I had really reasoned as Hall has conceived it—yes, then I very well understand his words: "The upshot of what is said here could constitute some rather devastating criticisms against Nygren's use of the scientific method." But now, as has been indicated, the whole depends upon a simple erroneous reading. As far as Hall is concerned the error that has been made, however, has not had such "devastating" effects. It means only that a few pages in his essay become confused. The splinter in the eye, which the erroneous reading has left, has meant that he cannot see clearly. It is a pity only that this should happen to that part which was to present my understanding of the meaning of the Christian ethic.

I have given some thought to whether there could be any factual problem which could lie near to this erroneous reading, and have thereby noticed the strange fact, that Christianity actually can have influenced *the very manner in which we put the ethical question*. In *Agape and Eros* I have very briefly called attention to this matter: "It is not difficult to see how *the meaning of the ethical question* has changed in the course of history. . . . For this change the ethical contribution of Christianity is chiefly responsible." Now according to our usual way of thinking the ethical *question* should remain what it is irrespective of Christianity, to which it would simply give its characteristic *answer*. How, then, could Christianity possibly have altered the way of putting the question? In and of itself there is nothing unreasonable about the fact that the question should to some extent be modified through empirical circumstances. Sometimes it has been asked if the theory of relativity does not require a revision of the conception of space and time and of the category of causality. Even if this should not be required, one is led to think that the great revolution which Christianity represents, and its nearly two thousand year influence on our modes of thought, also could have brought about certain shifts in the very manner of putting the ethical question. This would in such a case be an example of how the boundary between philosophy and Christianity has been crossed. But *if* this should be a case of a "crossing of the boundary," then in this instance it would be Christianity which has moved into the domain of philosophy, and not the contrary. What the case at this point is, can only be determined empirically. But a crossing of the boundary of this kind still does not mean any confusion between question and answer, between category and basic motif. In any case the questions which are connected with this whole matter are both complicated and interesting.

I feel honored that Professor Charles W. Kegley, the editor himself, has been willing to contribute an essay, and doubly honored in that he has had such a personal interest that he has written this essay despite the difficulties he encountered, in that several of my most important publications in ethics are to be found only in Swedish and thus were not directly available to him. I anticipated therefore that the essay would contain more general questions, which were only partially connected with my works. The more I read of Professor Kegley's essay, however, the more I became impressed by his questions and astonished that they in large part were just such questions as occupied me in my book, *Filosofisk och kristen etik* (1923). That his questions of the year 1969 and my questions and answers of the year 1923 correspond so well, is to a high degree encouraging. It shows more than anything else that they actually are essential questions and questions which give expression to the nature of the problems involved. An explanation for this correspondence naturally lies in the fact to which Kegley by way of introduction referred, namely that questions turning on the relation between morality and religion have come to the fore, and that the requirement of language analysis makes necessary a clarification of this relation. Now it was just problems of this kind which were the subject of my work, "Philosophical and Christian Ethics," and it was confusion with respect to these things which forced me to make a more thoroughgoing analysis. I must all the more regret that this work was never translated into English, in that its statement of the problem corresponds to such a high degree to the constellation of problems which has been sketched by Professor Kegley. Here it will only be possible briefly to refer to a few of the problems presented.

The difficulties encountered here are due chiefly to unclarity with respect to the scientific task of ethics. The purely philosophical (scientific philosophical) ethics' task is to clarify the *meaning* of the ethical judgment, or—as one now prefers to express it—its logical status. This is a genuine scientific and a genuine philosophical question. On the other hand, no philosophy and no science can express itself with respect to what *ought* ethically to be valued. The task of science is to understand and to describe, not to evaluate. The matter is complicated, however, in that a certain activity which goes under the name of philosophy, namely metaphysics (in this case metaphysical ethics), does claim to be able to set up objective, scientific norms for the ethical life and to give rules for ethical behavior. That one sets up ethical norms is not to be criticized. But that one claims this to be science—this is confusion, and against this philosophy must defend itself. In relation to the different ethical norms which have been set up in various places, science has the task to understand them, understand them as they have been intended, and present their meaning and inner coherence. Here theological ethics has *its* task: to seek to understand and present the ethical evaluation and pattern of behavior bound up with the Christian faith. He who believes in that God who is agape, and who has revealed his agape to us through Christ's giving of himself, has thereby received something new to reckon with, which cannot help but influence his basic ethical evaluation. It is in this way that agape becomes decisive for Christian ethics.

From the foregoing it follows, in part that it is difficult to put my understanding of ethics in any scheme of classification (e.g., Frankena's), in part because I cannot easily accept the characterization "agapism." This leads to the idea that theological ethics should set up an ethical principle or norm, while instead it only describes what the role and the implications of the Christian faith in God as agape are for the ethical life. All that belongs to human experience contributes toward creating our norm of evaluation. When the Christian faith in God as love is brought into this context, it can, as has been indicated, not help but influence the ethical evaluation—how could it possibly be otherwise! But this does not mean that the ethical evaluation is replaced by a religious evaluation, but that the ethical evaluation—just as *ethical* —is widened. Both religion and ethics retain their *autonomy*. But thereby also disappears the basis for the old poser: Is the good good because God wills it, or does God will it because it is good? This question gets its power from the fact that it does not reckon with the autonomy of the religious and the ethical, but it seeks to derive the one from the other. And it loses its power when one reckons with their autonomy. But thereby also a number of other things disappear: 1] any idea that there could be no genuine ethic other than on a religious (Christian) basis; 2] every claim for superiority—"graciously" or "less graciously"—of the religious (Christian) ethic over a nonreligious ethic; and 3] every presumptuous claim that the Christian should personally stand at a higher ethical level than the non-Christian; the contrary can often be the case—something which has nothing to do with the ethical outlook one has embraced. But 4] there disappears no less from the "philosophical" (i.e., pseudophilosophical) side the narrow-minded claim one sometimes encounters that a given philosopher's subjective evaluations should be solidly based on "reason." Before such pretentions, one can only call for more clarity of thought and greater moral humility.

Only a few of the questions presented have been answered, but what has been said should be sufficient to indicate in what direction even the answers to the others are to be found.

Cultural and Ecumenical Concerns

The two last essays are devoted, on the one hand, to "The Problem of Culture," and, on the other hand, to the church, issuing in "The Ecumenical Problem."

It is an extraordinarily difficult problem which Professor Søren Holm has been given to discuss. The difficulty is connected in part with the fact that I have nowhere given a comprehensive presentation of the problem of culture, in part in the fact that it, in accord with the general disposition of my investigations, must be a discussion on two levels, both the religio-philosophical and the theological. On the former level there is the general problem, "Religion and Culture," on the latter the concrete problem, "Christianity and Culture." In order to get any grasp at all on these widely branched-out problems, Holm must sweep over the whole field and thus take up the question of the different domains of experience or contexts of meaning, as well as the question of the motif contexts.

In philosophy of religion there is an intimate connection between religion and culture, but this connection occurs—it is well to notice—

always through the ultimate presuppositions of religion and the several cultural forms. Only in this way can the autonomy of religion, as well as that of the several cultural forms, be preserved. None exists apart from the other, but none is the same as the other. Each and every one stands under its *own* basic category, but the basic categories mutually condition each other. When Holm in this connection maintains "that religion cannot have any content which is not justified through one of the three autonomous forms of culture, viz., science, morals, and art," I can therefore not follow him. For in the final analysis this means a denial of the autonomy of religion, but this can only have as a consequence that the "cultural forms" become compromised. What kind of science would it be which presumed to "justify" the content of religion? In any case it would not be a science in any of the accepted meanings of this term.

When "the problem of culture" is brought over to the theological domain, it receives a wholly concrete content. During its almost two-thousand-year history the Christian faith has entered into relationship and interaction with widely differing cultures. This is inescapable and of the greatest significance for both parties. The risk is only that in this way a religious syncretism can creep in, which robs the Christian faith of its meaning and power. It is in this connection, but also only in this connection, that I have contrasted Christianity and idealism, in the sense that the latter, in addition to its philosophical meaning, has often also wanted to function as a surrogate of religion. It is to set up a defense against this that I have said yes to "cultural synthesis" and *no* to "religious synthesis," however difficult it may be to maintain this distinction concretely.

To this only one remark is to be added. When I have stated that God's agape is not motivated by man's greater or lesser value, this does not however mean that I "represent an anthropology which denies human value as such." We are no doubt all agreed that man has an infinite and irreplaceable cultural value—but it isn't this that calls forth God's love! It isn't these questions which we discuss when we seek to explain the meaning of God's agape and Christ's saving work!

If Professor Holm had a sparse and scattered material to work with, Professor Vilmos Vajta has had much more abundant material for his essay about the church and the ecumenical problem. With remarkable exactitude and care he has tracked down and gathered his material from the most widely scattered directions and from it formed a unified picture.

Vajta begins with an observation which is both correct and important. He points out that my student years in Lund came just during the years when the great church debate, "folk church—free church," was in full swing in Sweden, but that this debate, surprisingly enough, did not catch my interest or come to characterize my theological orientation. The explanation is not at all to be found, however, in any individualistic tendency. My being engaged at the time with other, religio-philosophical problems can explain this to some extent, but the actual explanation is even more the fact that this debate presupposed alternatives, which for me seemed to be false. What I missed above all was the concept, central for the New Testament, of the church as "the body of Christ." I was aware of this point of orientation, but I was not yet prepared to take up the question in its totality. In the philosophy of religion the question of the church could not find any place, since the church is a purely theological concept. Nor did the problem "Eros and Agape" offer the suitable starting point for an analysis of the concept of the church. Therefore it had to wait—although the problem was constantly before me through my participation in ecumenical discussions during this period.

The actual situation is hardly correctly described, therefore, if one speaks of "an ecclesiological vacuum." Vajta has more aptly expressed the matter when he says, "Nygren's theology in his first period was in principle open to take up the concept of the church," or, "he already has certain ideas implicitly available." Just the word "implicitly" states what is essential. For the openness in principle to take up the concept of the church depended on the fact that it from the very beginning (see, "Intellectual Autobiography," *Initium*) "implicitly" was there. When Vajta inquires about which *new* theological influence made itself felt, the answer is that it was the *old*, the original. What was earlier present "implicitly," became now the object of theological explication.

It now remains only to say a word about that which constitutes Vajta's main objection to my understanding of the church and the ecumenical question. It has to do with the Pauline idea of Adam-Christ in Rom. 5, and its possible connection with the idea of Christ as the head of the church. According to Vajta there is here no connection. Instead, he holds that one must sharply distinguish between Christ as Lord and Christ as head. Christ is the Lord of all, but only the *church's head*. This distinction, which is often encountered in the ecumenical discussion, I have of course had opportunity to examine. But it has shown itself to lack biblical foundation and legitimation. *It is not possible exegetically to maintain the desired distinction between Lord and head.* Christ is the head of the church, but also its Lord. And Christ is the Lord of all, but also its head. Here Col. 2:10 (cf. 1:15 ff. and Eph. 1:20–23) gives its clear witness: Christ has been placed by God as *head over all things.* This Christ, who thus is head over all things, God has now given to the church as its head. If we then go to Rom. 5, we find that this chapter actually has to do with Adam as head of the old humanity and Christ as head of the new humanity. Now it is true, that only the church is the body of Christ. But from this one may not draw the conclusion that Christ should therefore be the head only of the church. The dialectic here encountered I have dealt with more fully in an essay, "Christ the Head of the Church," in "The Rasmussen Festschrift" [3] where I have shown that "the juxtaposition, or contraposition, of 'head' and 'Lord' is only a rationalization which does not permit the biblical dialectic of the concept 'head' to come into its own." [4] In view of this discussion I can therefore let the suggestions that have been made suffice.

If one only takes seriously the facts that have been pointed out, many of the traditional difficulties both in the understanding of the church and the ecumenical encounter disappear. Thus there is no place, for example, for such a pseudoconcept as *corpus Christianum.* And – not of least importance – the church's relationship to the world and its task in the world comes forth in a clearer and more biblically determined light.

WE STAND at the end of the Reply. It began with the declaration that it is in the philosophy of religion that the great decisions are made. This is true with respect to the *scientific* (theological and religio-philosophical) discussion of religion and the Christian faith. Here muddled thinking has brought about much confusion, which can only be removed through philosophical-methodological clarification.

But in order that the expression *the great decisions* shall not give occasion to renewed confusion, and in order that the emphasis on the "scientific" task shall not give occasion to misinterpretation in the direction of "scientism," as if there should not exist any other manner of asking and answering than that of science, it is proper that this reply close with a personal word: *That which is most decisive is* – to use a New Testament expression – "to gain Christ and be found in him." This is that which is ultimately decisive. This is τὸ ὑπερέχον.

BIBLIOGRAPHY/NOTES/INDEX

BIBLIOGRAPHY OF THE PUBLICATIONS

OF ANDERS NYGREN TO 1970 [*]

Ulrich E. Mack

Abbreviations Used

STK	– *Svensk Teologisk Kvartalskrift*, Lund, Sweden
SU	– *Svensk Uppslagsbok*, Malmö, Sweden
SKD	– *Svenska Kyrkans Diakonistyrelses*, Bokförlag
Kristendomen o.v.t.	– *Kristendomen och vår tid*, Lund, Sweden
ZsystTh	– *Zeischrift für systematische Theologie*, hrsg. von C. Stange, Verlag Bertelsmann, Gütersloh
NZsystTh	– *Neue Zeitschrift für systematische Theologie, und Religionsphilosphie*, hrsg. von P. Althaus, L. Landgrebe, G. Nygren C. H. Ratschow, W. Trillhass, Verlag Alfred Töpelmann, Berlin
ThLZ	– *Theologische Literaturzeitung.* Monatsschrift für das gesamte Gebiet der Theologie und Religionswissenschaft, begründet von E. Schürer und A. von Harnack, Leipzig/Berlin
NTT	– *Norsk Teologisk Tidskrift*, Oslo, Norway
WKL	– *Weltkirchenlexikon*, Handbuch der Oecumene hrsg. von F. H. Littell and H. H. Walz, Stuttgart

Other Periodicals

Nordisk Teologisk Uppslagsbok, Lund, Sweden
Nordisk Familjebok, Stockholm, Sweden
Kirkeleksikon for Norden, Copenhagen, Denmark
Vår Lösen, Uppsala, Sweden

---

[*] This bibliography is based on a dissertation by Dr. Mack, submitted to Heidelberg University, 1964, entitled, "Motivforschung als Theologische Methode."

1918

1 "Den metafysiska filosofiens betydelse för religionsvetenskapen," in: *Bibelforskaren*, 35. årg. 1918, S. 131–57.

1919

2 "Det religionsfilosofiska grundproblemet," I–II, in: *Bibelforskaren*, 36. årg. 1919, S. 290–313.

1921

3 "Det religionsfilosofiska grundproblemet," III–IV, in: *Bibelforskaren*, 38. årg. 1921, S. 11–39.
4 "Det religionsfilosofiska grundproblemet," V–VIII, in: *Bibelforskaren*, 38. årg. 1921, S. 86–103.
5 *Religiöst a priori—dess filosofiska förutsättningar och teologiska konsekvenser*, Lund: Gleerupska Universitetsbokhandeln, 1921.
6 *Det religionsfilosofiska grundproblemet*, Lund: Gleerupska Universitetsbokhandeln, 1921 (special printing from "Bibelforskaren" 1919/21).

1922

7 *Dogmatikens vetenskapliga grundläggning med särskild hänsyn till den Kant-Schleiermacherska problemställningen*, Lund: C. W. K. Gleerup and Leipzig: Otto Harrassowitz, 1922, Lund Univ.:s årsskrift, N. F., afd. 1, Vol. 17, No. 8.
8 *Die Gültigkeit der religiösen Erfahrung*. Gütersloh: C. Bertelsmann 1922, Studien des apologetischen Seminars in Wernigerode, H. 8 (very shortened German treatment of 5).
9 *Det bestående i kristendomen*, Stockholm: Sveriges Kristliga Studentörelses Förlag, 1922, 2nd ed., 1956, Religionsvetenskapliga skrifter, 8.
10 "Till frågan om teologiens objektivitet," in: *Teologiska studier tillägnade E. Stave*, Uppsala: Almquist and Wiksell, 1922, S. 170–83 (contained in *Filosofi och motivforskning*, 1940, with the title "Om teologiens objektivitet," a.a.O., S. 168–86).
11 "Den religionsfilosofiska apriorifrågan" Reply, in: *Kristendomen och vår tid.*, 17. årg. 1922, S. 61–72.
12 "Är evighetskategorien en religiös kategori?," in: *Kristendomen och vår tid*, 17. årg. 1922, S. 220–41.

1923

13 "Religionen såsom 'Anschauung des Universums' hos Schleiermacher," in: *Studier tillägnade Magnus Pfannenstill*, Lund 1923, S. 132–39 (contained in *Filosofi och motivforskning* [=FM], 1940, S. 197–207).
14 *Filosofisk och kristen etik*, Lund: C. W. K. Gleerup and Leipzig: Otto Harrassowitz, 1923, 2nd ed., 1932, Lund Univ:s årsskrift, N. F. Afd. 1, Vol. 18, No. 18.

15 "Till frågan om den transcendentala metodens användbarhet imom religionsfilosofien," in: *Bibelforskaren*, 40. årg. 1923, S. 273–93.

1924

16 "Evangelisk och katolsk livstyp," in: *Kristendomen och vår tid*, 19. årg. 1924, S. 5–14 (contained in *Religiositet och kristendom*, 1926, S. 84 ff.).
17 "Kant och den kristna etiken," in: *Kristendomen och vår tid*. 19. årg. S. 159–79 (contained in *Etiska grundfrågor*, 1926, S. 98 ff.).
18 "Kant und die christliche Ethik," in: *ZsystTh*, 1. Jahrg. 1924, S. 679–99 (translation of 17).
19 "Biedermann," in: *Nordisk Familjebok*, 3. Aufl. Vol. 3, 1923 f.
20 "Biel," in: *Nordisk Familjebok*, 3. Aufl., Vol. 3, 1923 f.
21 "Kristendomens väsen i missionens belysning," in: *Den evangeliska missionen*, 78. årg. 1924, S. 169–70.

1925

22 "Det etiska omdömets ajälvständighet," in: *STK*, 1. årg. 1925, S. 38–60 (published also in *Etiska grundfrågor*, 1926, S. 5 ff., similarly in German, see 36).
23 "Ett standardverk inom Lutherforskningen" (review of K. Holl: *Gesammelte Aufsätze zur Kirchengeschichte*, I. Luther, 2. u. 3. Aufl., Tübingen, 1923), in: *STK* 1. årg. 1925, S. 99–107.
24 "Några reflexioner till Den allmänneliga kristna tron" (review of G. Aulén: *Den allmänneliga kristna tron*, 2. rev. Aufl.), in: *STK*, 1. årg. 1925, S. 182–97.
25 "Den fortgáende uppenbarelsen," in: *Kristendomen och vår tid*, 20. årg. 1925, S. 262–70.
26 "Colani," in: *Nordisk Familjebok*, 3. Aufl., Bd. 4, 1925.
27 "Kristendomen och den socialt-ekonomiska utvecklingen" (review of A. Runestam: *Kristendomen och den materiella nutidskulturen*, Stockholm, 1924) in: *STK*, 1. årg. 1925, S. 401–8.
28 "Ethische Literatur in Schweden," in: *Literarische Berichte aus dem Gebiete der Philosophie*, Erfurt 1925, Heft 5, S. 28–31.

1926

29 "Religionen såsom etisk drivkraft. Några principiella synpunkter," in: *Till Ärkebiskop Söderbloms sextioársdag, Stockholm, SKD* 1926, S. 410–19 (contained in *Etiska grundfrågor*, 1926, S. 84 ff).
30 "Det godas begrepp enligt evangelisk och katolsk áskådning," in: *STK*, 2. årg. 1926, S. 20–45 (contained in *Etiska grundfrågor*, 1926, S. 39 ff.; also in German translation in *ZsytTh* 1928, see 48).
31 Review of P. Marstrander: *Det teologiske studium*, Oslo, 1925, in: *STK*, 2. årg. 1926, S. 86–89.
32 "Wilhelm Wundt," in: *Kirkeleksikon for Norden*, 1926.
33 *Religiositet och kristendom*, Stockholm: Lindblads Förlag, 1926 (a collection and revision of four essays, the fourth of which appeared earlier as 16).
34 *Etiska grundfrågor*, Stockholm: Sveriges Kristliga Studentrörelses

Förlag, 1926 (a collection of essays, of which the first four were previously published as independent essays; see 17, 22, 29, 30; the last two sections may be found previously in *Filosofisk och kristen Etik*, 1923).

35 "Odölighetsproblemet" (collected review of eight works on the theme of the immortality of the soul by H. Scholz, H. Münsterberg, A. Ahlberg, C. Stange [3] and P. Althaus [2]), in: *STK*, 2. årg. 1926, S. 290–300.
36 "Die Selbständigkeit der ethischen Beurteilung," in: *ZsytTh*, 4. Jahrg. 1926–27, S. 211–34 (translation of 22).
37 "Den sociala samhällssynen och Guds rike," in: *Vår Lösen*, 17. årg. 1926, S. 251–55.
38 "Dansk systematisk teologi" (collected review of four Danish works by E. Geismar, P. Brodersen, H. Fuglsang-Damgaard and N. H. Søe,), in: *STK*, 2. årg. 1926, S. 385–94.

1927

39 "Söka och finna. Några reflexioner till Kant-tolkningen," in: *Festskrift tillägnad Hans Larsson*, Stockholm: Bonnier, 1927, S. 215–23 (contained in *Filosofi och motivforskning*, 1940, S. 187 ff.).
40 "Friedrich Ueberweg," in: *Kirkeleksikon for Norden*, 1927.
41 "Alexander von Oettingen," in: *Kirkeleksikon for Norden*, 1927.
42 "Egoism och religion," in: *STK*, 3. årg. 1927, S. 129–50 (contained in *Urkristendom och reformation*, 1932, S. 82–115, also in German translation in *ZsytTh* 1929/30; see 64).
43 "Religionen, andelivets konvergenspunkt," in: *Religionshistoriska studier tillägnade E. Lehmann*, Lund: C. W. K. Gleerup, 1927, S. 142–51.
44 "J. Ordings etik" (review), in: *NTT*, S. 130–34.
45 Review of Johannes Ording, *Kristelig etik*, Oslo, 1927, in: *STK*, 3. årg., S. 272–74.

1928

46 "Till den nyaste religionsfilosofiska litteraturen" (collected review of 15 works on Religious Philosophy by Bauch, Adolph, Tillich, Stavenhagen, P. Hoffmann, Rosenquist, Wobbermin, E. Brunner [2], Przywara [2], Wunderle, Geyser [2] and Hessen), in: *STK*, 4. årg. 1928, S. 52–74.
47 Karl Holl: *Luthers etiska åskådning: Översättning jämte förord av Anders Nygren*, Stockholm, 1928.
48 "Der Begriff des Guten nach evangelischer und katholischer Anschauung," in: *ZsytTh*, 5. Jahrg. 1928, S. 608–42 (translation of 30).
49 "Henri Bergson," in: *Kirkeleksikon for Norden*, 1928.
50 "Religionens sanningsfråga och religionsvetenskapen," in: *STK*, 4. årg. 1928, S. 198–206.
51 "Hur är filosofi som vetenskap möjlig?" in: *Festskrift tillägnad Axel Hägerström*, Uppsala: Almquist and Wiksell, 1928, S. 71–83 (contained in *Filosofi och motivforskning*, 1940, S. 9 ff.).
52 "Till förståelsen av Jesu liknelser," in: *STK*, 4. årg. 1928, S. 217–36 (contained in *Urkristendom och reformation*, 1932, with the title "Till tolkningen av Jesu liknelser," a.a.O., S. 51 ff.; appeared also

as "Das Zeugnis der Gleichnisse" in *Eros und Agape*, 2. Aufl. 1954,
S. 49 ff.).

53 "Är den religiösa sanningsfrågen ett vetenskapligt problem eller icke?"
in: *STK* 4. årg. 1928, 308–12.

54 " 'Religieusiteit' en Christendom," in: *Stemmen des Tijds. Maandblad
voor Christendom en cultuur*, Zestiende Jaargang, 1928, S. 600–620.

55 "Christentum und Religion," in: *Allgemeine evangelisch-lutherische
Kirchenzeitung*, 61. Jahrg. 1928, S. 1048–50, 1072–77.

56 *Het blijvende in het Christendom;* Uit het Zweedsch door J. Henzel
Amsterdam: H. J. Paris, 1928 (translation of 9).

57 *Religieusiteit en Christendom;* Uit het Zweedsch door J. Henzel Zeist:
G. J. A. Ruys' U-M, 1928 (translation of 33).

1929

58 "Kristendomen, frälsningens religion," in: *Nordiskt Missionsarbete*,
Helsingfors, 1929, S. 6–18.

59 "En landvinning för dogmatiken" (review of P. Althaus: *De yttersta
tingen*, 3. uppl., Uppsala, 1928), in: *STK*, 5. årg. 1929, S. 86–88.

60 "Tvenne Romarebrevs-Kommentarer" (review of Thomas Aquinas:
Kommentar zum Römerbrief, translation and introduction by H.
Fansel, Freiburg; and *M. Luther: Vorlesungen über den Römerbrief
1515/16*, trans. E. Ellwein, München, 1927), in: *STK*, 5. årg. 1929, S.
88–89.

61 Review of E. Åkesson: *Idéernas brottning*, Stockholm, 1928, in: *STK*
5. årg. 1929, S. 90–93.

62 "Christentum und Religion," in: *Luthers Kirche im Leben der Gegenwart*, Leipzig: Dorffling & France 1929, S. 131–44.

63 "Eros und Agape, Eine Skizze zur Ideengeschichte des Christentums,"
in: *ZsystTh*, 6. Jahrg. 1929, S. 690–733.

64 "Egoismus und Religion," in: *ZsystTh*, 7. Jahrg. 1929/30. S. 312–36
(translation of 42).

65 "Den kristna kärlekstanken hos Augustinus," in: *STK*, 5. årg. 1929, S.
203–28.

66 Review of P. Althaus: *Communio sanctorum, Die Gemeinde im
lutherischen Kirchengedanken*. I. Luther. München, 1929, in: *STK*,
5. årg. 1929, S. 291–96.

67 "Die Bedeutung Luthers für den christlichen Liebesgedanken," in:
Luther-Jahrbuch, XI, Jahrg. 1929, S. 87–133.

1930

68 Review of P. Althaus: *Communio sanctorum, Die Gemeinde im
lutherischen Kirchengedanken*. I. Luther. München, 1929, in: *THLZ*,
55. Jahrg. 1930, No. 2, Sp. 41–44 (translation of 66).

69 "Den kristna kärlekstanken hos Luther," in: *STK*. 6. årg. 1930, S. 3–31.

70 "Die kopernikanische Umwälzung Luthers," in: *Zeitwende*, 6. Jahrg.
1930, S. 357–65 (contained in *Urkristendom och reformation*, 1932,
S. 116 ff., as "Luthers kopernikanska omvälvning," similarly in *Eros
und Agape*, 2. Aufl. 1954, S. 538 ff. under the above-mentioned title).

71 "Eros och caritas" (review of H. Scholz: *Eros und Caritas*, Halle,
1929), in: *STK*, 6. årg. 1930, S. 205–8.

72 *Den kristna kärlekstanken genom tiderna. Eros och Agape* Första

delen, *SKD*, 1930, 2nd ed., 1938, 3rd ed., 1947, 4th ed., 1956, 5th ed., 1966.

73 *Eros und Agape. Gestaltwandlungen der christlichen Liebe, Erster Teil*, Gütersloh: G. Bertelsmann, 1930 (Studien des apologetischen Seminars Wernigerode, Heft 28) 2nd ed., Berlin: Evang, Verlagsanstalt, 1955 (translation of 72).

74 "Augustinus, Ett 1500—årsminne," in: *STK*, 6. årg. 1930, S. 223-30.

75 "Några reflexioner till problemet 'Urkristendom och religionschistoria' i anslutning till K. Holls framställning och R. Bultmanns kritik," in: *STK* 6. årg. 1930, S. 325-38 (contained in *Urkistendom och reformation*, 1932, S. 31 ff.).

76 "Tva nordiska arbeten i religionsfilosofi" (review of E. Geismar: *Religionsfilosofi*, 2. Aufl., Kopenhagen, 1930, also Chr. Ihlen: *Systematisk teologi i omriss*, Oslo, 1927), in: *STK*, 6. årg. 1930, S. 396-403.

1931

77 "Eros und Caritas" (review of H. Scholz: *Eros und Caritas*, Halle, 1929), in: *ThLZ*, 56. Jahrg. 1931, No. 2, Sp. 40-42 (translation of 71).

78 "Etik och verklighet" (review of Runestam: *Kärlek, tro, efterfoljd*, 1931), in: *STK*, 7. årg. 1931, S. 203-8.

79 "Eros och agape; ett beriktigande," in: *Vår Lösen*, 22. årg. 1931, S. 119-20.

80 "G. G. Rosenquiet såsom systematiker. Några minnesord," in: *Finsk teologisk tidsskrift*, 36. årg. 1931, S. 126-30.

81 "Origenes," in: *Nordisk Familjebok*, 3. uppl., 1931.

82 "Litteratur till etikens historia" (collected review of works by O. Dittrich [2], E. Howald, A. Dempf and T. Litt), in: *STK*, 7. årg. 1931, S. 290-97.

83 "Hellas och kristendomen" (review of G. Rudberg: *Hellas och Nya Testamentet*, Uppsala, 1939, also *Esaias Tegnér, Humanisten och hellenen*, Stockholm, 1930), in: *STK*, 7. årg. 1931, S. 298-303.

84 "Försoningens ord," in: *Ordet och tron, Till Einar Billing på hans sextioårsdag*, Stockholm: *SKD*, 1931, S. 108-23.

85 "Adolf Phalén," in: *STK*, 7. årg. 1931, S. 322-27.

1932

86 "En renässansteolog" (review of W. Dress: *Die Mystik des Marsilio Ficino*, Berlin/Leipzig, 1929), in: *STK*, 8. årg. 1932, S. 82-85.

87 "Syntes eller reformation? Till orientering i det närvarande andliga läget," in: *STK*, 8. årg. 1932, S. 103-20 (contained in *Urkristendom och reformation*, 1932, S. 145 ff., also as "Synthese oder Reformation" in *ZsystTh* 1933 [see 106], and as "Synthese und Reformation" in *Eros and Agape*, 2. Aufl. 1954, S. 456 ff.).

88 "Till den teologiska etikens problem" (review of P. Althaus: *Der Geist der lutherischen Ethik im Augsburgischen Bekenntnis*, München, 1930, also his: *Grundriss der Ethik*, Erlangen 1931, and by F. W. Schmidt: *Die theologische Bergrundung der Ethik*, Gütersloh 1931), in: *STK*, 8. årg. 1932, S. 181-85.

89 *Agape and Eros. A Study of the Christian Idea of Love*. Part I. Trans.

A. G. Hebert, London: Society for the Promotion of Christian Knowledge, 1932, reprinted 1937, 1941 (translation of 72).

90 "Tvenne frälsningsvägar," in: *STK*, 8. årg. 1932, S. 227–38 (contained in *Urkristendom och reformation*, 1932, S. 13 ff.).

91 "Amor proximi hos Augustinus" (review of H. Arendt: *Der Liebesbegriff bei Augustin*, Berlin, 1929), in: *STK*, 8. årg. 1932, S. 267–69.

92 "Luther och Scheler" (review of H. Eklund: *Evangelisches und Katholisches in Max Schelers Ethik*, Uppsala, 1932), in: *STK*, 8. årg. 1932, S. 269–81.

93 "En evangelisk socialetik" (review of G. Wünsch: *Evangelische Wirtschaftsethik*, Tübingen, 1927), in: *STK*, 8. årg. 1932, S. 281–87.

94 Review of: *Lutherischer Weltkonvent zu Kopenhagen vom 26. Juni bis 4 July 1929*. Denkschrift, hrsg. in *Auftrag des Ausschusses*, 1929, in: *ThLZ* 57. Jahrg. 1932, Sp. 480.

95 Review of H. Arendt: *Der Liebesbegriff bei Augustin*, Berlin, 1929, in: *ThLZ*, 57. Jahrg. 1932, Sp. 495–97 (translation of 91).

96 Review of K. Bornhausen: *Schöpfung*, Leipzig, 1930, in: *ThLZ* 57. Jahrg. 1932, Sp. 501–3.

97 *Försoningen, en gudsgärning*, Stockholm: Sveriges Kristliga Studentrörelses Bokförlag, 1932, 2nd ed., 1956.

98 *Urkristendom och reformation*. Skisser till kristendomens idéhistoria Lund: C. W. K. Gleerup, 1932 (collection of seven essays of which six were published previously as Nos. 42, 52, 70, 75, 87, and 90; the essay "Evangelisk bot" ["Evangelische Busse"] is found only in this pamphlet).

99 *Die Versöhnung als Gottestat*, Gütersloh: C. Bertlesmann, 1932 (Studien der Lutherakademie, Heft 5; translation of 97).

1933

100 "Systematisk teologi och motivforskning," in: *STK* 9. årg. 1933, S. 38–49 (contained in *Filosofi och motivforskning*, 1940, S. 73 ff.).

101 "Docent Eklunds Luthertolkning," in: *STK* 9. årg. 1933, S. 88–93.

102 "Luther och Scheler än en gang," in: *STK*, 9. årg. 1933, S. 101–12.

103 "Eros och pistis," in: *STK* 9, årg. 1933, S. 115–23 (contained in *Filosofi och motivforskning*, 1940, S. 90 ff.).

104 "Den nyaste Origenesforskningen" (review of W. Völker: *Das Vollkommenheitsideal des Origenes*, Tübingen, 1931, also H. Koch: *Pronoia und Paideusis*, Berlin/Leipzig, 1932), in: *STK*, 9. årg. 1933, S. 197–204.

105 "Till gamla kyrkans historia" (review of H. Lietzmann: *Geschichte der Alten Kirche. I. Die Anfänge*, Berlin/Leipzig, 1932), in: *STK*, 9. årg. 1933, S. 298–304.

106 "Synthese oder Reformation," in: *ZsystTh*, 11. Jahrg. 1933, S. 126–46 (translation of 87).

107 "Kristologi," in: *SU*, Vol. 16, Sp. 84–87.

108 "Kärlek, teol." in: *SU*, Vol. 16, Sp. 547–50.

109 "Det kyrkliga läget i Tyskland," in: *STK*, 9. årg. 1933, S. 320–49 (contained in *Den tyska kyrkostriden*, 1934).

110 "Lutherbilden i det nya Tyskland (Rezension von E. Vogelsang: *Luthers Kampf gegen die Juden*, Tübingen, 1933)," in: *STK*, 9. årg. 1933, S. 381–84.

386 THE PUBLICATIONS OF ANDERS NYGREN

111 "Lutherdom," in: *SU*, Vol. 17, Sp. 887.
112 "Luthers teologi," in: *SU*, Vol. 17, Sp. 896–901.

1934

113 "Reconciliation as an Act of God," in: *The Lutheran Church Quarterly*, Jan. 1934, S. 1–34 (translation of 97).
114 "Marcion," in: *SU*, Vol. 18, Sp. 244–45.
115 "Schleiermacher och det teologiska nutidsläget," in: *STK*, 10. årg. 1934, S. 71–76.
116 "Blodets och rasens religion. Reflexioner till den tyska kyrkostriden," in: *Kristen Gemenskap*, 7. årg. 1934, S. 57–60.
117 "Om det andliga ämbetet," in: *STK*, 10. årg. 1934, S. 120–27 (contained in *Filosofi och motivforskning*, 1940, S. 157 ff., also in German in *ZsystTh* 1934, see 128).
118 "Från den tyska kyrkostriden," in: *STK*, 10. årg. 1934, S. 152–64 (contained in "Den tyska kyrkostriden," 1934).
119 "En 'tysk teologi'" (review of Fr. Wieneke: *Deutsche Theologie im Umriss*, Soldin, 1933), in: *STK*, 10. årg. 1934, S. 178–82.
120 *Den tyska kyrkostriden. Den evangeliska kyrkans ställning i det "Tredje riket,"* Lund: C. W. K. Gleerup, 1934, 2nd ed., 1935.
121 "Motivforskning," in: *SU*, Vol. 19, Sp. 210–11.
122 "Nya födelsen" in: *SU*, Vol. 20, Sp. 328.
123 "Nåd," in: *SU*, Vol. 20, Sp. 440–41.
124 "Nådemedel," in: *SU*, Vol. 20, Sp. 441–42.
125 "Nådens ordning" in: *SU*, Vol. 20, Sp. 443–44.
126 "Omvändelse," in: *SU*, Vol. 20, Sp. 767.
127 "Origenes," in: *SU*, Vol. 20, Sp. 873–74.
128 "Vom geistlichen Amt," in: *ZsystTh*, 12. Jahrg. 1934, S. 36–44 (translation of 117).
129 *The Church Controversy in Germany. The Position of the Evangelical Church in the Third Empire*, trans. G. G. Richards, London: Student Christian Movement Press, 1934 (translation of 120).
130 Review of: *Kirche und Welt. Studien und Dokumente hrsg. von der Forschungsabteilung des Oekumenischen Rates.* Vol. I–III, in. *Kristen Gemenskap*, 7. årg. 1934, S. 157–58.
131 "Den evangeliska kyrkan i Tyskland 1933–1934," in: *Svenska Kyrkans Årsbok* 1935, 15. årg. S. 123–24.
132 "Pelagianism," in: *SU*, Vol. 21, Sp. 307–08.
133 "Person, 4. teol." in: *SU*, Vol. 21, Sp. 440–41.
134 "Pneumatisk, 2. teol." in: *SU*, Vol. 21, Sp. 821.
135 "Predestination," in: *SU*, Vol. 21, Sp. 1175–77.

1935

136 "Rationalism," in: *SU*, Vol. 22, Sp. 557–58.
137 "Religion," in: *SU*, Vol. 22, Sp. 731–32.
138 "Religionsfilosofi," in: *SU*, Vol. 22, Sp. 735–37.
139 "Religionsvetenskap," in: *SU*, Vol. 22, Sp. 741–42.
140 "Rättfärdiggörelse," in: *SU*, Vol. 23, Sp. 724–25.
141 "Salighet," in: *SU*, Vol. 23, Sp. 1003.
142 "Satisfaktion," in: *SU*, Vol. 23, Sp. 1261–62.

143 *Den tyska kyrkostriden* (2nd enl. ed.), Lund: C. W. K. Gleerup, 1935.
144 *De Kerkstrijd in Duitschland. De Positie van de evangelische kerk in het Derde Rijk*, Baarn: Bosch and Keuning, 1935 (translation of 143).
145 "Schleiermacher," in: *SU*, Vol. 24, Sp. 469–70.
146 "Semipelagianism," in: *SU*, Vol. 24, Sp. 1099–100.
147 "Skapelse," in: *SU*, Vol. 24, Sp. 1099–100.
148 "Skuld, teol.," in: *SU*, Vol. 25, Sp. 108.
149 "Ställföreträdande lidande," in: *SU*, Vol. 26, Sp. 647 f.
150 "Supranaturalism," in: *SU*, Vol. 26, Sp. 782.

1936

151 "Synd," in: *SU*, Vol. 27, Sp. 99–100.
152 "Systematisk Teologi," in: *SU*, Vol. 27, Sp. 153.
153 "Teocentrisk," in: *SU*, Vol. 27, Sp. 734 f.
154 "Teodicé," in: *SU*, Vol. 27, Sp. 738 f.
155 "Teologi," in: *SU*, Vol. 27, Sp. 745 f.
156 "Tertullianus," in: *SU*, Vol. 27, Sp. 813 f.
157 "Thomas ab Aquino," in: *SU*, Vol. 27, Sp. 916–18.
158 "Den evangeliska kyrkan i Tyskland 1935–1936," in: *Svenska Kyrkans Årsbok* 1937, 17. årg., S. 125–29.
159 *Den kristna kärlektanken genom tiderna. Eros och Agape.* Senare delen, Stockholm: *SKD*, 1936, 2nd ed., 1947, 3rd ed., 1966.
160 "Verkhelighet," in: *SU*, Vol. 29, Sp. 612.
161 "Verksynd," in: *SU*, Vol. 29, Sp. 615.
162 "Wobbermin," in: *SU*, Vol. 29, Sp. 1158 f.

1937

163 "Bekännelsetrohet och kristen gemenskap," in: *Kristen Gemenskap*, 10. årg. 1937, S. 1–9.
164 "Överhistorisk," in: *SU*, Vol. 30, Sp. 1091 f.
165 "Kristendom och idealism," in: *STK*, 13 årg. 1937, S. 154–66 (contained in, *Filosofi och motivforskning*, 1940, S. 208 ff.).
166 *Eros and Agape. Gestaltwandlungen der christlichen Liebe. Zweiter Teil.* Aus dem Schwedischen trans. Irmgard Nygren, Gütersloh: C. Bertelsmann, 1935; 2nd ed., Berlin: Evang. Verlagsanstalt, 1955 (translation of 159).
167 *Agape and Eros I*, to Japanese trans. Novuo Sato, Nagoya, Ichiryusha, 1937 (translation of 72; new Japanese translation, 1954, see 294).
168 *Die Versöhnung als Gottestat*, Japanese trans. Novuo Sato, Nagoya, Ichiryusha, 1937 (translation of 97).
169 "Barth, Karl," in: *SU*, Tillägsband, Sp. 150.
170 "Bodelschwingh, Friedr. v.," in: *SU*, a.a.O., Sp. 220.
171 "Dibelius, Otto," in: *SU*, a.a.O., Sp. 373 f.
172 "Hauer, Jakob Wilhelm," in: *SU*, a.a.O., Sp. 699.
173 "Hossenfelder, Joachim," in: *SU*, a.a.O., Sp. 748.
174 "Nygermansk religion," in: *SU*, a.a.O., Sp. 1063 f.
175 "Zöllner, Wilhelm," in: *SU*, a.a.O., Sp. 1311.
176 "En beslagtagen bok" (review of O. Dibelius/N. Niemöller: *Wir ru-*

fen Deutschland zu Gott, Berlin 1937), in: *STK*, 13. årg. 1935, S. 294 f.

177 "Svar på Ivar Alms "randanmärkningar" till Eros och Agape," in: *STK*, 13. årg. 1937, S. 302–8.

178 "Motivforschung als philosophisches und geschichtliches Problem," in: *Adolf Phalén in memoriam*, Uppsala: Almquist and Wiksell, 1937, S. 326–44 (appeared in Swedish with the title "Motivforskning som filosofiskt och historiskt problem" in: *STK* 1939 [see 186] and in *Filosofi och motivforskning*, 1940, S. 35 ff. [see 192]).

179 "Kyrkan och vigseln av frånskilda," in: *Vår Lösen*, 28. årg. 1937, S. 148–50.

180 "Lutherdomen inför kyrkorna. Från sommarens teologiska arbete i Edinburgh," in: *STK*, 13. årg. 1937, S. 311–23.

181 "Svar pa Ivar Alms genmäle," in: *STK*, 13. årg. 1937, S. 398–404.

1938

182 "Kyrkans frihet," in: *Vår Lösen,*" 29. årg. 1938, S. 54–57.

183 "Augustinus' Confessiones, dess litterära byggnad och dess tolkning," in: *Från skilda tider. Studier tillägnade Hjalmar Holmquist*, Lund: *SKD*, 1938, S. 405–24 (contained in *Filosofi och motivforskning*, 1940, S. 112 ff.).

184 *Agape and Eros*. Part II. *History of the Christian Idea of Love*. Vol. I, trans. Philip S. Watson, London: Society for the Promotion of Christian Knowledge, 1938 (translation of 159).

1939

185 *Agape and Eros*. Part II. *The History of the Christian Idea of Love*. Vol. II, trans. Philip S. Watson, London: Society for the Promotion of Christian Knowledge, 1939 (translation of 159).

186 "Motivforskning som filosofiskt och historiskt problem," in: *STK*, 15. årg. 1939, S. 3–21.

187 Review of C. Stange: *Erasmus und Julius II. Eine Legende*, Berlin, 1937, in: *STK*, 15. årg. 1939, S. 83 f.

188 "Simul iustus et peccator hos Augustinus och Luther," in: *Till Gustaf Aulen*, Lund: *SKD*, 1939, S. 245–62 (contained in *Filosofi och motivforskning*, 1940, S. 136 ff. and in German in *ZsystTh* 1940 [see 195]).

189 "Lutherin kopernikolainen vallankumous," in: *Raamatullinen aikakauskirja* 1939, S. 163–67 (translation of 70).

190 "Die Ehrenrettung von amor bei Augustin," in: *Dragma Martino P. Nilsson dedicatum* Lund: Håkan Ohlsson, 1939, S. 367–73 (as "Augustinus rehabilitering av amor" in *Filosofi och motivforskning*, 1940 S. 103 ff.).

191 "Det kristna ethos' egenart," in: *STK*, 15. årg. 1939, S. 299–307.

1940

192 *Filosofi och motivforskning*, Stockholm/Lund: *SKD*, 1940 (collection of essays [see 10, 13, 39, 51, 100, 103, 117, 178, 165, 178, 183, 188, 190]; the essay "Atomism eller sammanhang i historiesynen," S. 63 ff. appears only here).

193 Review of E. Benz: *Marius Victorinus und die Entwicklung der abendländischen Willensmetaphysik*, Stuttgart, 1932, in: *STK*, 16. årg. 1940, S. 219 f.
194 Review of E. Dinkler: *Die Anthropologie Augustins* Stuttgart, 1934, in: *STK*, 16. årg. 1940, S. 220 f.
195 "Simul iustus et peccator bei Augustin und Luther," in: *ZsystTh*, 16. Jahrg. 1940, S. 364–79.
196 "Romarebrevet och förkunnelsen," in: *STK*, 17. årg. 1941, S. 1–16.
197 "Denna tidsålder och den tillkommande," in: *STK*, 17. årg. 1941, S. 270–80.

1942

198 "Evangelisk gudstjänstform," in: *Kyrkomusikernas tidning*, 7, årg. 1942, S. 13–25.
199 "Luther och staten," in: *Svensk tidskrift*, 29, årg. 1942, S. 98–106 (appeared as "Staten och kyrkan" in *En bok om kyrkan*, 1942, S. 396 ff.).
200 "Evangelisk Gudstjenesteform," in: *Kirke och Kultur*, 1942, S. 402–12 (translation of 198).
201 "Corpus Christi," in: *En bok om kyrkan*, Stockholm: *SKD*, 1942, S. 396–407.
202 "Staten och kyrkan," in: *En bok om kyrkan*, Stockholm: *SKD*, 1942, S. 396–407.

1943

203 "Missionens plats i kristendomens centrum," in: *STK*, 19. årg. 1943, S. 113–26.
204 "Litterärkritisk studie till Romarebrevet," in: *STK*, 19. årg. 1943, S. 68–75.
205 a.) "Det självklaras roll i historien,"
b.) "Das Selbstverständliche in der Geschichte," in: *Kungl. Humanistiska Vetenskapssamfundets i Lund Årsberättelse*, 1943–44, a.) S. 1–12, b.) S. 12–24.
206 "Den rättfärdige skall leva av tro," ur ett bibelords historia genom två och ett halvt årtusende, in: *STK*, 19. årg. 1943, S. 281–91.
207 "Exegetisk och systematisk teologi i samarbete." Reflexioner till O. Lintons artikel "Systematisk teologi exegetiskt granskad," in: *STK*, 19. årg. 1943, S. 357–73.
208 "Missionens plats i kristendomens centrum," in: *Nordisk Missionstidskrift*, 54. årg. 1943, S. 236–43.
209 *Erôs et Agapé. La Notion chretienne de l'amour et ses transformations*, trans. Pierre Jundt, Paris: Aubier, 1944.
210 *Pauli brev till Romarna*, Stockholm: *SKD*, 1944 (Tolkning av Nya Testamentet, VI), 2nd ed., 1947.
211 "Tyska kyrkan och nazismen," in *Vår Lösen*, 35. årg. 1944, S. 409–19.
212 "Den rättfärdige skall leva av tro, Disskussionsinlägg," in: *STK*, 20. årg. 1944, S. 256.

1945

213 "Tyska kyrkan och nazismen," in: *Vår Lösen*, 36. årg. 1945, S. 45–48.
214 "Tro och vetande. Ur en diskussionsinledning," in: *Vår Lösen*, 36. årg. 1945, S. 166–73.

215 "Till tolkningen av Rom. 3, 25–26," in: *Svensk Kyrkotidning*, 41. årg. 1945, S. 355–56.
216 "Kristen syn pa förhållandet mellan man och kvinna," in: *Vår Kyrka*, 84. årg. 1945, No. 26, S. 5–7.
217 "Var kristna tro och vart samhällslivs framtid," in: *Kyrkor under korset*, 14. årg. 1945, S. 180–88.

1946

218 "Lutherakademien i Sondershausen. En blick bakom kulisserna," in: *Vår Kyrka*, 85. årg. 1946, No. 1, S. 2, 6, 7.
219 "Martin Luthers betydelse i teologi och folkuppfostran," in: *Vår Kyrka*, 85. årg. 1946, No. 7, S. 2.
220 "Filosofiens centrum och periferi," in: *Festskrift till Anders Karitz*, Uppsala/Stockholm: Almquist Wiksell, 1946, S. 123–35.
221 "Martin Luther, en aktuell gestalt," in: *STK*, 22. årg. 1946, S. 1–8.
222 "Martin Luther: a pertinent figure," in: *The Augustana Quarterly*, Vol. XXV, No. 4., 1946, S. 297–305.
223 *Sanningen om "kyrkonazismen." En granskning av "Svenska Landskommitténs,"* Stockholm: SKD, 1946.
224 *Ett tillägg till "Sanningen om kyrkonazismen."* Lund: SKD, 1946 (pamphlet).

1947

225 *Vår skola och kristendomen*, Göteborg, 1947 (pamphlet).
226 "Kristendomen och rätten," in: *STK*, 23. årg. 1947, S. 1–10.
227 "Lutherdomens framtidsuppgifter," in: *STK*, 23. årg. 1947, S. 101–15.
228 *Objawienie a Pismo Swiete.* Dwa Wykady, Lund: 1947 (pamphlet).
229 *Die Aufgaben des Luthertums in der heutigen Welt*, Berlin: Verlag Haus und Schule Gmb H., 1947 (pamphlet) (translation of 227).
230 "Uppenbarelsen och skriften," in: *En bok om Bibeln*, Lund: C. W. K. Gleerup, 1947, S. 85–95.
231 "Gamla Testamentet i Nya Förbundet," in: *En bok om Bibeln*, Lund: C. W. K. Gleerup, 1947, S. 96–115.
232 "Bibelforskning och praktiskt bibelbruk," in: *En bok om Bibeln*, Lund: C. W. K. Gleerup, 1947, S. 283–94.
233 "Kristus nådastolen," in: *Festskrift tillägnad prof. Joh. Lindblom*, Uppsala: Svensk exegetisk Årsbok, XII, 1947, S. 253–57.

1948

234 "Confessional Representation," in: *News Bulletin*, Geneva, Vol. III, No. 4.
235 "Über die konfessionelle Vertretung im Weltrat der Kirchen," in: *Nachrichtenblatt für die evangelisch-lutherischen Geistlichen in Bayern*, 3. Jahrgang 1948, No. 9/10.
236 "L'Eglise Lutherienne et le Problème de l'Oecumenisme," in: *Fraternité évangelique*, 27 me Annee 1948.
237 "Christianity and the Concept of Right," in: *The Augustana Quarterly*, Vol. XXVII, No. 3., 1948, S. 195–204 (translation of 226).
238 "Die heilige Schrift und das heutige Zeugnis der Kirche," in: *Der Weg von der Bibel zur Welt* (Bericht von zwei oekumenischen Studienta-

gungen, hrsg. von der Studienabteilung des Oekumenischen Rates der Kirchen), Zürich, 1948, S. 79–83.

239 "Lutheranisme en Oecumene," in: *Luthers Weekblad*, 3ᵉ Jaargang 1948, No. 33 (see 236).

240 *Luther's Doctrine of the Two Kingdoms*, Lausanne, 1948 (pamphlet).

241 "The Way to Christian Unity" in: *The Lutheran*, Vol. 30, No. 52, S. 15–17.

242 "Introduction," in: *The Lutheran World Review*, Vol. I, No. 1, 1948, S. 1 f.

243 "The Task of the Lutheran Church in a New Day," in: *The Lutheran World Review*, Vol. I, No. 1, 1948, S. 6–19 (translation of 227).

244 "Reflections in Connection with a Visit in America," in: *The National Lutheran*, Vol. 17, No. 3, 1948, S. 6–8.

245 "Die selbstverständlichen Voraussetzungen der Geschichte," in: *Universitas, Zeitschrift für Wissenshaft, Kunst und Literatur*, Jahrg. 3, 1948, S. 907–15.

246 "The Role of the Self-evident in History," in: *The Journal of Religion*, Vol. XXVIII, No. 4, 1948, S. 235–41 (translation of 205).

247 "Revelation and Scripture," in: *Theology Today*, 1948, Vol. V, No. 3, S. 318–26 (translation of 230).

248 "Lutherdomen och Ekumene," in: *Edvard Rodhe. En hyllning av ordinarie ledamöter inom Teologiska Fakulteten* (Lunds Univ:s Årsskr. N. F., Avd. 1, Bd. 45, No. 2) Lund, 1948, S. 5–16.

249 "Die Grundlage der Ökumenizität nach lutherischem Verständnis," in: *ThLZ*, 1948, No. 9 Sp. 523–26.

250 "Lutherdommens Framtidsoppgaver," in: *Det 7. Nordiske Prestemöte i Bergen*, Oslo, 1948, S. 167–88.

1949

251 "The Basis of Ecumenicity in Lutheran Theology" in: *The Lutheran World Review*, Vol. 1, No. 3, 1949, S. 15–18.

252 "Die Aufgabe des amerikanischen Luthertums," in: *Evang-lutherische Kirchenzeitung*, 1949, S. 27.

253 "Luthers Lehre von den zwei Reichen," in: *ThLZ*, 74. Jahrg. 1949, No. 1, Sp. 1–8.

254 "Luther's Doctrine of the two Kingdoms," in: *The Ecumenical Review*, Vol. I, 1949, S. 301–10.

255 *Herdabrev till Lunds stift*, Stockholm: SKD, 1949, 2nd ed., 1949.

256 *Commentary on Romans*, trans. Carl C. Rasmussen, Philadelphia: Muhlenberg Press, 1949. British edition, London: Student Christian Movement Press, 1952, reprinted 1955 and subsequently.

257 *Eros and Agape I*, Chinese trans. G. Sjöholm, Hong Kong, 1950 (translation of 72).

258 "Theology and Lutheran Unity," in: *The Lutheran World Review*, III, 1950, S. 57 f.

259 "Bischof Dibelius und die Oekumene," in: *Die Stunde der Kirche*, Berlin: Evang. Verlagsanstalt, 1950, S. 55 f.

1951

260 *The Gospel of God*, trans. L. J. Trinterud, London: Student Christian Movement Press, 1951 (translation of 255).

261 "Christus und die Verderbensmächte. Zugleich ein Wort zur Frage der Entmythologisierung," in: *Viva Vox Evangelii, Festschrift für H. Meiser,* München: Claudius Verlag, 1951, S. 50–61.
262 "Kristus och fördärvsmakterna. Tillika ett ord till kristendomens avmytologisering," in: *STK,* 27. årg. 1951, S. 1–11.
263 "Zum Geleit," in: *Lutherische Rundschau,* Jahrg. 1, 1951, S. 1–2.
264 *Der Römerbrief,* Göttingen: Vandenhoeck and Ruprecht, 1951, 2nd ed., 1954, 3rd ed., 1959; 4th ed., 1965 (translation of 210).
265 "Die Verwirrung zu Babel und die Einheit der Kirche," in: *Lutherische Rundschau,* Jahrg. 1, 1951, S. 41–46.
266 "Babels förbistring och kyrkans enhet," in: *Lutherhjälpen,* 1951, S. 65–70.
267 "Arbetet växer—enheten växer. Från Lutherska Världsförbundets Exekutivkommittee," in: *Kristen Gemenskap,* 24. årg. 1951, S. 130–32.
268 "Die theologische Bedeutung der lutherischen Weltkonferenz 1952" in: *Lutherische Rundschau,* Jahrg. 1, 1951, S. 102–4.
269 "Lutherska världsmötets teologiska betydelse," in: *Lutherhjälpen,* 1951, S. 129–31.
270 "Christus der Gnadenstuhl," in: *Ernst Lohmeyer in memoriam,* 1951, S. 89–93 (translation of 233).
271 "Christ and the Forces of Destruction, and a Word concerning the Demythologising of Christianity," in: *Scottish Journal of Theology,* Vol. 4, No. 4, 1951, S. 363–75 (translation of 261).
272 "Corpus Christi," in: *Ein Buch von der Kirche,* Göttingen: Vandenhoeck and Ruprecht, 1951, S. 15–28 (translation of 201).
273 "Staat und Kirche," in: *Ein Buch von der Kirche,* Göttingen: Vandenhoeck and Ruprecht (translation of 202).

1952

274 *Eros und Agape II,* Chinese trans. G. Sjöholm, Hong Kong, 1952 (translation of 159).
275 "Corpus Christi," in: *This is the Church,* Philadelphia: Muhlenberg Press, 1952, S. 3–15 (translation of 201).
276 "The State and the Church" in: *This is the Church,* Philadelphia: Muhlenberg Press, 1952, S. 294–306 (translation of 202).
277 *Das lebendige Wort Gottes. Ein Hirtenbrief—eine Laiendogmatik,* Stuttgart: Evangelisches Verlagswerk, 1952. Reprinted as, *Lizenfausgabe für DDR Berlin:* Evangelische Verlagsanstalt, 1953 (translation of 255).
278 "God's Word is for Today," in: *The Lutheran,* Vol. 34, No. 46, 1952, S. 14–16.
279 "Luther und Paulus," in: *Evang.-Luth. Kirchenzeitung* 1952, No. 14, S. 229–31.
280 "Objektives und Persönliches im Römerbrief," in: *ThLZ,* 78. Jahrg. 1952, Sp. 591–96.
281 *The Gospel and the New Era* (Chinese translation of "Lectures," Lutheran Press India, 1950), trans. D. Chu, Hong Kong: Lutheran Missions Literature Society, 1952 (pamphlet).
282 "On the Question of Demythologizing Christianity," in: *The Lutheran Quarterly,* Vol. IV, 1952, No. 2, S. 140–52.
283 "Andligt och världsligt regemente," in: *Nordisk Teologisk Uppslagsbok,* Vol. I, Lund, 1952, S. 92–97.

284 "Bergspredikan," in: *Nordisk Teologisk Uppslagsbok*, Vol. I, Lund, 1952, S. 326–30.

285 "Evangelium," in: *Nordisk Teologisk Uppslagsbok*, Vol. I, Lund, 1952, S. 813–15.

286 "Fader" in: *Nordisk Teologisk Uppslagsbok*, Vol. I, Lund, 1952, S. 833–36.

287 "Försoning," in: *Nordisk Teologisk Uppslagsbok*, Vol. I, Lund, 1952, S. 1024–31.

288 "Das lebendige Wort in einer verantwortlichen Kirche," in: *Offizieller Bericht der 2. Vollversammlung des Luth. Weltbundes*, 1952, S. 44–50.

289 "Det levande Ordet i en ansvarig kyrka," in: *Ny kyrklig Tidskrift* 1952, S. 45–55.

290 *Erôs et Agapé. La notion chrétienne de l'amour et ses transformations*, trans. Pierre Jundt. Deuxième partie, Livre I–II, Paris: Aubier, 1952 (translation of 159).

1953

291 "Der ökumenische Beitrag des Luthertums," in: *Informationsblatt für die Gemeinden in den niederdeutschen Landeskirchen*, 2. Jahrg., No. 12, 1953, S. 191 f.

292 "Missionen—Jesu mission och vår," in: *Den Evangeliska Missionen*, 1953, S. 81–84.

293 "Lutheranism and Ecumenicity," in: *The Christian Century*, 1953, S. 1108–9.

294 *Agape and Eros I–II*, trans. Philip S. Watson, Philadelphia: Westminster Press, 1953 (translation of 72 and 159).

1954

295 *Agape and Eros I*, Japanese trans. Ch. Kishi and H. Ouchi, Tokyo: Shinkyo Shuppansha Publ., Co., 1954 (new translation of 72; see 167).

296 "Christ—The Hope of the World" in: *Charisteria J. Köpp oblata*, Stockholm, 1954, S. 129–36.

1955

297 *Kristus och hans Kyrka*, Stockholm: *SKD*, 1955.

298 "Ragnar Brings teologiska insats," in: *Nordisk Teologisk Idéer och Män. Till Ragnar Bring den 10 juli*, 1955, Lund: C. W. K. Gleerup, 1955, pp. 293–96.

299 "Kärlek, Dogmhistoriskt och systematiskt," in: *Nordisk Teologisk Uppslagsbok*, Vol. II, 1955, Sp. 736–41.

300 "Luther, Betydelse och ställning i Kyrkans historia," in: *Nordisk Teologisk Uppslagsbok*, Vol. II, 1955, Sp. 881–93.

1956

301 "Till teologiens metodfråga (Diskussionsinlägg)," in *STK*, 32. årg. 1956, S. 20–35.

302 *Christus und seine Kirche*, Göttingen: Vandenhoeck and Ruprecht, 1956 (translation of 297).

303 *Christ and His Church*, Philadelphia: Westminster Press, 1956 (translation of 297).
304 "Ytterligare till teologiens metodfråga," in: *STK*, 32. årg. 1956, S. 133–60.
305 "Slutreplik angående teologiens metodfråga," in: *STK*, 32. årg. 1956, S. 313–22.
306 *Fridens evangelium.* Stockholm: *SKD*, 1956 (pamphlet).

1957

307 *Christ and His Church*, London: Society for the Promotion of Christian Knowledge, 1957 (see 303).
308 *The Gospel of God*, Japanese trans. M. Tanaka and Ch. Kishi, Tokyo: Nippon-Kiristokyodan-Shuppanbu; United Church of Christ in Japan Publisher, 1957 (translation of 260).
309 "Romarbrevet," in: *Nordisk Teologisk Uppslagsbok*, Vol. III. 1957, Sp. 355–60.
310 "Systematisk teologi," in: *Nordisk Teologisk Uppslagsbok*, Vol. III, 1957, Sp. 808–14.
311 "Uppståndelse," in: *Nordisk Teologisk Uppslagsbok*, Vol. III, 1957, Sp. 1066–72.
312 "Das Gespräch der Theologie," in: *Dokumente. Zeitschrift für übernationale Zusammenarbeit*, 13. Jahrg. 1957, S. 183–92.
313 "Kyrkans enhet. Till frågen om kyrko-och nattvardsgemenskap," in: *STK*, 33. årg. 1957, S. 65–74.
314 *En levande Gudstjänst*, Stockholm: *SKD*, 1957, 2nd ed., 1957.
315 "Die Einheit der Kirche. Über Kirchen-und Abendmahlsgemeinschaft," in: *Die Einheit der Kirche*, Berlin: Lutherisches Verlagshaus, 1957, S. 93–102 (translation of 313).
316 "Church Unity and Sacramental Fellowship," in: *The Unity of Church*, Rock Island, Ill., 1957, S. 75–85 (translation of 313).
317 *Tjänare och förvaltare. Några tankar om prästens kall*, Stockholm: *SKD*, 1957.

1958

318 "L'unité de l'Eglise," in: *Revue d'historie et de religion*, 1957, No. 4. pp. 283–93 (translation of 313).
319 "Der verantwortliche Dienst der Kirche," in: *Luth. Rundschau*, 7. Jahrg. 1938, pp. 364–69.
320 "The Church and Responsible Service," in: *Lutheran World*, Vol. IV, No. 4, 1958, pp. 342–46.
321 "Jes. 53 als Schlüssel zum Verständnis der Taufe," in: *Solange es 'Heute' heisst, Festgabe für Rudolf Hermann*, Berlin: Evanglische Verlagsanstalt, 1957, S. 210–13.
322 "Eros and Agape," in: *A Handbook of Christian Theology*, New York: Living Age Books, Meridian Books, Inc. 1958, S. 96–101.
323 "The Religious Realm of Meaning," in: *The Christian Century*, 1958, S. 823–26.
324 "Augustin und Luther. Zwei Studien über den Sinn der augustinischen Theologie," Berlin, 1958 (*Aufsätze und Vorträge zur Theologie und Religionswissenchaft*, hrsg. von E. Schott und H. Urner, Heft 3).

325 "Kristi närvaro i ordet och sakramenten," in: *STK*, 34. årg. 1958, S. 225–30.

326 "L'unité de l'Eglise," in: *Foi et Vie*, 57 Année, No. 6, 1958, Luthériens et Réformés (documents) Paris 1958, S. 432–46 (see 318).

1959

327 "Om Kristi närvaro (Diskussionsinlägg)," in: *STK*, 35. årg. 1959, S. 68–69.

328 *Pauli brev till Romarna*, Japanese trans. Ch. Kishi, Tokyo: Luther Sha, Luther Publ., 1959 (translation of 210).

329 "Luther's Doctrine of the Two Kingdoms," in: *Christus Victor*, London, 1959, No. 104, S. 3–10 (see 240).

330 "Gustaf Auléns teologiska gärning," in: *Bibliografi över Gustaf Auléns tryckta skrifter*, Lund: C. W. K. Gleerup 1959, S. 17–23.

331 "La Doctrine Luthérienne des deux Domaines," in: *Cahiers de la Réconciliation*, Paris: Luillet, 1959, S. 13–21 (translation of 240).

332 "Remarks on the 'Report of the Conversation concerning Holy Communion in the Evangelical Church in Germany,' " in: *The Ecumenical Review*, Vol. XI, No. 4, 1959, S. 428–29.

333 "Die Lutherforschung in Skandinavien," in: *Gott ist am Werk. Festschrift für Landesbischof Hanns Lilje zum 60. Geburtstag*, Hamburg: Furche-Verlag, 1959, S. 17–26.

334 "Dopet i ekumenisk belysning," in: *STK*, 35. årg. 1959, S. 209–21.

1960

335 "Amt, geistliches," in: *Weltkirchenlexikon* 1960, Sp. 43–46.

336 "Kirche," in: *Weltkirchenlexikon* 1960, Sp. 676–85.

337 "Den teologiska Faith and Order-Commissionen om 'Kristus och Kyrkan,' " in: *Kristen Gemenskap*, 33. årg. 1960, H. 1, S. 2–7.

338 "Carl Stange als theologischer Bahnbrecher," in: *NZsystTh*, 2 Vol. 2 Heft, 1960, S. 123–28.

339 *Essence of Christianity*, two essays, trans. Philip S. Watson, London: Epworth Press, 1960.

340 "Die Gegenwart Jesu Christi in Wort und Sakrament," in: *Bekenntnis zur Kirche. Festgabe für Ernst Sommerlath zum 70. Geburtstag*, Berlin: Evangelische Verlagsantalt, 1960, S. 294–98.

1962

341 "Emil Brunner's Doctrine of God" in: The Library of Living Theology, Vol. III. *The Theology of Emil Brunner*, ed. Charles W. Kegley, New York: Macmillan Co., 1962, pp. 175–86.

342 "Christianity and Law," in: *Dialog*. A Journal of Theology, Vol. I, 1962, Autumn, S. 36–45 (translation of 226).

1963

343 "Vad är det som förenar oss och håller oss samman?" in: *Svensk Pastoraltidskrift* No. 33, 1963, S. 535–38.

344 *The Significance of the Bible for the Church* (Facet Books, Biblical series 1) Philadelphia: Fortress Press, 1963 (44 s.) (pamphlet).

345   "From Atomism to Contexts of Meaning in Philosophy," in: *Philosophical Essays dedicated to Gunnar Aspelin*, Lund: C. W. K. Gleerup, 1963, S. 122–36.
346   "Kristus och kyrkan. Inför Montreal-konferensen," in: *Kristen Gemenskap*, 36. årg. 1963, S. 57–62.

1964

347   Review of Heinrich Bornkamm: *Luthers Lehre von den zwei Reichen im Zusammenhang seiner Theologie*, Gütersloh, 1958, in: *ThLZ*, 89. Jahrg. 1964, No. 5, Sp. 370 f.
348   "Vad är Kyrkornas Världsråd? Till frågan om Världsrådets ecklesiologiska status," in: *Kristen Gemenskap*, 37. årg. 1964, S. 3–6.

1965

349   *Der Römerbrief*, 4th ed., Göttingen: Vandenhoeck and Ruprecht, 1965.
350   "Trons Rättfärdighet," in *Till Bo Giertz*, 31/8/1965, Uppsala: Merkantil-Tryckeriet, 1965, S. 89–102.
351   "Christ the Head of the Church," in: *Essays in Honour of Carl Christian Rasmussen*, Lutheran Theological Seminary Bulletin, Gettysburg, Pa., Aug. 1965, No. 3, S. 17–21.
352   "Dopets innebörd. Introduktion," in: *En bok om dopet i ekumenisk belysning*. Utgiven av Svenska Faith-and-Order kommiten och redigerad av Torsten Bergsten, Stockholm: SKD, 1965, S. 11–20.
353   *Den kristne kaerlighedstanke*, trans. Erik M. Christensen, in: *Munksgaardsserien*, 13, Munksgaard, Kopenhagen, 1965 (translation of 72).

1966

354   *Pauli brev till Romarna*, Chinese trans. Y. C. Chung, Hong Kong: Taosheng Publishing House, 1966 (translation of 210).
355   *Eros och Ägape*. Pocketbook edition in "Verburn" and "Aldus" series, Stockholm: SKD and Bonnier, 1966.
356   *Kristus ja Hänen Kirkkonsa*, Suomentanut Vilho Ylijoki Kirjapaja— Helsinki (translation of 296).

1967

357   "Religion och metafysik," in: *Kristen Humanism. Årsbok 1967*, S. 34–46, Lund: C. W. K. Gleerup.
358   "Predikan hos Luther och i dag," in: *Tidskrift for Teologi og Kirke*, 38, årg. 1967, Oslo: Universitetsforlaget, S. 192–203.

1968

359   *Guds Ord i dag*, Svensk Pastoraltidskrifts Småskrifter Nr 13. Uppsala, 1968.
360   *Pauli brev till Romarna*, 3rd ed. in AB Verbum, Stockholm, 1968 (Tolkning av Nya Testamentet VI).
361   "Svenska Kyrkans Dopsyn," in *Dopet i Svenska Kyrkan*, Verbum, Stockholm, 1968, S. 9–13, 104–11.

362 "Framåt till Luther. Till frågan om Lutherska Världförbundets andliga profil" in: *STK* 44. årg. 1968, S. 6–15.

363 "Om det levande förflutna. Till Schleiermacherminnet 1968," in: *STK* 44. årg. 1968, S. 197–203.

364 "Die Rechtfertigung, der Schlüssel zum Evangelium." Japanese trans. in: *Gospel, Church and Luther. Essays in Honor of Prof. Chitose Kishi*, 1968, S. 226–44.

1969

365 "Avmytologisering av Nya Testamentet??" in: *Svensk Pastoraltidskrift*, 11. årg. 1969, S. 443–49.

366 "Luthers Lehre von den zwei Reichen" in: *Reich Gottes und die Welt. Die Lehre Luthers von den zwei Reichen*, hrsg. von *Heinz-Horst Schrey* (Wege der Forschung, Band CVII), 1969, S. 277–89.

367 *La Epistola a Los Romanos.* Comentario por Anders Nygren. Traducido de la versión alemana por Carlos Witthaus y Greta Mayena. Buenos Aires: Biblioteca de Estudios Teologicos. Editorial La Aurora, 1969 (Spanish translation of 210).

368 *Eros y Agape.* La noción christiana del amor y sus transformaciones. Traducción José A. Bravo. Barcelona: Sagitario, S. A. de Ediciones y Distribuciones, 1969 (Spanish translation of 72).

1970

369 *Tro och vetande.* Med inledning av *Lennart Pinomaa*. Luther-Agricola Sallskapets Skrifter B 6, Helsinki 1970.

370 *Agape and Eros.* Bologna: Il Mulino (Italian translation of 72).

371 *Meaning and Method. Prolegomena to a Scientific Philosophy of Religion* (Probable publication 1970).

372 *Religiöst Apriori.* Italian trans. "in preparatione." Bologna: Il Mulino (translation of 5).

Preface

[1] An earlier volume in The Library of Living Theology, *The Empirical Theology of Henry Nelson Wieman*, ed. Robert W. Bretall, has been published in paperback by Southern Illinois University Press, 1969.

Intellectual Autobiography

[1] For convenience, titles of books and articles have in most cases been translated into English. This does not necessarily mean that an English translation of the work exists (translator's note).

[2] Nygren's *Commentary on Romans* (Stockholm, 1944, published in English, London, 1952) formed part of this series. For its special form and purpose, see page 19 (translator's note).

[3] Because a large part of this autobiography relates to the University of Lund, it may be useful here to give a brief account of the stages of an academic career. The first degree in theology is *Teologie Kandidat* (Bachelor of Divinity), commonly taken in three or four years. Postgraduate work begins with the Licentiate's Degree (*Teologie Licentiat*) gained by examination and thesis; thereafter the Licentiate prepares his doctorate thesis. In due course the completed thesis is nailed up in the University (as Luther's 95 Theses were nailed up in Wittenburg), as an indication that the writer is prepared for a disputation on it. At the disputation, a public occasion, the thesis is subjected to criticism and defended by the writer. A thesis of sufficient merit earns for the writer not only the doctor's degree, but the higher degree of Docent, which brings with it the right to teach in the University. A docent duly appointed in a faculty is thus in the position of a lecturer or assistant professor (translator's note).

[4] The words *science* and *scientific* in this essay are used to translate the Swedish *vetenskap* and *vetenskaplig*, which have a wider reference than the common restriction of the English words to the natural sciences. For Nygren, *scientific* refers to a method and approach to scholarship that rigorously excludes all that is arbitrary and irrational (translator's note).

1. Anders Nygren's Philosophy of Religion

[1] Stockholm, 1922.

[2] We have no reason to discuss further the interpretation of Schleiermacher which Nygren gives. We proceed from his interpretation and critique of Schleiermacher in order to gain a point of departure for presenting Nygren's own philosophy of religion.

[3] It can parenthetically be pointed out that it has been affirmed that

Nygren has not given an adequate place for the *law* in Christianity. But according to Nygren, agape cannot be understood other than against the background of the law. Agape overcomes the false law, legalism, but it includes within itself the law which has been transformed and fulfilled in Christ. When the Christian basic motif is described using the idea of love as the point of orientation, and contrasting it with non-Christian ideas of love, this basic motif is defined from a particular point of view. The law could, of course, be used to provide a different point of orientation, though the nature of love would not be wholly clarified in such a case.

[4] See Anders Nygren, "Gamla testamentet i Nya förbunder," *En bok om bibeln* (Lund, 1947), pp. 96 ff.

[5] Anders Nygren, *Religiöst a priori*, acad. diss. (Lund, 1921).

[6] Stockholm, 1940.

[7] Anders Nygren, *Filosofi och motivforskning* (Stockholm, 1940), pp. 33–34.

[8] *Ibid.*, p. 34.

[9] Stockholm, 1923, p. 136.

[10] Trans. Philip S. Watson (Philadelphia, 1953).

[11] Anders Nygren, *Philosophical Essays Dedicated to Gunnar Aspelin* (Lund, 1963), pp. 122–36.

[12] Trans. Carl C. Rasmussen (Philadelphia, 1949).

2. Nygren and Linguistic Analysis: Language and Meaning

[1] Anders Nygren, "The Religious Realm of Meaning," *The Christian Century*, July 16, 1958, pp. 853–56.

[2] Anders Nygren, *Religiöst a priori* (Lund, 1921), p. 214.

[3] Note the article "Filosofi och Teologi hos Bishop Nygren," *Svensk teologisk kvartalskrift*, XXXII (1956), 284–312.

[4] Anders Nygren, *Det bestående i kristendom* (Stockholm, 1922). Trans. as *The Permanent Element in Christianity*, by Philip S. Watson, but included in a volume called *Essence of Christianity* (London, 1960), p. 23. Hereafter references will be to English translations, where these are available. Translations will be my own unless an English translation is cited in the footnotes.

[5] Anders Nygren, "The Religious Realm of Meaning," pp. 824 ff., for a later statement and *Religiöst a priori*, chapter 4, for an earlier (1920's). Also, *Dogmatikens vetenskapliga grundläggning* (Stockholm, 1922), pp. 69–91.

[6] Gustav Wingren, *Theology in Conflict*, trans. Eric H. Wahlstrom (Philadelphia, 1958), p. 15.

[7] *Ibid.*, p. 167. Nygren's protests against Wingren are exceedingly acute and decisive. Note *Svensk teologisk kvartalskrift*, XXXII and XXXIII (1956–57), for this spirited discussion between Nygren and Wingren.

[8] Anders Nygren, *Filosofisk och kristen etik* (Stockholm, 1923), especially pp. 115 ff. and his *Filosofi och motivforskning* (Stockholm, 1940), passim. Also *Agape and Eros*, Part I, trans. A. G. Hebert (London, 1932), p. 29. And in more purely theological contexts Nygren is anxious to show that Christianity is "not an ideology" e.g., Anders Nygren, *Christ and His Church* (Philadelphia, 1956), p. 31.

[9] Anders Nygren, *Agape and Eros* (1932), p. 28. Also Nygren, *Essence of Christianity*, p. 25: "these questions are inevitable and indispensible."

[10] The early writings, e.g., Anders Nygren, "Det religionsfilosofiska grundproblemet," *Bibelforskaren,* XXXVI (1919 and 1921) and in Nygren, *Religiöst a priori* stress the Kantian-like deduction whereas the later works are a little more descriptive. But this shift is not crucial to the issue I am raising.

[11] All of these circumstances are noted by Nygren in, *Essence of Christianity,* pp. 25-26.

[12] Note Nygren, *Essence of Christianity,* p. 25 and Anders Nygren, "Transcendentala metodens . . . ," *Bibelforskaren,* XL (1923), 273-74 and Anders Nygren, "Den metafysiska filosofiens betydelse för religionsvetenskapen," *Bibelforskaren,* XXXV (1918), 136-37.

[13] Ludwig Wittgenstein, *Philosophical Investigations,* trans. G. E. M. Anscombe, No. 544 (Oxford, 1953), p. 146.

[14] Nygren, *Filosofi och motivforskning,* p. 41.

[15] Nygren, *Essence of Christianity,* p. 26.

[16] Nygren, *Agape and Eros* (1932), I, 28.

[17] Nygren, *Filosofi och motivforskning,* p. 39. Here he says: "Philosophy is, in short, the logical analysis of presuppositions."

[18] The quotation is from *Tractatus Logico-Philosophicus,* 4.003. The passage is quoted in Nygren's interesting article "From Atomism to Contexts of Meaning in Philosophy," section 4. I have not seen the article in print and am quoting from the proof copy sent me by the author.

[19] Nygren, "Det religionsfilosofiska grundproblemet," and "Transcendentala metodens," especially pp. 273 ff.

[20] Anders Nygren, "Hur är filosofi som vetenskap möjlig?" in *Festskrift tillägnad Axel Hägerström* (Stockholm, 1928). This is an extremely clear statement in which he also declares his independence of metaphysics. Nygren's debt to Hägerström is apparently rather large.

[21] Nygren, *Filosofisk och kristen etik,* pp. 103 ff.

[22] Nygren, *Religiöst a priori,* pp. 230 ff. and Nygren, *Filosofisk och kristen etik,* especially pp. 147-48 and numerous other places in that book.

[23] Nygren, *Religiöst a priori,* p. 237.

[24] Nygren, *Filosofisk och kristen etik,* pp. 115 ff. Also note the article on the significance of metaphysical philosophy for theological studies: "Den metafysiska filosofiens betydelse för religionsvetenskapen," pp. 131-57.

[25] Wittgenstein, *Philosophical Investigations,* no. 77. Also one should note in this regard Einar Tegen's criticism of the "validity" concept; and he raises a question also about whether the "eternal" is really the same in all the contexts. His points are obscure, however. The first is discussed as though "validity" were a metaphysical concept and here Tegen is wrong. The second is a better logical point. Nygren answers the first very smartly. Einar Tegen, "Är en transcendental deduktion a religionen möjlig?" *Bibelforskaren,* XXXIX (1922), and XL (1923), 300-319 and 1-30.

[26] Wittgenstein, *Philosophical Investigations,* p. 81.

[27] Translated by Alan Carlsten (London, 1957).

[28] In the joint volume, *En bok om kyrkan* (Stockholm, 1942).

[29] Kant's *Religion Within the Limits of Reason,* quoted in *Christ and His Church* (1957), p. 22.

[30] Anders Nygren, *Christ and His Church* (1957), p. 23.

[31] *Ibid.,* p. 89.

[32] Anders Nygren, "Till frågon om teologiens objektiviet," in *Teologisk Studier, tillägnade Erik Stave* (Uppsala, 1922).

[33] Nygren, *Dogmatikens vetenskaplign grundläggning*, p. 11.

[34] Nygren has written variously about it, e.g., in *Kristendom och vår tid*, XVII (1922), 62–72. His article, "Den religionsfilosofiska apriorifrågan" concerns the question: Is the eternal the religious category?

[35] Nygren, *Essence of Christianity*, p. 50.

[36] *Ibid.*, p. 38. (Another interesting discussion of this is in *Agape and Eros* [1932], I, 30.)

[37] *Ibid.*, p. 61.

3. The Method of Motif Research

[1] Cf., Anders Nygren, "From Atomism to Contexts of Meaning in Philosophy," in *Philosophical Essays Dedicated to Gunnar Aspelin* (Lund, 1963), p. 135.

[2] Cf., Valter Lindstrom, "Distinktionen mellan lag och evangelium och fragan om kristendomens egenart," in *Vid Abdomens fot 1924–1949* (Abo, 1949).

4. Motif Research as a General Historical Method

[1] Anders Nygren, *Det religionsfilosofiska grundproblemet* (Lund, 1921), p. 71. Reprinted from *Bibelforskaren*, XXXVI (1919) and XXXVIII (1921).

[2] Anders Nygren, *Religiöst apriori, dess filosofiska förutsättningar och teologiska konsekvenser* (Lund, 1921).

[3] *Ibid.*, p. 109.

[4] *The Christian Century*, July 16, 1958, pp. 823–26.

[5] Anders Nygren, *Filosofi och motivforskning* (Stockholm, 1940), pp. 17, 39.

[6] Anders Nygren, "Transcendentala metodens användbarhet inom religionsfilosfien," *Bibelforskaren*, XL (1923), 273–74.

[7] Nygren, *Religiöst apriori*, pp. 234–36.

[8] *Ibid.*, pp. 238–40.

[9] Because our only concern at this point is to note the way in which Nygren's transcendental deduction of the religious category prepares the way for the development of the historical method of motif research, we shall not examine in any further detail the approach Nygren makes to the problem of religious validity. For a critical discussion of Nygren's transcendental deduction of the religious category, see Bernhard Erling, *Nature and History: A Study in Theological Methodology with Special Attention to Motif Research*, Studia Theologica Lundensia 19 (Lund, 1960), pp. 49–79, 159–91.

[10] Nygren, *Religiöst apriori*, p. 164.

[11] Anders Nygren, *Dogmatikens vetenskapliga grundläggning* (Stockholm, 1922), pp. 138–50.

[12] *Ibid.*, pp. 131–33.

[13] This monograph has been translated by Philip S. Watson and forms the first part of *Essence of Christianity* (Philadelphia, 1961).

[14] *Ibid.*, pp. 38–48.

[15] Anders Nygren, *Filosofisk och kristen etik*, 2nd ed. (Stockholm, 1932), pp. 237–300.

[16] *Ibid.*, pp. 244–52. Since a distinction is being made in this essay between Nygren's earlier descriptions of the historical content of the religious category and the later development of the method of motif research, the

question can be raised as to what extent the eros, nomos, and agape motifs which Nygren later describes in *Agape and Eros*, Sw. ed. 1930–36, rev. trans. Philip S. Watson (Philadelphia, 1953), are anticipated in the three forms of fellowship which the God relationship may manifest outlined in *Filosofisk och kristen etik*. Quite clearly the nomos and the agape motifs correspond to the legalistic and the love relationships. It is questionable, however, as to whether the eros motif may be identified with the despotic power relationship. One possible answer is to say that the eros motif is not a religion where the God relationship is one of fellowship. Nygren says that in this latter category are to be found not only primitive mana religions, but also many higher religions. *Filosofisk och kristen etik*, p. 244. The question would, however, remain as to where in terms of his later classification the despotic power type of religion would be found. Of interest in this connection is the fact that according to Nygren this kind of religion can take a degenerate form in which man seeks to gain power over God. *Ibid.*, p. 249. Furthermore in his distinction between three ethical types which correspond to the three religious types distinguished in *Filosofisk och kristen etik*, the power ethic is best illustrated in Nietzsche's ethics, *Ibid.*, p. 189, which at another point Nygren says is not without traces of Christian influence. *Ibid.*, p. 225. It would appear that it is especially with respect to Nygren's interpretation of this third type of religious and ethical orientation that the method of motif research reveals further development.

[17] *Ibid.*, pp. 266–67.

[18] *Ibid.*, pp. 276–82. The reference to "lost love" comes from a later essay, *Försoningen en gudsgärning* (1932), see Nygren, *Essence of Christianity*, pp. 124–26, and also appears again in *Agape and Eros* (1953), pp. 731–33. Yet it would appear to be simply a further development of the understanding of Christian reconciliation already set forth in *Filosofisk och kristen etik*.

[19] *Ibid.*, pp. 287–300.

[20] See *Religiositet och kristendom* (Uppsala, 1926), pp. 30–33. See also Erling, *Nature and History*, pp. 151–52.

[21] See Philip S. Watson's interpretation of the relation betwen the agape motif and the other motifs, "Translator's Preface," *Agape and Eros* (1953), pp. xiv–xv.

[22] Nygren, *Filosofi och motivforskning*, pp. 41–42; *Dogmatikens vetenskapliga grundläggning*, pp. 36–37.

[23] *Filosofisk och kristen etik* (1932), p. 126.

[24] *Filosofi och motivforskning*, p. 44; *Agape and Eros* (1953), p. 42.

[25] *Agape and Eros*, p. 43.

[26] *Filosofi och motivforskning*, pp. 40–45.

[27] *Agape and Eros* (1953), p. 42.

[28] *Filosofi och motivforskning*, pp. 45–46.

[29] *Ibid.*, p. 62.

[30] *Ibid.*, p. 72; *Agape and Eros* (1953), p. 32.

[31] *Filosofi och motivforskning*, p. 72.

[32] *Ibid.*, p. 78; cf. *Agape and Eros* (1953), p. 35.

[33] *Filosofi och motivforskning*, p. 65.

[34] Anders Nygren, "Det självklaras roll i historien," *K. Humanistiska Vetenskapssamfundets i Lund Årsberättelse* (1943–44), I, 1–12; German trans., 12–24.

[35] *Thus Spake Zarathustra*, ch. xxiv, trans. Thomas Common, *The Philosophy of Nietzsche* (New York, 1954).

[36] *Filosofi och motivforskning,* pp. 47–50.

[37] *Ibid.,* p. 50.

[38] For this terminology see Charles A. Beard, "Grounds for a Reconsideration of Historiography," *Theory and Practice in Historical Study: A Report of the Committee on Historiography,* ed. Merle Curti (New York, Social Science Research Council Bulletin 54, 1946), p. 5.

[39] *Filosofi och motivforskning,* pp. 52–60.

[40] *Agape and Eros* (1953), pp. 37–38.

[41] Nygren, "Det självklaras roll i historien," pp. 4–5.

[42] *Filosofi och motivforskning,* pp. 46–47.

[43] *Ibid.,* p. 50.

[44] "Det självklaras roll i historien," p. 4.

[45] R. G. Collingwood, *The Idea of History* (Oxford, 1951), pp. 266–82.

[46] An interesting discussion of the relation between a theological and a general approach to history, coming to some of the same conclusions as those of this essay, is to be found in Sidney E. Mead's "Church History Explained," first published in the March 1963 issue of *Church History* and reprinted in *New Theology No. 1,* eds. Martin E. Marty and Dean G. Peerman (New York, 1964), pp. 75–93. Mead calls attention to the canon of the historians that "every written history . . . is a selection of facts made by some person or persons and is ordered or organized under the influence of some scheme of reference, interest, or emphasis . . . in the thought of the author or authors," p. 82. Mead cites this canon from the above-mentioned *Theory and Practice in Historical Study: A Report of the Committee on Historiography,* p. 135 (see Note 38). He goes on to say, "It follows from these considerations that every written history is at least implicitly an explanation and defense of the allegiance—the faith—of the historian. It points to that to which the historian is committed. In this respect the Christian historian does not differ from the non-Christian historians. His conflict with them, if any, is a conflict of allegiances—of faiths—and should be recognized as such. This means that the basic differences between historians—or between schools of historians—are theological and / or philosophical and cannot be resolved by historical methods. This suggests at least that theology *is* the 'Queen of the sciences,' the final arbiter between the claims of the several disciplines and between the schools within disciplines," p. 83.

5. Literary Studies and the Use of Motifs in Nygren's Sense

[1] Anders Nygren, *Den kristna kärlekstanken genom tiderna. Eros och Agape,* Första delen (Stockholm, 1930); Senare delen (Stockholm, 1936). Anders Nygren, *Agape and Eros, A Study of the Christian Idea of Love,* Part I, trans. A. G. Hebert (London, 1932); Part II, Vols. I and II, trans. Philip S. Watson (London, 1938 and 1939).

[2] René Wellek, *Concepts of Criticism,* ed. and introd., Stephen G. Nichols, Jr. (New Haven and London, 1963), pp. 306–7.

[3] Arthur O. Lovejoy, *The Great Chain of Being, A Study of the History of an Idea* (Cambridge, Mass., 1936). Compare Lovejoy's Chain concept with a similar concept as developed by Nygren: The Alexandrian world-scheme; cf. indexes in the above-mentioned Parts I and II of *Agape and Eros* (see Note 1).

[4] Cf., e.g., Knut Erik Tranöy, *Wholes and Structures: An Attempt at a Philosophical Analysis,* Interdisciplinary Studies from the Scandinavian Summer University (Copenhagen, 1959).

[5] H. D. F. Kitto, *Form and Meaning in Drama, A Study of Six Greek Plays and of Hamlet* (London, 1956). Cf., index.

[6] Karen Blixen, *Out of Africa* (London, 1937, 1960), p. 280.

[7] Erik M. Christensen, *Ex auditorio, Kunst og ideer hos Martin A. Hansen* (Fredensborg, Denmark, 1965).

[8] Martin A. Hansen, *The Liar* (first publ. 1950), translated from the Danish by John Jepson Egglishaw (London, 1954), p. 199.

[9] Cf., the critical summing up in Thorkild Bjørnvig, *Forsvar for Kains Alter, En kritisk Efterskrift* (Copenhagen, 1965). See also, Erik M. Christensen, "Martin A. Hansen om kristendom," *Edda*, LXVI (Oslo, 1966).

[10] Anders Nygren, "Augustinus' Confessiones, dess litterära byggnad och dess tolkning," *Filosofi och motivforskning* (Stockholm, 1940), pp. 112–35.

[11] Nygren, *Agape and Eros*, Part II, Vol. II; pp. 398 ff.

[12] Jean-Louis Bellenot, "Les Formes d l'amour dans la Nouvelle Héloïse et La Signification symbolique des personnages de Julie et de Saint-Preux," *Annales de La Société Jean-Jacques Rousseau, tome trente-troisième* 1953–1955, Genève, pp. 149–208.

[13] Cf. e.g., M. Johann Nic. Meinhard, *Versuche über den Charakter und die Werke der besten Italiänischen Dichter*. Erster Theil, Neue Auflage, Braunschweig, 1774; "Uber die Poesien des Petrarca," p. 190:

> Diese Idee ist das System von der Schönheit und der Liebe, welches wir in den Werken der *Plato* finden, dieses Philosophen, der für empfindliche Leser so viel Reizendes hat; wie der eben so zärtliche als tiefsinnige Verfasser der Neuen Eloise aus seiner Erfahrung bestätigt. Diese Briefe kann man, im Vorbeigehen es zu sagen, als den besten Commentar über den *Petrarca* betrachten; sie sind mit dem Geiste ihres gemeinschaftlichen Lehrers, des *Plato* genähret.

6. Motif Research and the New Testament

[1] Anders Nygren, *Agape and Eros*, trans. Philip Watson (Philadelphia, 1953), p. 39.

[2] This methodology is a controversial issue. The philosophic implications and the question of its adequacy for the theological inquiry are special problems outside the field of this paper.

[3] Anders Nygren, "From Atomism to Contexts of Meaning in Philosophy" dedicated to Gunnar Aspelin on the occasion of his sixty-fifth birthday September 23, 1963, published in *Philosophical Essays Dedicated to Gunnar Aspelin* (Lund, 1963). (See also his latest book: *Meaning and Method: Prolegomena to a Scientific Philosophy of Religion* [Philadelphia, 1969]).

[4] *Agape and Eros* (1953), p. 35.

[5] *Ibid.*, p. 47.

[6] Anders Nygren, *Commentary on Romans*, trans. Carl C. Rasmussen (Philadelphia, 1949), pp. 81–92.

[7] Anders Nygren, *Significance of the Bible for the Church* (Philadelphia, 1963), p. 18.

[8] *Ibid.*, p. 26.

[9] Anders Nygren, *Christ and His Church* (Philadelphia, 1956), pp. 20–23.

[10] Anders Nygren, *The Gospel of God*, trans. L. F. Trinterud (London, 1951), pp. 28–31.

[11] *Ibid.*, pp. 34–47.
[12] *Agape and Eros*, pp. 61–75.

7. Agape in the New Testament

[1] All quotations are from the revised edition of the English translation by Philip S. Watson (London, 1953). Afterwards referred to as AE.

[2] For example, H. Scholz, *Eros and Caritas, Die platonische Liebe im Sinne des Christentums* (1929) and H. Preisker, *Die urchristliche Botschaft von der Liebe Gottes in der vergleichenden Religionsgeschichte* (1930).

[3] For the transcendental establishment of motif research see Anders Nygren, *Filosofi och motivforskning* (Stockholm, 1940); see the article "Motivforschung" by V. Lindström in *Die Religion in Geschichte und Gegenwart*, IV, No. 3, 1960, col. 1160–63, and the author's article, "Motiv" in the Lexikon für Theologie u. Kirche, VII, 1963, col. 663s.

[4] See, for example, on the subject of love, works by W. Lütgert (1905), J. Ziegler (1930–37), concerning doxa, J. Schneider (1932), H. Kittel (1934), G. Kittel in *Theologische Wortbuch (of the) New Testament*, II, 1935, 235–58; cf., B. Stein (Kebod Jahwe, 1939) about Charis G. P. Wetter (1913), J. Wobbe (1932) and on Justice (of God), Fr. Nötscher (1915).

[5] See, for example, L. Goppelt, *Judentum und Christentum im 1. und 2. Jahrhundert* (Gütersloh, 1954); W. Schmidthals, *Die Gnosis in Korinth* (Göttingen, 1956); R. M. Wilson, *The Gnostic Problem* (London, 1958); E. Peterson, *Frühkirche, Judentum und Gnosis* (Freiburg, 1959; R. M. Grant, *Gnosticism and Early Church* (New York, 1959). For the Qumran scrolls and their relation to the New Testament see especially A. P. Davies, *The Meaning of the Dead Sea Scrolls* (London, 1956); J. Daniélou, *Les manuscrits de la Mer Morte et le Christianisme* (Paris, 1957); K. Schubert, *Die Gemeinde vom Toten Meer* (München-Basel, 1956); R. Mayer and J. Reuss, *Die Qumranfunde und die Bibel* (Regensburg, 1959); J. Hempel, *Die Texte von Qumran in der heutigen Forschung* (Göttingen, 1962); K. Müller, *Qumran*, in Sacramentum mundi, III (Freiburg, 1969), col. 1–18.

[6] Thus the Protestant theologian, G. Eichholz, writes with reference to Cor. 13 in *Herr tue meine Lippen auf*" [Lord, open my lips] II[2] (Wuppertal, 1959), p. 174: "The desired specfication can by no means be achieved merely by following up the often confirmed contrast betwen Eros and Agape, or by tracing the difference in structure according to the pattern of Søren Kierkegaard or Anders Nygren, let alone that such a structure-analysis could only approach the limits of the unique truth in the love of which the Apostle Paul speaks. This love does not simply appear as the opposite of Eros' love. It issues forth from its own roots and its superiority would seem rather to be effaced by an antithesis, however clear-cut between Agape and Eros."

[7] See especially J. Burnaby, *Amor Dei* (London, 1938), M. C. D'Arcy, *The Mind and Heart of Love, A Study in Eros and Agape* (London, 1947), and Victor Warnach, *Agape, Die Liebe als Grundmotiv der neutestamentlischen Theologie* (Düsseldorf, 1951), passim, esp. pp. 184–203.

[8] More is to be found in Warnach, *Agape*, pp. 215–41 and recently in his article "Das Wirken des Pneuma in den Gläubigen nach Paulus" in "Pro Veritate" (*Festschrift* for the Archbishop L. Jaeger and Bishop Stählin), Münster-Kassel, 1963, pp. 156–202. Cf., R. Koch, *Geist*, in Bibeltheologisches Vörterbuch, 3rd ed, (Graz, 1967) pp. 474–506, esp. 487.

⁹ Regarding this and the general ontologic character of agape see Warnach, *Agape*, pp. 166–70, 247–77.

¹⁰ In his report to a group of Evangelical and Roman Catholic theologians the author specified this under the title "Was ist exegetische Aussage?" [What is an exegetic statement]; this was published in the review for controversial theology *Catholica*, XVI (1962) 103–30.

¹¹ Gabriel Marcel, who is strongly inspired by the Bible, also thinks similarly.

¹² From this point of view Nygren could avoid the sterile antithesis of the Pauline "Agape of the Cross" and the Johannine "Agape-metaphysics" (*Agape and Eros*, pp. 146–59); for both Paul and John agree in accepting the ontological-personal nature of agape in the deeper sense we indicated above.

8. Some Interpretations of Agape and Eros

¹ Cited by Anders Nygren, *Agape and Eros*, p. 59. All references to this book are to the one-volume version of the translation by Philip S. Watson (London, 1953).

² E.g., *Ibid.*, pp. 64–65, 200–203.

³ *Ibid.*, p. 163–65.

⁴ *Ibid.*, p. 186.

⁵ M. C. D'Arcy, *The Mind and Heart of Love* (London, 1962), p. 85.

⁶ *Agape and Eros*, p. 186.

⁷ *Ibid.*, p. 195.

⁸ *Ibid.*, p. 196.

⁹ *Ibid.*, p. 569.

¹⁰ *Ibid.*, p. 101.

¹¹ *Ibid.*, p. 711.

¹² *Ibid.*, p. 91.

¹³ *Ibid.*, p. 210.

¹⁴ John Burnaby, *Amor Dei* (London, 1938), p. 17.

¹⁵ Paul Tillich, *Love, Power and Justice* (New York, 1960).

¹⁶ Burnaby, *Amor Dei*.

¹⁷ Tillich, *Love, Power and Justice*, p. 31.

¹⁸ Books 8 and 9.

¹⁹ For *Philia* see C. Spicq, *Agapè, Prolégomenes à une Etude de théologie néotestamentaire* (Louvain, 1955), pp. 12–32. The dominant idea is that Philia is between equals.

²⁰ Tillich, *Love, Power and Justice*, p. 30.

²¹ Cf. D. N. Morgan, *Love: Plato, the Bible and Freud* (New Jersey, 1964), pp. 160–67.

²² Tillich, in *Love, Power and Justice*, p. 34, wishes to drop the term "self-love" altogether, replacing it by "self-affirmation," "self-acceptance" and "selfishness" according to the context. In the interest of avoiding a too elaborate phraseology I have retained the term "self-love" for Tillich's first two senses, only keeping "selfishness" apart. Naturally the problem will arise whether the Platonic sense of "self-love" is in fact equivalent to "selfishness" or not, or indeed whether *all* self-love is in fact selfishness. This will be considered later.

²³ Cf. J. M. Rist, *Eros and Psyche: Studies in Plato, Plotinus and Origen* (Toronto, 1964), pp. 38–39.

[24] For further discussion of nonappetitive love in the *Symposium* see R. A. Markus, 'The Dialectic of Eros in Plato's *Symposium*," *Downside Review*, 233 (1955), 219–30; A. H. Armstrong, "Platonic *Eros* and Christian *Agape*," *Downside Review* 239 (1961), 106–7; and Rist, *Eros and Psyche*, pp. 23–28, 34–36.

[25] Cf., A. H. Armstrong, "Platonic Love," *Downside Review*, 242 (1964), 203–4 and Rist, *Eros and Psyche*, p. 28.

[26] See in particlar Armstrong, "Platonic Love," pp. 199–201 for a more detailed defense of this interpretation.

[27] For these passages see Rist, *Eros and Psyche*, pp. 32–33.

[28] For a more detailed discussion of the *Timaeus* passage, with refutation of attempts to explain it away see Rist, *Eros and Psyche*, pp. 30–34, and Armstrong, "Platonic Love," pp. 204–6. Morgan (*Love*, pp. 18–19) rightly assumes that there is a creative *love* in the Demiurge but fails to make clear that in the *Timaeus* this is not stated explicitly.

[29] This is an interesting reminder that eros need not be a mere thirst for pleasure even in sexual love.

[30] These topics are treated in J. M. Rist, *Plotinus: the Road to Reality* (Cambridge, Eng., 1967).

[31] Rist, *Eros and Psyche*, p. 83.

[32] *Ibid.*, p. 85; A. H. Armstrong, "Platonic *Eros* and Christian *Agape*," p. 113.

[33] Cf. 6.7.35.25 and Rist, *Eros and Psyche*, pp. 94–100.

[34] Rist, *Eros and Psyche*, p. 95; cf. W. R. Inge, *The Philosophy of Plotinus* (London, 1929), p. 154.

[35] Rist, *Eros and Psyche*, pp. 71–73, 86–87.

[36] Nygren, *Agape and Eros*, pp. 569–70.

[37] Cf. the allusions at *In Rep.* 1.74 ff., *In Alc.* 3–6 (Westerink) and in Marinus' *Vita Procli* 15 and 30.

[38] Cf. Armstrong, "Platonic *Eros* and Christian *Agape*," pp. 116–17 and Rist, *Eros and Psyche*, pp. 215–16. Armstrong ("Platonic Love," pp. 120–21) suggests that the neoplatonist Hierocles also developed Plato's thought along "unappetitive" lines, but here there seems much more likelihood of Christian influence. If this is the case, then he cannot be taken as an example of the growth of nonappetitive trends in the purely Platonic tradition. For Christian influences on Hierocles see K. Praechter, "Christlich-neuplatonische Beziehungen," *Byzantinische Zeitschrift*, XXI (1912), 1–27.

[39] Cf. Spicq, *Agapè, Prolégomenes*, pp. 32–36 and new S. West, "A further note on ΑΓΑΠΗ in P. Oxy. 1380," *Journal of Theological Studies*, 20, 1969, 228–30.

[40] *Agape and Eros*, p. 68. I do not propose to consider Nygren's treatment of the relation between Christian and Jewish love. For a critique of his rigorous separation see Morgan, *Love: Plato*, pp. 69–71.

[41] *Agape and Eros*, pp. 86–88.

[42] *Ibid.*, p. 154.

[43] *Ibid.*, p. 735.

[44] Here is one of the reasons why Nygren (*Ibid.*, pp. 151–52) finds John 17:24 unsatisfactory.

[45] *Ibid.*, p. 711.

[46] *Ibid.*, pp. 100–101.

[47] The point is made by T. Gould, *Platonic Love* (New York, 1963), p. 47.

[48] Armstrong, "Platonic Love," p. 207.

[49] L. Streiker, "The Christian Understanding of Platonic Love, A Critique of Anders Nygren's *Agape and Eros*," *The Christian Scholar*, XXXXVII (1964), 334. Streiker compares Philippians 1:6; 2:12.

[50] Cf. D'Arcy, The Mind and Heart of Love, p. 96.

[51] About the fact that the nature of sin and its causes differ in Plotinus and in the New Testament there is no dispute. That is not the question, however, which concerns us here. It should be added also that Streiker's remark ("The Christian Understanding," p. 339) "In the end, as St. Thomas Aquinas recognized, in all that he loves, God loves himself," needs clarification if its truth-value is to be considered. The Plotinian One, of course, loves itself in all things. (Cf. Rist, *Eros and Psyche*, p. 82.)

[52] *Agape and Eros*, p. 720. It is hard to see what Nygren would have made of Philippians 2:12: "Work out your own salvation in fear and trembling."

[53] In his discussion of this problem Nygren concerns himself unduly with a rebuttal of Aquinas' views and insufficiently with the exposition of the New Testament as represented by Galatians 5:6. Nygren (*Agape and Eros*, pp. 656-57) cites a number of passages from Aquinas designed to show that the faith which justifies is given its form, in the Aristotelian sense, by God's *caritas*. An infusion of God's grace or *caritas* leads to the possibility of a free choice. And a free choice of God is faith in Him. According to Nygren this means that the infused *caritas* provides the *form* of faith. I take him to mean that when man becomes loving, he then has the form of faith. It is not our immediate concern to examine Aquinas' view, but if Nygren had considered Galatians 5:6 at this point he would have recognized a theory which sidesteps his own argument with Aquinas.

Elsewhere (p. 128) Nygren does comment on Galatians 5:6—he translates the relevant words as "faith working through love." He holds that this means that "in Paul the ethical life of the Christian, or his love for his neighbor, is referred to faith as its religious basis." The translation of the Greek is almost certainly satisfactory (cf., C. F. D. Moule, *An Idiom-Book of New Testament Greek*² [Cambridge, 1960], p. 26—the New English Bible has as a preferred reading "faith active in love"); but in Galatians not the ethical life of the Christian but justification is in question. The most natural explanation is that Paul is speaking of a certain kind of faith, a faith that shows itself by love, a faith in fact inseparable from love. We need not rely on the much-abused epistle of James (2:17-19) for the idea that there are other kinds of faith possible. Paul himself speaks of them (1 Cor. 13:2).

The attitude of Luther (the source of Nygren's schematization, Faith versus Love) can be seen from the following passage of his Lectures on Galatians, 1535, directed against such a supposed schematization (*Luther's Works*, Vol. 27 [St. Louis, 1964], 28): "In this manner they completely transfer justification from faith and attribute it solely to love as thus defined. And they claim that this is proved by St. Paul in this passage 'faith working through love'—as though Paul wanted to say: 'You see, faith does not justify: in fact it is nothing unless love the worker is added, which forms faith.'" That Luther himself recognizes, however, that Galatians is concerned not with faith versus love but with a loving faith is clear from his 1519 Lectures (*Luther's Works*, p. 335): "But the faith which our theologians call 'infused' is without love." The differences between our interpretation and that of Luther is basically only a semantic one. Luther says that loving faith is true faith which justifies; other faiths are feigned faiths. We say that there is a loving faith which justifies and other faiths which do not. The latter is the more scriptural formulation.

[54] *Agape and Eros*, pp. 124–25.

[55] Streiker, "The Christian Understanding," p. 337, following P. S. Watson in a translator's note to Nygren, *Agape and Eros*, p. 124.

[56] *Agape and Eros*, p. 96.

[57] Tillich, *Love, Power and Justice*, p. 25.

[58] E. Fromm, *The Art of Loving* (New York, 1956), pp. 49–50.

9. Amor in St. Augustine

[1] *Agape and Eros*, Part II, *The History of the Christian Idea of Love* (in the German, *Die Gestaltwandlungen der Christlichen Liebe*). English text (2 Vols.) trans. Philip S. Watson (London, 1938–39). All references are given to the pages of Vol. II in the English edition.

[2] *Agape and Eros: A Study of the Christian idea of Love*, Part I, trans. A. G. Hebert (London, 1932).

[3] *Ibid.*, II, pp. 250 ff.

[4] *Ibid.*, II, pp. 232 f., 252.

[5] *omnis homo vult esse beatus. Agape and Eros*, II, pp. 258 f.

[6] In the first of two essays published under the title *Augustin und Luther* (Berlin, 1958).

[7] *Agape and Eros*, II, pp. 258 ff.

[8] *Ibid.*, II, pp. 265, 276.

[9] *Ibid.*, II, pp. 283 ff.

[10] This is hardly substantiated by the single reference to *In Ev. Jo. Tr.* x1.10: *si deum digne amemus, nummos(!) omnino non amabimus.*

[11] *Agape and Eros*, II, pp. 292 f.

[12] *Ibid.*, II, p. 307.

[13] *Ibid.*, II, pp. 309 ff.

[14] *De Civitate Dei* xiv.42; *Serm.* xcvi.2.

[15] *Agape and Eros*, II, pp. 325 f. *In Ev. Jo. Tr.* cxxiii.5.

[16] *Ibid.*, II, pp. 331 ff. *De Doctrina Christiana* I.xxx.33.

[17] *Agape and Eros*, II, pp. 335 ff.

[18] Dr. Nygren's interpretation of Augustine's doctrine has been criticized especially by a number of Swedish scholars: most recently by Ragnar Holte of Uppsala in *Beatitudo och Sapientia* (Stockholm, 1958), of which a French version was published in 1962 by Etudes Augustinienness (Paris), and Augustinian Studies, Assumption College, Worcester, Mass. For much of what follows I have to acknowledge my indebtedness to this valuable study.

[19] *Ibid.*, I, pp. 162 f.

[20] *Enneads* I.iv.11: cf. Augustine, *Soliloquia* I.i.3: *"Deus beatitudo, in quo et a quo et per quem beata sunt quae beata sunt omnia."*

[21] *Beatitude et Sagesse* (Paris, 1962), pp. 250–71.

[22] *Beatitude et Sagesse*, pp. 252–56.

[23] *De Genesi ad litteram* xi.20.

[24] *De Civitate Dei* xiv. 28; xv.3.

[25] *Epist.* 211.12.

[26] *Serm.* 34, 8.

[27] *Agape and Eros*, II, pp. 331 ff.

[28] *Ibid.*, I, pp. 113 f.; 1 Corinthians xiii is not a digression after the doctrine of the one Body set forth in c.xiii; and cf. Eph. iv.1–6, and Col. iii.14, with Rom. xii.9 f.

[29] *In Ev. Jo. Tr.* lxv.3: John xvii.21.

[30] Augustine, *De Trinitate* VIII.vii.10.

[31] *Augustin und Luther.*

[32] *Augustin und Luther*, p. 30.

[33] *Ibid.*, p. 23.

[34] *Serm.* 71. 18.

10. Caritas in Augustine and Medieval Theololgy

[1] Anders Nygren, *Agape and Eros* (London, 1939 and 1954), p. 243. All subsequent page references to *Agape and Eros* in this chapter are to this edition.

[2] *Ibid.*, p. 244.

[3] *Ibid.*, p. 244.

[4] *Ibid.*, p. 281.

[5] *Ibid.*, p. 476.

[6] *Ibid.*, p. 479.

[7] *Ibid.*, p. 500.

[8] *Ibid.*, p. 501.

[9] *Ibid.*, p. 503.

[10] *Nicomachean Ethics*, I:7.

[11] *Agape and Eros*, p. 183.

[12] *Ibid.*, p. 508.

[13] *Ibid.*, p. 511.

[14] *Ibid.*, p. 510.

[15] *Ibid.*, p. 511.

[16] De spiritu et littera, cap. 64: maior notitia/maior dilectio.

[17] *Agape and Eros*, p. 546.

[18] *Ibid.*, p. 533.

[19] *Ibid.*, p. 539.

[20] In *Ev. Jn* tract, CXXIII. 5., cf. Nygren, *Agape and Eros*, p. 543.

[21] *Agape and Eros*, p. 544.

[22] *Ibid.*

[23] *De lib. arb.* 3, 76; cf. *Serm.* 142, 3.

[24] *Agape and Eros*, pp. 555 f.

[25] *Ibid.*, pp. 526 ff.

[26] *Ibid.*, p. 526.

[27] *Ibid.*, pp. 526 f.

[28] *Ibid.*, p. 527.

[29] *Ibid.*, p. 559.

[30] *Ibid.*, p. 563.

[31] *Ibid.*, p. 609.

[32] *Ibid.*, p. 619.

[33] *Ibid.*, p. 620.

[34] *Ibid.*, p. 639.

[35] *Ibid.*, p. 640.

[36] *Ibid.*, p. 642.

[37] *Ibid.*, p. 643.

[38] *Ibid.*, p. 645.

[39] *Summa theologica*, 1, 2 q. 94 a.2: Quaelibet substantia appetit conservationem sui esse. Cf. q. 48 a.l; *Met.* 1:1: Unaquaeque res naturaliter appetit perfectionem suam. Cf. *C. gent.* 3:16; *In Div. Nom.* 9, 4; etc.

[40] *Summa theologica*, 1, 2 q.l a.2: Nihil enim reducit se de potentia in actum. *Phys.* 7:10: Non reducit quod est in potentia in actum nisi per id quod est in actu. Cf. *C. gent.* 1, 16: 2, 16.

[41] Cf. Steinbuchel, *Der Zweckgedanke in der Philosophie des Thomas* (1912), (Beitrage z. Geschichte der Philosophie des Mittelalters, 11:1), p. 27: "Even when outer goals are achieved, it is done for an immanent goal, for self-perfection" (translated by the author).

[42] *Summa theologica*, 1, 2 q. 26 a.4: Sic ergo motus amoris in duo tendit, scilicet: in bonum quod quis vult alicui, vel sibi vel alii, et in illud cui ult bonum. Cf. 1, 2 q.20 a.1 ad 3; 1, 2 q. 77 a.4 ad 3; *De perf.* 13.

[43] *Summa theologica*, 1, 2 q.26 a.4: Ad illud ergo bonum, quod quis vult alteri, habetur amor concupiscentiae; ad illud autem cui aliquis vult bonum, habetur amor amicitiae. Thomas's terminology is not quite consistent. Sometimes he signifies a misdirected love in Augustine something like cupiditas as amor concupiscentiae, and love to another person than oneself as amor amicitiae.

[44] *Ibid.*, 1, 2 q.28 a.4.

[45] The problem is dealt with more exhaustively in my dissertation: *Person och gemenskap enligt romersk-katolsk och luthersk grundaskadning* [Person and community according to basic Roman and Lutheran conceptions] (Stockholm, 1947), pp. 121 ff.

[46] *Summa theologica*, 1 q.60 a.4: Illud autem quod est unum cum aliquo, est ipsumet; unde unumquodque diligit id quod est unum sibi.

[47] For a more detailed account of the ordo Caritatis in Thomas, see my above cited work (Note 45), pp. 174 ff.

[48] This contrast is excellently described, although in other terms, by Joseph Klein in his booklet, *Die Caritas-lehre des Johannes Duns Scotus* (Munster, 1926).

11. Agape in Luther

[1] Anders Nygren, *Den kristna kälestanken* genom tiderna. *Eros och Agape.* I (Stockholm, 1930, 1947; II, Stockholm, 1936, 1948). Quotations from English translation by Philip S. Watson: *Agape and Eros* (London and Philadelphia, 1953).

[2] *Agape and Eros*, II, 681–741. Cf., also Anders Nygren, "Die Bedeutung Luthers für den christlichen Liebesgedanken," *Luther-Jahrbuch*, XI (Munich, 1929), 87–133.

[3] See *Agape and Eros*, I, p. 48.

[4] Even in the Synoptic Gospels (*Agape and Eros* I, pp. 61–104) and John (*Ibid.*, pp. 146–59) the agape motif does not find expression in perfect purity. In them, besides God's love, love for God (which in Paul, as in Luther, is replaced by faith) plays a part. In John, moreover, God's agape easily passes into a metaphysical conception of the Father's temporal love for the Son, so that it loses something of its "spontaneity." At the same time love of neighbor, restricted to love of the brethren, easily becomes particularist: God's agape is directed only towards the limited circle of his own, not towards the world.

[5] *Ibid.*, pp. 105–45.

[6] *Ibid., II*, pp. 254–88, 335–48.

[7] *Ibid.*, pp. 289–316, 349–92, 409–46.

[8] *Ibid.*, pp. 613–64.

[9] *Ibid.*, pp. 449–562.

[10] *Ibid.*, p. 682.

[11] *Ibid.*, p. 683.

[12] On the New Testament, see: C. H. Ratschow, "Agape: Nächstenliebe und Bruderliebe," *Zeitschrift für systematische Theologie*, XXI (1950), 160–82; Victor Warnach, *Agape, Die Liebe als Grundmotiv der neutestamentlichen Theologie,* (Düsseldorf, 1951); W. Thimme, *Eros im Neuen Testament*, in: Verbum Dei manet in aeternum, *Festschrift für Otto Schmitz* (Witten, 1953), pp. 103–16.

On the History of Theology, cf. M. Fuerth, *Caritas und Humanitas: Zur Form und Wandlung des christlichen Liebesgedankens* (1933). G. Hultgren, *Det evangeliska kärleksbudet hos Augustinus* (Stockholm, 1939). M. C. D'Arcy, *The Mind and Heart of Love, A Study in Eros and Agape* (London, 1945, and 1947). See also *Religion in Geschichte und Gegenwart.* Tübingen, J. C. B. Mohr, 1957–62. Ed. K. Galling, II, 605.

[13] On method, cf. H. U. v. Balthasar, "Eros und Agape," *Stimmen der Zeit*, No. 136 (1938), 389–402. J. Burnaby, *Amor Dei* (London, 1938). K. Leese, "Eros und Agape," *Zeitschrift für systematische Theologie*, XIX (1938), 319–39. V. Lindström, "Distinktionen mellan lag och evangelium och frågan om kristendomens egenart," in: *Vid Abdomens fot* (Helsinki, 1949), pp. 112–31. G. Wingren, *Teologiens metodfråga* (Malmö, 1954). (German trans.: *Die Methodenfrage der Theologie,* [Göttingen, 1957]). V. Lindström, "Motivforschung," *Die Religion in Geschichte und Gegenwart,* IV, 1160–63.

[14] The figures in parentheses in the remainder of the first section of this paper refer to the relevent pages in *Agape and Eros*, II.

[15] *Martin Luthers Werke: Kritische Gesamtausgabe* (Weimar, 1883), cited as WA, 56:157, 2 ff.: "The summary of this epistle is to pluck up and to break down and to destroy and to overthrow all wisdom and righteousness of the flesh (whatever we are in the sight of men, or even to ourselves), however genuine and sincere, and to plant and to build up and to magnify sin (however little it may exist, or was previously thought to exist)."

[16] Nygren, "Bedeutung," p. 95. Cf. *Agape and Eros*, II, p. 699.

[17] In *Agape and Eros*, II, pp. 717 ff. and "Bedeutung," pp. 89 ff., Nygren discusses the charge, raised by both Catholics (Mausbach) and Protestants (Runestam), that Luther has destroyed the Christian idea of love, or at any rate greatly diminished its scope in the interests of faith. In answer to this Nygren shows how Luther has repudiated only a particular, egocentrically oriented, idea of love which it is wrong to describe as "Christian," to make room for the genuine, specifically Christian, idea of love. He finds Luther's opposition to Catholic Christianity more clearly revealed in his treatment of the idea of love than anywhere else ("Bedeutung," 87, 89).

[18] On this, cf. R. Schwartz, *Fides, Spes und Caritas beim jungen Luther.* Unter besonderer Berücksichtigung der mittelalterlichen Tradition, *Arbeiten zur Kirchengeschichte* 34 (Berlin, 1962), pp. 358–88: Luther's controversy with Gabriel Biel, was deep-seated and Luther carried it into great detail; he is attacking Biel's claim that "Deum diligere super omnia" is a natural possibility for man as he is.

[19] Cf., "Bedeutung," pp. 89 ff.

[20] *Ibid.*, pp. 92 ff.

[21] *Ibid.*, p. 88.

[22] See above, Note 17.

[23] "Bedeutung," p. 116: "In demolishing the Catholic view of 'fides caritate formata' and dethroning love from the place within the doctrine of justification which Catholics have been so ready to assign it, Luther can be said to be actually building up Agape-love. For in the process he has validated first God's Agape as absolutely sovereign, spontaneous, and unmotivated, and secondly Christian love as pure and free from all egocentric calculations." In this Luther must be respected as "the builder and renovator of theocentric Agape-love."

[24] Cf. the criticism which F. K. Schumann, "Natürliche Liebe und christliche Liebe," in: *Um Kirche und Lehre* (Stuttgart, 1936), pp. 175–201, brings against this claim, though without mentioning Nygren by name.

[25] "Bedeutung," p. 120.

[26] *Agape and Eros*, II, pp. 683 ff.: In contrast to Augustine and the Middle Ages, Luther drew the features of love in the Christian sense not from man, but entirely from God's act in Christ.

[27] "Bedeutung," p. 127.

[28] On this, cf. T. Harnack, *Luthers Theologie mit besonderer Beziehung auf seine Versöhnungs und Erlösungslehre.* Erste Abteilung, *Luthers theologische Grundanschauungen* (1862). New edition (Munich, 1927); R. Seeberg, *Lehrbuch der Dogmengeschichte*, IV/I, 5th ed. (Basel, 1953), 178–85; W. v. Loewenich, *Luthers theologia crucis* (1929), 4th ed. (Munich, 1954); W. Elert, *Morphologie des Luthertums* I (1931), 2nd ed. (Munich, 1952), pp. 186 ff; L. Pinomaa, *Der Zorn Gottes in der Theologie Luthers: Ein Beitrag zu der Frage nach der Einheit des Gottesbildes bei Luther* (Helsinki, 1938); H. Bandt, *Luthers Lehre vom verborgenen Gott: Eine Untersuchung zu dem offenbarungsgeschichtlichen Ansatz seiner Theologie* (Berlin, 1958).

[29] Cf. W. Maurer, *Von der Freiheit eines Christenmenschen: Zwei Untersuchungen zu Luthers Reformationsschriften* 1520/21 (Göttingen, 1949), pp. 113 f.

[30] G. Aulén, *Den kristna gudsbilden* (Lund, 1927), German trans., *Das christliche Gottesbild in Vergangenheit und Gegenwart* (Gütersloh, 1930), pp. 160 ff., seems to me at this point to do greater justice to Luther, when he speaks of different religious "motifs" (power, justice, love) in Luther's picture of God, which Luther in a tense "dynamic synthesis" concentrates on the motif of love, yet does not reduce. Cf. Seeberg, *Lehrbuch*, pp. 180 f. Cf., also Lindström, "Distinktionen," and Wingren, *Die Methodenfrage der Theologie*, both of whom are critical of Nygren and opposed to the elimination of law from God's activity in favor of an undialectical exposition of the motif of love.

[31] Seeberg, *Lehrbuch*, p. 293.

[32] Cf. W. Maurer, *Freiheit*, p. 102, in connection with the passage in Luther's Exposition of the Magnificat, WA 7:556, 30 ff.

[33] Cf. Seeberg, *Lehrbuch*, p. 255; Schwartz, *Fides*, p. 398. For Luther the fact that God gives and makes possible spontaneous love shows that his *demand* for love does not apply to acts.

[34] Cf., *Agape and Eros*, II, pp. 692 ff.

[35] Cf., Schwartz, *Fides*, pp. 388–413.

[36] Cf., Schumann "Natürliche," pp. 193–98: Genuine love, which does exist in the natural man, is nevertheless carried out by a "crooked will," and only when this has been exposed as what it is and destroyed can God's transforming love obtain a foothold in us and make our imperfect love for our neighbor a genuine love from the heart. In faith and hope we acknowledge our existence as sinful and have faith that God causes his love to pass through our sinful existence. In this way, God's activity is neither simply opposed to natural love, nor does it merely sublimate it, but it meets our natural love and transforms its whole basis.

[37] Cf., *Agape and Eros*, II, pp. 734–37.

[38] On this, cf., e.g., R. Prenter, *Spiritus Creator: Studien zu Luthers Theologie* (Kopenhagen, 1944, 1946), German trans. (Munich, 1954), pp. 91 ff. P. Althaus, *Die Theologie Martin Luthers* (Gütersloh, 1962), pp. 121 ff. These suffice to confirm the same point in principle.

[39] Warnach, *Agape;* and Thimme, *Eros.*

[40] WA 7:556. Cf. A. Peters, *Glaube und Werk*. Luthers Rechtfertigungslehre im Licht der Heiligen Schrift, *Arbeiten zur Geschichte und Theologie des Luthertums VIII* (Berlin, 1962), pp. 190 f.: The distinction is one that Luther makes between a servant's love and a son's, which loves God, his father, for his own sake alone. Pages 193, 196, 198, 200: Therefore fear of punishment or hope of reward can play no part in genuine love for God. P. Althaus, *Die Theologie*, p. 114: God's love, according to Luther, as simple, existential acceptance of God's divinity. Especially in his frequent expositions of the First Commandment Luther has acknowledged that there is a special and indispensable place for love towards God alongside fear and faith. For this, cf., J. Meyer, *Historischer Kommentar zu Luthers Kleinem Katechismus* (Gütersloh, 1929), pp. 178–83. He quotes Tischveden 2:395 f.: "Fear, that we may not offend, love as the feeling that God loves us and gives us good gifts, faith as confidence that good things are promised us."

[41] Cf. the principle involved in the raising of the question "What is the Christian understanding of love for God?" In N. H. Søe's, *Christliche Ethik Ein Lehrbuch* (Danish, 1942, 1946, German trans. Munich, 1949), pp. 143–46.

[42] W. Elert, *Das christliche Ethos: Grundlinien der lutherischen Ethik* (1949), 2nd ed. (Hamburg, 1961), pp. 360–69: "Love for God and the First Commandment."

[43] *Ibid.*, pp. 360–63. The figures in parentheses in my text refer to the pages in Elert's *Ethos*. The italics are for the most part mine.

[44] On this, see, Schumann, "Natürliche," pp. 191 f.: "The word love, which comes from the world of nature, does not in principle acquire its Christian meaning when it is applied to a new attitude of men as Christians, but when it describes this union with us of God in Jesus Christ. Love in the Christian sense means in the first place, and decisive over all other linguistic usage, God's love for us." What it means to speak of the Christian's love follows from this. It is love fashioned by God's love. Love in the Christian sense means to be in God's love, to "abide" in God's love, and *so* to love. "Our love . . . is nothing but abiding in his love. Our abiding in his love is what enables us . . . to love."

[45] On this, cf., Althaus, *Die Theologie*, p. 233: "Enlightened by the Holy Spirit, 'I heartily rejoice in the First Commandment through the grace which Christ has brought me, while I believe in him.' I no longer stand impotent, and so in despair, before this commandment of God's, but

through. It yearns for Christ, receives consolation, and loves him in return" (WA 7:29). "Through faith the soul is made pure, and caused to love God; yet she wishes that all things were pure. . . . Yet the deeds are not the real essence of being good, and it is not true that they make a man dutiful and righteous before God. Rather he does them voluntarily and freely, out of love, in order to please God. His only object is to seek to do what pleases God, whose will he gladly does as well as ever he can" (WA 7, pp. 30 f.). "Lo, that is how love and joy in God flow out of faith, and how love gives rise to a free, eager, and glad life of serving one's neighbor without reward" (WA 7, p. 36).

[52] "Without this grateful, blessing, enriching love, faith is dead, not because it is then unable to accomplish anything, but because it is then not faith at all. For faith means to accept the whole of life, with all its earthly content, as a gift." (Elert, *Ethos*, p. 359). On Luther, cf., R. Prenter, *Spiritus Creator* and A. Peters, *Glaube und Werk*, pp. 198 f. Both allude also to the danger which Luther saw in the separation of love from faith. If the direction of our love towards God, which faith includes in itself, is lost, it may itself become a "work"!

[53] Cf., e.g., Luther's Sermon on Good Works, 1520, WA 6, pp. 204–7, pp. 210–13; or Luther's *Large Catechism*, 1529, WA 30/1, pp. 180 f. Cf., W. Maurer, *Freiheit*, p. 61, with reference to Luther's treatise on The Freedom, 1520: "The inner man has become one with God. He is joyful and glad on account of Christ, who has done so much for him. All his pleasure consists in serving God in return, without reward, and out of unconstrained love."

[54] Cf., H. M. Müller, *Erfahrung und Glaube bei Luther* (1929).

[55] On this, cf., Seeberg, *Lehrbuch*, pp. 382 f.; Maurer, *Freiheit*, pp. 100–102; Prenter, *Spiritus Creator*, pp. 81 f. In the *Large Catechism* (1529) Luther says: When by God's good gift "we know and feel his fatherly affection and unfathomable love for us, this would warm our hearts, and inflame them with a desire to offer up thanks, and to use all we possess in God's honor and praise" (WA 30/1 1, p. 185).

[56] Elert, *Morphologie*, p. 153.

[57] See the examples given by Elert, *Morphologie*, pp. 146–54.

[58] *Ibid.*

[59] On its meaning in the New Testament, cf., R. Bultmann, *Das christliche Gebot der Nächstenliebe* (1930), in *Glauben und Verstehen*, I, 2nd ed. (Tübingen, 1954), 229–44.

[60] Cf., *Agape and Eros*, II, pp. 727 ff.; "Bedeutung," p. 88. See above, Note 33.

[61] Cf. Althaus, *Die Theologie*, pp. 119–27, 235–38.

[62] On this, cf., A. Hardeland, *Das Erste Gebot in den Katechismen Luthers* (1916). Also his "Luthers Erklärung des Ersten Gebots im Lichte seiner Rechtfertigungslehre." *Theologische Studien und Kritiken* (1919), pp. 201 ff. H. Bornkamm, "Christus und das Erste Gebot in der Anfechtung bei Luther," *Zeitschrift für systematische Theologie* (1927/28), pp. 452 ff. H. M. Müller and H. Bornkamm, "Diskussion über das Erste Gebot bei Luther," *Theologische Blätter* (Bonn and Leipzig), 1927, pp. 269 ff.; 1928, pp. 37 ff. P. Althaus, "Gottes Gottheit als Sinn der Rechtfertigungslehre Luthers," *Luther-Jahrbuch*, XIII (Munich, 1931), pp. 1–28. A. Siirala, *Gottes Gebot bei Martin Luther: Eine Untersuchung der Theologie Luthers unter besonder Berücksichtigung des Ersten Hauptstückes im Grossen Katechis-*

mus (Helsinki, 1956). (Further literature in E. Schlink, *Theologie der Lutherischen Bekenntnisschriften*, 3rd ed. [Munich, 1948], pp. 112 f., and in Elert, *Ethos*, pp. 360, 589.)

[63] Althaus, "Gottes Gottheit," p. 119. On this, cf., Althaus, *Gebot und Gesetz* (Gütersloh, 1952) and W. Joest, *Gesetz und Freiheit: Das Problem des tertius usus legis bei Luther und die neutestamentliche Parainese*, 2nd ed. (Göttingen, 1956).

[64] On this, cf. especially Althaus, *Die Theologie*, pp. 120–27, with illustrations from Luther showing how God's loving will reaches man as a helpful command (as distinct from "law"). "Faith shows itself in this . . . that man strives to fulfill God's commandment, thus wishes for love. We are meant to love—the action commanded is shaped by this fact, not only as regards its content, but also as regards man's personal attitude to it. For God's commandment further demands that the will be moved by God's good will *alone*, in other words by pure delight in his law, and that it shall be entirely man's *own* will" (124).

[65] Cf. Althaus, *Die Theologie*, pp. 232 f. In this connection mention must be made of two important studies by P. Althaus, in which he examines with the greatest care Luther's exposition of two New Testament passages. In each of these, in addition to faith, or rather within faith, there is an express call for love: (a) "and if I have all faith," 1 Cor. 13:2 in Luther's exposition. *Gedenkschrift für W. Elert* (Berlin, 1955), pp. 128 ff.; (b) Love and the assurance of salvation, 1 John 4:17a in Luther's exposition. *Festgabe J. Lortz*, I (Baden-Baden, 1958), pp. 69 ff. Both are now reprinted in Althaus, *Die Theologie*, pp. 357–71 and pp. 372–85.

[66] Althaus, *Die Theologie*, p. 361.

[67] This point of view is emphasized by Seeberg, *Lehrbuch*, pp. 321 f., 330 f. On the basic point at issue, cf., Schumann, "Natürliche," pp. 175–201.

[68] Seeberg, *Lehrbuch*, p. 321.

[69] *Ibid.*, pp. 330 f.

12. Systematic Theology and Motif Research

[1] This essay is an adaptation and considerable expansion of an article by the author on "The Scientific Theology of Anders Nygren," published in *The Expository Times* in May, 1963, and used here by kind permission of the editor of that journal.

[2] An English translation of this appears in Anders Nygren, *Essence of Christianity* (London, 1960).

14. Nygren's Ethics

[1] Stockholm, 1923.

[2] Stockholm, 1926.

[3] The term "scientific" is used here in the broad sense common to the European scene and not as limited to the natural sciences. Nygren's approach is, in fact, characteristic of the methodology of the so-called Lundensian school of theology. Cf., my study of the Lundensian methodology as represented in the thought of Ragnar Bring, *A Framework for Faith* (Leyden, 1969).

[4] *Filosofisk och kristen etik*, p. 2.

[5] *Ibid.,* p. 3

[6] *Ibid.,* p. 9.

[7] *Ibid.,* p. 10.

[8] *Ibid.,* p. 13.

[9] *Ibid.,* p. 33.

[10] Reference is made to *Politische Ethik und Christentum,* 1904.

[11] *Filosofisk och kristen etik,* p. 70. The term "method" is used with a certain equivocation in Nygren's discussion at this point. In one context, *Ibid.,* p. 74, he uses it in the general sense of "purpose" or "interest," while a few pages above he uses it in the more special sense of "approach," *Ibid.,* p. 71. This accounts for the confusing fact that philosophical and theological ethics are at one point said to be "perfectly different in form and *method,*" while in another context both are said to be "scientific in *method.*" The distinction in "method" which Schleiermacher is seen to point out here is the difference in "purpose" or "interest."

[12] The phrase "scientific Christian ethics" is defined by Nygren as the systematic exposition of what is essentially and characteristically Christian ethics. *Ibid.,* p. 72.

[13] *Ibid.,* p. 84.

[14] Pages 101 ff.

[15] Title of chap. 1 in *Filosofi och motivforskning* (Stockholm, 1940), first published in the *Festskrift* for Axel Hägerström, 1928.

[16] *Ibid.,* p. 13.

[17] *Filosofisk och kristen etik,* p. 108. This is not a particularly happy formulation by Nygren, for it might indicate that experience can be considered problematic and needs to be *established* as valid, namely by reference to certain *proven* presuppositions. Such scepticism with regard to experience is expressly rejected by Nygren. Cf. "Den religionsfilosofiska apriorifrågan," *Kristendomen och vår tid,* XVII (17 årg., 1922), 68. The most fundamental philosophical assumption made by Nygren is that human experience is valid and that significant judgments can be made from it. *Filosofi och motivforskning,* p. 17; *Det religionsfilosofiska grundproblemet* (Lund, 1921), pp. 67 f; *Religiöst apriori* (Lund, 1921), pp. 210 f. However, at times he expresses himself in such a way as to give the impression that the categorical presuppositions are not only sought as means to *understand* valid experience but to *serve as foundation for* its validity. The step is not long from this approach to the use of categories as *proof of* and *criteria for* the validity of experience, a position which Nygren himself would consider as unworthy of critical philosophy.

[18] I am saying "metaphysics of this sort," recognizing that there are other ways of defining metaphysics. Nygren has not to my knowledge expressed himself with regard to Heidegger's form of metaphysics, but there are indications that Heidegger's "ontology," defined as a formal transcendental phenomenology in contradistinction from the "ontic" considerations of the positive sciences, is very close to Nygren's own concept of philosophy as a universal science, even though the terminology is quite different.

[19] The concept of "validity" is actually the central idea in Nygren's philosophical structures. However, it is probably one of the most problematic aspects of the whole system, partly because it is capable of equivocation in itself, and partly because it is used by Nygren in several different ways (see Note 26).

[20] Cf. *Die Gültigkeit der religiösen Erfahrung* (Gütersloh, 1922), chap.

5, "Die transzendentale Methode," pp. 53 ff; and *Religiöst apriori* (Lund, 1921), pp. 206 ff.

[21] I choose this formulation carefully so as to agree with Nygren's basic assumption, (Note 17), that human experience *is* valid and that the philosopher seeks not to *establish* experience as valid, but simply to *understand the presuppositions for its being so*. I minimize, therefore, Nygren's more careless remarks to the effect that this validity must be "proven," *Filosofisk och kristen etik*, p. 135, "justified," *Ibid.*, p. 136, or "tried," *Ibid.*, p. 143.

[22] Nygren's method is, of course, inspired by Kant initially. But Nygren has made no secret of his intention to go beyond Kant, in method, *Etiska grundfrågor*, pp. 107, 114, 118, 123 f, as well as in content, *Ibid.*, pp. 15 ff, 98 ff, 102. Any question concerning the appropriateness of calling Nygren's method Kantian, is for this reason, irrelevant. As Nygren commented in a conversation with this author: "Kantian or not, I would rather that one would discuss the method itself."

[23] *Filosofisk och kristen etik*, p. 107. This is again a formulation which has some unhappy implications. Cf., Note 17.

[24] "Only that has the right to stand as a philosophical principle or a primary presupposition of which it can be said that on the basis of its acceptance alone are experience and validity at all possible." *Filosofi och motivforskning*, p. 31.

[25] *Ibid.*, p. 40.

[26] *Ibid.*, underlined here. The exact wording of this phrase should be noted. Nygren has at no point indicated that he is out to define an inclusive category, only an inclusive theory of the categories. Thus E. Tegen's criticism of Nygren, *Bibelforskaren*, XXXIX–XL (1922–23), 305 ff, on the grounds that he follows only Kant's "narrow" deduction of the a priori principles of validity within the several areas of experience and does not take seriously Kant's "broad" deduction, designed to show that beyond the multiplicity of ultimate presuppositions there is a mutual implication by which they are all united in an interdependent system, is only partly justified. Nygren *is* interested in the "broad" interrelationship between the categories. Cf. "Till frågan om den transcendentala metodens användbarhet inom religionsfilosofien," *Bibelforskaren*, XL (1923), 273–93. However, his emphasis falls on the *methodological* correlation of the transcendental categories and not on the *material* combination of all categories within one supercategory. *Ibid.*, p. 289. Cf. *Filosofi och motivforskning*, pp. 34 f., for Nygren's critique of Kant's attempt to define a synthetic principle of apperceptive unity in terms of an "oberste Prinzip alles Verstandesgebrauchs." Such attempts, to Nygren, constitute a break with the original intentions of criticism and serve only to compromise its scientific openness in the direction of metaphysical definitions. As for his own deductions, he will have no room for a "broadening" of this sort.

This has not always been recognized by Nygren's interpreters, due perhaps to some lack of care in the study of Nygren's terminology. For example, when Nygren is seen to play with the thought that "eternity" might serve as the ultimate principle of categorical unity, he is careful to point out that this transcendental use of the concept "eternity" must be distinguished from its use as the form of the religious category. "Är evighetskategorien en religiös kategori?" *Kristendomen och vår tid*, XVII (1922), 220–41. It appears that Nel F. S. Ferré, *Swedish Contributions to Modern Theology* (1939), p. 201, and Bernhard Erling, *Nature and History*

(Lund, 1960), pp. 33, 177 ff, who both find Nygren to claim that the religious category is the fundamental principle of transcendental unity, have both overlooked the confusing but important equivocation which Nygren is eager to have recognized.

Perhaps because of the easy confusion of the two ways "eternity" is intended, Nygren has turned more and more to the concept "validity," using qualifiers like "original," "primary," or "transcendental" to indicate what he means when using it as the principle of categorical correlation. Cf. *Filosofisk och kristen etik*, pp. 136, 138, 140, 148. However, even this is capable of confusion, particularly because "validity" is also used in two or three other ways, namely to describe the validity of the individual categories (which is "primary validity" with reference to each particular area of experience, investigated by the various branches of critical philosophy), and to denote the validity of individual experiences (which is "secondary" or "derivative validity," legitimately the concern of the scientific disciplines of understanding, illegitimately of the normative disciplines of thought). Cf. *Filosofisk och kristen etik*, pp. 148, 150 f. Bernhard Erling, *Nature and History*, has again been confused by Nygren's fine distinctions at this point. He makes the elementary mistake of introducing into the concept of validity not only the content-defined distinction of valid/invalid, *Ibid.*, pp. 30 f., thus losing its openness, but also the assumption that it really only applies in the theoretical area of experience, where the general acceptance of causality and mathematical necessity form the objective presuppositions for its claims, as well as for Nygren's subsequent attempts to establish the validity of the religious and ethical categories. *Ibid.*, p. 74. Nothing could be further from Nygren's intentions. His problem is not to establish the validity of religious or ethical experience; that is already assumed by Nygren. His problem is the transcendental deduction of the presuppositional categories underlying valid experience, and for this purpose he finds it helpful to refer to the theoretical category of causality, *not as a material starting-point* in the transcendental deduction of the religious or ethical categories, but simply *as an analogical* example of how the deduction can take place. Cf. *Religiöst a priori*, pp. 206–15; *Dogmatikens vetenskapliga grundläggning* (Stockholm, 1922), pp. 70–74. Erling's attempt to show that Nygren fails in the deductions of the religious and ethical categories primarily because of his timidity in regard to the category of causality is apparently intended to clear the ground for his own theory that, with a concept of causality softened and broadened by the impact of recent progress in the field of quantum mechanics, these deductions are not only possible but will result also in the establishment of clear conceptions of the necessary causal connections between ethical ideals and valid ethical judgments. *Nature and History*, pp. 48, 80, 89, 91, 120. By proceeding in this direction, Erling has gone on to a position so thoroughly unlike Nygren's as to propose the possibility of a *normative* ethics, based on the assumption that a necessity of some sort parallel to the relation of cause and effect within logic and mathematics must be operative in the relation of the ethical category and valid ethical judgments. *Ibid.*, pp. 102 ff, 115.

[27] This is Nygren's general description of the ethical category. Cf. *Agape and Eros*, pp. 42 f; *Etiska grundfrågor*, pp. 43. However, at times he gives the impression that the good must be given more specificity, particularly when he uses "fellowship" as the presuppositional form in his own reflections. *Filosofisk och kristen etik*, pp. 188 ff. One should observe that

Nygren regularly refers to "ethical categories" in the plural. *Ibid.*, pp. 150, 184, 322, *Etiska grundfrågor*, p. 114, selecting one specific form, namely *"gemenskap"* (fellowship), simply for the purposes of his own analysis. *Ibid.*, p. 188. One ought not, therefore, to think of "fellowship" as the definition of the essential substance of ethics according to Nygren. It is only one of the ways (though to Nygren a very useful way) in which the formal structure of the category of the good can be conceptualized.

²⁸ Nygren consistently uses this description of the religious category although the concept "eternity" does not seem particularly clear. Furthermore, there are several conditions which would seem to impinge upon its formal and "open" character. In the first place, the term "eternal" carries certain metaphysical connotations which might compromise its openness toward forms of religion which find their point of orientation within time and space. Secondly, the concept "eternity" is so characteristic of certain central Christian affirmations that its delineation may easily be slanted toward this particular content. There are indications that Nygren has had difficulty in holding the formal category and the particular Christian interpretation of religion from falling into an illegitimate identity. However, one should note that Nygren does not exclude the possibility of speaking of the religious category in differing terms. He is quite aware of the arbitrariness of his own particular point of view when selecting the category of "eternity" as his concept of the religious a priori. Cf. *Dogmatikens vetenskapliga grundläggning*, pp. 150 f; *Filosofisk och kristen etik*, p. 238.

²⁹ *Filosofisk och kristen etik*, pp. 151, 188; *Etiska grundfrågor*, pp. 107 ff, 123.

³⁰ One of the recurring criticisms against Nygren's theory of the "areas of experience" has been that it tends to isolate religion or ethics from other areas of life. His primary emphasis has clearly been to avoid categorical confusion and to show the autonomy of these experiences. He may have done so in a way which jeopardizes the further task of structuring the inclusive categorical scheme. However, Nygren's emphasis on autonomy must rank as his major contribution to critical philosophy, and in Nygren's thought the groundwork is established even for the development of a theory of categorical interrelationships. Ragnar Bring sees the development of such a theory to be the primary task of present-day critical philosophy. *Wie ist nichtmetaphysische Philosophie möglich?* (1940), pp. 34, 40; "Anders Nygrens teologiska gärning," *Svensk teologisk kvartalsskrift* (1940), pp. 317 ff. Cf., my attempt to bring the Lundensian tradition one step further, *A Framework for Faith* (Leyden, 1969), chap. 9.

³¹ *Filosofisk och kristen etik*, pp. 111 ff.

³² *Ibid.* This is not to say that critical ethics is to be a normative discipline. Cf. Note 37. When Nygren speaks of a "trial" of ethical experience, he is not arguing for an evaluational scrutiny of it, but simply for "a critical investigation in order to find out whether the ethical attitude as such is to be seen as a legitimate attitude, and whether it has the right to claim that it represents a generally valid experience. It must examine on what presuppositions the ethical experience can claim validity." *Ibid.*, p. 115.

³³ *Ibid.*, pp. 115 ff.

³⁴ *Ibid.*, p. 120.

³⁵ *Ibid.*, p. 116. Cf. Nygren's diagram.

³⁶ *Ibid.*, pp. 123 ff.

³⁷ Nygren's sharp distinction betwen normative and critical ethics helps

to clarify a confusing equivocation in the use of the concept "validity." Both these disciplines are concerned with validity, but in a different sense: "Normative ethics seeks to prove that certain ethical norms or rules are valid, (while) critical ethics, on the other hand, (shows) that the ethical (experience) at large and as such is a valid experience. Normative ethics will establish that this or that, with justification, is evaluated as ethically good; critical ethics only seeks to reveal that the ethical is rightly evaluated, i.e., that the ethical category is rightly used as principle of validity." *Filosofisk och kristen etik*, p. 135.

38 *Ibid.*, pp. 39 ff.

39 *Ibid.*, p. 46.

40 *Ibid.*, p. 51.

41 See Nygren's essay "Kant och den kristna etiken," reprinted in *Etiska grundfrågor*, pp. 98-127.

42 *Ibid.*, pp. 108 f.

43 *Ibid.*, p. 118.

44 "Thus Kant has left the chief question of critical ethics, the question concerning the validity of ethical experience, unanswered as a testament to his successors. At this point contemporary critical ethics must begin." *Ibid.*, 124.

45 *Filosofisk och kristen etik*, p. 152.

46 *Ibid.*, p. 186.

47 *Filosofisk och kristen etik*, pp. 160-83; *Etiska grundfrågor*, pp. 128-55.

48 *Filosofisk och kristen etik*, p. 161.

49 Cf. Note 37, for an explanation of what might be called the "critical evaluation" of an ethical condition.

50 *Ibid.*, p. 167.

51 *Ibid.*, p. 170. One should observe that Nygren has slid from the analysis of the "elements" of the ethical condition to the definition of its "center."

52 *Ibid.*, p. 171.

53 *Ibid.*, pp. 172, 176.

54 *Ibid.*, p. 184.

55 *Ibid.*, p. 190.

56 *Ibid.*, pp. 192 ff, chap. 4.

57 *Ibid.*, p. 213.

58 *Ibid.*, p. 193.

59 *Ibid.*, p. 215.

60 Nygren's discussions of the history of Christian ethical thought is simply intended to set the pure type, namely "evangelical" ethics, over against the impure types, represented variously by Roman Catholic thinkers, by the Protestant left wing, or by Ritschlian liberalism. Cf. *Filosofisk och kristen etik*, pp. 194 ff; *Etiska grundfrågor*, pp. 39 ff, 53 ff.

61 *Filosofisk och kristen etik*, p. 208.

62 *Ibid.*, p. 213.

63 *Ibid.*, pp. 230 ff.

64 *Etiska grundfrågor*, p. 97.

65 *Filosofisk och kristen etik*, p. 246.

66 Note 28. Cf. *Filosofisk och kristen etik*, p. 238.

67 Note 27. Cf. *Filosofisk och kristen etik*, p. 241.

68 *Filosofisk och kristen etik*, p. 244.

69 Cf. Notes 26, 30.

70 *Filosofisk och kristen etik*, p. 258.

[71] *Ibid.*, pp. 250, 259.

[72] *Ibid.*, p. 264.

15. *Interpretation and Criticism of Nygren's Ethics from a Philosophical Standpoint*

[1] H. D. Lewis, *Morals and Revelation* (London, 1951); William K. Frankena, *Faith and Philosophy*, ed. A. Plantinga (Grand Rapids, 1964), chap. 9; *Ethics* (Englewood Cliffs, 1963); and *Philosophy* (Englewood Cliffs, 1964), pp. 345–65. See also, Paul Ramsey, *Deeds and Rules in Christian Ethics* (Edinburgh and London, 1965 and 1967), chap. 5. It scarcely needs adding that more than a few critics of religion have vigorously stated their negative judgments, for example, Walter Kaufmann and Kai Nielsen. A strong version of Nielsen's argument is "God and the Good: Does Morality Need Religion?" *Theology Today*, XXI, 1 (April, 1964).

[2] *Religion*, ed. Paul Ramsey (Englewood Cliffs, 1965), p. 343.

[3] Nygren's two main books in the field of ethics proper, as distinguished from the enormously provocative and relevant passages in *Agape and Eros*, are *Filosofisk och kristen etik*, and *Etiska grundfrågor* (see Bibliography). Neither of these last two have appeared in English, and I apologize for the injustices which may thereby occur in the present comments. Some small consolation derives from the thought that the very ineptness of the English-speaking writer may capture a few of the questions many other non-Swedish reading authors would likely pose. I also gratefully acknowledge my indebtedness to Bernhard Erling's extended analysis of Nygren's system, *Nature and History* (Lund, 1960), and also to its author for patient and perceptive suggestions, as also to Thor Hall.

[4] Erling, *Nature and History*, p. 100.

[5] Scholars have wrestled with the problem of the interrelationship of the various types of ethics described by him. In the absence of agreement among them, I certainly shall not be presumptuous enough to attempt to sort them out. It is fortunate that Nygren can himself clarify the schema in his "Reply" if he considers it necessary.

[6] As I shall indicate shortly, Nygren is aware of certain present-day efforts to develop new types of metaphysics, i.e., empirically grounded interpretations which seek to identify the generic traits of reality.

[7] *The Nature of Metaphysics*, ed. D. F. Pears (London, 1957), p. 144.

[8] See also, Toulmin, Hepburn, and Macintyre, *Metaphysical Beliefs* (London, 1957); *Prospect For Metaphysics*, ed. Ian Ramsey (New York, 1961); *Metaphysics*, ed. W. E. Kennick and Morris Lazerowitz (Englewood Cliffs, 1966), especially the introduction and part 8; *Metaphysics and Explanation*, ed. W. H. Capitan and D. D. Merrill (Pittsburgh, 1966).

[9] See Paul Tillich's *Morality and Beyond* (New York and Evanston, 1963), and *Love Power and Justice* (New York, 1960).

[10] In *Philosophical Essays* (Lund, 1965). The second is the title of his latest book. See, in this connection, the concluding section of Paul Holmer's essay.

[11] "The Christian Ethos: Its Source, Nature and Authority," Study Department of Universal Christian Council for Life and Work (June 1939), 3, E. 39, p. 6.

[12] *Ibid.*, p. 5.

[13] *Ibid.*, p. 6.

[14] See, Pelikan, Jaroslav, *From Luther to Kierkegaard* (St. Louis, 1963).

[15] "The Christian Ethos," p. 42. *Essence of Christianity*, trans. Philip S. Watson (Philadelphia, 1961), p. 30. The first three chapters of this latter book are pertinent to the question here under discussion. I do not think that the ambiguity is removed, however, because the autonomy of the theoretical, aesthetic, and the ethical is affirmed while at the same time these spheres of experience are said to be based upon the religious experience and its unique engagement with the eternal.

[16] See "The Autonomy of Ethics," in *Prospect For Metaphysics*, ed. Ian Ramsey.

[17] *Ibid.*, p. 39.

[18] One of the genuinely discerning American ethicists, William Frankena, who is by no means hostile to theism, has shrewdly pointed out that the most articulate of the Christian ethicists, the Niebuhrs and Tillich, for example, have a hidden naturalistic and noncognitive ethics. That means to say that, when the chips are down, these authors are really saying that we ought to live the life of love *"because this means* loving is necessary for the fulfillment of my essential nature."* (Frankena, *Philosophy*), p. 426 passim.

16. The Role of Culture in the Thought of Anders Nygren

[1] I have dealt with this in my book *Religionsfilosofien i det tyvende Aarhundrede* (1952), II, pp. 127–62. I have discussed Nygren's Eros Theology in the paper "Ethos og Agape," printed in my book *Om Filosofi og Religion* (1942).

[2] The present author has tried to avoid this in his own book *Religionsphilosophie* (German trans., 1960), pp. 224–57, in which it is claimed that religion cannot have any content which is not justified through one of the three autonomous forms of culture, viz. science, morals, and art.

17. Christ's Church and the Churches in Nygren's Theology

[1] G. Aulén, *Hundra års svensk kyrkodebatt* (Stockholm, 1953), pp. 7 f.

[2] G. Aulén, *Till belvsning of den lutherska kyrkoidén* (Uppsala-Leipzig, 1912).

[3] Aulén, *Hundra*, p. 8.

[4] The foremost representative of the concept of the folk church in Sweden during this period was Einar Billing. See especially his *Den svenska folkkyrkotanken* (Stockholm, 1930). For a theological analysis of Billing's concept of the church see O. Krook, "Die Erneuerung des Kirchenbegriffes in der schwedischen Theologie," *Ein Buch von der Kirche*, ed. G. Aulén, et al. (Göttingen, 1951), pp. 274 ff., and S. von Engeström, "Einar Billings Kirchenverständnis," *Ein Buch von der Kirche*, pp. 258 ff.

[5] He became *teol. kand.* (candidate of theology, roughly equivalent to the American bachelor of divinity) in Lund in 1912.

[6] He was born in Gothenburg, which is the center of the west-Swedish, churchly oriented type of Christianity, influenced by Henric Schartau.

[7] With respect to the so-called Lundensian high-churchliness, see Erik Wallgren, *Individen och samfundet*, Studia Theologica Lundensia 16 (Lund, 1959). Cf., Holsten Fagerberg, *Bekenntnis: Kirche und Amt in der deut-*

in faith in Christ I know that I can fulfill it; indeed, in my faith I have already begun to do so (WA 46:662; 39/1:373; 2:492). The 'law begins to be a thing of joy,' the Christian willing from his heart to fulfill it" (WA 39/1:375). "The Christian does what the law wishes of his own free will, not because the law demands it, but out of love for God and for righteousness" (WA 7:760; 39/1:434).

[46] On this, see Schwartz, *Fides*, p. 401: "In the obedient will, that is in Caritas, the spiritual law is the fulfillment and end of the law. For through Caritas the will is 'in the law of the Lord'" (Ps. 1:2); p. 406: "that Caritas, which through the Holy Spirit is written in our heart as the law of the spirit, is the living will of obedience or the presence of the will in the law. Grace and charity are fully bound up with one another. They are both the fulfillment of the law, in that they set the will free from itself, that is to say, from its self-seeking desires, for that selfless obedience which no longer seeks its own, but what is God's. Here the point has been reached at which Luther's observations (frequent even at this period) on the free, willing, and glad obedience of grace or love have their place."

[47] For this reason God's love never comes to us merely as overwhelming, but always at the same time making a personal appeal to us, wooing and inviting us, and so there belongs to the essence of faith, in Luther's sense of the word, a certain (when rightly understood) legitimate egoistic side of salvation. (On this, cf. Elert, *Morphologie*, pp. 61 f. and pp. 189 f.)

[48] Cf. Maurer, *Freiheit*, pp. 61 ff. Schumann, "Natürliche," pp. 192–96, where he shows differentially how God's love overflows upon us and passes through us, so that in the process it actually becomes *our own love!*

[49] On this, cf. Seeberg, *Lehrbuch*, p. 334; P. Althaus, *Die Theologie*, p. 374; Schwartz, *Fides*, p. 358.

[50] Cf., Schwartz, *Fides*, pp. 251 f.: "The double movement from discerning faith and active love is accomplished within the unity of both." "God creates obedience in us by giving us through the Holy Spirit a law for our mind and implanted in our heart, by which we *discern and love* his will. . . . The obedience of faith is fulfilled where God's work is *loved* above everything. Here, in obedience, faith and love are one." Page 254: "It is faith which justifies, but hope and charity, which are worked by God together with faith before any merit of ours, *prove* that we actually are righteous as the result of faith only when we love God and set our hope on him." Pages 255 f.: "Only faith, hope, and charity in their unity . . . constitute a man's relation to God. The man who believes in Christ—in God—and wins his affections away from all things, from pleasure, riches, honor and life itself and fixes his hope and love on Christ alone, he it is who fulfills the First Commandment, a possibility which is, of course, only open to him through God's activity in grace." Page 257: "Charity is . . . inherent in the very meaning and obedience of faith."

[51] There is for Luther no real faith in God in which love for God "with all our heart" is not present. It is in love that the joyful and warm side of faith, which comes from the heart and attaches itself to God as a person, finds expression. Thus Luther frequently says, with reference to faith and activity based on faith, that "desire and love" must be in it. On this see Seeberg, *Lehrbuch*, pp. 312 ff.; Elert, *Morphologie*, pp. 128 f.; Althaus, *Die Theologie*, pp. 127, 204 f. (cf. also Note 45 above); R. Schwartz, *Fides*, pp. 250–55. From Luther's treatise, *On the Freedom of a Christian*, 1520: "For when our heart hears about Christ in this way, it must rejoice through and

schen konfessionellen Theologie des 19. Jahrhunderts (Uppsala, 1952).

[8] Nygren's doctoral dissertation, on the basis of which he became docent at the University of Lund, is called *Religiöst apriori* and was published at Lund in 1921.

[9] *This Is the Church,* ed. Anders Nygren, trans. Carl C. Rasmussen (Philadelphia, 1952), pp. 3–15.

[10] He participated in the first Faith and Order conference in Lausanne (1927) and later in the two ecumenical conferences in Oxford and Edinburgh (1937) for Life and Work, and Faith and Order, respectively.

[11] Anders Nygren, *Agape and Eros,* trans. Philip S. Watson (London, 1953).

[12] *Det bestaende i kristendomen* constitutes the first part of *Essence of Christianity,* trans. Philip S. Watson (Philadelphia, 1961). On pp. 46 f. and 56 f. Nygren uses the concept "vital fellowship" to designate the distinctive character of religion.

[13] *Ibid.,* pp. 49–62.

[14] *Ibid.,* pp. 32 f.

[15] *Försoningen, en Gudsgärning* (1932) constitutes the second part of *Essence of Christianity.*

[16] See especially E. Billing, *Försoningen,* 2nd ed. (Stockholm, 1930) and G. Aulén, *Christus Victor,* trans. A. G. Hebert (London, 1945).

[17] *Essence of Christianity,* p. 81.

[18] Anders Nygren, *Filosofi och motivforskning* (Stockholm, 1940), pp. 157 ff.

[19] *Ibid.,* p. 166.

[20] *Ibid.,* p. 160.

[21] *Ibid.,* p. 165.

[22] *Ibid.,* p. 158.

[23] See above, Note 11.

[24] As far as I can see, a reference to Eph. 5:25 occurs for the first time in Nygren's *Christ and His Church,* trans. Alan Carlsten (Philadelphia, 1956), p. 91. See also the essay, "Church Unity and Sacramental Fellowship," *The Unity of the Church* (Rock Island, Ill., 1957). In the essay "Corpus Christi" (1942) "walking in love" (Rom. 14:15 and Eph. 5:2) is identified with the responsibility of members of the body of Christ. *This Is the Church,* p. 14. Cf. *Christ and His Church,* p. 103: "Love is, so to speak, the blood stream of the body of Christ."—2 Cor. 5:14, however, is used only in a context where neighbor love in general is being discussed. *Agape and Eros,* pp. 129, 131.

[25] In the discussion of Luther's critique of the concept of the sacrifice of the mass, holy communion is an illustration of the concept of agape and is not introduced under the perspective of the concept of the church. *Agape and Eros,* pp. 695 ff.

[26] The most important passages in Nygren's writings are found in the following works: *Etiska grundfrågor* (Stockholm, 1926), pp. 184 ff.; *Urkristendom och reformation* (Lund, 1932), pp. 40 ff.; *Essence of Christianity,* pp. 83 ff., 101 ff., and passim.

[27] Pages 61 ff.

[28] Aulén's *Hundra,* pp. 99 ff. and 135 ff. has shown this to be the case for both Einar Billing and Nathan Söderblom, the two most important Swedish church leaders of the 1930's.

[29] *This Is the Church,* pp. 3 ff. The influence of the essay is significant

even in this respect, that G. Aulén, who previously had not related christology to the concept of the church, now due to Nygren's influence introduces a new chapter on this subject in his dogmatics. See G. Aulén, *The Faith of the Christian Church*, trans. from the 4th Swedish ed. (1943) E. H. Wahlstrom and G. E. Arden (Philadelphia, 1948), pp. 329 ff., esp. pp. 332 f.

[30] For further discussion of this matter, see P. E. Persson, *Kyrkans ämbete som Kristus-representation*, Studia Theologica Lundensia 20 (Lund, 1961), esp. pp. 167 ff.

[31] *This Is the Church*, p. 4.

[32] *Ibid.*

[33] *Ibid.*, p. 5.

[34] *Ibid.*

[35] *Ibid.*, p. 6.

[36] *Christ and His Church*, p. 31. See esp. pp. 89 ff.

[37] *This Is the Church*, p. 8.

[38] Anders Nygren, *Commentary on Romans*, trans. Carl C. Rasmussen (Philadelphia, 1949), pp. 16 ff. and 210 ff.

[39] *Ibid.*

[40] *Ibid.*, p. 210, cf. p. 217.

[41] *Ibid.*, p. 213. See also especially the interpretation of Rom. 5:15 on pp. 219 ff.

[42] *Ibid.*, p. 213. Nygren sees this possible parallel clearly suggested in Paul's expressions "the sinful body" and "this body of death" (Rom 6:6 and 7:24). This reference appears in his essay, "Dopet i ekumenisk belysning," *Svensk teologisk kvartalskrift*, XXV (1959), p. 218, and in *Christ and His Church*, pp. 101 f.

[43] *This Is the Church*, p. 9.

[44] See also, e.g., the document which Nygren prepared for the 1947 assembly of the Lutheran World Federation in Lund. It was published with the title, "Den lutherska kyrkan i världen just nu," in *Svensk teologisk kvartalskrift*, XXIII (1947), p. 175. The formulation was also approved in the final report of the same assembly. See *Proceedings of The Lutheran World Federation Assembly, Lund, Sweden, June 30–July 6, 1947* (Philadelphia, 1948), pp. 44 f. See further A. Nygren, "Uppenbarelsen och Skriften," *En bok om Bibeln* (Lund, 1947), pp. 90 ff., and *The Gospel of God*, trans. L. J. Trinterud (Philadelphia, 1951), pp. 38 ff. Finally, see also *Christ and His Church*, pp. 93 ff.

[45] A. Fridrichsen, "Försoningen och kyrkan i Nya Testamentet," *Den nya kyrkosynen* (Lund, 1945), p. 42.

[46] *Ibid.*, pp. 60 f. Nygren is not mentioned in this context. Yet to a certain extent his theology is also vulnerable to this critique.

[47] *Ibid.*, p. 61.

[48] See especially R. Newton Flew, *Jesus and His Church* (London, 1938).

[49] *Christ and His Church*, pp. 89 f. See also his essay in *The Unity of the Church*, p. 77.

[50] *Christ and His Church*, pp. 97 ff.

[51] *Ibid.*, pp. 99 f.

[52] *Ibid.*, p. 101.

[53] *Ibid.*, p. 102.

[54] *En bok om Bibeln*, p. 91.

[55] *Ibid.*, p. 92.

[56] *The Gospel of God*, pp. 31, 69 ff.

[57] Anders Nygren, "The Living Word in a Responsible Church," *The Proceedings of the Second Assembly of The Lutheran World Federation, Hannover, Germany, July 25–August 3, 1952* (Geneva, 1952), p. 47.

[58] *En bok om Bibeln*, p. 88.

[59] *The Gospel of God*, pp. 31 f.

[60] *En bok om Bibeln*, p. 91.

[61] Nygren deliberately limits his discussion in this way in *Christ and His Church*, p. 11. The few places where the Spirit is nonetheless mentioned are pp. 103 and 118.

[62] About this see further in my pamphlet, *Anders Nygren—Ein Glaubensbote des Luthertums, Ökumenische Prophile*, Heft V/2 (Berlin, 1952).

[63] *Christ and His Church*, pp. 108 ff. Cf. also "Church Unity and Sacramental Fellowship," pp. 75 ff.

[64] *Commentary on Romans*, pp. 420 ff.

[65] *Christ and His Church*, p. 120.

[66] *Ibid.*, p. 113. The italics are mine.

[67] *Commentary on Romans*, pp. 230 ff.

[68] "The Living Word in a Responsible Church," p. 43.

[69] Anders Nygren, "Luthertum und Ökumene," *Luthertum*, Heft 1 (Berlin, 1951), p. 14.

[70] *Ibid.*, p. 12.

[71] *Ibid.*, p. 13.

[72] *The Gospel of God*, p. 93.

[73] *Christ and His Church*, p. 113.

[74] *Ibid.*, p. 114. Cf. "Church Unity and Sacramental Fellowship," p. 82.

[75] "Church Unity and Sacramental Fellowship," pp. 122 f. Partially rev. trans.

[76] *Ibid.*, p. 113. Partially rev. trans.

[77] *Ibid.*, p. 120.

[78] *Ibid.*, p. 118.

[79] *Ibid.*, p. 117.

[80] *The Gospel of God*, p. 94.

[81] "Dopet i ekumenisk belysning," p. 209.

[82] Anders Nygren, "Bekännelsetrohet och kristen gemenskap," *Kristen Gemenskap* (1937), p. 7.

[83] "Den lutherska kyrkan i världen just nu," p. 175.

[84] "Bekännelsetrohet och kristen gemenskap," p. 7.

[85] "Luthertum und Ökumene," p. 10.

[86] This thesis of Nygren's retains its truth even in view of the most recent ecumenical development. In this connection see my essay "Confessional Loyalty and Ecumenicity," *The Ecumenical Review*, XV (1962–63), pp. 26 ff.

[87] Anders Nygren, "Lutherdomen inför kyrkorna. Från sommarens teologiska arbete i Edinburgh," *Svensk teologisk kvartalskrift*, XIII (1937), p. 312.

[88] *Christ and His Church*, p. 10.

[89] In addition to Nygren's article cited above in Note 86, see also J. Nörregaard's article about Edinburgh in *Kristen Gemenskap* (1937), pp. 120 ff.

[90] See his lecture at the Hannover Assembly (Note 57 above), pp. 42, 48.

[91] *Christ and His Church*, p. 124.

[92] "Church Unity and Sacramental Fellowship," p. 83.

[93] *Christ and His Church*, p. 125.

[94] Nygren has in this connection always emphasized the important role of theology in the ecumenical enterprise. See e.g., "Luthertum und Ökumene," pp. 6 f. and 9. See also *Christ and His Church*, pp. 118 f.

[95] Thus, e.g., in India and in Holland. See Nygren's own references in "Luthertum und Ökumene," pp. 6 f.

[96] *E.g.*, in "Church Unity and Sacramental Fellowship," pp. 82 ff. and in *Christ and His Church*, pp. 124 f.

[97] "Church Unity and Sacramental Fellowship," p. 84.

[98] *Ibid.*, p. 82. Cf., *Christ and His Church*, p. 114.

[99] *Christ and His Church*, p. 123.

Reply to Interpreters and Critics

[1] *Religiöst a priori* (Lund, 1921), p. 208.

[2] *Bibelforskaren*, 1923, pp. 22 ff. The full documentation of each and every work of Anders Nygren is given in the Bibliography at the conclusion of this volume.

[3] *The Lutheran Theological Seminary Bulletin*, Aug. 1965, pp. 17 ff.

[4] *Ibid.*, p. 21.

INDEX

Aesthetics, 41

Agape: and eros, problem of, 6; Christian, 6; in a Christian context, 18; God's, 51, 60; and eros, 52; Christian motif of, 96–97; in the universe, 125; Christian, 145; with eros, 146–47; lack of motivation in the, 149–50; nature of, 160; doctrines of, 161; God's "uncaused," 177–78; eros in Christian, 205; expression of, 231; theology of, 238–59; Nygren's concept of, 323; Christian faith in, 352; mentioned, 58, 65, 68, 107, 112, 116, 117, 122, 127, 128, 359, 360, 363

Agape and Eros: forms of love in, ix; mentioned, 11, 19, 54, 67, 84, 99, 143, 161, 186, 203, 230, 231, 232, 233, 239, 324, 358–65 passim, 366–67

Aiken, Henry, 286

Alcibiades, 165

Anachronism, 110

Analytic philosophy, use of, 70–91 passim

Anthropology, 155

A priori: concept of, 14; question of, 15; judgments, 42; religious, 45–47, 50, 99; mentioned, 45, 55, 101, 309

Aquinas, St. Thomas, 33, 111, 114, 198, 201

Arbitrariness: criticism of, 269; mentioned, 49, 98

Aristotle, 33, 145, 158, 162, 189–90

Arseniev, N. V., 26

Art: literary, 120; mentioned, 225, 243

Athanasius, 243

Atheoretical domains, 108, 109

Atonement: doctrine of, 7

Augustine, St.: pivotal position of, 174; search for God, 176; and God's love, 179; and love of neighbor, 183–84; *Caritas,* doctrine of, 362–63; mentioned, 9, 127, 243–44

Aulén, Gustav, 17, 143, 145, 232, 319, 328

Austin, J. L., 88, 89

Authorianism, x

Barth, Karl: and Nygren, 150

Basic motif, 96–97

Beauty, 73, 75, 82, 87, 102, 108, 157, 164, 165, 270, 295, 296

Being: presuppositions of, 248; mentioned, 176

Bergmann, Gustav, 88

Bible: spiritual interpretation of, 64–65; motifs in the, 116; Gospel of the, 137; mentioned, 40–42, 49, 68, 240

Billing, Einar, 328

Black, H., 88

Blixen, Karen. *See* Dinesen, Isak

Bredvold, Louis, 122

Bring, Ragnar, xi, 17, 19, 143, 348–52

Brunner, Emil, vii, xiii, 287, 289

Buchler, Justus, 286

Buddhism, 38, 104, 229, 315

Bugge, F. W., 7

Bultman, Rudolf, vii, xiii

Burnaby, John: on Nygren, 161; quoted, 364; mentioned, xi, 162, 362

Calvin, John, 314

Caritas: discussed, 175–86 passim; Augustine's doctrine of, 187–202, 362–63; mentioned, 215, 243, 253

Category, 72, 77

Catholicism: love in, 204–5; mentioned, 185

Christensen, Erik M., xi, 357

Christian faith: love in, 231; theology of, 233; authentic, 239; denied, 249; borders expanded, 266; and ethics, 280; history of, 373–75; mentioned, 18, 33, 43, 44, 57, 63, 154, 271, 352, 367

Christianity: central point of, 14; is religion of love, 18; essence of, 39; a concrete religion, 40; rejected, 43; concepts of eternity in, 52; truth of, 54, 234–37, 309, 366–67; Christian feeling of guilt, 58; message of, 60; basic motif of, 67, 99, 100, 356; conception of, 69; agape in, 75; distinctive character of, 105; and Christian

Index

434 INDEX

Weiss, Paul, 286
Weizäcker, E. F. von: quoted, 355
Wellek, René: quoted, 121; mentioned, 122
Whitehead, Alfred North, 249
Wieman, Henry Nelson, vii
Wilamowitz-Mollendorff, Ulrich von, 10, 156, 159, 304, 360, 361, 362

Wingren, Gustav: criticisms of, 74; mentioned, 72
Wittgenstein, Ludwig: quoted, 79, 82, 83; Nygren on, 129–30; mentioned, 28, 61, 71, 73, 76, 77, 88, 89, 90, 288, 354
World Conference on Faith and Order, 25